READINGS ON MERGERS AND TAKEOVERS

READINGS ON
MERGERS AND TAKEOVERS

Edited by J M Samuels
Professor of Business Policy at the Graduate Centre for Management Studies at the Universities of Birmingham and Aston in Birmingham
on behalf of The Acton Society Trust

Paul Elek Books Ltd
London

First published in 1972 by Paul Elek Books Ltd
54–58 Caledonian Road
London N1 9RN

ISBN 0 236 17619 6

Set in 10/12 pt. IBM Press Roman, printed by photolithography, and bound in Great Britain at The Pitman Press, Bath

CONTENTS

PART C
A POLICY TOWARDS MERGERS

PART D
THE INTERNATIONAL ASPECTS OF MERGERS

PART E
THE EVIDENCE

INTRODUCTION

The 1960s witnessed a dramatic change in the British government's economic policy. Previously, economic management had sought to maintain and increase competitiveness within industry by means of the Monopolies Commission, the Restrictive Trades Practices Court and by such acts as the abolition of resale price maintenance. Suddenly this was superseded by a policy aimed at securing the nation's economic growth and international competitiveness through widespread rationalization which would result in fewer but larger industrial units. The 'cult of bigness' was manifested in government circles by the creation of the state-financed Industrial Reorganization Corporation, but it was pursued with equal fervour in the private sector which was swept with an unprecedented wave of mergers and takeovers.

The Acton Society Trust, which had published studies on the effects of earlier mergers, was concerned about the implications of this new and greater spate of industrial amalgamations. It therefore commissioned various experts to examine the economic, financial, social and trade union consequences of this activity. The results of their findings, presented at a Conference held in London in May 1970 and subsequently updated, comprise the major part of this book, and together they provide the first comprehensive review of the impact of mergers on public policy, industrial performance and organized labour in Britain.

Britain has not been alone in experiencing a topical growth in mergers and takeovers. The United States, too, have been similarly infected. The opportunity has been taken in this book to include a number of important articles from leading American business and economic journals which enables the reader to compare and contrast the experiences of both countries. Additional material from British sources is also included, and two chapters that have not previously been published.

The papers included in this study are concerned with establishing the reality of the present situation. There are many changes taking place in the industry and economy of the developed countries, and the relationship between mergers and takeovers and these changes needs to be examined. Five trends can easily be identified: the increasing interference of government in the affairs of companies; the gradual reduction in the importance of the small firm in that the percentage of the employment provided and output accounted for by small companies is falling: the increasing importance of the institutional investor; the formation of countries into large trading blocks; and the emergence of the large multi-national corporation. It is the speed and extent of these changes which will determine the structure of industry in the future. Certain trends are the result of mergers; others provide the inducement to merge. This book considers the most important of the issues involved.

The study is divided into five parts. Part A deals with the findings of a number of empirical studies into the impact of mergers. The first chapter, a review of the literature on the success or failure of mergers and takeovers, makes the point that a surprising number of mergers are found to be unsuccessful. The same point is made in Chapter Two by Dr. Newbould whose analysis of the takeovers effected in the UK in 1967 and 1968 indicates that very large increases in the earnings of the acquired companies must be obtained in order to justify the price paid by the purchaser. Dr. Newbould is one of the few researchers working on mergers in the United Kingdom and the results reported in his paper, originally presented at the 1970 Conference, are a part of the larger study fully detailed elsewhere. Here, however, he concerns himself with two particular financial aspects of mergers: first, the extent to which directors, in defending the company against a takeover bid, can force up the offer price and so benefit their own shareholders; secondly, the fact that because the price which has to be paid for a company is often relatively high, the rate of growth that is required in the earnings of the purchased company often needs to be high if the purchasing company is to receive a normal rate of return.

Chapters Three, Four and Five report research conducted in the United States. There is no reason to suppose that these findings would substantially differ from what might be obtained if similar studies were undertaken in the UK: the fact that the scarcity of UK research into the success or failure of mergers drives one to use American findings does not in itself make their relevance suspect. The study by Professors Weston and Mansinghka is based on the performance of conglomerate companies – which have, of course, over the last few years been the most active acquirers – and suggests that, on average, conglomerates perform as well financially as other companies. In Chapter Four, Mr. Kitching examines the performance of a wider classification of merged companies. He takes as his criteria not just financial performance but also the objectives of the managers involved, in terms of what they hoped to achieve by the merger, and the extent to which these objectives have been realized. Kitching finds a high probability of success with certain categories of merger, but a low one with others.

In Chapter Five Professor Levinson looks at various psychological aspects of mergers, thereby making explicit the perhaps vague but growing awareness that it is not possible, and certainly not advisable, to explain mergers purely in economic terms. This analysis of the motives and feelings of the individuals involved in a merger reveals a number of the difficulties encountered in making it a financial success, and shows why so many mergers can be regarded as failures.

Mr. Briston and Mr. Rhys in Chapter Six suggest that because of statistical problems the study of mergers in aggregate is not worthwhile, and therefore each particular case should be studied separately. This is exactly the approach adopted in Part B of the book where Mr. Bhaskar studies in detail three companies which engaged in takeover activity some years ago, and whose investments can now reasonably be judged in terms of success or failure.

Chapter Seven provides three case studies never before published. Each is concerned with a particular merger. The aim is to assess the extent to which an outsider is able to judge the success of a merger. Because a certain time must be allowed to elapse after an acquisition in order for any economies of scale, rationalization or reduced risks through diversification to be reflected in the financial performance of the company, the three mergers examined all date back to around 1960. The three were chosen purely on the grounds of their importance, interest and the availability of data. There is no suggestion that these particular mergers are especially representative of all acquisitions that took place at about that time, though their experiences are certainly not unique, and similar results would undoubtedly emerge from an investigation of many other mergers that took place during the last decade.

Two of these case studies illustrate mergers which in the opinion of the case writer could be regarded as unsuccessful. Such an opinion however is based only on an analysis of the company's financial reports. The companies concerned were not approached to seek the opinions of the executives involved. The cases illustrate the difficulties of an outsider attempting to judge the success of management's decisions when the only knowledge that can be obtained is through the company's financial reports.

The third part of the book, which concerns mergers and their implications for the relative positions of the different interested parties, offers various recommendations on future policy. In Chapter Eight Professor Beesley and Mr. White consider the problem of deciding when a merger is in the national interest and when it is not, and show how the technique of cost benefit analysis might usefully be applied to this area. They also analyse merger control in the United Kingdom, offering suggestions as to how this could be improved.

The importance of management in determining the success of a merger is emphasized in a number of chapters. The co-operation of the Trade Unions is of hardly less vital importance, particularly in the early stages of reorganization, yet this is a generally neglected subject in the literature. The attitude of Trade Unions towards mergers is examined by Mr. Hughes in Chapter Nine.

In Chapter Ten Mrs. Dev deals with the position of the shareholders in mergers and demonstrates the need for more information to be made available at the negotiating stage. The quantitative information which reaches shareholders on the benefits expected from the change in control is negligible; this reticence may, however, reflect nothing more sinister than that the companies themselves have not quantified the benefits and are only aware of the broad categories of possible benefits. When mergers involve quoted companies, the air of secrecy which must surround any negotiations often denies the companies the opportunity of exchanging the information which would make the quantification of benefits possible. The large uncertainty which must therefore obscure any anticipated benefits must also undermine the confidence of the shareholders, and indeed, as Hogarty has found, the shareholders of the average actively acquiring company have not been as financially successful as the shareholders of the average non-actively acquiring company.* Mrs. Dev argues that more information should accompany profit forecasts made by the merging companies so that the shareholders can assess the uncertainties involved.

The position of shareholders of the merged companies is of course extremely complex. The code of behaviour which operates in the City is designed to protect the shareholders of the company to be purchased; this code is examined by Mr. Blanden in Chapter Eleven. The shareholders of the acquiring company are in fact

---

*Hogarty, T. F., 'The Profitability of Corporate Mergers', *Journal of Business*, July 1970.

not so well protected, it being (perhaps naively) assumed that the merger is being carried out in their best interests; whether or not the shareholders are in a position to evaluate the benefits of the merger is the question examined by Mrs. Dev.

Chapter Twelve by Mr. Goodman is concerned with the influence of mergers on the people working in industry; it is taken from his book *The Impact of Size* which deals with a more general problem – the conditions affecting people working in large companies. In this book Mr. Goodman recommends a number of ways of improving the working environment and boosting morale. He stresses particularly the importance of providing increased opportunities for the creative use of individual skill and imagination, arguing that the creation of such an environment, with real scope for individual achievement, would inevitably lead to improvements in performance. The particular chapter that is reproduced in this book is concerned with the taming and controlling of economic power. Mergers are seen as the consequence of a desire for power on the part of industrial leaders, and this objective is pursued regardless of any real benefit to the community. Not all would see Mr. Goodman's fear of large-scale business as entirely justified, but before agreeing or disagreeing with his thesis it is necessary to appreciate the possible advantages and disadvantages of size. These are reviewed in Chapter Sixteen.

Part D is concerned with the international aspects of mergers. In Chapter Thirteen Dr. Brooke, in examining the problems of managing multi-national companies, reports on part of a very much larger research study conducted with Dr. Remmers into the strategy of multi-national enterprise. He discusses the changes in national attitudes to foreign investment and the difficulties of organizing large international operations, and suggests that there may be a trend towards breaking up these large multi-national concerns.

Chapter Fourteen aroused considerable interest when published originally as an article in the US business journal *Fortune.* Entitled 'Europe's Love Affair with Bigness', it explores the supposed infatuation of European businessmen with the idea of running large companies. It is suggested that one of the reasons for this is pure nationalism, the wish to have a company large enough to compete on equal terms with the US giants; but that this nationalism will, at the same time, create a barrier to integration on a European scale.

In Part E, Chapter Fifteen Dr. Murray examines the subject of the effect of the internationalization of business on the British economy: to what extent does the large multi-national company undermine the integrity of the national state as an economic unit? He concludes that the effectiveness of the government in controlling the economy has been weakened by this internationalization.

Chapter Sixteen consists of a new survey of the literature that has appeared on economies of scale and the size of companies. This section focuses attention particularly on the economic logic behind the trend towards 'bigness' and concentration, with an analysis of the implications at both a micro and macro level. This aspect of industrial organization still causes heated controversy. The review chapter will help to clarify some of the issues that continue to cause debate.

PART A

EVIDENCE ON THE SUCCESS OR FAILURE OF MERGERS

Chapter One

THE SUCCESS OR FAILURE OF MERGERS AND TAKEOVERS*

J. M. Samuels

Professor of Business Policy, Graduate Centre for Management Studies, Universities of Birmingham and Aston in Birmingham

The Conservative Government ended the life of the Industrial Reorganization Corporation, the body brought into existence in 1966 which considered mergers as an indispensable device for reorganizing the industrial structure. The Corporation encouraged mergers that would not otherwise have taken place; they used their considerable financial resources to enable one company to purchase another company when the money could not be obtained from other sources. No statement has yet been made which indicates how, if at all, the Conservative Government intends to 'rationalize' the industrial structure. If the policies of this government in other areas are any guide they will simply leave it to market forces to bring about any mergers. It is doubtful if the government will see its role as one of a merger broker.

With this possible change in policy it would seem a good time to examine the evidence on the success or failure of mergers and takeovers. The first fact that emerges is that there have been comparatively few studies on this subject, and it is perhaps surprising that the Labour Government was prepared to operate such a strong policy in this area when evidence to support the policy was so limited. All would agree that there is a need to encourage greater efficiency in British industry, but not all would agree that encouraging firms to merge necessarily achieves this result.

The policy of the Labour Government seemed to be an acceptance that the majority of mergers have a neutral or beneficial effect. This may well be so, particularly in view of the fact that the majority of mergers involve small, often private companies, whose growth prospects it is often thought can be limited. Because of this belief, however, only few of the mergers involving large companies were investigated and fewer still were actually prevented from taking place.

The theme of this paper is that the evidence on the success of mergers is far from conclusive. The Monopolies Commission themselves believe that the present merger activity is 'leading to the continued absorption of medium sized companies not necessarily accompanied by gains in efficiency'. Not only are the social welfare

*Reprinted from the *Journal of Business Policy,* Spring 1971.

results of mergers unclear; the benefits to the shareholders of the buying and selling companies are far from certain.

To justify a merger in the eyes of public opinion it seems all that is necessary is to quote the magic words 'economies of scale' and 'rationalization'. But the Monopolies Commission has often been frustrated by the unwillingness or inability of the companies engaged in merger discussions to quantify the expected economies and benefits. The Commission only looks at a very small proportion of mergers, and one must wonder how much planning by the companies concerned has gone into the mergers the Commission does not examine. One factor on which the success of a merger depends, according to all researchers on the subject, is advanced planning. Yet in such an important proposed merger as Unilever/Allied Breweries[1] the Commission states that there was a reluctance on the part of the companies to quantify the expected benefits. In mergers where the management is less expert and the merger exempt from public scrutiny one cannot be sure that the results will be beneficial to the public interest.

The evidence on economies of scale is far from conclusive. But even if the potential gains are there, they do not materialize automatically. Their realization depends almost entirely on the expertise with which management handles the multiple problems of organization and cooperation so that economies of scale can result. Management is the key factor in determining the success of mergers. It is hoped in this analysis of the success and failure of mergers to indicate why certain mergers fail. This should assist in any future planning of mergers by pointing out the mistakes that should not be repeated. If it is possible to identify a class of mergers that have the necessary conditions for success this would indicate the type of mergers that should be encouraged. Before attempting to estimate the probability of success of a merger it is necessary to determine why the merger took place. Which are the companies that become involved in mergers? What are the objectives of the mergers?

1. Companies Involved in Takeovers and Mergers

Theory would suggest that the companies being taken over are the less efficient firms, those wasting scarce resources. With better management, gains in economic performance are bound to follow. If the economic benefits are passed on to consumers, if social welfare is increased, then few could argue against the merger. A difficulty lies in deciding which firms are inefficient. Accounting profits are, unfortunately, not good guides. Amey has shown the danger of using the accounting measure of return on capital employed as a measure of efficiency.[2] The reported profit of a company depends on its accounting practices and the opportunities open to it in the market, and the figure given is a static one reflecting the position at one point in time. The Monopolies Commission has difficulty in interpreting profit rates: as Rowley points out, the Commission looks at the static situation, underestimating the possible impact of potential competition.[3] One reason for a merger can arise when the stock market is underestimating the real value of a company. If the company is not too conscious of its stock market valuation, and its stock market price is low in relation to its potential, it is an ideal victim for a takeover bid. The purchaser may be of the opposite type: keenly conscious of its stock market valuation, which it is anxious to keep high, and always reporting to show the best position. A merger or takeover between two such companies does not automatically result in real gains for the economy. The point being made is that the victims in takeovers and mergers are not necessarily the firms failing to make the best use of their resources. The victims could be firms using their assets to their best advantages, but their stock market price is low, because of stock market actions and lack of knowledge. They are being purchased because they are a good investment.

Marris has advanced the hypothesis that a 'share price may favour a radical change in the voting distribution, i.e. a takeover raid. Takeover raids are difficult and risky, but if the prospective gain is large enough, the attempt will seem worthwhile'.[4] In a recent study[5] the Marris hypothesis was examined. It is possible that the feature that distinguishes the companies that receive takeover bids from the other category of companies is simply that the former are undervalued. There are, of course, other reasons for takeovers, such as the much-discussed, but difficult to measure, rationalization of an industry's structure. But even with the other reasons behind a takeover bid, which may be classed as prime motivating factors, the relative price of the shares to be purchased cannot be overlooked, and an overvalued company would be less attractive even in the rationalization process. It is recognized that it is perfectly possible to find a company's shares correctly valued or even overpriced, with the current expectations of future returns, and for it still to be a good purchase for a takeover bidder. If the prospective purchasers can use the assets, including the management, of the company more profitably, then they may be prepared to purchase shares classed as overvalued in terms of present market knowledge.

The results of the study, based on only a small sample of the companies that were taken over, show that on the pre-bid market price 80 per cent of the companies were classed as undervalued. This would indicate that at the time the purchasing company is considering possible companies to take over, the valuation of the share price, based on estimates of future earnings and dividends, and historic earnings and dividends, is a relevant factor. The fact that 80 per cent of companies that were purchased were classed as undervalued on a pre-bid share price shows that it is in this category that takeover victims are to be found.

As a result of takeover negotiations the price that eventually has to be paid is higher than the pre-bid price. When a comparison is made between the valuation of a company's shares and the price paid for the purchase of the shares, a different picture emerges. The price paid for the company exceeds the valuation of the company in 90 per cent of the cases. This could mean that the purchasing company has higher expectations of the growth of the acquired company than has been estimated for the model. The growth expectations in this research were based on past growth rates. The purchasing company in bidding this higher price than would be expected from the model, is showing a more optimistic view of the future, perhaps based on expectations of their own ability to manage the new subsidiary.

In a recent study, Gort advances the hypothesis that 'forces which generate discrepancies in valuation are decisive in determining variations in merger rates both among industries and over time'[6]. He is suggesting that the phases of widespread merger activity occur simply because a number of companies are being undervalued. Gort accepts the point that 'particular mergers may result from the pursuit of monopoly power, economies of scale, or yet other sources of gain' but he does not find these as important reasons explaining periods of merger activity.

For a merger to take place the buyers and/or sellers of firms must expect their wealth to increase as a result of the two companies being brought together. This can happen in one of two ways. First, the market value of assets of the combined firms may rise because of the merger. Second, the valuation of buyers and sellers may differ, with the result that each expects to gain from the purchase. The first of these arguments is the result of expected economies of scale. The second of the arguments is similar to Marris's theory.

Gort tests these reasons for mergers to see which offers the best explanation of the varying merger rate. Seven explanatory variables were selected to test the hypothesis that the frequency of mergers is a function of either economic disturbances that lead to valuation discrepancies, or economies of scale. The results support the valuation discrepancy hypothesis, and 'argue against an important role for economies of scale in determining variations in merger activity'.

The particular economic disturbances which were found to give rise to valuation discrepancies were changes in technology, barriers to entry in an industry and growth in an industry. When there are changes in technology, leading to new products or new processes, past records give little guidance as to future performance. Consequently, one can expect variations in price due to the uncertainty of investors about the future. When barriers to entry in an industry are high, there can be wide differences between the capitalized value of a firm's future earnings and the cost of its assets; hence, again, there can be a range of valuation differences.

Newbould has shown that because the price which has to be paid to purchase a company is often comparatively high, the rate of growth required in the earnings of the purchased company needs to be dramatically high if the purchased company is to receive a normal rate of return.

Gort and Newbould's work suggests that there is too much emphasis on economies of scale as a result of mergers. The motivation in all mergers is, of course, gain, but if this materializes it may be because of valuation differences, not necessarily because of the realization of possible long-term economies. The economies of scale statements that are made at the time of mergers are simply attempts to justify the action in terms of national gains. Kitching quotes an 'experienced acquirer': 'We are quite sceptical about the existence of synergy. When we are testing the potential earnings of a company, we don't place any value on the benefits which might accrue from synergy.'[7] It appears that words like 'rationalization' and 'economies of scale' are reserved for public statements. The analysis suggests that the companies being taken over were initially approached because they were regarded as good buys, even with their existing future growth potential, on assessments of the growth the market may reasonably expect to result from the companies' existing management and utilization of resources. This does not mean that synergy is not possible after the integration of the two companies; it may be an additional benefit for the shareholders of the acquiring company.

The position of the shareholders of the merged companies is extremely complex; there is a code of behaviour operating in the City, which is designed to protect the shareholders of the company to be purchased. The shareholders of the acquiring company are not so well protected; it is of course assumed that the merger is being carried out in their best interests. However, once a company enters into takeover negotiations the reputation and image of those initiating the move become involved, and this often makes it difficult for the bidding company to withdraw.

Vested interests become involved in going through with the purchase. Analysis would suggest that the companies often finish up paying more for the victim than a valuation would warrant. Advantages may still accrue from the merger, but the traditional synergy formula (2 + 2 = 5) should perhaps be written 2 + 2½ = 5!

The motivation for certain mergers may not be economic, and so it would not be surprising, if one tried to measure the success of mergers in terms of purely financial returns, to find a number of merged companies classed as failures. Levinson quotes two reasons for mergers which would not normally be given as justification.[8] One is fear, the fear of being taken over, which results in the defensive pursuit of bigness. The company becomes bigger by becoming fatter, but it will not necessarily be more efficient; this was not, in any case, its main aim. A second of these psychological reasons is 'obsolescence'. Organizations age and become inflexible, so they begin to take over other companies to infuse new blood (new profits) into the system. A study of the motives for a merger can give guidance in assessing the chance and degree of financial success; some motives are less likely to lead to gains for the shareholders than others.

2. The Financial Performance of Merged Companies

Firms can be classified into a number of groups, beginning with a basic firm, consisting of one product, one plant and a single market. This then extends into multi-market and multi-plant firms, moving through various stages of diversification to the investment company (Investment Trust). The classifications of firms that result from diversification are first, concentric firms, which are the result of market or product extension, but which allow carryover from one interest to the other of research, engineering, production, marketing and financial management capabilities. Second are 'managerial conglomerates', with management specialist groups, interacting with and providing services for the individual operating entities; and thirdly, 'financial conglomerates', where the corporate level provides finance and maintains financial responsibility and control, but does not attempt to interfere with the managerial decisions.

The vast majority of mergers and takeovers result in firms that can be classified in one of these three categories. Weston carries out various tests on the performance of sixty conglomerate firms over the period 1958 to 1967.[9] He concludes that the earnings performance of conglomerates, measured by return on total assets and return on net worth, is not significantly different from that of all manufacturing companies; but given the unfavourable earnings opportunities in industries from which conglomerates emerged, the performance is favourable.

Weston finds therefore that in financial terms, on average, conglomerates perform no better than the average industrial company. What, however, is surprising is the range of performance of these conglomerates: 'The great diversity in the conglomerates' performance has important implications'.

The results of some mergers are a success, others a failure. It is important not to consider mergers and takeovers as either wholly a good or a bad thing, but to be able to differentiate the mergers that have a high probability of success from those that could well fail. The probability of success, or of economic benefits, from concentric mergers is very high. The results of financial or managerial conglomerates are less predictable but Weston believes that the criticisms of them have not been substantiated, and so there are no grounds for prematurely raising barriers against them.

In any case, Weston claims, the shakier mergers will be weeded out by a healthy system: market forces will see to it that they either improve or disappear. This weeding out process is however by no means automatic; many mergers and takeovers are themselves defensive in motivation. They are undertaken in an attempt to prevent the normal processes of the market from taking place.

Even if one could argue that the market mechanism will eliminate the unsuccessful conglomerate, it is not necessarily in the best interests of the economy to allow the merger to take place and then wait for the market to pass judgement on it. It may be be a better policy to decide in advance of the merger whether it has a high probability of success.

An analysis by Pamela Farrent[10] of the thirty major acquirers in the UK showed that they mostly operate in industries where one could not expect a rapid growth in earnings (except in the case of Rio Tinto-Zinc), such as the paper, publishing, motors, breweries, and food and drink industries.

Kitching used two methods to determine whether a merger could be classified as a success or failure.[11] He obtained the financial results of the companies, in order to compare the actual performance with forecasts made before the merger. In addition he used interviews with the key management to discover the hopes they had of the merger, and the results they wanted to obtain. This latter approach was subjective, involving an assessment of success or failure against some original strategy or original hopes. Kitching's results are interesting. He shows a high incidence of failure with certain types of mergers, particularly conglomerate mergers. Simple vertical and horizontal mergers are usually successful. Concentric mergers come in between these two extremes of failure and success.

Kitching found support for the theory of Ansoff on 'critical mass', there being a size mismatch when the acquired company's sales were less than 2 per cent of the parent company's sales volume before the merger. This size mismatch 'occurs in 84 per cent of acquisitions considered failures'. Some of the other findings of Kitching on the reasons for failure in mergers are given later in this chapter.

In a study by Hogarty the investment performance of active acquiring companies is compared to that of their respective industries.[12] Investment performance is in this case purely concerned with the returns earned by the shareholders, where returns are defined to include both capital gains and cash dividends. The findings of the study are that the investment performance of the heavily merged firms is worse than the average performance of firms in the respective industries. The period investigated was from 1953 to 1964, and so was before the recent disenchantment of investors with conglomerate-type companies. Hogarty finds that 'while most active acquirers do not obtain an attractive return, a few do'. These few obtain very large returns, which appears to tempt other firms into merger activity.

3. Reasons for Success and Failure in Mergers

A large amount of research has been undertaken in the attempt to prove or disprove the existence of economies of scale. Theoretically there are economies of production, marketing, research and finance. Economies should mean that the larger the organization, the lower the unit costs and the greater the proportional returns. The reasons put forward to justify the vast majority of mergers can be interpreted as attempts to obtain increased economies of scale.

There is, however, no automatic reason why economies should emerge when two companies are brought together. There may be possible advantages from large-scale operation, but this does not mean that all large organizations can achieve them.

Synergy does not automatically arise. The opportunities may be there, but the success of the merger depends upon the management's ability to take advantage of these opportunities to realize the potential economies. Kitching concluded that 'the type of merger is not the determining factor in the success or failure of an acquisition. The primary cause must be sought elsewhere'.[13] The key factors determining success found by Kitching were the quality of both planning and management. It seems that all research into post merger performance emphasizes the same fact, that success depends on planning and management. Profits are not produced by machinery, buildings or products. It is people that give life to these otherwise dormant assets. The key to the success of a merger turns out to be the people involved, the amount of thought and planning that has gone into the merger, and the ability of the people involved.

Searby points to the first trap leading to a failure, a disregard, or inadequate appraisal of the complexities before the merger takes place, combined with the tendency to relax after it.[14] Wallace estimated that a single merger may involve 2,000 changes and 10,000 major non-routine decisions.[15] Large companies, especially when taking over smaller ones, often ignore such complexities until the advantages that appear so obvious on paper fail to materialize.

On the psychological level, Levinson points to the two kinds of fear that dominate the outlook of many large, rigid organizations, and which may be at the root of many merger failures:[16]

(i) Fear of a general kind breeds a belief that the way to become stronger is to become bigger. This leads to a process of accretion at organizational level, as companies resort to taking over others as the quickest means of growth. This creates additional problems and inflexibilities.

(ii) The fear of obsolescence specifically, in a large, rigidly structured firm with exaggerated notions about the successes of its rivals, will again lead to a renewed effort to take over more companies and infuse new blood into the system.

These two kinds of fear, which lie behind many mergers, often result in a condescending attitude towards the junior partner and a desire for bureaucratic control. The senior partner acts aggressively in trying to assert authority and 'forgets' many of the promises to the junior partner; the latter feels betrayed and exploited, and many of its talented personnel, which the larger company sought to acquire, resign or leave. Disillusionment brings further controls to remedy the situation, resulting in general apathy and a stifling of initiative. In a small company people tend to identify themselves with the organization. If the senior partner fails to understand the value system of the small company that gives it its 'organizational pulse', there is an identification crisis and the merged company ends up with no organization. Levinson then maintains that this type of 'selling the other party' accentuates the fear-and-obsolescence syndrome and the parent company in a vicious urge seeks to devour more companies. This eventually becomes self-defeating. Levinson argues that the psychological powers of companies are independent of size, and if acquiring companies fail to grasp this and act accordingly they will suffer from loss of initiative and imagination and a floating population of executives, with negative consequences for the organization and for society as a whole.

Ansoff considers that 'diversification typically leads to basic changes in the nature of a firm's management problems. The firm may move into product areas where the research, design and production technologies may be quite new, and where the marketing, financial and economic problems involved may differ significantly. Diversification, therefore, often brings on substantial extra costs and financial risks; and for that reason should not be undertaken unless the firm has carefully analysed the motives for diversification and proceeds only after it has carefully reviewed diversification opportunities'.[17] There is some doubt as to whether all British managements carry out such a review before embarking on a merger.

Weston makes the same point concerning the importance of management and planning and attempts to generalize about the relationship.[18] He examines the possible carryover from one industry to another of managerial capabilities. The extent to which synergy may arise depends on the extent of carryover of the management functions from one industry to another.

Managerial capabilities can be classified under five headings: Financial, General, R & D and Engineering, Manufacturing and Marketing. Weston divides industries into four groups; Defence, Producers' Durables, Producers' Material, and finally Consumers' Durables and Non-Durables. The finance carryover from one industry to another is always high, whatever the industry groups involved. The general management carryover can vary from high – from, say, Defence to Producers' Durables – to moderate, from Defence to Producers' Materials. Engineering carryover can vary from high – from, say, Producers' Durables to Defence – to low, from Producers' Durables to Consumers' Durables. Both Marketing and Manufacturing carryover is never high, unless of course to a firm in the same industrial class, and in many instances the carryover is regarded as having a negative effect.

Where the managerial capabilities involved in the diversification or merger are similar, the carryover can be substantial. Hence, market extension mergers, and product extension mergers can have high carryover. Concentric diversification or mergers also involve a high degree of carryover. But it is obvious that mergers involving companies in certain industries are not likely to result in management carryover for certain functions, at least in the early years of the merger. The results would suggest that a takeover where it is claimed the benefits are based on a manufacturing or marketing expertise being used in the acquired company, should be looked on with suspicion, the similarity between the companies should be examined, and at best the returns should not be expected to arise until some time has elapsed.

Kitching suggests that the primary reasons why acquisitions succeed or fail are:

(a) The existence of managers of change. The managers of one of the companies involved must be able to deal with changing circumstances. 'In the period immediately following the merger, the quality of management talent determines the success or failure of the venture.' It is careful planning at this stage that enables any possible synergy potential to be realized.

(b) The organization after the merger. The most successful acquisitions seem to be distinguished by three characteristics:
   (i) The parent company appoints a top executive to 'ride herd' immediately after the acquisition.
   (ii) The reporting relationship between key people in both the acquired and the parent companies is immediately made clear.
   (iii) At the outset the buying company places major emphasis on 'information reporting' rather than on budgets. It uses the control system that is found on acquisition, but immediately asks for a few additional reports.

(c) The acquisition should be part of a plan. Companies have a higher success rate if acquisition is part of strategy of growth and diversification, rather than a mere reaction to an opportunity for buying. The first type could be called 'crystal ball' mergers, the second 'golf course' mergers. For success in a merger it is necessary to have an objective, consistent acquisition criteria. This means that decisions following the acquisition will be based on some clear directive.

(d) There must be careful analysis of future needs. Kitching's study showed that the successful companies make a careful analysis of their subsidiaries' future requirements for parent company funds.

To conclude with the findings of Searby, who believes that there is a tendency for management to relax after a merger has taken place, rather than respond to the change: 'The real risk in managing the post-merger period is not the danger of a colossal failure but the possibilities that the merger will not end with a bang – but a whimper. Considering the high cost of most current mergers half successes can be costly indeed.'

4. British Companies and Mergers

With all the emphasis on planning it is surprising when looking at the Monopolies Commission reports on certain mergers in the United Kingdom to find the casual way in which many mergers are approached. These reports are the most detailed records available on proposed mergers. One must assume that they are indicative of what would be found if other mergers were investigated, although one suspects that because these mergers in particular are to be examined, more detailed research and planning goes into them by the companies concerned than is likely in other mergers.

The main purpose of the proposed Unilever/Allied Breweries merger was the establishment of an international drinks business. The report on the proposed merger reveals that though discussions on the advantages of the merger had taken place between the companies, there was reluctance on their part to quantify the benefits. To quote the report: 'Unilever emphasized to us (the Commission) that much detailed research and planning would have to be done in the overseas markets concerned before the final shape of the proposed operation could be established and that, since in the course of planning there might be substantial modifications to its present thinking, it would be premature to state exactly how the intended development would be carried out. . . . A principal object of the proposed merger is to combine Allied's technical skill and experience as brewers with Unilever's skills in the techniques of mass marketing and its experience in, and detailed knowledge of, overseas markets for consumer goods. . . .' It was stated that it was not possible to quantify the benefits which should accrue as a result of Unilever's contribution to Allied's research, nor was it possible to quantify the expected savings which should result from access by Allied to Unilever's distribution and transport services. In advertising it appeared that there might be some advantages to be gained from the merger, although Unilever could not expect any increase in advertising discounts.

This is probably one of the mergers with the most detailed advanced planning, and yet the Monopolies Commission considered that in both the technical field and the marketing field 'there is a certain vagueness on the part of the two companies as to precisely what form the expected benefits will take and this in turn has led to some overstatement of what these benefits may amount to'. However, the Commission considered it understandable, because of the early stage of the discussions, that they should be unable to formulate in precise terms the benefits to result.

This conclusion by an independent body relates not only to the benefits to be gained from the economies of the proposed merger, but to the financial returns that will result for the acquiring company. They also cast doubts as to whether it was financially worthwhile for Rank to take over De La Rue. One must wonder how many other takeovers not scanned by the Commission would appear to be unprofitable if the facts were known in detail and an attempt made to quantify them.

Further evidence of the reluctance or inability of companies to quantify benefits was found by Sutherland.[19] He recommends that 'the Monopolies Commission should press hard in all cases for quantification of the cost savings expected to flow from the merger – for an explanation of why the merger is necessary to secure them

– and for an exposition of the scheme of rationalization expected to be carried out to secure them'.

It could be argued that it should be left to the companies concerned and the stock market to sort out whether a merger is likely to be a success or not. If, after the event, the stock market is not satisfied with the performance of a merged company, this will be reflected in its price and shareholders will be able to act to express their dissatisfaction at the management's inability to achieve the desired performance. But some weaknesses would be better diagnosed before the event; the motives for mergers, for instance, do not always coincide with the public interest, particularly if such factors as fear, obsolescence or personal aggrandizement play a major part. Some form of government interference can thus be justified. If a proposed merger appears to be against the public interest, or the probability of its success is low, the government may have good grounds for intervening before the merger is concluded. Government interference with the structure of industry should take the form not of a new I.R.C. but with encouraging a climate of economic growth and competition, and with strengthening the powers of the Monopolies Commission to ensure the mergers that take place are in the national interest.

Chapter Two

IMPLICATIONS OF FINANCIAL ANALYSES OF TAKEOVERS*

Gerald D. Newbould

Reader, Manchester Business School

The financial aspects of a takeover are of concern to many and perhaps the people most readily identified are those deeply involved in the financial terms: the shareholders and the managers. Necessarily, therefore, any implications of financial analyses of takeovers will involve primarily these two groups of people; but, some of the implications which follow in this paper could be taken up more widely, for takeover activity has become so important to so many companies that all of us are involved as employees or consumers. If any of the implications do form the subject of wider discussion some benefit will have been achieved, for I believe there is a great danger that the present attitude in the UK – that takeovers and mergers are regarded too favourably as a solution to a variety of economic and managerial problems – will continue. I think one can here contrast the USA and the UK. The United States, like the UK, has been through periods of merger 'fever' but now a much more critical, and realistic, attitude is being adopted. When the UK imitates this, more benefit will be derived from takeover and merger activity.

The analyses in this paper are based upon takeovers and mergers which occurred in the UK in 1967 and 1968.[1] Data relating to every takeover and merger were collected through an analysis of the financial press. During these two years there were 2501 completed takeovers and the total consideration paid was over £5200 million. In each situation a *primum mobile* firm and a victim firm were selected. The aim of selecting a *primum mobile* firm was to form a basis from which managerial intentions and economic impact could be measured. The term 'victim' firm implies too much submission in the majority of cases but it is a clear designation for that firm which was not the *primum mobile* firm. Where the bid was not a surprise, the reported comments of the managements of the firms normally gave the best clues to their relative roles in the takeover situation (and from here onwards in this article the term 'takeover' is used to describe all forms of 'merger', 'takeover', etc.). If this failed the smaller of the firms was designated as the 'victim', on the assumption that the management of the larger would have a greater say in the running of the enlarged firm. Usually, of course, the firm identified as the *primum mobile* was the larger.

*Paper presented at the Conference on 'Mergers and Takeovers', London, 28 and 29 May, 1970.

While there were 2,501 takeovers in the two years under study, the following analyses are restricted to under 250 of these. The ones excluded are those where the consideration involved was less than £1 million and those in which required data were not available, e.g., the *primum mobile* firm and the victim firm did not possess stock exchange quotations for their equity shares, or earnings had not been published.

Numerically there are many exclusions but the analyses below cover just about every 'important' takeover in the UK in 1967 and 1968.

PART 1

Share Prices: Victim Firms and Bidding Firms

This section is devoted to the first analysis concerning share prices. The share prices are those of the victim firm and the bidding firm in each takeover. The question is a relatively simple one: 'Which firm was relatively weaker in terms of share price at the time of the first bid?' There is no deep implication to be obtained from this first analysis but this part and the next are necessary prefaces to the analyses in later parts. 'Bidding' is substituted for '*primum mobile*' from this point for the sake of brevity. 'Bidding' would be an incorrect legal description in the case of a true merger, i.e., where A and B form C to takeover each. A or B is the *primum mobile*, now 'bidding', firm; C is economically irrelevant.

Share prices were chosen as a measure of 'weakness' in the absence of any more amenable data. Asset value cannot be used, for quite apart from the well-known accountancy conventions which underlie disclosed asset values, a feature of takeover situations is the 'discovery' of new asset values which were just about to contribute to the improving prospects for the firm. A conceptual objection to the use of assets is that the real value of the assets is the discounted value of the net earnings which the assets are expected to produce and hence a separate calculation would be needed for each firm. The nearest approximation to this discounted value is the share price which is objective and easily obtainable, but restricts the analysis to quoted companies.

To obtain a share price which is representative of investors' expectations a test of minimum marketability was applied. There had to be several 'marks' at the time in question. This further reduces the number of takeovers which can be examined, but only by nineteen.[2]

Part of the following analyses depends upon the type of takeover, where type is defined by examination of the nature of the opposition to the takeover. Three types were distinguished: 'uncontested' takeovers include all those where the directors of the victim firm did not show, in public, any opposition to the takeover. These would include, therefore, the ones often regarded as 'deals' or 'true mergers' as well as those where there was overt or covert acquiescence on the part of the directors of the victim firm. The second type covers those 'contested by directors'; for a takeover to be included in this group the directors of the victim firm had to be seen to be contesting the bid. It is possible therefore that some vigorous but undisclosed contests have remained in the 'uncontested' category. The final type covers those 'contested by third parties'. This includes takeovers in which more than one bidding firm was involved. In the comparisons in this paper only the successful bidding firm is included. On the occasions where the directors of the victim firm threatened, but did not effect the arrival of a second bidding firm, the takeover remains in the type 'contested by directors'; the ploy was treated as another legitimate tactic of defence. The numbers of takeovers in each type and the total analyzed in this section are shown in Table 1.

Table 1

Takeovers examined in respect of share prices

	Uncontested	Contested by directors	Contested by third parties	All
No.	161	27	35	223

The first date chosen in the comparison of the relative weakness of the share price of the victim firm to the share price of the bidding firm is that four weeks before the first public announcement of the intention to proceed with a takeover.[3] This lapse of four weeks is given in order to remove the effect of leaks or accurate anticipation on the part of investors. The share price at this date for each victim firm and each bidding firm was compared with the price which marked the year's high for each firm.

Table 2

Relative weaknesses in share prices
(Year's high compared with price four weeks before first bid)

	Uncontested	Contested by directors	Contested by third parties
Victim firms:			
Mean	0·899	0·846	0·847
Variance	0·0176	0·0157	0·0256
Bidding firms:			
Mean	0·931	0·930	0·925
Variance	0·0069	0·0049	0·0075

Table 2 shows the means for these comparisons for victim firms and bidding firms according to the type of the takeover. For example, the mean of 0·899 for uncontested mergers indicates that the share prices of victim firms four weeks before the first bid were on average at 89·9 per cent of the year's highs.

It can be seen that for each type of takeover the mean of the victim firms' share prices was lower than the mean of the bidding firms' share prices.

In addition to the means, the variances are also shown in Table 2. Variance is a measure of the variability of the observations used to form the mean. The higher the variance, the more variability there is in the observations used in the calculation.

It can be seen that for each type of takeover the variance of the victim firms' share prices was higher than the variance of the bidding firms' share prices.

In other words, the bidding firms' share prices were not only nearer to their individual highs on average, but also they were consistently nearer.

Before any conclusion such as the one implied by the previous paragraph can be accepted, one must take account of chance and the vagaries of the sampling procedure. There is, of course, an inherent variation in share prices and the means shown in Table 2 could be the chance outcomes of this variation. Whenever any analysis is being carried out on the basis of observed data, the possibility exists that the results have arisen by chance and therefore one must apply statistical tests to measure the relevance, or *significance*, of observed results. One test of significance relates to a difference between means (as in Table 2), and to the extent to which the observed difference between two means (such as between 0·899 and 0·931) can arise by chance. The hypothesis that one sets up is a *null* hypothesis: that there is no real difference between the two means. The appropriate tests using the number of observations and the variance will then indicate the probability of getting the observed difference in the means (such as 0·032) simply by chance. With a probability of 10 per cent or higher (5 per cent, 2 per cent and 1 per cent are the usual ones), an observed result is said to be 'significant'; one rejects the null hypothesis and regards the chance of obtaining the observed difference as too high to be acceptable.

Table 3

Comparisons of weaknesses in share prices of bidding firms and victim firms

Comparison	Observed difference	Level of significance
Uncontested bidders v. victims	0·032	2%
Contested by directors bidders v. victims	0·084	1%
Contested by third parties bidders v. victims	0·078	2%

The results of tests of significance on the differences in the means in Table 2 are shown in Table 3. The differences between the means are seen to be highly significant (2 per cent or 1 per cent) and thus one accepts that the differences are too large to be the result of chance.

One can conclude therefore that the victim firms in any type of takeover were on average relatively weaker in terms of the share price than the associated bidding firms.

One possible interpretation is that the victim firms were intrinsically weaker but another is that each bidding firm tended to time its bid to take advantage of the relative weakness of the victim firms' share price and the relative strength of its own. Either way, there is more reason for a firm to act in a way consistent with maintaining a strong share value.

PART II

Share Prices: Victim Firms in Different Types of Takeover

It will be observed from Table 2 that the mean for victim firms in different types of merger also varies (0·899, 0·846, 0·847) indicating a priori that the relatively weaker victim firms might be involved in contested bids either by the actions of their own directors or by the entry of rival bidding firms.

In the same way as in Part I, tests of significance can be carried out upon the observed differences. First, however, a comment must be made about correcting share prices by means of a computed index of share prices. In Part I, it was immaterial whether a correction by an index was applied or not, because the same correction would have been applied to each share price in each pair of observations. In this section, however, the comparison is between columns rather than between rows, and different corrections would be applied to each reading in each column. It is usual to apply such a correction, but it has not been done here. The reason is that the takeover activity was so widespread and so many firms which are included in the normal share price indices were involved, or were anticipated to be involved, that the indices would be moved by their actual or anticipated involvement. In any case, inspection did not suggest that any type of takeover was associated with any type of movement in share prices overall. Thus without correcting the figures given in Table 2, the results of tests of significance are shown in Table 4. Clearly, with the very small difference in the means of the share prices of victim firms in the two contested types of takeover, the difference could very easily arise by chance. However, when comparing the mean of the share prices of victim firms in uncontested takeovers with the mean in either of the contested types, a significant result is obtained.

Table 4

Comparisons of weaknesses in share prices in victim firms in different types of takeover

Comparison	Observed difference	Level of significance
Uncontested v. contested by directors	0·053	10%
Uncontested v. contested by third parties	0·052	5%
Contested by third parties v. contested by directors	0·001	none

The conclusion is, therefore, that the bids which drew in a rival bid were for firms which were relatively weak in terms of the share price; and those takeovers which were contested by the directors of the victim firms were for firms which were also relatively weak in terms of the share price.

The possible interpretations are that rival bids were attracted by the sign of a 'bargain'[4] and the directors who contested regarded the weakness as 'temporary' and contested on this ground. Equally, tactical considerations could account for the results; rival bidding firms took the opportunity to close in, or the directors contested because the weakness was only tactical.

The results of this section reinforce the implication of the previous section: a firm should act in a way consistent with maintaining a strong share price – an implication not consistent with the behaviour implied in Part IV.

PART III

Share Prices: Effect of Opposition by Directors

The analyses in the previous section concerned the share prices of the involved firms at two dates before the takeover bid commenced. The analysis is now extended to include the final price paid for the victim firm. The measurement is the premium represented by the final bid price over the prebid share price paid by the bidding firm. The average premium measured first as the final bid price over the price four weeks before the first bid and, second, as the final bid price over the year's high share price for each type of takeover is shown in Table 5. The interpretation of the figure shown for the mean is that, for example in the case of uncontested takeovers, a premium of 33·4 per cent over the price four weeks before the first bid, was paid.

Table 5

Premiums paid for shares of victim firms

	Uncontested	Contested by directors	Contested by third parties
Final/four weeks before			
Mean	1·334	1·770	1·739
Variance	0·0686	0·2263	0·0734
Final/year's high			
Mean	1·207	1·487	1·456
Variance	0·0704	0·1833	0·2163

Concentrating first upon the premium paid over the price four weeks before the first bid, it can be seen that the average premiums in the two types of contested takeover exceed that in the uncontested type. Thus, the average premiums are, 77 per cent and 73·9 per cent, where there is a contest by directors and third parties respectively, and only 33·4 per cent where there is no contest.

Again one is dealing with observed results and the vagaries of the procedure must be recognized. Consequently, tests of significance on these differences in the premiums need to be carried out. The results are in Table 6.

Table 6

Comparisons of premiums paid for shares of victim firms in different types of takeover (Final/four weeks before)

Comparison	Observed difference	Level of significance
Contested by directors v. uncontested	0·436	1%
Contested by third parties v. uncontested	0·405	1%
Contested by directors v. contested by third parties	0·031	none

The average premium paid, or achieved, in either of the types of contested takeover are significantly higher than that in the uncontested type of takeover.

Before pursuing this, it will be recalled that victim firms in contested bids were, on average, relatively weaker before the takeover than victim firms in uncontested bids (see Table 4); the differences in the premiums could be therefore the result of making-up ground forfeited before the bid. The way round this possibility is to compare the final bid price with the year's high price. The average premiums using this comparison were shown in Table 5 and were 20·7 per cent, 48·7 per cent and 45·6 per cent for 'uncontested', 'contested by directors' and 'contested by third parties' respectively.

There is therefore still a substantial difference in the premiums paid in contested takeovers compared with uncontested takeovers. Tests of significance show that these results too are unlikely to be the outcome of chance alone (see Table 7).

Table 7

Comparisons of premiums paid for shares of victim firms in different types of takeover (Final/year's high)

Comparison	Observed difference	Level of significance
Contested by directors v. uncontested	0·280	1%
Contested by third parties v. uncontested	0·249	1%
Contested by directors v. contested by third parties	0·031	none

The results are therefore identical to those achieved using the first method of measuring the premium and any implications need not be modified due to the use of an alternative method of measurement.

Before setting out the implications, it is necessary to make a note of another point. In Tables 6 and 7 the differences between the two types of contested takeover prove to be not significant at any level. For practical purposes, therefore, one cannot distinguish between the effects of opposition by directors and the effects of competitive bidding between rival firms.

The conclusions of this section are definite. It has been shown that there is no difference between the mean increase in the share prices of victim firms in takeovers contested by directors and in takeovers contested by third parties. This would suggest that a premium of between 74 per cent and 77 per cent, or 46 per cent and 49 per cent (depending upon the starting point) was achievable in the period under study.

These levels of premium were achievable for the shareholders of the victim firm either through opposition by their directors or by open competition between rival bidding firms.

The directors could achieve, on average, through their own efforts, terms equivalent to those in a full-scale bid battle. When the directors did not contest, the premiums paid to their shareholders were significantly lower.

The implication is that the following issue must be raised: whether the directors who did not contest a bid are guilty of trading personal security (through non-opposition to the bidding firm) for inferior terms for their own shareholders, or of some neglect of duty through insufficient activity.

PART IV

Equity Earnings: Current Difficulties for Successful Bidders

The previous parts have looked at takeover activity, in terms of share prices, before each takeover and at the time of each takeover. The next analysis starts at the time of the takeover and looks forward at the operations of the enlarged firm over its first five years of operation.

For a management to take over another firm a variety of motives will exist. Whether the motives are rational (in economic language) or purely personal, there is a constraint on the takeover activity exerted by the necessity of delivering, at least once a year, financial reports.

Because of the attention paid to these financial reports and to the financial performance implied therein, the management of an individual firm must attempt seriously to achieve annual increases in a variety of ways which can be regarded as indicators. Some indicators of financial performance are gross measures – the level of profits, the level of sales, the level of dividends, etc. – and some are ratios – rate of return on capital employed, earnings per share, etc. It may be impossible to achieve across-the-board improvements every year but, in general an effort will be made to improve financial performance in order to avoid the odium associated with declining financial performance, and to gain the approval and recognition accorded to individuals at the highest level of successful management by the press and those in public office.

Underlying each measure of performance are the following facts: a firm is involved in a bundle of projects, the projects will be managed individually and in divisions, and the achievements of the divisions will be aggregated to form the reports delivered for public scrutiny and comment. It is, therefore, essential that each division should contribute positively to the aggregate performance, rather than absolutely negatively, as in the case of a loss-making division, or relatively negatively as in the case of a division falling below par. At takeover, the bidding firm takes on another division, and takeover can improve or hinder performance.

In some cases the individual projects in the victim firm will be allocated to the appropriate divisions in the bidding firm, but this only complicates the essentially simple point, that the victim firm is an additional division of the acquiring firm. Like any other division of that firm it will have to be managed so as to contribute positively rather than negatively to the aggregate results. Consideration in the form of cash and/or securities will have been paid for the new division and this is a relevant figure in determining whether the division's contribution is to be a positive one.

A simple measure of positive contribution is the rate of return, expressed in terms of the earnings of the division (gross, net of corporation tax, or net of its share of corporation tax) as a percentage of the cost of the division. This may produce, in many cases, a measure which indicates a low rate of return immediately on takeover, because the management of the bidding firm is expecting to increase the earnings of the newly acquired division. In other words, the simple rate of return ignores the improvements which most managements would think that they could effect.

A better measure would therefore take into account the subsequent increases. This is impossible because even now (May 1970) some of the takeovers were effected only 18 months ago. If it were possible to wait for, say, five years, it might be difficult to unscramble the results of the divisions even if a deeper investigation than that provided by the published accounts of the firms could be carried out.

What is possible is to reverse the procedure. Instead of asking whether the (expected or unscrambled) increases produce an acceptable rate of return, it can be asked what increases[5] must be achieved from the date of the takeover in order to produce an acceptable rate of return.

The discussion in previous parts of this paper was confined to ordinary shares and here attention is also focused on the consideration for the equity of the victim firm and the earnings accruing to that equity. The first step is to choose an acceptable rate of return. Let us take 10 per cent net of corporation tax; this is chosen, more than any other figure because it is a round number. What would be better is a rate appropriate to each firm, but 10 per cent is a good working figure. The second step is to guess the period of time over which the enthusiasm of the management can be expected to concentrate upon the newly acquired division. Again, a round number, five years, has been chosen, but neither the five years nor the 10 per cent are anything more than figures which can be changed at will. To be definitive in the following exercise an estimate of the rate of inflation is required. The most common rate used in financial exercises is 3½ per cent per annum.

The known data and assumptions are:

C = the cost of the victim firm
E = the earnings of the victim firm at the time of the takeover (net of interest charges, net of corporation tax)
r = the required rate of return (10 per cent)
n = the period over which the increases are to be measured (5 years)
g = the rate of inflation (3½ per cent)
and there remains the figure which is being sought:
g^* = the required rate of growth of earnings.

Formally, their relationship is:

$$C = \frac{E}{(1+r)} + \frac{E(1+g^*)}{(1+r)^2} + \frac{E(1+g^*)^2}{(1+r)^3} \cdots + \frac{E(1+g^*)^{n-1}}{(1+r)^n} + \frac{E(1+g^*)^{n-1}(1+g)}{(1+r)^{n+1}} + \frac{E(1+g^*)^{n-1}(1+g)^2}{(1+r)^{n+2}} \cdots$$

In basic terms, this formula shows the required rate of growth in earnings that is necessary over a planning period in order to produce a given rate of return.

This formula was applied to all the victim firms for which a consideration of £1 million or over was paid and for which the earnings, interest and tax data were available on Moody's Cards. There were 242 firms. (The additional 19 firms over the 223 in the earlier parts is due to the absence of a test of minimum marketability of the equity shares.) The result for the firms is shown in Table 8, allocated into categories of required rates of growth. The range of required rates of growth extends from under 3½ per cent per annum to over 50 per cent per annum. For perspective one can bear in mind the rate of growth due to inflation (3½ per cent per annum) or the rate of growth of profits of UK companies over the previous five years (1962–66: 4 per cent per annum).

From Table 8 it can be seen that 53 of the 242 firms need growth at less than the rate of inflation to achieve a 10 per cent rate of return on their acquisition expenditure. A further 23 need growth of 3½ per cent to 7 per cent per annum to achieve this rate of return. There are therefore around 76 of the 242 firms (31 per cent) where the required rates of growth are less than double what had been achieved previously. A priori, this would seem an achievable task, given the premise that there would be management interest in the new opportunities.

But this leaves 166 out of the 242 in which the managements have to achieve increases of more than double what had been achieved previously.

Among these are 63 cases where the required rates of growth are between 20 per cent and 50 per cent per annum and another 22 where they are in excess of 50 per cent per annum. These 85 (63+22) firms comprise 35 per cent of companies resulting from major takeovers in the UK in the two years under study.

Table 8

Required rates of growth of earnings to achieve 10 per cent rate of return

Required rate of growth of earnings % p.a. compound	Number of firms
Less than 3½	53
3½–	23
7–	17
10–	30
15–	34
20–	63
50–	22
	242

These rates of growth are *not* once-and-for-all increases; they are compound annual rates of growth.

The conclusion is that there are a substantial number of managements which are at the moment likely to be facing severe difficulties if they are to justify in financial terms a takeover concluded in 1967 and 1968.

The implications are more serious. It is likely that the conclusion reflects a lack of serious analysis preceding a takeover: otherwise such requirements as those in this section would not be found. It is also likely that some of the disappointing results of some companies currently being published can be traced to over-ambitious – or rash – acquisition expenditure and that more disappointing results are likely to appear.

It is perhaps as well to repeat at this point that the figures for just about every 'important' takeover in the UK in 1967 and 1968 are included in Table 8; thus everyone, not just the shareholders and managers directly involved, will be affected by the misallocation of resources resulting from an eagerness to acquire at any price.

PART V

Equity Earnings: Effect of Opposition by Directors

In Part III, substantially inferior terms were noted as being obtained by shareholders when their directors did not contest a proposed takeover. There, the analysis was in terms of share prices. In this section the required rates of growth of equity earnings can demonstrate the same conclusion.

If the firms in Table 8 are distributed according to the three categories, 'uncontested', 'contested by directors' and 'contested by third parties' (as used earlier), their required rates of growth by type can be plotted on a graph. The clearest way to show this is by a 'more-than' ogive curve. The interpretation of any point on such a curve is that for any given required rate of growth of earnings, x per cent of that type of takeover required 'more-than' this rate of growth.

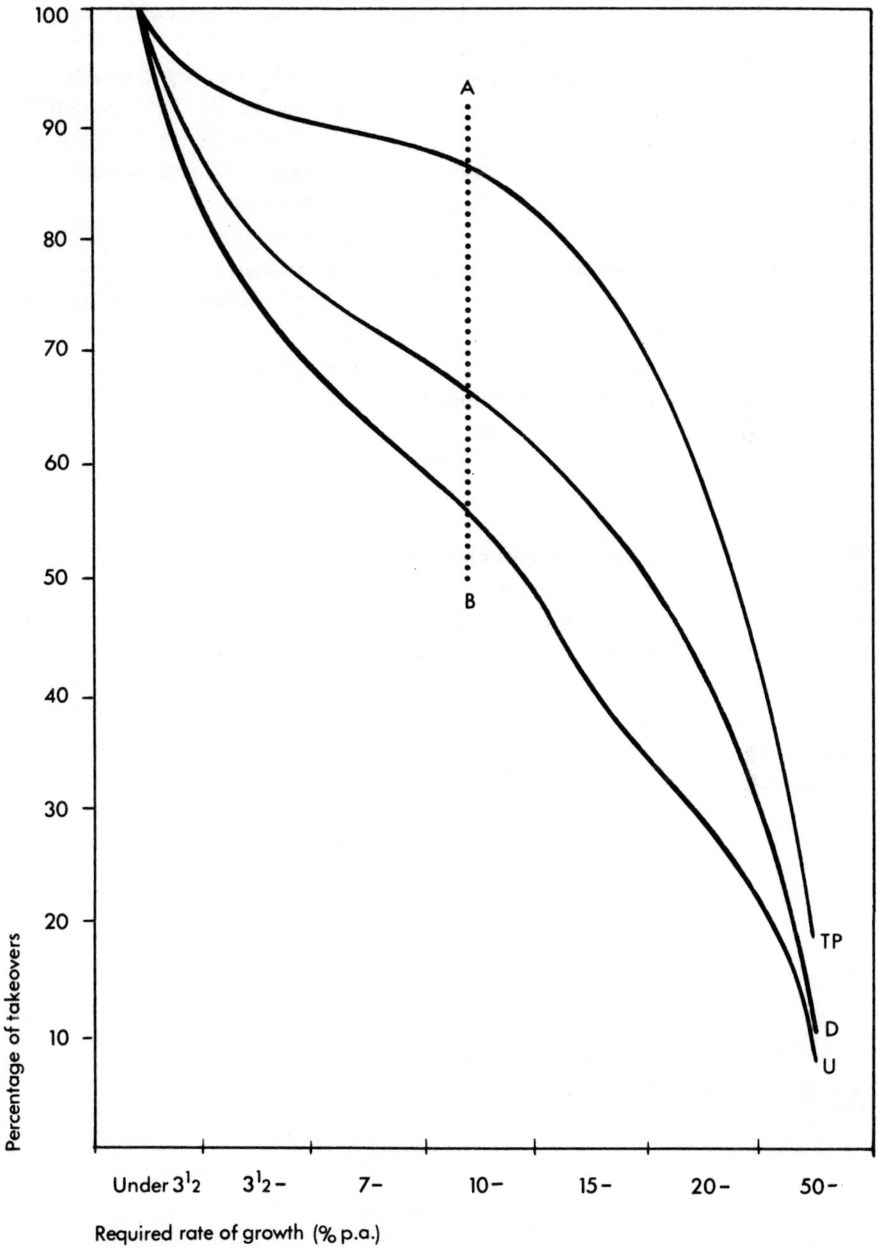

Figure 1. 'More-than' ogive curves for required rates of growth of equity earnings.

The 'more-than' ogive curves for the 'uncontested', 'contested by directors' and 'contested by third parties' types of takeover are drawn in Figure 1, shown as U, D and TP respectively. As an example of interpretation, take the vertical line AB drawn over the '10 per cent' required rate of growth category. Thus 55 per cent of uncontested takeovers required a rate of growth in excess of 10 per cent per annum to produce an acceptable rate of return, whereas the percentage for takeovers contested by directors is 65 and that for takeovers contested by third parties is 86. Therefore the greater the curvature of a line in the diagram, the higher is the proportion of firms in that type of takeover requiring a particular rate of growth.

It can be seen that there is greater curvature for the two contested types of takeover than for the uncontested type, thus confirming the analysis of Part III.

The implication is that the management of a bidding firm has to work that much harder after the takeover if there is opposition to it. Conversely, when there is no opposition, the management of a bidding firm has an easier task at the time of the merger because of the lack of opposition, and an easier task subsequently since it pays relatively less for the victim firm.

SUMMARY

The analyses in this paper have used only financial data which are publicly available. With these data, some serious and some less serious implications have resulted. One main implication concerned the duties of the directors of a firm which is the subject of a takeover bid. The directors have a clear legal duty to their shareholders to represent them financially. It is also clear that when the directors did not oppose the bid their shareholders received significantly inferior terms. Another main implication concerns the willingness of bidding firms to pay prices for acquisitions which in many cases could never be justified to their shareholders or to the public at large.

Chapter Three

TESTS OF THE EFFICIENCY PERFORMANCE OF CONGLOMERATE FIRMS*

J. Fred Weston

Professor of Business Economics and Finance, University of California at Los Angeles,

and

Surendra K. Mansinghka[1]

Assistant Professor of Finance, University of California at Riverside

Many aspects of conglomerate firms have now been studied. The literature on portfolio theory is relevant for appraising diversification aspects of conglomerate firms performance.[2] Other aspects of the economic theory of conglomerates have been treated in various papers.[3] A comprehensive analysis of legal aspects has been made.[4] Business motivations for conglomerate diversifications have been described.[5] The conglomerate merger movement has also received considerable scrutiny with regard to its public policy effects.[6] Most empirical work tests aspects of the effects of mergers generally.[7] Only three statistical studies of conglomerate performance have been published.[8]

Professor Samuel R. Reid's studies include data evaluating a sample of conglomerate firms for the decade ending in 1961. He utilized three measures that he characterized as reflecting the interests of managers and three reflecting the interests of stockholders. Professor Reid concluded that more actively merging firms and firms that diversified to a greater extent in their merging activity scored higher on the criteria related to managers' interests and lower on criteria related to stockholders' interests.[9]

Lorie and Halpern studied the performance of 117 mergers taken from the Federal Trade Commission listing for 1954–67 of all mergers in manufacturing and mining in which the acquired firm had $10 million or more of assets.[10] In their study the focus is particularly on the possibility of 'deception of investors'. The mergers which they studied were therefore those in which the shareholders of the acquired company received relatively complicated instruments such as convertibles or warrants rather than cash, common stock, ordinary preferred stock or bonds.[11]

The investment return to stockholders of the acquired firms was analysed on various bases comprehended in the period six months prior to the merger to two

* Reprinted from the *Journal of Finance*, September 1971.

years after the merger. In general, the investment return performance to stockholders of the acquired firms was superior to the market performance of broad market indexes for comparable periods of time. For example, the mean rates of return for the periods 12 and 14 months subsequent to the mergers were 9·34 per cent and 9·52 per cent, respectively, while corresponding rates for the market index were 7·7 per cent and 7·38 per cent.

Smith and Schreiner compared the efficiency of portfolio selection by conglomerates with that of investment companies.[12] Their findings indicated superior portfolio performance for investment companies. Their data on investment companies was based on actual industry distributions of investments. However, the study of the portfolio results of the conglomerates was a simulation study based upon the industries in which the conglomerate firms appeared to be operating. Further, the distinctive economic function of conglomerates is not portfolio diversification. Indeed, it has been demonstrated that 'home-made diversification' is an effective substitute for corporate or other institutional diversification under the assumptions of perfect capital markets.[13]

Since the data of the previous empirical studies ended predominantly in the early or mid-1960s, an updating is clearly required.[14] Also, most of the studies dealt with mergers generally. Of the three empirical studies dealing with conglomerate mergers, the Lorie and Halpern study is specialized to cover the point of view of stockholders in acquired companies. The Smith and Schreiner study focuses on aspects of conglomerate diversification under a form of simulation for conglomerates. Only the Reid study is directly comparable to this paper.

To evaluate the findings of the previous studies and related issues, the present study begins with a comprehensive empirical analysis of the performance of conglomerate firms. We employ a number of measures, paralleling the performance measures, presuming to reflect the interests of managers and individual stockholders as well as institutional investors. However, our greatest emphasis is on criteria related to economic efficiency. After our results are presented, an evaluation is made of Professor Reid's study. Next, some supplementary data sources for evaluating conglomerate performance are presented. Finally, some comments on the significance of our findings are made.

1. Identification and Selection of Conglomerate Firms

The term 'conglomerate' heretofore has been ambiguous and its implications have undergone a substantial transformation.[15] The confusion is aggravated by the classification system employed by the Federal Trade Commission in reporting on merger activities in three categories. *Horizontal mergers* involve firms in the same industry. *Vertical mergers* represent firms at different levels of the production process in the same industry. *Conglomerate mergers* are 'all other' mergers. Conglomerate mergers are further divided into 'product extension and geographic extension' and 'other' mergers.

Much of the ambiguity stems from the emphasis in the Census Standard Industrial Classification (SIC) system on the characteristics of products for defining 'industries'. The more relevant consideration from the standpoint of the economic effects of mergers is the extent to which research, manufacturing, marketing and other managerial capabilities are extended or complemented in a merger.[16] From this standpoint it would be more informative to label product and market extension mergers as 'concentric' or 'congeneric'. These terms suggest that the merging firms possess related characteristics.

Since the word 'conglomerate' carries some ambiguity, we attempt to give some explicit content to the term.[17] We are focusing on firms that have entered into a broad program of diversification achieved to a substantial degree by external mergers and acquisitions rather than by internal development. In selecting the companies to be included in the study two criteria are therefore relevant. The first is the extent to which growth was achieved from external sources and the second is the degree of diversification represented by the external mergers and acquisitions.

To implement these criteria, we first compiled a list of all firms involved in three or more mergers during the period 1960 through 1968.[18] In making our compilation we sought to adjust for underreporting. If a firm's assets grew at a rate greater than ten per cent per year, the possibility of growth by merger was further investigated. In addition, if acquisitions, adjusted for post-merger growth, aggregated more than $500 millions, or if the firm appeared to have been involved in at least two major acquisitions or a number of smaller acquisitions as indicated by the increase in the number of subsidiaries listed in Moody's in the period between 1960 and 1968, we judged it to be a candidate for application of our two screening rules.

Screening Rule No. 1 required that twenty per cent or more of the increase in total assets of a firm during the period 1960–68 be accounted for by external acquisitions. In view of the fact that the acquired or merged firms would have continued to grow separately if the merger had not taken place, we attempted to adjust for this factor. The total assets of the acquired or merged firms for the years subsequent to acquisition were adjusted by the subsequent growth in their total assets calculated at the growth rate of their industries.[19] Screening Rule No. 2, the diversification criterion, required that in 1968 the firm was involved in ten or more 3-digit SIC industry categories or in five or more 2-digit SIC categories.[20] Application of these criteria led to the selection of sixty-three firms as conglomerates listed in Table 1.[21]

Two control samples were selected, one of industrial companies only and one combining both industrial and non-industrial companies. Since most of our companies were included in the *Fortune* 500 Industrial Companies list, our control sample of industrial companies was selected by applying a table of random numbers to the *Fortune* lists of 500 largest industrial companies excluding, of course, the companies already included in our conglomerate study. To provide a further check, we selected a second control group from the combined directory of large corporations from *Fortune* which in 1968 constituted 500 industrial companies and 250 non-industrial companies.[22] The two random sample groups were chosen as control groups for the comparisons of performance next presented.[23]

Table 1

List of conglomerate companies

Company Name

1 AMK	33 Kidde (Walter)
2 American Metal Climax	34 Kinney National Service, Inc.
3 American Standard	35 Ling-Temco-Vought
4 American Tobacco (Brands)	36 Lear Siegler
5 Avco	37 Litton Industries
6 Avnet	38 Martin Marietta
7 Bangor Punta	39 Midland-Ross
8 Boise Cascade	40 Monogram Industries, Inc.
9 Cities Service	41 National Distillers & Chemical
10 City Investing	42 National General Corporation
11 Colt Industries	43 North American Rockwell
12 Consolidated Foods	44 Northwest Industries
13 Continental Oil	45 Occidental Petroleum
14 Dart Industries (Rexall Drug & Chemical)	46 Ogden
15 Diamond Shamrock	47 Olin Mathieson Chemical
16 Dresser Industries	48 Rapid-American
17 Eaton Yale & Towne	49 Reliance Electric
18 Eltra	50 Republic Corporation
19 Emerson Electric	51 SCM
20 Emhard (Amer. Hardware Co.)	52 Signal Companies
21 FMC	53 Singer
22 Fuqua Industries	54 Studebaker-Worthington
23 GAF	55 Teledyne
24 General Telephone & Electronics	56 Tenneco
25 Genesco	57 Textron
26 Georgia-Pacific	58 Transamerica Corporation
27 Glen Alden	59 TRW
28 Grace (W.R.)	60 US Industries
29 Gulf & Western Industries	61 US Plywood-Champion Papers
30 Houdaille Industries	62 White Consolidated Industries
31 Indian Head	63 Whittaker
32 International Tel. & Tel.	

2. The Comparative Performance of Conglomerate Firms

Since previous studies measured growth, we have done so also. Our main reason for so doing is to test our hypothesis that the findings of some of the previous studies of lower growth in the earnings per share or market price of conglomerate firms were due to the relatively early terminal dates of the studies.[24]

Data on comparative growth rates

Arithmetic means of growth rates were calculated for (1) total assets, (2) sales, (3) net income, (4) earnings per share, and (5) market price based on the yearly high, the yearly low and the arithmetic mean of the annual high and low prices.[25] The periods covered were 1958–68 and 1960–68.[26] The growth rates for the conglomerate firms were higher on all items. But a meaningful comparison of the results requires analysis of the statistical significance of the differences between the means. F-statistics were calculated, comparing the conglomerate firms with each sample separately and jointly.

Table 2 shows a consistent pattern between both time periods. The arithmetic means of growth rates were significantly higher for the conglomerates as compared with Sample 1 or Sample 2 separately or jointly.[27] The differences in the growth rates between the two random samples were generally not significant.

Table 2

Means of Growth Rates in Key Financial Items, 1958–68 and 1960–68

	Sample means of growth rates			F-statistics			
1958–1968							
	C	R1	R2	C, R1	C, R2	R1, R2	C, R1, R2
Total Assets	22·8%	12·6%	10·2%	16·25S^1	26·56S^1	2·53	18·28S^1
Sales	24·0	11·6	10·1	22·13S^1	27·60S^1	1·01	21·72S^1
Net Income	20·7	10·4	11·6	19·50S^1	15·74S^1	·413	13·57S^1
Earnings per share	12·6	8·7	8·9	4·86S^{10}	4·59S^{10}	·008	3·33S^{10}
Market Price-High	15·6	11·9	9·8	4·52S^{10}	13·28S^1	1·77	6·40S^1
Market Price-Low	16·8	12·0	10·5	5·98S^5	12·96S^1	·760	6·52S^1
Market Price-Average	15·9	11·8	10·0	5·16S^5	13·25S^1	1·30	6·47S^1
1960–1968							
	Sample means of growth rates			F-statistics			
	C	R1	R2	C, R1	C, R2	R1, R2	C, R1, R2
Total Assets	26·0%	12·8%	11·1%	23·06S^1	30·27S^1	1·09	23·07S^1
Sales	28·7	12·0	10·9	22·36S^1	26·38S^1	·471	22·12S^1
Net Income	26·1	12·8	11·4	11·83S^1	15·80S^1	·555	12·26S^1
Earnings per share	18·7	10·8	8·5	7·48S^5	14·42S^1	2·02	9·46S^1
Market Price-High	16·9	10·3	9·1	11·44S^1	17·98S^1	·564	10·77S^1
Market Price-Low	16·3	10·4	8·6	8·61S^1	17·85S^1	1·11	9·55S^1
Market Price-Average	16·6	10·4	8·9	10·55S^1	18·20S^1	·790	10·53S^1

The notation used in the table:

C represents the conglomerate firms: 61 firms in 1958, 63 in 1968.
R1 represents the random sample of industrial firms: 61 in 1958, 63 in 1968.
R2 represents the random sample of industrial and non-manufacturing firms: 58 in 1958 and 63 in 1968.

S after the F-statistic indicates that the relationship is significant at the level indicated by the number shown: S^1 indicates significance at the 1% level, etc.

Source: Moody's *Handbook of Common stocks*; Standard & Poor's *Stock Market Encyclopedia*; Individual Company annual Reports; Moody's Investment Manuals.

No great importance is attached to these measurements of the differential growth rates. For any of the measures calculated the difference in growth rate is primarily a function of the degree of merger activity of the conglomerate firms. This applies to the growth rates of the earnings per share as well as the growth rates in market price per share. The more critical measurements reflect the effectiveness of the economic utilization of resources by the three groups.

Comparative performance measures

Earnings performance measures for the years 1958 and 1968 for 63 conglomerate firms were compared with those of the two other samples of firms. Multiple measures are provided, representing alternative methods of measuring earnings performance. To measure earning power before the influence of financial leverage, the earnings are related to total assets. Since this represents all forms of assets financed by debt or equity, the costs of sources of funds utilized to finance total assets must be included in the numerator.[28] Our first measure is the ratio of earnings before interest and preferred stock dividends to total assets. Whether the numerator should be before or after taxes is a matter of dispute in the financial literature, so we made the calculations both ways.[29] For 1968, we calculated the returns on net worth by two methods, including and then excluding preferred stock.

Table 3

Significance Tests for Earnings Performance Measures, 1958, 1968

	1958						
	Sample means			F-statistics			
	C	R1	R2	C, R1	C, R2	R1, R2	C, R1, R2
1 EBIAT/Total assets	5·8	9·2	6·8	9·83S^{1}	1·10	6·12S^{5}	6·21S^{1}
2 EBIT/Total assets	8·7	16·7	12·6	17·13S^{1}	5·47S^{5}	4·52S^{10}	9·54S^{1}
3 Net inc/net worth	7·6	12·6	10·7	10·52S^{1}	4·30S^{10}	2·08	6·05S^{1}
	1968						
	Sample means			F-statistics			
	C	R1	R2	C, R1	C, R2	R1, R2	C, R1, R2
1 EBIAT/Total assets	10·4	8·5	7·6	0·44	0·93	1·37	0·70
1a EBIAT/Total assets*	9·4	8·2	7·5	0·21	0·50	0·80	0·37
2 EBIT/Total assets	15·1	15·6	13·3	0·02	0·38	2·33	0·44
3 Net inc/net worth	13·3	12·4	12·0	0·81	1·98	0·12	0·85
4 Net profit/equity	14·2	12·4	12·2	0·99	1·44	0·06	0·98

Abbreviations have the same meaning as in Table 2. New measures introduced: EBIAT refers to earnings before interest and preferred stock dividends, but after taxes. EBIT refers to earnings before interest, preferred stock dividends and taxes. Net inc refers to net income plus preferred stock dividends. Net worth includes preferred stock. Net profit to equity represents net income less preferred dividends to net worth excluding preferred stock.

Total assets* represents total assets plus the difference between the balance sheet values of preferred stock and estimated book value of preferred stock. The additions to total assets were respectively $5·7, $0·5, and $1·7 billions for the conglomerates, sample 1 and sample 2.

Source: Moody's *Handbook of Common Stocks*; Standard & Poor's *Stock Market Encyclopedia*; Individual Company annual Reports; Moody's Investment Manuals.

In Table 3, statistical tests of the significance between the means of the earnings ratios are set forth. For the year 1958, the earnings rates of the sample groups were significantly higher than the earnings rates of the conglomerates firms.[30] By 1968, there were no significant differences observed in earnings performance among the three groups.[31]

Two possible explanatory influences on earning power performance are examined in Table 4. Price/earnings ratios are calculated, along with their significance measures, on two bases. The first set of price/earnings ratios included all firms. In the second set of calculations, unusual price/earnings ratios were excluded.[32] For 1958, in the early stages of the conglomerate movement, there were no significant differences between either of the two sets of price/earnings ratios.[33] In 1968, at the height of the popularity of conglomerate firms, the difference between the means of their price/earnings ratios and the means for Random Sample No. 1 remained non-significant, but became significant compared with Random Sample No. 2.

Table 4

Significance Tests of Factors Influencing Earnings Performance, 1958, 1968

	1958						
	Sample means			F-statistics			
	C	R1	R2	C, R1	C, R2	R1, R2	C, R1, R2
1 Price/earnings ratios	15·2X	14·6X	18·3X	0·02	0·37	0·96	0·36
2 Price/earnings, adjusted*	17·2X	14·9X	15·8X	0·83	0·34	0·22	0·51
3 Debt/net worth incl. P/S**	95%	56%	155%	8·19S[1]	2·13	6·24S[5]	4·33S[5]
	1968						
	Sample means			F-statistics			
	C	R1	R2	C, R1	C, R2	R1, R2	C, R1, R2
1 Price/earnings ratios	19·4X	18·7X	16·7X	0·10	4·60S[10]	0·74	0·97
2 Price/earnings, adjusted*	19·4X	20·2X	16·7X	0·26	4·61S[10]	4·22S[10]	2·82
3 Debt/net worth incl. P/S**	169%	87%	201%	10·25S[1]	0·33	5·45S[5]	3·46S[10]
4 (Debt + P/S)/equity	233%	94%	210%	5·95S[5]	0·09	5·67S[5]	3·00S[10]

* The adjustment for the price earnings ratios was to exclude ratios exceeding 100 times and those with negative values exceeding 50 times.

** P/S refers to preferred stock. Other abbreviations have the same meanings as in Tables 2 and 3.

Source: Same as Table 2.

These data are contrary to the general impression that one of the reasons for the high growth in earnings per share of the conglomerate firms is that they were able to play the differential price/earnings ratio game. On the contrary, their price/earnings ratios as a group average were not significantly different from the price/earnings ratios of other groups of industrial firms.

A dilemma confronted the conglomerate firms with depressed price/earnings ratios. If they merged with firms with higher price/earnings ratios, the conglomerates would suffer dilution in earnings per share which would at least initially depress growth rates in earnings per share. The disadvantage of a differentially lower price/earnings ratio in merger activity can be offset by offering non-equity forms of securities in exchange or utilizing delayed equity forms such as convertibles and warrants.

Table 4 provides information on this point also. Debt to net worth ratios were measured on two bases in 1968. On the first basis, preferred stock was included in net worth, but not in debt. With net worth including preferred stock, the predominant portion of which for conglomerates was convertible, the ratio of debt to net worth was 169 per cent. This compared with 87 per cent for Random Sample No. 1 and 201 per cent for Random Sample No. 2.[34] The leverage ratios of the conglomerate firms were significantly higher than those of Random Sample No. 1 firms in both 1958 and 1968. In 1958 the debt ratios of the conglomerate firms were significantly lower than those of Random Sample No. 2, including non-industrial firms, but they were not significantly different in 1968. As compared with industrial firms, therefore, the conglomerate firms employed higher debt ratios, both in 1958 and in 1968. In addition, as compared with both samples, the debt ratios of the conglomerate firms grew more rapidly during the decade.

3. Implications of Defensive Diversification

Some preliminary implications of the data in the foregoing tables may be indicated. The conglomerate firms had lower profitability rates in the late 1950s. On the average, their price/earnings ratios were not significantly different from the price/earnings ratios of other firms. Utilizing leverage, however, they were able to raise the return on their net worth. But measurement of returns on total assets, which is free of the effects of financial leverage, is a more meaningful figure. The returns on total assets for the conglomerates in 1958 were generally significantly lower than for the other samples. However, by 1968 the returns on total assets were not significantly different.

This improvement in earnings performance is evidence consistent with the successful achievement of defensive diversification by the conglomerate firms.[35] Defensive diversification may be defined as diversification to avoid adverse effects on profitability from developments taking place in the firm's traditional product market areas.[36] Hence the foregoing data are consistent with the proposition that the conglomerate firms perform the economic function of preserving the values of ongoing organizations as well as restoring the earning power of the entities.[37] In addition, the conglomerate firms avoid the costs of bankruptcy.[38]

Analysis of the backgrounds and acquisition histories of the conglomerate firms suggests that they were diversifying defensively to avoid (1) sales and profit instability, (2) adverse growth developments, (3) adverse competitive shifts, (4) technological obsolescence, and (5) increased uncertainties associated with their industries. These potentially unfavorable developments occurred in various degrees and combinations in a number of industrial categories.

The largest single category of firms came from the aerospace industry. This industry is subject to wide fluctuations in total market demand as well as abrupt and major shifts in its product mix. Excess capacity developed, aggravated by entry of firms from other industries. The industrial machinery and auto-parts companies were also subject to considerable instability in sales.

Low growth prospects were associated with a major secular decline in some markets. This was characteristic of the railway equipment industry, textiles, movie distribution (at an earlier period), and the tobacco industry. A related problem was slow growth in sales or declining profit margins due to persistently unfavorable excess capacity conditions in these (and other) industries. A number of firms sought to diversify in the attempt to acquire access to the new technologies that had developed after World War II. Illustrative was the need of firms in the electrical industry to develop an electronics capability.

Another large category of conglomerates is composed of firms originally based in the natural resources industries. These industries are characterized by instability in demand and supply relationships resulting in substantial fluctuations in product prices and in profit margins. In addition, rising corporate tax rates stimulated them to seek diversification in order to utilize more fully the tax shelter afforded to natural resource operations.

The classification of these diverse firms into a small number of forms of defensive diversification involves some over-generalization. In addition to factors such as tax considerations, some of the conglomerates pursued positive programs such as applying advanced technology in industries and firms were technology had lagged (e.g., Litton Industries). Others were attempting to utilize effectively special capabilities in financial planning and control (e.g., IT & T and Transamerica).

But defensive diversification was a strong motivation among the conglomerate firms. Consistent with the important role of defensive diversification are our findings that profitability of the conglomerate firms was below average in the late 1950s and had improved to average levels by 1968. In this connection, Professor Reid found that on measurements similar to those employed in the present study the conglomerate firms had less favourable performance on profitability measures. In the following section, therefore, the Reid study will be examined.[39]

4. Managerial vs. Stockholder Benefits of Conglomerate Mergers

Professor Reid's analysis distinguished between tests that represented the interests of the managers of the firms and those that represented the interests of the owners of the firms. The three measures Professor Reid used to reflect managers' interests are (1) growth in sales, (2) growth in assets, and (3) growth in employment. The three measures he uses to reflect stockholders' interest are (1) growth in the market value of shares, (2) growth in the ratio of net income to total assets, and (3) growth in the ratio of net income to sales. Professor Reid found that growth rates in the three measures reflecting managers' interests were favorable for conglomerates compared with other companies, while the conglomerates performed less effectively on measures reflecting the stockholders' interests.

But Professor Reid's conclusions are at variance with his own data. In his detailed industry analysis, the results for his measures of performance were either not significant or significant in the wrong direction for ten or more of the fourteen industries for each of his six measures.[40] When Reid does not group his firms by industry, his data on the conglomerates compared to non-merging firms is consistent with his generalization. But the performance of the conglomerate firms, by his own data, was more favorable for all six ratios than for firms engaging in other forms of merger activity.[41] Furthermore, the fact that the data grouped by industry shows no significant difference between the conglomerate firms and all other firms suggests that it is the greater weighting of a small number of industries that produced the results for his total sample.

Conceptual difficulties mar two of his three measures purporting to reflect stockholder interests. Professor Reid measured profitability by calculating net income available to common stockholders divided by total assets. If profits are to be related to total assets, financial charges should be added back to reflect other sources of funds utilized to finance total assets.[42] Otherwise the measure of net income divided by total assets penalizes firms with greater leverage and in particular firms that are increasing leverage over the time period measured. Since the conglomerate firms were utilizing more debt and they were increasing their debt at a faster rate over time than other firms, dividing net income available to common stockholders by total assets biases the performance of the conglomerate firms downward.

Professor Reid's other measure of profitability was the time trend in the ratio of profits to sales. This ratio has little economic significance in the context of the present analysis. The ratio of profit to sales varies greatly among industries, depending primarily upon the characteristic sales to asset turnover. On the average, industries with high ratios of profits to sales are capital intensive with a low turnover of assets, and conversely for industries with high turnovers.[43] Trends in the ratio of profits to sales, therefore, reflect primarily the industry mix of the firms rather than any measure of inherent profitability or managerial performance. Since the conglomerate firms were by definition changing their product mix, Reid's measure of the ratio of profits to sales simply reflects the fact that conglomerate firms were moving into product areas with higher asset turnover, characteristically associated with lower profit margins on sales than industries with lower total asset turnovers.

Thus, two of the three measures purporting to reflect stockholder interests contained conceptual defects. The third test Reid employed was growth in market price of common shares – a measure which suffers from the defect of the early terminal year (1961) for the data. Professor Reid's conclusion, therefore, that the conglomerates operated effectively for the managers, but not for the stockholders has no valid empirical basis. Nor is his implication that conglomerate firms were not efficient supported by the data. The data from our own studies support the conclusion that the performance of the conglomerate firms, on the average to date, satisfies the criterion of efficient economic performance. However, the question may be raised whether the terminal year of 1968 is too early to reflect the critical impacts on conglomerates during 1969. Data were not available for 1969 while our study was in progress. However, from a number of other sources, data through 1969 for segments of the analysis performed in our broader study are available as a check on our results.

5. Other Empirical Evidence on Conglomerate Performance

Forbes, Fortune and *News Front* magazines compile annual performance results for up to 1,000 firms. These data provide a basis for further analysis of conglomerate performance.[44]

The Forbes Data[45]

Forbes compiles data which permit calculation of six performance measures for 500 or more firms as well as for two categories termed by *Forbes* 'conglomerates' and 'agglomerates'.[46] The *Forbes* measures summarized in Table 5 permit comparisons with each of the major categories of analysis employed in our study. *Forbes* calculates a five-year annual increase in sales.[47] The median values of the growth

Table 5

Performance comparisons between multi-industry companies and Forbes' total large firms, 1963–1969*

	Forbes' firms		*Multi-industry companies*	
	1962–64 to 1968	1963–65 to 1969	1962–64 to 1968	1963–65 to 1969
Number of companies	500	578	38	47
1 Five-year annual increase in sales	9·0%	9·9%	20·0%	19·05%
2 Five-year annual increase in per-share earnings	8·6	7·05	12·7	12·2
3 Price gain for five-year periods	70·5	17·15	140·0	60·2
4 Five-year average combined return on debt and equity	9·7	9·6	10·0	9·6
5 Five-year average return on equity	12·4	12·5	12·6	13·4
	1968	1969	1968	1969
6 Last year's return on equity	12·0	11·65	12·2	11·85

* Median values compared on all items.

Sources: *Forbes*, Vol. 103 (January 1, 1969), pp. 37–41, 53–66, 78, 80, 91.
Forbes, Vol. 104 (January 1, 1970), pp. 44–81, 96–9, 227–31.

rates in sales of the multi-industry companies were at least double the growth rate in sales for the broader sample of firms. The growth rate in earnings per share for the multi-industry companies ranged from 12·2 per cent to 12·7 per cent for the two five-year periods, ending in 1968 and 1969, respectively, about 50 per cent better than the performance by the total of the *Forbes* firms. *Forbes* measured the gain in market price in terms of a total percentage increase for a five-year period. The multi-industry companies performed more than twice as well as the broad sample; growth for both declined when 1969 is taken as the terminal year.

Forbes calculates three profitability measures. The first profitability measure is a five-year average combined return on debt and equity. This is comparable to our measure of earnings before interest and preferred stock dividends but after taxes, to total assets, except that the *Forbes* denominator does not include current liabilities. The results confirm the findings of our analysis. The five-year average combined return on debt and equity for the multi-industry companies for the period ending in 1968 was slightly higher than the *Forbes* broader group. For the period ending in 1969 there was no difference in the median values of the five-year average returns for the two groups.

The results of the *Forbes* data on the other two measures of earning performance were also the same as for our study. Both the five-year average return on equity and last year's return on equity for the multi-industry companies was slightly higher than the earnings performance of the *Forbes* total number of large companies. The *Forbes* data, therefore, provide confirmation of the results of our study.

The News Front Data

News Front compiles data on the 1,000 largest manufacturing companies in the United States.[48] The firms are grouped by SIC categories. In its 1969 presentation *News Front* presented a category, SIC 3999, 'diversified/conglomerate companies', in which are listed 47 firms. Presenting data for 1968, the diversified/conglomerate averaged a return on stockholders' equity of 12·1 per cent, compared to 12·2 per cent for 'average manufacturing'.[49] The difference between the performance of the multi-industry companies and 'average manufacturing' described by *News Front* is negligible.

The Fortune Data

Fortune magazine each year calculates the ten-year compound annual growth rates of earnings per share for its sample of 500 industrial firms and the ratio of net income to net worth. These results are summarized for our sample of conglomerate firms compared with the total *Fortune* 500 firms for the most recent five years through 1969. The results are tabulated in Table 6. For the ten-year periods ending in 1965 and 1966, the compound annual growth rates of the *Fortune* 500 companies were higher than for the conglomerate firms. Beginning in 1967, the conglomerate firms began to out-perform the *Fortune* 500 firms by relatively large differentials.

For the ratios of net income to net worth, the conglomerates were higher than the *Fortune* 500 in every year but the differences are not significant.

Table 6

Comparisons of the performance of conglomerates with the *Fortune* 500 firms, 1965–1969*

	Ten-year compound annual growth rates of EPS			Net profit to stockholders' equity		
Years ended	*Fortune* 500**	Conglom-erates	Conglom-erates less *Fortune* 500	*Fortune* 500	Conglom-erates	Conglom-erates less *Fortune* 500
1969	7·10	9·91	+2·81	11·3	11·8	+0·5
1968	8·71	11·98	+3·27	11·7	12·9	+1·2
1967	6·59	8·57	+1·98	11·3	12·4	+1·1
1966	6·09	5·99	−0·10	12·7	13·2	+0·5
1965	6·04	5·74	−0·30	11·8	12·4	+0·6

* Medians of the growth rates or percentage returns for each group of companies are reported.
** Comparisons with our two random samples does not change the direction of the differences, but the magnitudes are sometimes larger, sometimes smaller.

Source: *The Fortune Directory*, 1966–70.

5. Conclusions

Most of the earlier studies of mergers covered periods ending in the early or mid-1960s. The present study, supplemented by compilations from *Forbes*, *Fortune* and *News Front* magazines, extends the analysis through 1969. Our empirical findings suggest three generalizations.

1. The conglomerate firms out-performed samples of other firms or broader groups of firms on all of the growth measures. Contrary findings of some other studies resulted from their early terminal dates, before the mid-1960s. However, we do not attach great significance to these measures, since they reflect primarily the extent of past merger activity by the conglomerate firms. More important will be the growth in market price per share over a period of years in the future, after the ability of the conglomerate firms to sustain a growth rate in earnings per share over an extended period has been tested.

2. The earnings performance measured by the ratio of net income to net worth is somewhat higher for conglomerate firms, but the difference is not statistically significant. This somewhat higher return on net worth did not result from the differentially higher price/earnings ratios of conglomerate firms in mergers because on average the price/earnings ratios of conglomerate firms were not significantly different from the price/earnings ratios of other samples of firms. The higher returns on net worth of the conglomerate firms resulted from the larger and increasing percentage of leverage employed by them during the decade of the 1960s. The

effects of the higher leverage of conglomerate firms on their longer-run success has not been fully tested.

3. We attached greatest significance as a measure of the economic performance of conglomerate firms to the ratios of profitability free of the influence of leverage. The earnings rates of the conglomerate firms in the late 1950s or the early 1960s were significantly lower than the earnings on total assets or net worth-plus-long term debt for other groups of firms. However, by 1968 no significant differences in earnings performance were observed.

It appears, therefore, that an important economic function of conglomerate firms has been the raising of the profitability of firms with depressed earnings to the average for industry generally.[50] This function was particularly important in connection with defensive diversification. A large proportion of the conglomerate firms developed out of industries in which adverse developments in their economic environments had either taken place or were in prospect. Therefore, the most appropriate test of the earnings performance of conglomerate firms is not superior earnings performance, but whether they were able to achieve at least average earnings performance.[51]

In many respects the conglomerate movement may be regarded as the development of a new industry. Economic principles predict, therefore, that the earning power of this group of firms would tend to be equal to the earning power of firms on the average. Theory also predicts great variations in earnings performance among individual conglomerate firms.

The superior performance of individual firms in new industries has characteristically attracted an excess number of firms and firms without the requisite managerial or product characteristics for survival. Hence, as a new industry, one would expect the failure rate among conglomerates in the near future to be somewhat higher than in industry generally. But there will be individual conglomerate firms that will achieve higher-than-average profitability over periods of time. The success of individual conglomerates, as is true of firms generally, will depend upon the relative abilities of their managements for achieving operating efficiency and for making the shifts in their product-markets required by the changing economic environment.

Editor's note

The September 1971 edition of the *Journal of Finance* included not only the above article, but also a reply by Professor S. R. Reid.[52] The Weston/Mansinghka article criticized certain of the research work of Reid,[53] and the reply presents evidence which attempts to refute their observations.

Reid points out that his work tested the hypothesis that, 'the form of growth as well as the type of merger will have differential effects upon the resulting growth of firms and particularly upon their profitability patterns'. He believes that there is a conflict of interests between owners and managers of large publicly held merging firms, and in particular that firms using the conglomerate strategy for growth tend to be size maximizers rather than profit maximizers. The results of his study 'indicate that the conglomerate merger is a special case among the various merger types with the firms using it displaying unique performance patterns in comparison with firms using alternative growth strategies. While the profit-to-stockholders variables were stronger in this group than in the other merger type groups, size maximization appears to be a particularly strong factor in the conglomerate group.'

Reid found that although conglomerates may have out-performed firms that grew by other forms of acquisition strategy, the firms that showed the best performance from the point of view of stockholders were those that did not merge at all. The firms that followed a pure 'internal growth' strategy, although small in number, benefited their stockholders better than companies that followed any type of acquisition policy. This finding is similar to that of Hogarty.[54]

It is, of course, on this latter point that Reid and Weston/Mansinghka disagree. The above article finds evidence that suggests that conglomerates do perform as well in terms of profitability as the average firm.

The reply of Reid's discusses the criticisms of his profit-to-stockholders variables. He examines a recent period, 1960–9, using the Weston/Mansinghka data and the variables of his previous study and comes to the same conclusions as he did in his earlier study. He concludes the reply with the same statement as in his original study: 'Since it appears that if such a thing as synergy does exist, the synergistic benefits are serendipitous, then stockholders, whose objectives are more economic and rational, should be better able to allocate resources'.

It is unfortunate that the disagreement has arisen. There is far too little empirical research on the advantages or otherwise of mergers and takeovers, and the fact that two of the more detailed studies into one form of merger policy, namely the conglomerate, appear to have conflicting results can only delay any public reaction or government action. It is possible to try to explain why these different results arise; for example, Weston/Mansinghka and Reid chose different methods to select their control groups. However, the important point is that more research is still needed into the impact of conglomerates which it is hoped will provide conclusive evidence one way or the other.

Chapter Four

WHY DO MERGERS MISCARRY?*

John Kitching

Independent Consultant on Mergers and Acquisitions

Acquisitions are in fashion. Large corporations are creating special posts with titles like 'director of acquisitions'. Smaller companies now list the responsibility for acquisitions high among the duties of the vice president for corporate planning and investment. A host of fashionable terms have sprung up in connection with the acquisitions movement – for instance, 'conglomerate', 'concentric', 'defensive', and 'a key part of diversification strategy'. Academics argue learnedly about 'synergy' in acquisitions. And there is even a journal devoted to mergers and acquisitions.[1]

Some impressive figures underscore the popularity of corporate weddings. For example:

In 1966 there were 2,377 corporate consolidations – an increase of 75 per cent over 1963.[2] (These figures include divisional spin-offs and partial acquisitions. The Federal Trade Commission lists 1,628 *full* acquisitions in 1966.)

Of those consolidations, an estimated 98 involved acquisition of a company which either had assets in excess of $10 million or was purchased for more than that figure.[3]

As a rough estimate, assets amounting to $4·5 billion were acquired last year [1966] in the manufacturing and mining fields, and the compound growth rate in the value of assets bought is running at 15·5 per cent annually.

In isolated incidents, growth and diversification by means of acquisitions has led to Justice Department investigation. But, generally, the progress toward more and bigger acquisitions seems inevitable, and socially and economically acceptable. It's about time, therefore, that someone took a close look at this royal progress and asked the question. 'Has the king any clothes?' Or, putting it more plainly, are companies really getting what they paid for?

Research Scope and Methods

The research was divided into two parts – a survey of the management literature and field interviews with executives of twenty-two companies. Interestingly, the literature

* Reprinted from the November–December 1967 edition of the *Harvard Business Review*

search revealed that research to date has concentrated only on the events leading up to and immediately following acquisition. However, since the results of an acquisition are not apparent until two years after it has taken place, according to the majority of the managers interviewed, an accurate evaluation of its success or failure cannot possibly be made on the basis of results obtained in the weeks or months immediately following the merger. So the literature is virtually silent on the real causes of success or failure of acquisitions. Accordingly, this research focused on the experience of companies two to seven years following an acquisition, since that amount of time is required for an acquisition to become stable enough to be evaluated accurately.

The field research was done with the generous cooperation of twenty-five top-level executives. Company chief executives, senior vice presidents for finance, controllers, treasurers, directors of corporate planning, and directors of acquisitions all contributed their time and experience.

The industries covered included textiles, electronics, communications, automotive supply, marketing, recreation products, toiletries, food, aviation products, tobacco, finance, retailing, rubber goods, building supplies, and chemicals. The sales volume of these companies ranged from $25 million to $2 billion. Acquisitions were classified as follows:

Horizontal – Same industry as buying company, with approximately the same customers and suppliers.

Vertical integration – Major supplier or customer of the buying company and in the same industry.

Concentric marketing – Same customer types as buying company but different technology.

Concentric technology – Same technology as buying company but different customer types.

Conglomerate – Customers and technology different from those of buying company.

The interviews were divided into two parts. The first part dealt with the top manager's *qualitative* assessment of the success or failure of the acquisition program, measured against the original strategy. Particular attention was given to the most and the least successful acquisitions; in these situations, the top manager was asked to give his opinion as to the major causes behind the success or failure. The second part of the interviews focused on the *financial results* actually obtained, compared with the forecasts made before the merger (where these existed), and on the ease and dollar payoff of the synergy achieved. This procedure was designed to cross-check the manager's subjective judgement on the acquisition's success or failure (though acquisition objectives could sometimes be successfully reached without achieving financial targets).

Clearly, this methodology cannot yield really definitive statements about the causes of success and failure in acquisitions. (Such work is already under way in the Carnegie Institute of Technology, under the direction of H. Igor Ansoff.) What it can do, however, is to identify trends or patterns in the experience of several companies. This 'common experience' may prove useful to managers contemplating acquisition. And it can form the basis for more extensive research into the acquisition process.

The names of the companies contributing to this study have been withheld in order to protect their confidence. Instead, they are designated by initials, such as 'Company M', and their various subsidiaries are differentiated by subscripts, such as 'M_1', 'M_2', and so on.

Research Aims and Findings

This article is based on discussions with top executives of 22 companies, and draws on their experience in acquiring and managing a total of 181 companies in the period 1960–65. It audits in detail the *actual results* of 69 acquisitions made by 20 of the 22 companies sampled.

The objective of this survey was not only to sample the results of acquisitions, but also to establish the underlying causes for variations in performance. The magnitude of such variations seems to be great. For an example of success, take the following report (digested from an actual memorandum, with italics added) to the president of a corporation which I shall call Company S:

'*Earnings of acquired companies.* The final earnings for 1966 are $7·22 per share, unchanged from the preliminary earnings submitted last month. The average from the 22 companies we acquired is *approximately* 78 per cent *above the per share earnings of Company S as a whole*'.

Compare this success story with the long drawnout agony hinted at in Company M's published annual reports. The following excerpts concern an acquired company, which I shall call M_1 (italics are added for emphasis):

1962: 'Company M acquired M_1, for 200,000 shares. M_1's products are sterile and disposable. We hope that disposable products is a growth field. With M's strength in product creativity and design, plus high quality manufacturing and packaging at low unit costs, we trust there will be an increase in our sales and profits in this new field. And also an interchange of product development. . . with our overseas company'.

1963: 'Our medical supply operations in the United States increased sales, but *made no contribution to company earnings'.*

1964: 'Company's disposable surgical products business continued to build position in highly competitive industry. We *do not expect important contribution to earnings from this activity* in the near future'.

1965: 'Our disposable surgical products activity registered gain in overall sales volume; *results not a significant factor in company's total earnings picture'.*

1966: 'Disposable surgical products gained in overall sales volume, but *significant results from this activity not expected in the near future'.*

Need for concrete data

The scope and methods of the research are described at the beginning of this article. Two considerations influenced the approach which I took:

1. The top executives I interviewed seemed uneasy about their companies' acquisition activities. In the use of mergers, their companies had a fashionable tactic, and one which looked good to stockholders – either as a strategy for growth or as a defensive move. But the executives were uneasy about the relatively high degree of risk associated with investment in an acquisition compared with an equivalent investment in, say, a new plant. They wished to know what the 'track record' of other companies had been, before attempting to undertake or expand their own acquisition programs. And if there were any general rules to be learned from the experience of others – either about avoiding pitfalls or about taking positive action to help ensure success – then they wanted to know about them.

2. The research seemed important from the standpoint of testing out unproven academic hypotheses. For example, to what extent do acquisitions lead to economies of scale? Can the concept of synergy, so widely held, be proved out in practice? And is there any relationship between the type of acquisition and its success or failure?

Overview of results

Before going into the study in detail, let us take a look at some of the major findings. These can be classified under the headings of objective results (obtained from statistical evidence) and subjective results (drawn from top executives' reflections on their experience). Turning first to the *objective* results:

Nearly half of the mergers (45 per cent of the sample) were of the fashionable conglomerate type. Horizontal acquisitions were the next most common (25 per cent), followed by concentric technology (14 per cent), concentric marketing (13 per cent), and vertical integration (5 per cent). There is a relatively high risk of failure in concentric acquisitions, and a relatively low one in horizontal mergers.

A 'size mismatch' (where the acquired company's sales were less than 2 per cent of the parent company sales volume before the merger) occurs in 84 per cent of the acquisitions considered failures. This reinforces the 'critical mass' theory advanced by H. Igor Ansoff, but there are, of course, organizational methods for dealing successfully with 'mismatch'.

In 81 per cent of the failures, the organizational format (either the reporting relationships established after the merger or the extent of autonomy allowed) is disturbed at least once after the acquisition is first brought into the new family.

Theoretically, synergy in mergers should be greatest where production facilities are combined, because economies of scale are possible. Combinations based on technology (process know-how and R & D transfer), marketing, organization (personnel economies and productivity increases), and finance (additional and lower-cost capital) should be of diminishing value, in that order. According to top managers, however, the ease with which synergy is actually released occurs in the reverse order; that is, synergy is most easily accomplished where financial resources are pooled, and is most difficult to achieve where production facilities are combined. Furthermore, the dollar payoff is actually lowest, on the average, where production and technological resources are put together; highest, where financial resources are combined. What about the *subjective* results? They can be crystallized into six major points:

1. The element critical for success is not the potential amount of synergy to be released in combining two companies. Rather, it is the existence or absence of 'managers of change' – men who can catalyze the combination process. In the most successful mergers, either the acquiring company brought in new managers of change or it motivated the old management to introduce profitable change.

2. According to the executives interviewed, failure occurs in a pattern that might be formularized as follows: the *sum* of the managerial competence in the parent company plus that of the acquired company fails to equal or exceed the demands of the management tasks found in the newly merged organization. This pattern was so universally and firmly stated that it gains almost the stature of a physical law. And although the 'law' may seem obvious, the appraisal techniques to which its acceptance gives rise are highly sophisticated. Furthermore, it had been overlooked by almost all the companies whose acquisitions failed.

3. The nature of the reporting relationships set up between parent and acquired companies, along with the organizational responsibilities and control systems established, is a dominant influence on the success or failure of the merger.

4. Companies that merely react to opportunities to purchase are less successful in their acquisitions than those with an overall strategy which includes an acquisition program. The more successful companies will often actively solicit the sale of companies which they wish to purchase.

5. Successful companies formulate a set of acquisition criteria which are consistent with overall strategy, and then rigorously apply them. This is hard to do in the atmosphere of secrecy and emotion which surrounds negotiation, but experienced acquirers have nonetheless evolved valuable techniques for cool appraisal.

6. Even in the case of successful acquisitions, parent companies tend to underestimate their subsidiaries' future requirements for additional funds; often, too, the demands on the parent's management time are underestimated. The result is that return on investment is less than expected.

Performance Patterns

Now let us examine the objective results of the study in more detail. Analysis of the data gathered in the study shows some interesting facts, many of which are summarized in Table 1 (pp. 46-9). Although, as earlier indicated, a larger sample is needed for definitive statements, it is quite probable that these results present a fair picture of the total acquisition movement in the United States.

Varying failure rates

Table 2 shows the breakdown of the sample among the various categories of acquisition, as well as the incidence of failure for each type. (Acquisition types are defined on page 41).

Interestingly, the greatest proportion (45 per cent) of acquisitions consists of the conglomerate type. This suggests that the move to diversify and spread risk is well under way. But this strategy is in itself risky, as the Table shows, since 42 per cent of all the failures occurred in this group. Risk reduction evidently bears its own risks!

The proportion of horizontal acquisitions is surprisingly high (25 per cent), inasmuch as this type is the one most likely to be accused of having a restraining effect on trade. However, the Justice Department does not generally discourage horizontal mergers among smaller units of an industry. The results shown here are probably indicative of a continuing movement among firms with smaller market shares in the direction of merging with larger companies to improve their industry standing. The encouragingly low incidence of failure in this group is probably due to the fact that the parent company is familiar with the market and the technology.

Table 2

Which types of acquistion have the highest incidence of failure?
[As reported by executives]

Acquistion type	Per cent of total	Per cent of failures
Vertical integration	3%	0%
Horizontal	25	11
Concentric marketing	13	26
Concentric technology	14	21
Conglomerate	45	42

The greatest incidence of failure occurs in the concentric acquisition. Those companies with common customers, the 'concentric marketing'group, represent only 13 per cent of the sample, but their failures constitute 26 per cent of the sample total. Similarly, the 'concentric technology' group has 21 per cent of the failures, although it represented only 14 per cent of the sample. Apparently, what happens is that the parent company, feeling it 'knows the market backwards', gets lulled into a false sense of security and neglects the technology aspect, or vice versa.

The type of merger, however, is not the determining factor in the success or failure of an acquisition. The primary cause must be sought elsewhere.

Size mismatches and organization

Several executives attributed acquisition failures to mismatches of size. For example, frequent comments were made to the effect that the acquired company 'was so small no one in corporate headquarters could get interested in it', or 'we couldn't get these little entrepreneurs to think like big businessmen'.

In 84 per cent of the failures, as previously stated, the acquired company's sales volume is less than 2 per cent of the parent company's at the time of acquisition. Certainly, where there is a great difference in size between the parent company and the acquired company, management needs to be particularly thorough in developing

Table 1. Results of merger

Subsidiary code name	Date of merger	Type of merger	Performance	Management of acquired company: Organization
A_1	1960	Conglomerate	Failure	Autonomous; then grouped
A_2	1961	Horizontal	Success	Grouped
B_1	1963	Conglomerate	Success	Autonomous
B_2	1963	Conglomerate	Success	Autonomous
B_3	1963	Conglomerate	Success	Autonomous (formed own group)
B_4	1963	Conglomerate	Success	Autonomous
C_1	1965	Concentric technology	Success	Autonomous
D_1	1964	Conglomerate	Success	Autonomous
E_1	1960	Concentric marketing	Failure	Merged with parent
E_2	1963	Concentric marketing	Failure	Merged with E_1
E_3	1963	Concentric marketing	Failure	Merged with parent
E_4	1962	Horizontal	Success	Grouped with existing company in Canada
F_1	1965	Conglomerate	Success	Parent company officer appointed chairman of subsidiary's executive committee
F_2	1964	Conglomerate	Success	
F_3	1965	Conglomerate	Success	
G_1	1962	Conglomerate	Success	Grouped
G_2	1965	Conglomerate	Failure	Grouped & merged with another company
H_1	1965	Vertical	Success	Autonomous
I_1	1961	Horizontal	Success	Merged
I_2	1963	Concentric marketing	Success	Merged
J_1	1961	Concentric technology	Failure; then success	Autonomous; then merged
K_1	1961	Concentric technology	Success	Autonomous
K_2	1965	Concentric technology	Success	Autonomous
L_1	1961	Horizontal	Success	Merged
L_2	1965	Horizontal	Failure	Merged
M_1	1962	Conglomerate	Failure	Autonomous
N_1	1965	Horizontal	Success	Merged
N_2	1964	Horizontal	Failure	Autonomous; then merged
N_3	1964	Horizontal	Success	Merged
N_4	1961	Concentric technology	Failure	Grouped as a division
N_5	1961	Concentric technology	Failure	Grouped as a division

Table 1. Results of merger

Key to synergy scores: H = High M = Medium L = Low O = Nil

Subsidiary manager reports to:	Sales volume as percent of parent Sales volume	Synergy released in organization (ease of achievement): Motivation	Efficiency	Synergy released in other functions (ease of achievement/dollar payout): Finance	Marketing	Technology (including R&D)	Production
President at first; then group vice president	0·5%	O	M	H/$L	O/$O	O/$O	O/$O
Group vice president	2·0%	M	M	H/$L	L/$L	O/$O	O/$O
'Face to face' meetings with holding company executive team	29·0%, 9·0%, 31·0%, 4·2%	H	M	H/$H	M/$M	O/$O	L/$L
President	7·0%	H	M	H/$H	M/$L	L/$L	O/$O
Senior vice president	3·0%	H	O	H/$H	L/$M	O/$O	O/$O
Group vice president at first, then president, North America	6·7%	O	M	H/$L	M/$O	O/$O	O/$O
	0·2%	O	M	H/$O	M/$O	O/$O	O/$O
President, North America	0·4%	O	M	H/$L	L/$O	O/$O	O/$O
President of international corporation	3·6%	M	L	H/$H	M/$M	L/$L	O/$O
Senior vice president	12·3%	M	O	H/$H	O/$O	O/$O	O/$O
	5·3%	M	O	H/$H	O/$O	O/$O	O/$O
	1·8%	M	O	H/$H	O/$O	O/$O	O/$O
Group vice president	16·0%	H	L	H/$H	L/$O	L/$M	O/$O
Group vice president	10·0%	H	L	H/$L	M/$L	M/$L	L/$O
Area vice president	2·0%	M	L	H/$O	M/$O	O/$O	H/$H
Senior vice president	35·0%	O	L	H/$H	H/$H	M/$L	M/$L
Senior vice president	12·0%	H	L	L/$L	H/$M	M/$L	L/$L
President at first; now area vice president	29·0%	H	L	L/$L	H/$H	L/$M	L/$L
Senior vice president, operations	37·0%	H	L	H/$M	L/$L	H/$L	O/$O
Senior vice president, operations	66·0%	H	L	H/$M	L/$L	M/$M	O/$O
Executive committee	8·0%	M	M	H/$M	O/$O	O/$O	O/$O
Executive committee	10·5%	M	M	H/$O	O/$O	O/$O	O/$O
Executive committee & 3 separate officers	1·0%	L	L	H/$L	O/$O	M/$O	O/$O
Division manager	0·2%	H	H	H/$M	H/$H	M/$M	M/$M
Corporate headquarters at first; then division manager	0·3%	O	O	L/$O	L/$L	L/$O	O/$O
Division manager	0·5%	M	M	M/$M	H/$H	H/$H	L/$L
Group vice president at first; then corporate vice president	0·6%	O	L	O/$O	M/$O	H/$O	H/$O
	0·6%	O	L	O/$O	M/$O	H/$O	H/$O

* Net income as % of parent net income.

Table 1. Results of merger

Subsidiary code name	Date of merger	Type of merger	Performance	Management of acquired company Organization
N_6	1961	Concentric technology	Failure	Grouped as a division
N_7	1962	Conglomerate	Success	Merged
N_8	1964	Concentric technology	Failure	Merged; then autonomous
N_9	1965	Conglomerate	Success	Autonomous
N_{10}	1965	Conglomerate	Success	Grouped
N_{11}	1965	Conglomerate	Success	Grouped
N_{12}	1965	Conglomerate	Success	Grouped
O_1	1963	Vertical	Failure; then success	Autonomous; then merged
P_1	1961	Concentric marketing	Success	
P_2	1960	Conglomerate	Success	
P_3	1960	Conglomerate	Failure	Autonomous; then grouped
P_4	1960	Conglomerate	Success	
P_5	1960	Horizontal	Success	
P_6	1960	Concentric technology	Success	
Q_1	1962	Conglomerate	Failure	Autonomous
R_1	1965	Concentric marketing	Success	Grouped
R_2	1965	Conglomerate	Failure	Semiautonomous
S_1	1965	Conglomerate	Success	
S_2	1963	Conglomerate	Success	
S_3	1964	Conglomerate	Success	
S_4	1963	Concentric marketing	Success	
S_5	1963	Horizontal	Success	
S_6	1965	Conglomerate	Failure	
S_7	1965	Conglomerate	Success	
S_8	1963	Conglomerate	Success	
S_9	1961	Conglomerate	Success	
S_{10}	1963	Horizontal	Success	
S_{11}	1964	Horizontal	Success	
S_{12}	1961	Horizontal	Success	
S_{13}	1962	Concentric marketing	Failure	
S_{14}	1965	Horizontal	Success	
S_{15}	1964	Concentric technology	Success	
S_{16}	1965	Horizontal	Failure; then success	
S_{17}	1964	Horizontal	Success	
S_{18}	1965	Concentric marketing	Failure	
S_{19}	1965	Horizontal	Success	
T_1	1965	Conglomerate	Failure	Various forms of grouping
T_2	1960	Conglomerate	Success	Semiautonomous

Table 1. Results of merger

Key to synergy scores: H = High M = Medium L = Low O = Nil

Subsidiary manager reports to:	Sales volume as percent of parent Sales volume	Synergy released in organization (ease of achievement) Motivation	Efficiency	Synergy released in other functions (ease of achievement/dollar payout) Finance	Marketing	Technology (including R&D)	Production
Group vice president at first; then corporate vice president	0·5%	O	L	O/$O	M/$O	H/$O	H/$O
Division manager	0·6%	L	H	M/$L	M/$M	L/$L	M/$M
Division manager at first; then group president	1·8%	O	L	O/$O	O/$O	M/$O	O/$O
Group vice president	6·0%	M	M	H/$H	O/$O	L/$L	O/$O
Group manager	–	L	M	H/$M	M/$M	L/$L	M/$M
	2·0%	L	M	H/$M	M/$M	L/$L	M/$M
	–	L	M	H/$M	M/$M	L/$L	O/$O
Parent company president	1·0%	O	L	H/$L	H/$L	L/$O	O/$O
President at first; after 1965, group vice president	0·1%	H	H	H/$L	H/$L	O/$O	H/$L
	10·0%	H	M	H/$H	M/$M	L/$L	M/$H
	0·5%	H	M	H/$L	H/$L	L/$O	H/$L
	2·0%	H	H	H/$H	M/$M	L/$L	H/$H
	3·0%	H	H	H/$H	M/$H	M/$H	H/$H
	2·0%	M	M	H/$H	M/$M	L/$L	H/$M
Two different parent company executives	1·0%	O	L	H/$L	O/$O	O/$O	O/$O
Group manager	10·0%	M	M	H/$H	M/$L	O/$O	M/$H
(Several reporting relationships)	0·4%	O	O	H/$L	H/$M	O/$O	O/$O
Product group vice president	2·7%		–	–	–		–
Product group manager †	3·8%	H	M	H/$H	L/$H	O/$O	O/$O
Product group manager †		–	–	–		–	–
Group vice president at first; then product group manager	4·6%	–	–	–	–	–	–
Product group manager †	2·2%	H	H	H/$H	M/$H	O/$O	O/$O
Various group vice presidents	0·1%	L	O	H/$L	O/$O	O/$O	O/$O
Executive vice president							
Product group manager †	3·3%	H	H	H/$H	L/$H	O/$O	L/$L
Group vice president at first; then product group manager	0·7%	–	–	–	–	–	–
Group executive	3·1%	–	–	–	–	–	–
Product group manager †	0·6%	–	–	–	–	–	–
Product group manager †	1·8%	–	–	–	–	–	–
Product group manager †	0·3%	M	H	H/$M	M/$M-$L	M/$H	H/$H
Group vice president	1·8%	–	–	–	–	–	–
Product general manager	0·1%	–	–	–	–	–	–
Product group manager †	0·1%	M	M	H/$L	H/$M	O/$O	O/$O
Product group manager †	0·1%	H	M	H/$H	M/$H	O/$O	O/$O
Product group manager †	0·01%	–	–	–	–		–
(Merged with existing division)	0·6%	–	–	–	–	–	–
Vice president automotive group	1·1%	H	O	M/$L	L/$L	O/$O	O/$O
Executive vice president	4·0%	H	M	H/$H	M/$M	M/$M	L/$L

†After period of autonomy

its plans for integrating the new company. As an example of the consequences of mismatch when the acquired company is not carefully meshed with its new parent, take this comment from a top manager in Company N:

'This little group of companies didn't cost much to buy, but since 1961 I reckon they have lost us £10 million, plus the drain on management time'.

Size mismatch *can* be overcome with the use of the right organizational structure and reporting relationships, as we shall see later, but frequently the wrong action seems to be taken. It is worth noting that in 81 per cent of the failures, the organization structure has been changed – usually in the direction of greater consolidation – or else the chief executive's reporting relationship has been altered. The danger is that such action will create confusion at the subsidiary level and a lack of knowledge at the parent company level – two factors which help to explain the failures of these acquisitions. Moreover, such changes are usually symptomatic of a lack of adequate planning at an earlier stage. What usually happens is that when failure appears imminent, reorganization efforts are made to 'try to get the mixture right'. But it is poor planning, and poor appraisal of executive talent, which caused the mixture of the two organizations to go wrong in the first place.

Synergy – fact or fiction?

Everyone knows about synergy. Putting 2 and 2 together to make 5 sounds like 'a good 20 per cent return' to the businessman. But do such happy results ever actually occur? To quote an experienced acquirer, the senior vice president for finance of Company K:

'We are quite skeptical about the existence of synergy. When we are testing the potential earnings of a company, we don't place any value on the benefits which might accrue from synergy.'

The survey probed both the ease with which synergy is released and the dollar value of the synergy in each of five business functions. The objective results contradict the usual notions about synergy.

Most managers would consider the potential for synergy highest in the case of production mergers. This is because of the economies of scale that can be achieved as a consequence of longer runs, the increased purchasing power made possible (quantity discounts), the justification of more expensive, more efficient machinery, and the opportunity to close down inefficient lines and transfer production to other factories.

Technology would appear to be the next most profitable area for mergers because of the possibilities of sharing R&D know-how and of transferring technical processes. Mergers of marketing organizations, where there are opportunities to sell two complementary product lines through one distribution channel and with one sales force, would seem to have the third greatest synergistic potential. And mergers in the organization area might rank fourth, since they provide opportunities for eliminating duplicated functions and releasing human creativity through improved motivation. Finally, financial mergers appear to offer possibilities of achieving synergy, since additional capital may enable high-risk, high-payoff projects to get off the ground; and, with two sets of assets as collateral, borrowing power goes up and the cost of money goes down. But there was a general impression that the synergistic potential of financial mergers is not as high as that of other types just mentioned.

Table 3

Which functions produce the biggest dollar payoff from synergy after acquisition?
[As scored by executives]

Type of merger	Finance	Marketing	Technology (including R&D)	Production
Conglomerate	100	58	20	32
Concentric technology	100	72	72	27
Concentric marketing	100	100	57	72
Horizontal	96	100	41	29
All categories	100	74	33	36

Note: Executives scored the dollar payoff of synergy as 'high', 'medium','low', or 'none' for each acquisition case. The scores were converted into arbitrary units, with 100 representing the score for the highest rated function. Thus the table shows *relative* payoff values for each function. Vertical integration is excluded because the sample is too small. Organizational efficiencies are excluded from the payoff area because they are too difficult to quantify, and management motivation is similarly excluded because it is the prime cause of the dollar payoffs in the other areas.

However, the research findings show that practice just about reverses hypothesis. As *Table 3* shows, far from producing the biggest payoff, production and technology are at the bottom of the list of dollar producers through synergy; marketing shows up better; and finance is clearly the area where synergy has the biggest payoff.

Finance: Why should finance have the greatest payoff? Part of the answer is revealed in *Table 4,* which relates to the ease of synergy release. In financial mergers, synergy is achieved with greater ease than in any other type of merger. This is understandable when we consider that additional funds are much easier to obtain when the asset backing of the merged companies is larger. And the cost of capital – due to lower interest rates and longer repayment times – can be lowered. Frequently, too, the parent company has surplus capital which can be used to finance what the senior vice president for finance of Company T calls 'the subsidiaries' frustration list' of projects previously denied funds. The resultant growth usually occurs in the area of high-margin sales and may lead the subsidiary to the 'take-off' point of generating its own substantial profits. Little wonder, then, that top managers see financial synergy as having achieved the greatest payoff.

Other functions: Marketing seems to have the next biggest dollar payoff. This again is related to the ease of achievement. It is not difficult to train a sales force to sell another product line, or to get the distribution channels to handle the acquired company's products (although several horror stories were told to me about product lines which produced the opposite of a synergetic effect in the distribution channels or among the sales force). Advertising economies can still be found. And it is relatively easy to save money in physical distribution, too, when one is able to take advantage of lower unit costs or to eliminate duplicate field sales offices. Furthermore, product lines sometimes reinforce each other, as in the case of Company I and its subsidiary, I_2, where the previously separate product lines are now marketed together as a package deal to appeal to one sector of the leisure market.

Technology and production – the two areas which theoretically should pay off most handsomely – do not do so in fact. Although the whole point of the technology-based concentric merger is to pool R&D knowledge and to transfer any specialized process know-how, the actual dollar payoff of so doing is rated, in *Table 3*, below that of finance and equal to that of marketing.

Table 4

In which function of a business is it easiest to release synergy?
[As scored by executives]

Type of merger	Finance	Organization		Marketing	Technology (including R&D)	Production
		Motivation	Efficiency			
Conglomerate	100	67	42	42	18	24
Concentric technology	65	70	55	75	100	65
Concentric marketing	100	52	79	74	21	47
Horizontal	100	73	70	67	33	24
All categories	100	68	55	59	33	34

Note: Scores are tabulated as explained in *Table 3.*

With regard to the area where traditional economics suggests that synergy should be greatest – namely, in production – many of the managers echoed these comments of an executive of Company I:

'Economies of scale are a highly overrated concept. They do occur. For example, certain technologies are possible when certain volume breaks occur; that is, the trade-off between hand labour and mechanical methods is worthwhile at certain volume levels. But most of the so-called fixed costs are actually volume variable, so that the profit leverage in expanding production volume in one factory or the other after acquisition is actually limited.'

Motivation and efficiency: One of the most interesting aspects of *Table 4* relates to the gains in organizational efficiency and the extent to which the motivation of the subsidiary managers is seen to be changed. (These payoffs can be included in *Table 4* because we are dealing here with opinions and impressions, not financial performance.)

There are two ways in which organization change can release synergy. One way is to centralize control, legal, public relations, and other services at the corporate level. To quote an executive of Company T, this move 'frees up the managers of subsidiaries to do the things they are best at'. The second way of releasing synergy is to change the management environment so that previously conservative or frustrated men are now motivated to become managers of change and to make more effective and profitable use of resources.

One cautionary note should be sounded in connection with the findings obtained in this study. The sample deals with companies acquired two to seven years ago. It probably takes longer to effect production economies than any other type. For example, closing down a factory or transferring a production line is a lengthy process. Conceivably, therefore, the relatively low dollar payoff in production may in time improve as major changes are decided and implemented. Also, conglomerates constitute 45 per cent of the sample, and these acquisitions by definition do not combine companies with the exact same production or technological skills. In these particular cases, the synergistic effects in production or technology cannot be expected to rank very high.

Causes of Success and Failure

What are the primary reasons that acquisitions succeed or fail? While the judgements of the executives interviewed cannot be quantified, a common pattern or thread runs through their beliefs. The pattern can be summarized in six main points.

(1) *Managers of change*

In the time period immediately following the merger, the quality of management talent determines the success or failure of the venture, and it is at this time that careful planning allows the synergy potential to be released, if it is released at all.

An interesting finding of the survey is that few top managers regard synergy as being inherent in a situation; most feel that synergy is a product or result of superior management. As the director of acquisitions in Company S puts it, 'The key variable for success is managing the company better after the acquisition than it was managed before'.

As for the ease of achieving synergy release, consider this comment of the senior vice president for operations of Company T: 'Don't think it's hard to release synergy; it's not. It's damn near impossible. This executive went on to say that it required stock option incentives in front and 'a red hot poker behind' to motivate his line managers sufficiently to do the hard work, make the changes, and produce a synergistic effect.

It does not matter whether these managers of change are provided by the parent company or by the subsidiary. But whichever company provides them, the supply of managerial talent must be carefully husbanded. I was told by an executive of the highly successful Company G:

'We appraised our position when we started on the acquisition trail and found that our major strength was in management, whereas we had a negative working capital position. So we used preferred stock to buy companies in trouble at distress prices. Then we put our superior management in and turned the situations around. The results were so successful that we are now able to borrow long-term and pay for our acquisitions in cash. Now we have a very positive working capital position – *but no managers to spare*. So, we buy well-managed companies these days.'

If the needed executives come from the subsidiary company, they may need a little stimulation before they can become effective managers of change. Sometimes this stimulation is accomplished by frequent exposure to parent company management philosophy. An executive of Company K, which has had an annual growth rate in sales of 32 per cent and in profits of 33 per cent, attributes his company's success with subsidiary K_1 to this process:

'We just kept meeting with them and communicating our ideas on growth. And finally they stopped thinking about plateaus, and started thinking about mountains.'

Sometimes a pruning operation to remove dead wood at the top is necessary. Many of the success stories with acquisitions started this way. By the same token, failures are often characterized by the presence of old or conservative managements who will not, or cannot, change. Evidently Company Q suffered from this kind of paralysis, as the comments of one of its executives reveal:

'In Q_1 there was a great deal of potential for synergy. It had a revolutionary product which was starving for capital, and there was great potential for additional parent company sales, since the subsidiary used the parent company's product in fabrication. Money was pumped in, and later on the subsidiary's president died. But apart from that, nothing happened. It was a classic case of synergy potential that was never realized. We finally sold the company.'

(2) *Skills for the task*

The sum of management skills must be greater than the joint management task. A common mistake is to underestimate the demands a merger will make on management time; executives erroneously believe that, because the company to be acquired is smaller than the buying company, its problems will require proportionately less management time. The consequences of believing in this fallacy are revealed in these comments by the senior vice president of company Q:

'We made the great mistake with Q_1 of thinking that its problems – and therefore its demands on our top management time – were proportional to its size. It didn't get the attention it needed, and it died on us.'

Another illustration of the dangers of a misfit between management tasks and skills is this account of Company M's experience:

'For the first several years, operating and management problems appeared faster than we were able or willing to solve them. The subsidiary's chief executive was not strong enough to build up the company profitably, using the parent company's resources. Six months after the acquisition was made, we were in our well-known marketing battle – which meant that the parent company management was too fully occupied to cope with the subsidiary's problems. The results have been continuing losses.'

How, then, to guard against the danger of not having enough competent managers to do the job? Consider:

The first step is to have a policy based on recognition of the problem. Note how managerial manpower resources are specifically taken into account in the strategy of Company K, as described by one of its executives:

'We just don't have enough managers up here at headquarters to send in to turn a poor situation around. Our policy therefore is one of autonomy. We buy the company for its management. We don't intend to push managers around after we have acquired a company. We will be neither wreckers nor resurrectors.'

An acquisition policy must include some good method of appraising subsidiary company management before the purchase is made. An executive of Company T, which is a highly successful conglomerate, describes the 'track record' approach used by his company:

'We can't spare anybody from headquarters to go in and operate a company. So the managements of the companies we acquire have to have a good track record – on the down side of the business cycle as well as the up side. Their performance, judged on the basis of return on assets, must be as good as, or better than, the industry average. We buy demonstrated performance – because we don't have enough spare management talent to do anything else.'

A final refinement is to make an independent audit of subsidiary management's competence before the merger takes place. This step is expensive, and it involves delay. But it reinforces the 'track record' approach, providing a detailed evaluation of individual managers. This is how an executive of Company F, which diversified from a service to a manufacturing industry, describes his company's reasons for using this approach:

'We couldn't tell you which men have what competence level. Sure, we know if the company is a leader or laggard in its industry. But we don't have the industrial know-how to say that Jones is weak while Smith is strong. So what we do is to hire some consultants to make an organization study. The company we're negotiating with invites the consulting firm in, but we pick up the tab. After the study, we know whom we'll want to keep, and where we'll need fresh talent.'

Of course, not every company has the time or money for so thorough an approach. Perhaps this is another way of saying that not every company can afford to take the risks of the acquisition game. For if managerial competence and the requirements of the to-be-purchased organization are not evaluated before the merger, the chance of failure increases markedly. As the executive of Company J who was put in charge of J_1 after its early failure comments ruefully:

'If our evaluation of J_1's top management had been as thorough as the one we made of its product line, we would have had no problem.'

(3) *Management relationships*

The most successful acquisitions seem to be distinguished by three characteristics in the relationships between the parent company management and the subsidiary management.

'Riding herd': First, the parent company appoints a top executive to 'ride herd' *immediately* after the acquisition. The necessity of appointing a key person to this post, and of doing so right away, can be seen in this account of Company H's experience with H_2 (a subsidiary not included in *Table 1* because of insufficient data), as related by an executive of the parent company:

'When Company H bought H_2, it discovered several skeletons in the closet. There had been a good deal of dishonesty at the time of negotiations. Luckily, Mr. X [a parent company vice president] was assigned the responsibility for the company. We didn't see him around H for several months – he was full time in the acquired company. And now H_2 is coming around. Experience shows us how important key people are in the acquired company, and so are those assigned to ride herd on the new acquisition.'

An executive of another corporation, Company R, described to me a case with a less happy ending:

'When R bought R_2, there were already two strikes against our success. First, the R group manager who was to control the new acquisition was not consulted about it before the acquisition was made. Secondly, R_2's facilities were out on the West Coast, too far from the parent company to allow detailed surveillance. Add to this the fact that the chief executive of R_2 was not what he represented himself to be, and you have a good situation for an acquisition going right out of control. We were sure that the top management of the company we bought was very good; and we felt there was no need to watch it closely. We learned – the tough way.'

Reporting procedures: The second characteristic of successful mergers is that the reporting relationship between key people in both the acquired company and the parent is immediately made clear. When subsequent changes in reporting relationships occur, they are made on a planned basis.

There are many different ways of handling this matter after a company has been acquired. Clearly, there is no one ideal method; the approach chosen must be tailored to the environmental conditions encountered and the capabilities of the executives concerned. What *must* be avoided, however, is the setting up of unclear reporting relationships and the temptation to change them often; such action was present in 81 per cent of the failures. Here are some of the methods which successful companies have employed:

Autonomous-direct – The president of Company P had the presidents of newly acquired companies report to him directly. He explains:

'All of these presidents wanted to report to me directly. Up to the time we acquired their companies, they had been entrepreneurs, and they were only accustomed to dealing with the top man in an organization. Although this was bad for my health, and it gave me a span of control of which no consultant would approve, it just had to be this way for the first few years.' (Later on – say, when the original top management of the acquired companies retires – the system may be changed.)

Group approach – Company R, which calls itself 'a series of small companies', groups the organizations on a product-line basis. When a new small company is acquired, it is assigned to a group manager who is more capable of understanding the problems of the firm than are executives at the remote headquarters of the parent.

In some cases, as in Company J and Company T, group management helps to produce acquisition proposals, that is, the closeness of subsidiaries with similar product lines, along with the natural interest of the group manager in fortifying and rounding out these lines, serves to bring new acquistion prospects to top management's attention and create more aggressiveness in commencing purchase negotiations.

Merged channels – Only a relatively few companies try the 'total absorption' route, i.e., meshing the new organization into the existing corporate reporting format. This requires substantial parent company management effort – plus an understanding of the subsidiary's business. Therefore, as one might predict, it is more common among horizontal and vertical acquisitions than among conglomerates or concentrics. In our sample, most of the concentric and conglomerate acquisitions in which the parent and the subsidiary were totally merged were failures. There are some exceptions, of course, as *Table 1* shows; but most of these can be explained by rather extraordinary efforts on the part of parent company executives to learn the new business and to get on top of it.

Unsuccessful acquisitions are often characterized by shifts in responsibility at the parent company level and by confusion at the subsidiary level as to which executive in the parent company is in charge of managing the new enterprise. Let us now examine the reporting relationships found in two companies that failed in their acquisition efforts. An executive in Company M states:

'During the first three years, Company M left the original top manager of M_1 in command. In that time he reported to *three* different people or committees in Company M. And he had two different parent company managers ride herd on him.'

When Company R acquired its subsidiary, R_2, there was split reporting on the R&D function. In this case, as in many other cases of failure, R_2 was geographically remote from its parent. An executive from Company R reports:

'We had an extraordinary situation. R_2 was spending a great deal of money on R&D and producing nothing. The R&D department in R_2 was headed by two men, neither of whom would speak to the other. Each reported to a different R location – one man reported to the engineering department, and the other to the research department.'

Plans and controls: The third distinguishing characteristic of successful acquisitions is the approach of the buying companies to installing a system of controls. At the outset they place major emphasis on *information reporting* rather than on budgets. This system is put into operation immediately. But no hard-and-fast rule is followed. Successful companies vary their requirements according to the situation.

Obviously, the small company which is introduced suddenly to the full paraphernalia of large company planning, including, perhaps, ten-year planning assumptions, five-year business plans, a one-year profit plan, and 200 activity reports to group or corporate management, finds itself faced with a big problem. As the manager of one recent Company S acquisition remarked, 'Suddenly our biggest product is paper reports'. And companies can sink under the strain of the paper work involved, or at least lose what an executive of Company G, in referring to the management of one of its acquisitions, has termed 'the feral instinct for profit'.

The successful approach to planning and control seems to be typified by the method used by Company K. An executive of that company describes it this way:

'We use the control system we find when we acquire the company. But we immediately ask for a few additional reports to corporate headquarters. These constitute our top management control system and are common throughout the company. Also, we insist on the underlying figures being of high quality, and we insist on timeliness. We install no further requirements beyond these unless we are sure the system won't be overloaded.'

If the organizational and reporting policies just described are critical for success, as this study suggests, then we have an interesting question. Is the determinant of success in acquisitions really the strategy used, as pronouncements on this topic have generally indicated in the past, or is 'managing the company better afterward than it was managed before' what really guarantees success? This hypothesis is worth testing. Certainly, some of the successful acquisitions reviewed in this study were made without any strategic planning, simply in response to an opportunity that came up involving a company which, while having no strategic 'fit' with the parent company, had great potential for improvement.

(4) *Reactors vs. planners*

However true the foregoing hypothesis may turn out to be, it should not increase the unemployment rate among strategic planners. For the study shows a distinct difference in the success rate of companies with a strategy for growth and diversification, of which an acquisition program may be only a part, and that of companies which merely react to opportunities to buy.

Before discussing the two different approaches, which were neatly characterized by one executive as 'crystal ball mergers' and 'golf course mergers', respectively, it may be worthwhile to put strategic planning into perspective. Managers who have lived through the experience of making a success out of their acquisitions feel that superior strategic planning has been helpful. It has provided acquisitions that 'fit' parent company management capability and that are consistent with corporate goals. The key variable for success, however, is not superior strategy; it is the managers of change, who can take an unplanned acquisition whose resources are related only indirectly to those of the parent company and make a success of it. This should be kept in mind in the discussion that follows.

'Golf course' mergers: The react-to-opportunity approach is illustrated by the actions of Company O. According to one of its executives:

'Representatives of O_1 came to us with a proposal that we buy their company. It seemed a pretty good idea. O_1's product was a major part of the manufacturing cost of sales of our product, and I could see the economies to be obtained from this vertical integration. The research people in O_1 looked pretty good – all kinds of academic qualifications. And the product samples they gave us all worked beautifully.

'So we bought the company and gave its product range the full marketing treatment. O_1's products sold through our sales force like hot-cakes – once. Then the complaints came in. The manufactured items just didn't meet the specs that the laboratory 'one-offs' had. And all those Ph.D.'s weren't worth a damn when it came to making the production item perform. Eventually we had to close down the company, redesign the product, and redo the production engineering. Now we make the line ourselves, under our own roof. It's a success; but was the effort worth it?,

Sometimes the opportunity arises through a broker. A top executive of Company Q recounts this experience:

'A broker telephoned to tell us about Company Q_1. This firm had a new product which was really revolutionary. In addition to its intrinsic potential, there was the fact that it used our product as its major ingredient, so we thought we could get a two-way payoff. We had one of the big consulting firms study the market. Their report was very thorough, and the prospects looked great.

'It wasn't until we bought it for a fancy price that we realized (a) we were now competing with our major customers, and (b) we didn't have anybody we could spare to manage the new acquisition.

'We shut it down eventually. It cost us a few million dollars.'

Many companies still operate – and quite successfully – on this philosophy, and the preceding examples by no means prove it does not work. Nevertheless, the 'golf course' approach seems to be going slowly out of style.

'Crystal ball' mergers: There is a noticeable trend toward treating acquisitions as a part of the overall corporate strategy. Decisions are influenced by the answers given to these questions: What business are we in? What business *should* we be in? Instead of reacting to offers to sell, in other words, management focuses on the recommendations made by such a person as a director of corporate planning; he indicates desirable fields for entry and suggests specific companies whose purchase would open the gate to these fields. Here are two examples as described by executives I interviewed:

'Company N used to count mainly on reacting to offers to sell. All this has changed. I now have a plan which details the areas of greatest potential. These are not expressed in terms of products but, rather, in terms of human needs. For example, we don't say that closed-circuit TV or teaching machines are the products with the greatest potential. Instead, we see the area of educational aids as a whole as the greatest field of potential. Closed-circuit TV and learning machines are just two ways of entering this field. If we are going to offer a well-rounded product line, however, we are going to have to acquire much more competence than these two items will give us. For instance, we will need a book publishing company, someone who can write programmed learning texts, and so on.'

'By accident Company F backed into a manufacturing-type acquisition in the 1950s. It was quite profitable as it happened. Then we saw a slowing down in our main business; competition got more vigorous, too, and we had spare funds, which is worse than having excess capacity in manufacturing.

'So, influenced by our fortuitous success with the manufacturing operation, we made a strategic decision in 1963 to get into other businesses. We set the appraisal criteria carefully – we had to – and it's worked out well. Now 18 per cent of our profits come from our diversification through acquisition program, and we have pinpointed the companies we'd like to have for further diversification.'

There is probably a greater chance of success when the responsibility for developing an acquisition program is some top executive's main job – resting with, say, a vice president of corporate development, rather than with a senior vice president of finance. The reason is that when a corporate officer has his own full-time job to do in addition to this new job, the task of evaluating a proposed acquisition – from the standpoint both of its 'fit' with corporate goals and of its intrinsic worth – can easily be skimped. As the president of Company P said, 'An acquisition is equally as important as building a new plant. But most managements do not give the acquisition a fraction of the time or the analysis that goes into putting up a new plant.'

(5) *Effective criteria*

A key factor for success is having acquisition criteria that are consistent and that are rigorously applied. Otherwise, acquisition decisions are likely to be distorted by impulses and emotions, and acquiring companies victimized by the environment which typically surrounds purchase negotiations. This environment, with its atmosphere of necessary secrecy, of cards being held close to the chest, and the outside world (especially the financial press) being kept firmly at bay, has a low emotional flash point. The acquiring company is playing for high stakes; the performance record of the managers concerned will be greatly affected by the results of the deal. The management team of the potential subsidiary is wondering what will happen to it afterwards, and perhaps is playing for a high payoff (where the managers own the stock). Unlike most sale-purchase situations with high risk (e.g., house buying, or bidding on large contracts), the lifetime careers of top executives are bound up in the results.

It is hardly an atmosphere conducive to rigorous application of objective criteria. Yet successful acquirers manage to do a thorough job. The first, and most important, task is to develop a set of acquisition criteria beforehand. Armed with this, the successful acquiring company *selects* rather than *reacts*. An example is Company T. A top executive of that company outlines its criteria as follows:

'1. Management's track record in the company being considered for acquisition should be better than the industry average in terms of return on assets – on the down side, as well as on the up side, of business cycles.

'2. We will only buy into old industries which are 'non-glamour'.

'3. We will buy companies with low price-earnings ratios. [The actual average in this case is 6·5 times earnings!]

'4. We seek to buy assets which are readily convertible into cash.

'5. The top executive of the company in question *must* stay on.

'6. These shall be our minimum sales volume criteria:

(a) For entry into a new field – $100 million.

(b) For entry into a new market – $20 million.

(c) To round out a product line, if already in market – $1 million.'

Another successful company which has fairly specific acquisition criteria is Company K, where application of these criteria is encouraged by requiring key parent executives to state their recommendations in writing before a deal is closed. A Company K executive states that his company will purchase another company when:

'Its marketing ability and products have been established as better than average.

'The company's sales volume is larger than $1 million (unless our senior vice president for operations has outlined – in writing – a plan as to how he will operate this company).

'The management of the company can be left to run the company by itself.

'The company will increase the parent company's earnings per share.'

Companies which have made a success of their acquisitions are distinguished by their top managements' ability to weigh the strengths and weaknesses of potential acquisitions in a short period of time. Time pressures are great for two reasons. First of all, the secrecy necessarily surrounding negotiations dictates that lengthy visits and conversations with the top management of a potential subsidiary be ruled out. Secondly, long delays may be costly. As Company T's senior vice president of finance says, 'The longer we wait, the less chance there is of making a deal' – and the survey results certainly bear him out. Only an estimated 10 per cent of the companies were 'courted' over several months. If the premerger evaluation is not thorough, however, postmarital problems can result. One regret frequently voiced is, 'If only subsidiary managers looked as good now, when they are on our side of the table, as they did on theirs when we were bargaining'.

The need for both speed and thoroughness poses an apparent dilemma. Fortunately, it has been neatly solved by the more experienced companies. One technique often used where both companies' stocks are publicly traded is to peg the level at which any stock will be exchanged, using as the basis the figures put out by the company to be bought. Since the 'exchange rate' between the two stocks is fixed, a leisurely – and public – evaluation of the opportunity will not cause the acquiring company any additional expense. Room can be left for subsequent adjustment, usually on a contingent basis.

Another technique is for management to hold a portion of the purchase price 'in escrow' until the acquired company makes the profits it has forecasted (assuming such a forecast enters into purchase price negotiations). For instance, Company R pays the price its estimators feel is 'right'. Then, if and when the acquired company reaches the profit target on which it based its asking price (which is invariably higher), Company R pays over the difference between the bid price and the price asked.

(6) *Analysis of future needs*

Finally, this study shows that *successful companies make a careful analysis of their subsidiaries' future requirements for parent company funds.* Statements of financial results of a number of the acquisitions were compared with the returns projected at merger time. This provided a check on the failure-success rating given the acquisition (see *Table 1*). But it also brought to light a really significant finding – that is, the great extent to which the future capital requirements of the acquired company are often underestimated. As an executive of Company K noted sadly:

'We made the sales and profits targets for K_1 easily. But I underestimated the capital requirements of the new company by a factor or two.'

Clearly, companies acquiring smaller companies in the future would do well to pay more attention to their estimates of the capital required for plant and machinery, as well as that needed to finance additional sales. This finding reinforces the earlier one on the necessity of establishing appropriate plans and controls. When decent budgetary control has not been set up, it is all too easy for the new acquisition to say, in effect, 'Papa is rich. Let's go buy four new tape-controlled machine tools'. And when the investment half of the ROI fraction goes up, in such cases, the ROI itself usually goes down.

Conclusion

What, then, are the general implications of these research findings for management? The study points to the following suggestions for analysing an acquisition:

Above all, match the managers of change available with the tasks in the newly merged enterprise. This requirement makes it important to:

1. Identify the nature of the management tasks.
2. Evaluate the managers in the new organization against the tasks to be accomplished, and decide which managers should be let go.
3. Specify which managers in the buying corporation can be spared to take care of the new acquisition, and decide whom to hire in addition.
4. Also motivate the new team to manage change.

Specify the control system to be used, and stick to it. Name the top executive who is to ride herd. Put in the appropriate planning and control systems. Decide on the right organization structure, keeping in mind that problems of size mismatch can probably be avoided by grouping the new organization with other subsidiaries having similar product lines, marketing structures, or other vital operations. (In this event, get group management involved at the negotiating stage.)

Allocate the strategic planning responsibility, preferably on a full-time basis, to a top-level officer, and ask him to develop acquisition criteria which are consistent with overall corporate policy. When a specific acquisition opportunity arises which looks interesting, ask each executive in charge of a major function for a formal appraisal of the company.

In evaluating the ROI projections for the new company:

1. Treat the forecasts of production and technology dollar payoff with skepticism.

2. Make sure that the marketing synergisms (especially those expected to arise out of combining the two companies' sales forces, distribution channels, and advertising) can be realized in practice.

3. Give the greatest weight to the dollar payoff expected in the finance area (through cheaper borrowing, liquidating unused assets, and financing new ventures formerly starved for capital).

4. Finally, if the acquiring corporation is new to the game, why not tap the skills and experience of the sophisticated acquirers, especially their knowledge in the area of risk reduction at negotiation time?

Chapter Five

A PSYCHOLOGIST DIAGNOSES MERGER FAILURES*

Harry Levinson

Visiting Professor of Business Administration, Harvard Business School

Caught up in all the hoopla and glamor which have characterized the great merger spree in recent years, business executives have been preoccupied with the strategies, tactics, and techniques of acquiring, merging, and selling—yet, frequently the really crucial factor, people, has been superficially dealt with. Nowhere is this shallowness more evident than in those mergers that have been outright mistakes with destructive consequences for both parties. Such failures have usually been attributed to rational, technical problems.

However, I contend that the unrecognized psychological problems, often heavily weighted by fear and obsolescence, are the real culprits and lead to attitudes which are expressed in words like these:

'We're smarter and better than they are. After all, we're buying them.'

'We've got to control them. They need our managerial know-how.'

'They're out to get all they can from us. They want to be free to do things their own way, but they don't want to be responsible for the results.'

Such condescending attitudes on the part of the senior organization lead to efforts at manipulation and control which, in turn, produce disillusionment, disappointment, and a feeling of desertion in the junior partner. Loss of morale, personnel, and profits soon follows. This is not to say that all mergers which fail do so for these psychological reasons. Obviously, in some cases sheer incompatibility or the unwillingness of the junior partner to cooperate is more than a rationalization.

In this article, I shall examine some of the psychological shoals and suggest ways of avoiding them. Since the trend towards mergers is not likely to abate in the near future, it will become increasingly important to consider carefully how mergers might be handled with greater mutual satisfaction and success.

First, however, let me acknowledge that many mergers have been mutually advantageous to both parties. Thus my focus here—from the perspective of the dominant partner—is on the many others that have been mutually disappointing.[1]

Psychological Shoals

Any discussion of the failures of mergers rightfully begins with the question: Why merge? There are, of course, many important reasons for merging. For example, there are valid economic considerations: to acquire access to more capital, better professional management, or greater product and technical sophistication; to meet competition more effectively; to acquire new products or round out an existing product line; to acquire innovative capacity or tax benefits; to foster growth; and so on.

In addition, there are many personal reasons for merging: to realize capital gains or protect an estate; to assure the continuity of an organization; to demonstrate one's managerial or financial competence, or both; to become the chief executive officer of a larger organization; and so forth.

Unrecognized motives

Between the lines of these rational reasons for acquisitions, often there are two more subtle reasons which are rarely discussed in these terms: *fear* and *obsolescence.* These unrecognized feelings constitute psychological traps because they lead to impulsive actions which compound the very problems that a merger is intended to resolve.

Fear: One pressing wish to merge derives from the feeling that unless the company grows, larger companies will destroy it. Following this logic, destruction is to be avoided only by becoming more powerful. And the fastest way to become more powerful is to buy others.

This sets in motion a process of accretion, and I use the word advisedly, for the process is psychologically similar to that of a man who seeks to become bigger by becoming fatter. Such a man eats too much because unconsciously he is afraid of being so little. There is much folk wisdom to the saying that beneath the bulk of the fat man is hidden a tiny one. While the fat man may be physically large to begin with, he perceives himself to be small for many unconscious reasons and acts accordingly.

So it is with organizations. The initial size of the company may make little difference in this feeling on the part of those in the positions of leadership. The important point is that they feel threatened.

But one of the problems with getting bigger by accretion, whether it happens to an individual or an organization, is loss of flexibility and additional burdens on the internal systems. More than one organization has found itself bigger, with more managerial problems, and with few—if indeed any—long-term gains to show in, say, earnings per share or innovation.

Obsolescence: As organizations age, they develop bureaucracies and become more rigidly systematic in the way they define jobs, delineate objectives, and narrow task focus and responsibility. The more rigidly the system functions as a system—that is, the better the way in which matters are measured, counted, and controlled—the less room there is for individual initiative and spontaneity. In fact, the purpose of bureaucratizing the system is to reduce individual variation and to foster known, standard modes of action.

Inevitably, organizations, like ageing people, become more stereotyped in their ways, less adaptable to changing conditions, and less flexible in their efforts to cope with their environments. In a word, they become obsolescent. The executives, too, become obsolescent. One way of obtaining enterprising new blood, they decide, is to buy an enterprising organization.

All well and good, but behind these two—fear and obsolescence—there are frequently underlying unconscious attitudes which are the actual destructive forces. When a person is fearful, his first unconscious step in fighting fear is to deny his fear and tighten up. The word 'uptight' aptly characterizes this feeling. When a person becomes obsolescent, he tends to adopt a defensive attitude of superiority and to re-intensify his customary efforts. The fact that he is the dominant party, together with his denial of fear and his air of superiority, leads to the kinds of condescending attitudes we noted earlier.

Controlling Behaviour

Condescending attitudes lead to behaviour which implements them. The attitudes of top management are taken for gospel by staff people, who concretize them in the form of practice. Thus the pivotal issue becomes one of controls. The dominant organization must, they argue, have the same processes and procedures in all of its components. The newly merged junior organization must serve the system. Ergo, no sooner bought than controlled.

As the dominant organization imposes control systems from its established bureaucracy, it stifles in the junior the very quality it sought to obtain and becomes even more obsolete. The very words 'control' and 'controller' specify the problem. They assume by definition that someone must police, ride herd, and keep people in some kind of box.

Some managements from the very beginning intend to impose controls and to make arbitrary changes in keeping with their own ways of doing business. However, they never convey such thinking to a prospective merger partner because they know the prospect would hardly be likely to merge under those circumstances. Thus they begin by wooing the prospect, promising him they will change nothing. When the merger is sealed, the original intentions are acted on, and the new partner feels he has been 'conned'. The underlying contempt of the senior partner for the junior one becomes magnified; the junior now feels he has let himself be taken in.

Perpetuation problem

Fundamentally, the problem to be dealt with in a merger is the same task every organization always has—namely, to build in perpetuation. This means that from the beginning of the relationship one must create conditions conducive to perpetuation, and develop the capacity in people to assume responsibility.[2] If perpetuation is the basic focus, then control systems and modes of management must foster that intent.

However, if the basic focus is 'How do I control the new organization?' then the control devices become the overriding concern. The method is rational, its purpose, fine; and its outcome, efficient control. Therefore, it *should* work. Only when it does not do people begin to ask questions, and then they usually project solutions which fail to fit the problem: higher salaries, profit sharing, competition, and so forth.

I have no brief against controls or controllers *per se,* but every form of control, like every other managerial process, is based on some implicit conception of motivation. A control system based on policing assumes people must be whipped into shape and kept there by someone else. It conveys to the people who are controlled that they are regarded as inadequate and incompetent, and are therefore not to be trusted.

Contrast this with a conception of accounting data as feedback on performance by which the people can control their own behaviour. The person (or department) that furnishes such information might be better called a 'facilitator'; and the service stance that goes with it, 'facilitating'—provided that is what he really does.

Family integration

From a psychological point of view, the phenomenon of merging is similar to forming a new family. From the dominant organization's point of view, it is much like adopting a foster child. From the other point of view, it is akin to getting a new stepfather.

If the parent is concerned with how to make his child good, he will concentrate on goodness at the expense of the child's development. If he is concerned with rearing the most mature, most capable, most flexible child, then he must be concerned with facilitation of growth, not with control.

This is not to say that controls are bad. To be sure, all children need to be controlled and to learn self-control. Rather, it is to say that when control is the purpose, the whole point is missed. The result is a blob of human clay instead of a living being. Clay may respond to someone else's manipulation; it has no growth potential.

Furthermore, the stepfather who assumes he is going to have to beat the child into shape is in for a running battle. The child will feel deserted and betrayed by the stepfather who promised him affectionate esteem. He will fight if he can, withdraw in anger if he cannot, and leave the family at the first opportunity. So it is with merged managements and even line executives. Suddenly, the dominant management finds itself bereft of the very innovative men it had thought it had acquired.

In many mergers, therefore, one finds organizations left with the hollow shells of their name and structure, and with the necessity of bringing in a completely new management group. However, the kinds of managers brought in as replacements will tend to be more bureaucratic or 'take-charge' types. They are unlikely to be people who have started organizations themselves or who have established records of imaginative innovation.

If those in the merged, junior company were previously in an innovative organization either because they could not work under more bureaucratic controls in the first place or because such controls inhibited their creativity, they will now feel that someone is always looking over their shoulders, or that they have become puppets. Even if they remain, they will no longer trust the organization or its leadership. They will spend the rest of their careers going through the motions. Some, with their backs up, will have to be fired or retired early, while others will have to be placed on some innocuous managerial shelf.

I have observed organizations, even as long as twenty years after a merger, in which there was still residual anger at being taken over. Some employees who had been members of the acquired company were still idealizing the old company and comparing the 'new' unfavourably with their former circumstances. In their view, everything had been so much better before.

A case illustration

Here is a typical example of an outcome which was not what the dominant management intended. It illustrates that, however rationalized, control focus on the part of the parent organization is essentially self-defeating:

A small scientific organization, which had operated with relative success in its own naive way because its scientists and technicians were free to be innovative, was acquired by a larger company. The major stockholders of the small organization wanted to realize capital gains and long-term appreciation. The purchasing corporation wanted to diversify.

Following the merger, the dominant management discovered that the junior's financial picture was not as good as it had thought. The immediate response to this discovery was quick imposition of controls by a new take-charge president who had demonstrated previous successes in salvaging losing situations. He imposed all of the usual textbook methods and standards on his new organization, and he promptly began to lose its key people.

Fortunately in this case, he was quick to call for help. Then, to work the situation through, he shifted from trying to control the new people to facing them with the realities of what the organization was up against.

Knowing what they faced and being responsible people, they dug in and brought the company back into the black. The realities of their financial circumstances were control enough; they did not need a whip.

What about the parent organization's leaders in such a situation? They had the fantasy that *everything* would go up—sales, rate of return, profits. They fully expected that the people in the smaller organization would love them for being merged into their larger, more protective nest with its greater advancement opportunities. They were disillusioned, angry, and frustrated when the opposite occurred.

After all, they were not ogres—or were they? If not, then why did people desert them when they were only trying to do what was right to save the smaller organization from its own follies?[3]

Manipulation of Personnel

Although there have always been mergers (the usual practice has been simply to incorporate one company within the other) where little thought was given to the consequences, this is no longer advisable. When organizations merged, say, twenty-five or thirty years ago, people stayed, even if they did not like the new parent company. Furthermore, most jobs were routine and promised to remain that way, even at the middle- and upper-management levels.

Today, the traditional, heavily dependent employee-management relationship based on loyalty and long service is outmoded. Competence alone now counts. If there is competence in the junior organization, no management can afford to squeeze it out by doing what it did years ago. If it does, it denies people's expectations about gaining greater opportunity out of the merger, in terms of their growth and development, their responsibility, and their advancement.

What one needs, in contrast to the stability of a pre-World War II organization is one characterized by flexibility and adaptability. This requires adaptive, innovative people, and a context in which they can solve problems.

'Identification crisis'

There is an additional factor to be dealt with, which I shall call the 'identification crisis'. In earlier years, people were less likely to feel it was their organization. It was clearly the boss's organization, and they were seen by him all too often as chattels. In more recent times, managements have gone to great lengths to integrate people as members of the corporate family, to encourage them to identify themselves with the organization, and to see it as their own.

Even when people felt that the organization belonged to the boss, they had some feeling of obligation to him. Later, that obligation was reinforced by paternalism. Now, with dispersed ownership, there is less likely to be a feeling of obligation and loyalty, and a merger undermines that even more. In fact, the stronger the identification, the greater the possibility of the feeling of being deserted when merger takes place.

One response to this is mobility. People begin to look for the best 'other-pastures' break. Newspaper articles are already beginning to report 'floating middle management', and too many good executives are spontaneously retiring early to the dismay of their superiors. There are two problems here:

1. With the decreasing age of company presidents, the potential for mobility declines earlier, so organizations tend to retain people who cannot move but who also have no enthusiasm. This means many hit a plateau. It also means much disillusionment in the very people who should be making contributions. When people

do move, largely because they feel hemmed in or without challenge, they are saying, at the most elementary level, 'The organization doesn't love me. It doesn't use my talents. It uses me as an expendable device.'

2. There is need for continuous reorganization and regrouping to maintain flexibility to cope more easily with new problems. Regrouping is harder when people basically cannot trust the organization. No matter what work groups people find themselves in, the basic identification must be with the organization, or there is no organization.

Vicious circle

When managements do not see their own tacit con game assumptions—the product of their trying to 'sell' the other party, and their own fears—they are left to suffer the consequences without beginning to understand why they occurred. Manipulation as a technique suffers from the fact that it always carries the seeds of its own destruction.

For some organizations, this process has now reached frightening proportions. They buy others, impose controls, lose key managers, put in a new leadership group, lose innovative capacity, and then go out to buy more to make up for the new burdens. This vicious circle hinges on an underlying fallacy: controls *produce* profits. Controls are necessary for guidance. When they become the major method of staying profitable, they eventually become self-defeating.

Profitability and survivability derive in the last analysis from adaptation to the market-place. The greater the attention management directs inwardly on the organization, the less attention it gives to the outside world. People become pre-occupied with contemplating their own navels. They are taught to beat themselves, to go on economic diets.

To be sure, contemplation and control are highly important, but such self-preoccupation is more characteristic of monks than merchants. Self-flagellation is no substitute for innovative imagination and aggressive pursuit of those dreams. By the time all the internal squeezing is done, whatever the temporary contribution to profits, skill in coping with the outside is lost. To make matters worse, people feel driven. Morale declines. People have the feeling no one cares and that they are working only for the dollar. Ultimate financial objectives are seriously threatened.

Some organizations can get away with the manipulation process for a long time—squeezing cash reserves, manipulating accounting methods, selling off less profitable units, and so on. Large organizations with assured resources—like banks, insurance companies, and public utilities—can continue for many years unaware of their losses. But even the largest manufacturing organizations are now having difficulty, as repeated complaints about quality control testify, and the largest financial institutions are having difficulty getting young people; in addition, they have already been outflanked by newer types of financial organizations.

Reality gap

Fundamentally, the problem is: What does the senior president want? If he wants to evolve a more adaptive organization, he can't get there by the usual means executives have been following. If he merely wants to be a big man and is not concerned about the price, then he is like the man who does not care about his family so long as he gets the income.

How does such a problem come about? Why is there such a gap between the 'real' and the psychological? Why is it so difficult to reconcile the two?

The business executive is fundamentally a rationalist. He is heavily trained in business method and economic logic. He is largely unaware of the fact that with every technique or process he uses—whether or not it is rational in its own right—he is making an assumption about motivation. The problem is that his assumptions often do not fit people's actual motivations and feelings.

While it is true *theoretically* that the shortest mathematical distance between two points is a straight line, it is equally true *practically* that while the shortest distance, in terms of time, between two points may be a superhighway, one may have to make many circles to get on it. When it comes to matters psychological, all too often the executive is unwilling to make the necessary circles. He thinks he is more practical and direct when he does not; but he is neither, as repetitive efforts to solve the same old problems show.

The self-defined realist equates real with palpable, material; measurable and visible. That which is more subtle is to him 'unreal' and therefore easily disregarded. But that is like trying to treat polio only with warm baths or external medication. The executive, like the physician, must evolve ways of seeing that which is not readily visible to the naked eye and of grasping its reality.

There are other reasons for the gap between the real and the psychological. Executives as a breed tend to run scared. They are continuously trying to 'make it'. They fear failure. In addition, they feel themselves to be under tremendous pressure for results by forces outside themselves. They feel they must respond fast and on the basis of hard facts. As a result, they have not learned to delay action long enough to think about its psychological meaning. They tend to look on such considerations as a luxury they cannot afford.

Minimizing the Impact

There are, then, two major problems to be dealt with: (a) the executive's anxieties, and (b) the meshing of two organizations into one so that the marriage yields a family and not merely an association of convenience. Obviously, there are problems in all mergers, as in all marriages. The concern is not to eliminate all problems. Rather, it is to make the choices more rational and the modes for coping with the problems more effective. Here are four suggestions that may be helpful in minimizing the negative psychological impact of mergers.

(1) *Introspective assessment*

Every management which is thinking of buying up another company should ask itself seriously why it is doing so. 'Of course,' you say, 'every management does that.' It does–it asks itself about everything except the psychological issues in the situation. While much thinking goes into the financial and marketing analyses and into evaluating the managerial and product potentials of the organization to be acquired, almost never does the same kind of thinking extend to introspection, particularly with respect to such issues as aspirations, fears, and wishes for power.

After determining why it really wants to merge, every management should then ask itself if it wants to merge for the wrong reasons. If it wants simply to get bigger, out of fear, is fear alone a sufficient motivation? Are there not more rational ways to deal with fear? How rational is the fear? How much of a panic psychology is it paying out? If the motivation is fear, then that underlying pressure is likely to continue, resulting in the whipping of the smaller organization and thereby destroying the very goal management wants to attain. If the motivation is to add zest to a sluggish organization, is it not more reasonable to rejuvenate the old one than to fight obsolescence by merger?

(2) *Projected assumptions*

Having assessed its own motivation, the prospective parent organization should next ask itself what assumptions it is making about the other party. It can infer these from its attitudes toward the other organization and what it is keeping to itself for fear that the other will refuse to merge if all of the intentions are clear. How are these assumptions likely to get management into trouble?

The prospective parent organization must take an honest look at its own control intentions and–beneath those–its assumptions about its projected partners (read 'subordinates' instead of 'partners' to understand the unconscious motivation better). If the parent management follows the strategy that it will persuade or sweet-talk the other president into merging and, then, that it will show him what *real* management is, it is laying the groundwork for its own failure. Such an attitude is often found when the junior company has behavioural flexibility–such as dress and time freedoms–which is unacceptable to the senior organization.

If the assumption could be put into words, it might go something like this: 'You crazy scientists who won't come to work on time, we'll show you.' Behind such a statement would be the anger of the parent company toward the others for their success in spite of being so crazy, anger about being dependent on such types, and anger over the need to prove itself better than they in order to justify its own existence.

If a management has such feelings, it would do well to examine them critically. Why have such feelings? How justified are they? What will happen if they are sprung after the merger is made? What resentment and resistance will follow? What will be the cost of the consequences?

(3) *Organizational pulse*

If management is going to make an assessment of a company which looks attractive, in addition to assessing financial, marketing, and management talent, it should ask itself what the other company is all about psychologically. Why are these people here? Why are they together? What gratifications are they getting? What is their perceived image of themselves? What is their feeling about the organization of which they are a part? Management should not stop with the top executive structure. How do lower level people feel about these issues? Management will have to live with them, too. This does not necessarily mean taking an opinion survey of the whole organization or talking to each individual.

For example, in the small scientific organization I cited earlier in the case illustration, turnover at both managerial and worker levels was very low despite the fact that similar companies were paying higher salaries. This suggests that something was holding those people together; if it had held them together over a long period of time while others nearby were earning more, it constituted a psychological cement.

However, the purchaser failed to examine and take seriously the basis of that solidarity. When he failed to recognize the underlying value system and sense of common purpose, and instead tried to institute seemingly rational managerial goals and controls, he chipped away some of the psychological cement and the whole organization began to crumble.

One can sense the pulse of an organization very easily by the spirit of its people, the way they talk to each other, what they talk about, and their attitude towards strangers. If the plant abruptly shuts down cold and tight for a coffee break—regardless of work in process—and if the people rush madly for the door at quitting time, these are elementary signals of how people feel about their work.

Part of the problem is that organizations try to be too rational about the things they can measure. Most of the critical elements of an organization being acquired have to do with people's feelings, and these are not so easily measured. Most executives will say, 'Yes, I know feelings are important', and then promptly go about disregarding them.

(4) *Harmonious atmosphere*

Having assessed some of the feelings of the junior organization, what are the differences between the way *those* people feel about their organization and the tenor and tempo of the prospective parent organization? This is not to say which one is right, but only to ask, 'How do they differ?' A hard-nosed, no-nonsense, high-pressure sales organization will have a difficult time assimilating one that depends heavily on service and customer consideration. This is one of the critical points at which a clash is likely to arise.

At the bargaining table, the prospective partners would do well to indicate to each other what they wish from the merger, how they see each other's organizations, how they feel about apparent differences, and how important those differences are to them. In particular, both organizations should be able to answer with psychological honesty, 'What does he want me for, really?' Then the prospective partners can jointly evolve their modes of compromise and integration. Such a process also creates a mechanism for the continuing solution of problems which arise subsequently.

All organizations need devices for solving problems at critical integration points.[4] This is as true for organizations which merge as it is for divisions or units within a company. For example, the personnel department of the smaller organization, which may have had certain ways of doing things in response to its top management, now has to deal with the personnel department of the larger organization as well.

How are such issues to be resolved with mutual satisfaction? How are future issues to be confronted? The larger organization must be able to hear the anxieties and pains of the smaller. Where does it hurt as a result of this merger, or where is it likely to hurt?

Most organizations woo the other, persuade it, effect the merger, and then go about business as usual—their way. This is often further compounded when the negotiations are first carried on between presidents, and the president of the smaller organization is assigned to report to a vice president of the larger one. Here is what happens:

The vice president, responding to the demands of his own boss for greater control, profitability, and productivity, in turn makes similar demands on the president of the smaller company. The latter now has to deal with his feelings of being deserted, in addition to whatever feelings he may have about being conned and taken over. These feelings may become more acute when whatever he wants to try innovatively is now squashed by fiat from someone he did not bargain for and with in the first place. His one channel, short of pounding the table or quitting, is through the man to whom he is reporting.

With these contemporary events, there is a growing general feeling that expectations in mergers are not being fulfilled. This feeling may in turn make it more difficult to consummate mergers as time goes by. Even worse, people may enter mergers as a good many enter marriages these days: 'I'll take a chance, and if it doesn't work, I'll leave.' That kind of a tentative commitment inevitably undermines a marriage; it will inevitably undermine a merger. It usually means that the relationship is bound by all kinds of secret clauses and reservations, as well as hidden expectations, which then continually burden both parties.

Complicating these forces is an increasing frequency of feelings of guilt on the part of presidents who sell out after having built organizations that are loyal to them. The long-term identification is exploited by the senior organization, control modes are introduced, procedures are changed arbitrarily, and the cohesive organization, with the close relationships people had with each other, now becomes just another place to work.

In such cases, people have learned an important lesson: it does not pay to be loyal, to identify, to invest themselves in an organization or its leadership. They will be sold down the river.

The old presidents are then angry with themselves for what they have done and communicate this anger to others who may be in the same position. The old presidents fight as long as they can, but ultimately quit or are eased out. They are left with residual feelings of anger, guilt, and resentment, and the depression which follows.

Of course, many presidents will disregard such experiences. They are like middle-aged maiden ladies still looking for a husband for security. They are prone to take whatever comes along, later finding the price too high to pay, and, subsequently, seeking ways out.

Thus it is important not to try to con the junior organization's managers. The senior partner may buy them, but it will also lose them. Even if the senior partner acquires the people, the products, and the plants, it will have unwilling, resentful partners who feel they have been taken. They will buck every way they can, and the senior partner will have lost their trust permanently.

The dominant management needs to be as straight and as factual as it can, and not withhold information about what it plans to do. It will only be kidding itself.

In fact, the senior partner would do well to let the junior's managers examine its own organization and talk to a wide range of people. Above all, management should never promise more than it can deliver. That is a business failing. For example, many organizations these days are promising young people creative possibilities, but most are not organized to permit such innovation. They therefore get rapid turnover and mutual disillusionment. Who needs it?

A contemporary example of this fourth suggestion being put into practice, at least according to a published account,[5] was the merger of AMK and United Fruit. Eli M. Black, President and Board Chairman of AMK, it is reported, operates with the philosophy that the best way to win such a company is to win its management. After proffering the merger, Black told John M. Fox, Board Chairman of United Fruit, that he would make no further moves toward gaining control without the approval of United Fruit's management. There would be no raids, no end runs, no fights. AMK wanted only a minority position, not control, on the UF board.

The two managements met daily during the negotiating process, and Black invited the UF management to visit AMK in New York. Black's whole concern was to create an atmosphere of harmony and rapport. In that he succeeded, for, according to Fox, 'Black never went back or changed a single thing he had promised us. He never acted without consulting us. He lived up to his word.'

Conclusion

There are many reasons for merger, including psychological reasons. Many mergers have been disappointing in their results and painful to their participants. These failures have been attributed largely to rational financial, economic, and managerial problems.

I contend that some psychological reasons for merger not only constitute a major, if unrecognized, force toward merger, but that they also constitute the basis for many, if not most, disappointments and failures. At least those that have turned sour, or have the most dangerous potential for turning sour, are those that arise out of some neurotic wish to become big by voraciously gobbling up others, or out of obsolescence.

Such mergers flounder because of the hidden assumptions the senior partner makes, and the condescending attitudes toward the junior organization which then follow. These result in efforts at manipulation and control which, in turn, produce (a) disillusionment and the feeling of desertion on the part of the junior organization, and (b) disappointment, loss of personnel, and declining profitability for the dominant organization.

To cope with these issues, I have suggested that senior executives of the dominant company should:

Probe their own motivations for merging.

Review the psychological assumptions that they have about the other party in the merger.

Assess the psychological relationships and attitudes of the people in the junior organization, and note how they may differ from those in the senior organization.

Out of open, honest discussion of these motivations, assumptions, and differences, create a harmonious atmosphere in which problem-solving mechanisms are set up so that the anguish of the junior organization can be heard and acted on, and operating modes can be evolved rather than imposed.

These suggestions depend for their validity on the recognition of the reality and power of feelings, and particularly on the fact that both the senior and the junior organization will be equal in psychological power despite vast differences in economic power. Either the senior management understands the psychological power of its partner and acts accordingly, or it stands to lose what it sought in a merger.

The importance of these considerations goes beyond corporations *per se*. If contemporary modes of merger result in widespread loss of initiative, increased constriction of imagination, and floating populations of executives, this has not only self-defeating implications for organizations, but also has powerful negative effects on society.

Chapter Six

PROBLEMS IN THE ANALYSIS OF STATISTICS RELATING TO TAKEOVERS AND MERGERS*

R. J. Briston

Senior Lecturer in Finance, Bradford Management Centre

and

D. G. Rhys

Lecturer in Economics, University of Hull

In recent years considerable attention has been paid to takeovers and mergers. Attempts have been made to classify them into different categories; to determine whether there are any significant relationships between the level of takeovers and various economic indicators; and to analyse the success of mergers. In particular, a great deal of concern has been expressed regarding the increased concentration which may result from a high level of merger activity for, without a corresponding increase in the numbers and importance of new firms, mergers lead to the concentration of net assets into fewer hands. The official surveys on merger activity conducted by the Board of Trade and the Monopolies Commission point to a significant increase in such concentration. For instance the Monopolies Commission (Ref. Note 1 (c)) produced figures for manufacturing companies alone covering firms which held about 80 per cent of total net assets in the period 1961 to 1968 inclusive. Firms qualified for inclusion in the survey on a size basis, the base date being taken as 1961. Firms meeting the size qualification *after* 1961 were not included but it was held that this would not have had a significant effect on the conclusions drawn from the survey data. In 1961 the population of companies in the survey was 1,312; at the end of 1968 the figure was 908, a fall of 31 per cent. Furthermore, in 1961 the largest 28 companies held 39 per cent of the net assets included, while in 1968 the 28 largest companies held over 51 per cent of net assets.

---

*Paper presented at the conference on Mergers and Takeovers, London, 28 and 29 May, 1970.

However, the Board of Trade statistics for 1969 suggest that diversification is becoming a more important feature of merger activity:

Table 1

	Same industrial group		Different industrial group	
	No. of mergers	Value £m.	No. of mergers	Value £m.
1968	348	1527·6	290	785·1
1969	484	454·6	407	651·7

Considering the situation in the 1960s as a whole, the 1969 figures may either represent a new and significant development or merely an isolated instance of a movement against the trend. However, the recent growth of conglomerates in the United States suggests that diversification may continue to be an important feature.

The basic aim of this paper is to assess the information available regarding takeovers and mergers and to try to determine how that information may be analysed in order to answer questions relating to takeover activity. In Part I the scope of the official statistics regarding acquisitions is outlined. Part II explains some models which have been applied to these statistics in an attempt to establish whether they can be explained by any of the main economic indicators. In Part III the dangers of aggregate analysis of this sort and the inconsistencies of the available data are stressed. Part IV concentrates upon the problems of analysing the success of mergers, while in Part V we advocate that a case-study approach is the only satisfactory method of determining such crucial factors as the purpose of mergers and the extent of their success.

PART I

The Scope of Official Statistics on Takeovers

Official figures on mergers have emanated mainly from the Central Statistical Office and the Board of Trade. Between 1949 and 1960 the figures related to companies with a stock exchange quotation. From 1961 companies with assets of under £0·5 million or with incomes of £50,000 or below were excluded. Consequently between 1949 and 1960, if a firm in the manufacturing, distributive and service trades had a stock exchange quotation it was included in the survey population. In addition, as companies went 'public' they were immediately included. The 1961 change excluded 400 companies each with assets of less than £0·5 million. However, they accounted for less than 5 per cent of assets and income of quoted companies taken in total; in 1960 they had spent £23 million on purchasing subsidiaries out of a total expenditure of £338 million.[2] In other words the change in the population may have reduced the annual value of officially reported merger activity between 1961–4 by around 6·6 per cent compared with 1960. Moreover, any firm becoming large enough after

1961 to warrant inclusion in the survey after the base date, was not, in fact, included. So as mergers and bankruptcies continued the sample covered a declining population between 1961 and 1964. Subsequently the survey's base was changed to 1964 so that companies in manufacturing, distribution, construction, transport and certain other services with assets of £0·5 million or greater, or with an income of £50,000 or more in 1964 were, therefore, included. This tended to widen the population again, given the fall in the purchasing power of money and new 'qualifiers'. In 1968 a few non-quoted companies were included for the first time. Perhaps the most significant development was the extension of the Board of Trade's analysis of merger activity in 1969 to cover acquisitions reported in the press by all industrial and commercial companies instead of confining the survey as previously to those companies covered by the Board of Trade's regular analysis of company accounts. The categories included for the first time were companies mainly trading overseas, most industrial holding companies, shipping and agricultural companies, plus some smaller firms. This important development meant that data worked out on the basis of the 1969 population, compared with that of 1964, has increased the value of merger activity by almost £198 million or some 21·8 per cent while the actual number of mergers 'caught' increased from 612 to 891.

PART II

The Application of Models to Takeover Statistics

In order to take our analysis of the motivation behind mergers one stage further, we constructed a few simple models in order to test the validity of a number of hypotheses. As our dependent variable we took the real value of expenditure on mergers over the period 1956 to 1968. As our independent variables we took real national income at factor cost, real gross profits, bank advances and the money supply both measured in real terms plus a proxy variable to take out the time trend. We also ran the first differences of the data leaving out the time trend of course. Our final independent variable was the *Financial Times* index of ordinary share prices and again we used crude data and the first difference. Our models utilized two and, at the most, three independent variables; as we only used thirteen observations, any attempt to use larger devices would have utilized too many degrees of freedom. As it was, the multi-colinearity in the data remained a problem.

The models used and the conclusions reached were as follows with each variable given these characters:

E = Real expenditure on mergers[1]
Y = Real national income at factor cost[2]
G = Gross real profits[3]
F = *Financial Times*–Actuaries ordinary share index[6]
A = Bank advances[4]
M = Real money supply[5]
T = Time trend[4]

[1] Basic data derived from *Economic Trends,* Board of Trade.
[2, 3] Sources: *National Income and Expenditure Blue Book 1969.*
[4, 5] Sources: Financial Statistics, C.S.O. *Bank of England Quarterly.*
[6] *Annual Abstract.*

In all cases the first differences are given by Δ. The corrected data is summarized in *Table 2*.

Table 2

(£ million)

Variable year	Real expenditure on mergers	Real nat. income	Gross profits	Bank advances	Money supply	F.T. ord. share index
1956	154·47	20927	3539·7	2317·6	9732·9	94·0
1957	154·09	21295	3512·5	2290·9	9660·2	100·0
1958	133·2	21102	3385·9	2297·1	9728·3	110·6
1959	332·5	21772	3629·1	3017·5	10255·4	151·1
1960	356·5	22791	3932·6	3729·4	10362·6	183·9
1961	375·4	23605	3883·7	4007·3	10260·3	189·1
1962	335·7	23882	3770·2	4035·7	10263·5	175·2
1963	319·0	24906	4108·0	4495·3	10745·0	186·3
1964	414·2	26186	4475·7	4877·7	11093·2	198·7
1965	398·4	26851	4520·3	5043·3	11309·1	186·9
1966	569·2	27229	4255·0	5015·2	11625·4	188·5
1967	801·8	27550	4188·7	6752·4	11995·6	201·3
1968	1543·7 (2068·87)*[1]	28278	4530·4	7343·0	12534·0	284·5

*[1] Figure from a new Board of Trade series.

From this data we tested the following relationships:–

Model one	:	$E = b + c\,Y + d\,G + e\,T$
Model two	:	$E = b + d\,G + g\,A + e\,T$
Model three	:	$E = b + d\,G + h\,M + e\,T$
Model four	:	$\Delta E = b + c\,\Delta Y + d\,\Delta G$
Model five	:	$\Delta E = b + d\,\Delta G + g\,\Delta G$
Model six	:	$\Delta E = b + d\,\Delta G + h\,\Delta M$
Model seven	:	$\Delta E = b + c\,\Delta Y + g\,\Delta A$
Model eight	:	$\Delta E = b + c\,\Delta Y + h\,\Delta M$
Model nine	:	$E = b + c\,Y + k\,F + e\,T$
Model ten	:	$\Delta E = b + c\,\Delta Y + k\,\Delta F$

With the result that:–

Model one	$E = 2182{\cdot}2 - 0{\cdot}13\,Y + 0{\cdot}175\,G + 114{\cdot}9\,T$
	This model has a Durbin-Watson D. Statistic of 1·83
Model two	$E = -294{\cdot}7 - 0{\cdot}05\,G + 0{\cdot}30\,A - 52{\cdot}06\,T$
Model three	$E = -4698{\cdot}3 - 0{\cdot}4\,G + 0{\cdot}56\,M - 51{\cdot}2\,T$
Model four	$\Delta E = 39{\cdot}7 - 11{\cdot}01\,Y + 6{\cdot}1\,G$
Model five	$\Delta E = 22{\cdot}15 + 4{\cdot}6\,G - 0{\cdot}34\,A$
Model six	$\Delta E = 29{\cdot}25 + 1{\cdot}15\,G + 9{\cdot}7\,M$
Model seven	$\Delta E = 3{\cdot}9 + 6{\cdot}1\,Y - 0{\cdot}11\,A$
Model eight	$\Delta E = 28{\cdot}7 + 1{\cdot}2\,Y + 11{\cdot}4\,M$
Model nine	$E = 469{\cdot}02 + 0{\cdot}07\,Y + 21{\cdot}23\,F + 8{\cdot}7\,T$
Model ten	$\Delta E = 23{\cdot}56 + 6{\cdot}6\,Y + 2{\cdot}95\,F$

Quite clearly the first three models are of very little use. With only thirteen observations and nine degrees of freedom the multi-colinearity between the variables is very strong. Moreover, the low Durbin-Watson statistic in model one shows the existence of some degree of auto-colinearity. In terms of the T statistic the relatively high figures attached to the time trend component in models one to three suggests that the high multiple correlations of between 0·87 and 0·978 are largely due to the time trend. However, model one gives a high T statistic of 8·54 for national income and a partial correlation value of –0·94.

The first difference models four to eight are rather more interesting as we can discount the time trend component. What is shown quite clearly here is that, using the data in the way presented, the T statistics for every independent variable in models four to eight range between 0·11 and 1·51. Given the small number of observations a T statistic in excess of 2·5 is needed before we can say that we have a satisfactory explanatory model. What is perhaps interesting is that the incidence of merger activity is often a negative function of national income, or the positive relationship is a weak one. In other words, national income is not a significant explanatory variable of merger activity in the first instance.

Models nine and ten are perhaps the most interesting. In model nine the T statistic for the time trend at 0·32 suggests that this component is unimportant as an explanatory variable while the T statistic for the *Financial Times*–Actuaries ordinary share index is 5·11. In model ten national income has a T statistic of 1·09 and a partial correlation of –0·33 whereas the T statistic for changes in the F.T.–Actuaries ordinary share index is 4·67 with a partial correlation coefficient of 0·83. In other words, changes in merger activity may be significantly and positively correlated to changes in the F.T.–Actuaries ordinary share index. Of course it could be argued that the independent variable here should be takeover activity. In other words, changes in share prices mainly reflect changes in merger activity rather than changes in share prices affecting merger activity. In order to try to resolve this problem we lagged the data with merger activity in year t being regressed on the share index for t – 1. Clearly it is unrealistic to say that takeover activity in, say, 1958 depends on *actual* share prices in 1959. However, if a close relationship appeared, then there may be a case for saying that share prices in 1959 reflected merger activity in 1958; in other words the link was from merger activity to share prices and not vice versa. In the event, lagged data produced a partial correlation of changes in merger activity associated with changes in the F.T. share index of 0·10 and a T statistic of 0·30. Consequently it is more likely the changes in share prices have more of a causal effect on mergers than vice versa. The mechanism could be something like this. With an upward movement in the share index, firms feel that the high value of their own equity makes it easy to persuade another enterprise to join them, either through share exchange, cash purchase or both. In addition, merger by share exchange may be quite easy to arrange and a cheap way of acquiring subsidiaries if the buyers shares are moving up relatively to those of the acquired firm. The elasticity between changes in the F.T.–Actuaries ordinary share index and changes in merger activity is 0·167, i.e., a 1 per cent change in the share index leads to a 0·167 per cent change in expenditure on mergers.

From these simple models it would appear that the partial correlation coefficients between gross profits and merger activity vary between 0·11 and 0·42, that for bank advances between 0·07 and 0·21, that for the money supply between 0·32 and 0·45, and that for national income between 0·04 and 0·23. Only the F.T.–Actuaries ordinary share index gives us a reasonably close relationship. Even here, however, there is the drawback that the share index is expressed in monetary and not real terms unlike the remainder of the statistics. Moreover, as explained below, it is doubtful whether annual averages give a satisfactory picture of the pattern of behaviour during each year.

It would appear then, that the main motivation behind mergers lies outside the variables which we have considered. In particular it is likely that the prime objectives behind a merger vary from case to case and that they are likely to be behavioural and strategic rather than easy to categorize and quantify.

PART III

The Dangers in Building Aggregate Models

Although it is very tempting to apply increasingly sophisticated statistical techniques to data relating to takeovers and mergers, the dangers of establishing spurious relationships should not be under-estimated. In particular, the following areas present exceptional difficulties.

(1) *Discrepancies between statistical series*

The main statistics are produced by the Board of Trade for the years from 1964 onwards. These initially related to acquisitions of subsidiaries by companies engaged mainly in manufacturing and in the distributive and service trades, whose shares are quoted on a United Kingdom stock exchange. From 1961 onwards the statistics excluded about 400 companies each with assets of less than £0·5 million. The series was extended in 1969 to cover acquisitions reported in the press by all industrial and commercial companies instead of (as previously) only by those covered by the Board of Trade's regular analysis of company accounts. The main categories now included for the first time are companies mainly trading overseas; most industrial holding companies; shipping and agricultural companies; and some smaller companies. Also there was a change in the basis of recording, as explained below, as a result of which the 1968 figures are not comparable with earlier years. In addition to this basic data, J. B. Tabb in a PhD thesis prepared at Sheffield University, has listed the companies quoted on the London Stock Exchange which were taken over between 1945 and 1965. His figures are significantly different from those of the Board of Trade, largely because he includes plantations, estates, shell companies etc. In 1959, for instance, the Board of Trade shows 98 public companies as having been taken over, while Tabb has identified 206 such companies. In an article in Business Ratios, M. A. Utton provided figures relating to quoted companies which were acquired by firms in the manufacturing industry between 1954 and 1965. In most years these figures were lower than those described above because he excludes companies in the distributive and service trades. Nevertheless, for 1961, he shows 65 companies with assets of £328·71 m. as having been acquired, compared with Board of Trade figures of 64 companies with a total consideration of £225·4 m.

(2) *The choice between series based on numbers of takeovers and those based upon values*

The problems in this area can be demonstrated by the Board of Trade statistics for the period 1964–8:

Table 3

	No. of companies acquired			Total consideration (£m.)		
	Non-quoted	quoted	total	Non-quoted	quoted	total
1964	868	71	939	240	262	502
1965	920	75	995	160	347	507
1966	727	78	805	117	330	447
1967	577	84	661	151	630	781
1968	458	140	598	137	1516	1653
1969	–	–	891	–	–	1106

The 1967 figures have since been adjusted to show total consideration of £882 m. and neither the 1968 nor the 1969 figures can be compared with those of earlier years. Even if, notwithstanding this lack of continuity, one wished to use the above data for a regression analysis it is clear that virtually any relationship could be established if the appropriate series was chosen. The number of quoted companies acquired, for example, rose steadily between 1964 and 1967 and then shot up by two thirds in 1968. On the other hand, the total number of companies acquired declined rapidly each year between 1965 and 1968 but increased substantially in 1969. At the same time the total consideration was virtually unchanged between 1964 and 1965, fell during 1966, rose by about 80 per cent in 1967, more than doubled during 1968 and fell back by one third in 1969. Clearly the important data here is that relating to the value of acquisitions, for the actual number of acquisitions is irrelevant. Here again, however, there are many problems. Even if it were possible to identify all acquisitions, full information about the cost is not always available. In the case of some non-quoted companies, for example, the Board of Trade has had to base the valuation upon the nominal value of the shares acquired. In other cases the value has been based upon market value. This would, of course, lead to an over-statement of the level of activity in years with high stock market values, for a company would be prepared to pay an inflated price for another company if it could use its own over-valued shares for this purpose. This probably explains why shares and loan stock financed 84 per cent of the total consideration in 1968 compared with 40 per cent in 1964. Another problem occurs where less than 100 per cent of the shares of another company are bought. If, for example, a 51 per cent holding is acquired, should the subsidiary be valued at the cost of that holding or should the value of the entire capital be computed at the price per share paid for the 51 per cent holding? Each of these is probably incorrect, though the second gives a better indication of the value of the assets over which control has been acquired. Nevertheless it is probable that the value per share of a majority holding is higher than that of a minority holding.

Similar problems occur where a company with a high level of vote-gearing is acquired. If, for example, a company has assets with a market value of £1,000,000, which are financed by £500,000 debentures, £100,000 preference shares, £300,000 non-voting ordinary shares and £100,000 voting ordinary shares, that company could probably be controlled through an expenditure of less than £100,000. In such a case the cost of acquiring control bears no relation to the value of the assets acquired and would be an inappropriate figure for measuring the economic impact of the takeover.

A further problem relates to the valuation of mergers. The Board of Trade method is as follows:

The merger of companies A and B to form C is treated as the acquisition by C of A and B. The value included, therefore, covers both A and B, whereas if A acquires B, only the value of B is included.

This treatment seems to involve double counting and it would be more consistent if the smaller of the merging companies were regarded as having been acquired. Certainly it seems strange that one particular legal method of implementing what is often in effect a disguised takeover should receive double the weight of a more overt acquisition.

(3) *The problem of timing*

When endeavouring to establish causal relationships between data relating to the number or value of acquisitions and various economic indicators, it is crucial that the exact date of acquisition should be determined. For analytical purposes the date at which the acquiring company decided to make the bid is most relevant. But this information cannot be obtained from any of the available statistical series. Failing this, the date at which the bid was publicized seems most appropriate. If this date is used it must be appreciated in any analysis of managerial motivation that the intention to bid was formed a considerable time earlier. In any case the Board of Trade statistics have only recently begun to record acquisitions by the date of announcement of the bid. Between 1954 and 1967 the data was compiled from the accounts of acquiring companies whose financial years ended within the twelve months to the 5th April following the end of the calendar year. Thus not only was it impossible to analyse acquisitions on a monthly or quarterly basis, but also many acquisitions might be allotted to a year different from that in which they were actually made. Moreover, no information is available regarding unsuccessful bids, which are of obvious importance when attempting to determine the factors which motivate takeover bids. Since 1968 the Board of Trade has produced quarterly statistics based upon information extracted from the financial press supplemented by special inquiries. The date of acquisition was the date on which the bid was successful, which will often, of course, be a considerable time after the bid was decided upon.

The publication of quarterly statistics represents an enormous improvement and the fluctuations between quarters reveal how dangerous it is to base conclusions upon annual data. The quarterly figures for 1968 and 1969 are as follows:

Table 4

		No. of companies acquired	Consideration £m.
1968	First quarter	159	768·9
	Second quarter	134	248·2
	Third quarter	145	620·8
	Fourth quarter	200	674·8
	Total for year	638	2312·7
1969	First quarter	247	419·1
	Second quarter	252	297·7
	Third quarter	197	233·4
	Fourth quarter	195	156·1
	Total for year	891	1106·3

The 1968 figures differ from those shown in *Table 3* in that they include mergers and property companies. The information in *Table 4* gives a much clearer picture of takeover activity than that given by annual figures. The figure for the first quarter of 1968 is artificially high for it includes £455 m. for the merger of the British Motor Corporation and Leyland Motors into The British Leyland Motor Corporation. The data suggests that takeover activity rose to a peak during the second half of 1968 when share prices were rising to ridiculously high levels. When the market broke in early 1969, so takeover activity declined and by the end of the year was running at almost the level of 1964 and 1965. Although this supports the positive correlation with stock market prices shown in Part II, this could not be definitely established unless the dates on which bids were made were available for comparison with the value of the F.T. index at the same date.

(4) *The definition of control*

The legal definition of control normally involves the holding, beneficial or otherwise, of more than 50 per cent of the voting shares of a company. This definition is used for the Board of Trade statistics, probably because it has the advantage of certainty. However, economists have long argued that control may be wielded through a much lower holding of voting stock. Berle and Means,[2] for example, have argued that a company may be controlled through the ownership of a dominant minority of the voting stock and they suggested that a holding of between 20 per cent and 50 per cent would be sufficient for this purpose. R. J. Larner, analysing the ownership of the 200 largest non-financial corporations in 1963, argued that the lower limit of 20 per cent for minority control was too high in view of the increased dispersion of stockholdings. In his study he classified a firm as immediately controlled by minority stock ownership if 10 per cent or more of its voting stock is held by an individual, family, corporation, or group of business associates.[3] P. Sargant Florence[4] also recognized the existence of minority control and suggested that where either the single largest shareholder, or connected persons among the twenty largest shareholders, or companies among the twenty largest shareholders, held 20 per cent or more of the votes, such control would probably exist.

Although the point at which control would exist is vague, it seems reasonable that a large minority holding would often give effective control due partly to the direct pressure which may be brought to bear on the directors and partly to the impotence of the other shareholders because of the dispersion of their holdings. Many shareholdings classified as trade investments may, therefore, be disguised acquisitions in economic terms and should be analysed as such. Similarly where a company formally takes over another in which it already has a substantial minority holding, the acquisition in real terms may have been made with the purchase of the minority holding, but for all of the statistical series it will not be regarded as made until legal control is achieved. This argument is not, of course, intended to criticize the statistics, but only to point out the difficulties in drawing economic conclusions from data which is, of necessity, based upon law rather than economics.

(5) *The concentration upon deals in companies as opposed to assets*

Where statistics of acquisitions are based upon the takeover of companies as opposed to assets, many instances of rationalization, concentration etc., will be omitted. This attention is being paid to transactions in shares rather than changes in the ownership and use of assets. Unfortunately, however, economists are more concerned with transactions in assets and a statistical series which includes such transactions if they are carried out indirectly through the purchase of the shares which confer ownership of those assets, but excludes them if the assets are purchased directly, is bound to be defective for many types of analysis. The types of inconsistency which may occur are obvious. If a parent company allows its subsidiaries to retain their corporate identity and then sells one of them to another company this would be a takeover. If, on the other hand, it is organized into divisions and sells one division to another company, this would not be a takeover, though exactly the same transaction is taking place in economic terms, the only difference being the legal method of transfer. Because of the concentration upon companies rather than divisions, if two or more companies merge, the merger is recorded in the statistics (with the value placed upon the transaction depending upon the legal form which the merger takes), while, if two or more divisions merge, as when the computer interests of English Electric, I.C.T., and Plessey were merged to form International Computers Ltd, the transaction would be ignored. Similarly, if a company sells its assets to another company and then liquidates this would not be a takeover, though if the second company were to buy the shares of the first company instead of purchasing the assets directly, this would be regarded as an acquisition.

PART IV

The Analysis of the Purpose and Success of Mergers

(1) Much of economic analysis of acquisitions has been directed at the purpose of the takeovers, distinguishing particularly between concentration and diversification. In the Board of Trade statistics, each company included in the analysis is allotted to an industry group, corresponding generally to an Order of the Standard Industrial Classification, 1968. If a company has diverse activities it has been classified to the industry in which its main activity lies; but for some companies the classification is a very arbitrary one. On this basis the Board of Trade breaks down the total of acquisitions between those within the same industry group and those from a different group. The main problem is that the use of industrial groups only gives the barest indication of the purpose of a takeover. In the first place the industrial categories are so broad that what appears to be a horizontal merger is often, in fact, diversification. The problem of industrial classification has already been admirably explained by M. A. Utton,[5] so the point will not be stressed further here. Another major problem is the number of different definitions applied to mergers and acquisitions. The Board of Trade statistics distinguish only between concentration and diversification, though it is admitted that many of the takeovers classified under diversification would have represented vertical integration had more information been available concerning the activities of the companies concerned. The Monopolies Commission 1[(c)] suggests that mergers should be categorized under:–

(*a*) Horizontal mergers – mergers between companies that sell the same products (or products which can be easily substituted for each other);
(*b*) Vertical mergers – mergers between companies of which one is an actual or potential supplier of the other.
(*c*) Conglomerate mergers – mergers between companies that do not produce similar products and where neither is an actual or potential supplier of the other.

However, it is admitted that in application to particular cases, these broad working definitions need further refinement, since many companies are considerably diversified and consequently a predominantly vertical merger may have horizontal or conglomerate elements, a horizontal merger may be in part conglomerate, possibly with vertical features as well, or a conglomerate merger may have vertical or horizontal aspects. Even in a conglomerate merger, there could be common elements apart from finance or management – the merging companies might, for instance, be operating in the same technological field or supplying complementary products or, at any rate, selling to markets within the same general class or in the same overseas areas.

The Bureau of Economics of the U.S. Federal Trade Commission also classifies mergers by horizontal, vertical and conglomerate. Conglomerate mergers are subdivided into three categories – product extension, market extension and other. The product extension and market extension categories represent acquisitions in which the acquired and acquiring firms are discernibly related in a production and marketing sense. The 'other' category represents combinations in which such relationships are not discernible.[6] These broad categories are also used by S. R. Reid,[7] though he refers to the product and market extension category of conglomerates as a circular merger. He also makes the point that what appears to be a horizontal merger may, in fact, be geographical diversification where the companies involved make the same product but are situated in different markets.

The main drawbacks to these definitions are that mergers may fall into more than one category (in which case there is no recognized method of apportionment) and that the categories themselves are too broad, particularly where diversification is concerned. Ansoff, for example, defines six types of diversification:

(*a*) Horizontal diversification with same type of customers and related technology.
(*b*) Horizontal diversification with same type of customers and unrelated technology.
(*c*) Concentric diversification – marketing and technology related.
(*d*) Concentric diversification – marketing related only.
(*e*) Concentric diversification – technology related only.
(*f*) Conglomerate diversification – new market and unrelated technology.[8]

Even these definitions are very arbitrary and rigid, for they depend upon the impersonal characteristics of the companies concerned rather than upon the subjective purpose behind the merger. For instance, a merger which appears to be motivated by 'conglomerate diversification' might, in fact, be the result of one of a variety of motives. It may have been induced by financial factors such as cash-raising or obtaining a stock exchange quotation. The main object may have been the purchase of land to expand production of the company's existing product. On the other hand, the motive may be the expansion of an existing product into which the company has previously diversified, or it may be completely new diversification caused by fear of the collapse of the company's main market. Another objective may be the stabilization of earnings, for earnings should fluctuate less the more the number of unrelated products which a company sells. In such a case the company may intend to allow its subsidiaries to operate independently or it may hope to obtain managerial economies. Finally the intention may be the more aggressive one of maximizing sales or assets.

Unfortunately, the more one extends the number of classifications of purpose the more difficult it is to categorize acquisitions purely on the basis of their industry. Ultimately, it will prove necessary for a meaningful classification to approach the bidding company direct for information.

(2) In analysing the success of a merger it is tempting to argue that vertical and horizontal mergers are intended to increase efficiency and that they should result in higher profits than those of the individual companies added together; while conglomerate mergers are intended mainly to reduce fluctuations in earnings. These assumptions, if made purely on the basis of industrial classifications, are dangerous, partly because of the difficulties of defining the purpose of a merger as outlined above, and partly because the success of the merger depends upon a comparison with the results which would have been achieved had the merger not taken place, and this information is simply not available.

Nevertheless it is very common for economists to attempt to analyse the success of mergers by comparing the performance of merging firms with that of unitary growth firms in the same industry. We, therefore, examined the performance of companies in the motor vehicles industry to discover whether the companies which had grown by merger had performed noticeably better or worse than those which had grown by means of internal expansion.

Taking the profit record of merger intensive and unitary growth firms mainly from the private car sector of the industry, over the period 1957–67, Table 5 shows the results.

Table 5

	Merger intensive			Unitary growth	
	BMC	Leyland	BMC & Leyland	Ford	Vauxhall
1957	100	100	100	100	– Losses in 1957
1958	221	104	171	134	– Slight recovery 1958
1959	140	94	118	175	100
1960	240	119	199	183	104
1961	90	82	102	121	51
1962	36	58	62	120	85
1963	138	102	142	125	110
1964	195	170	219	69	133
1965	210	195	242	46	131
1966	183	157	209	172	102
1967	–130	187	87	138	90
1968			195		
1969			205		

The base period for the merged firms takes account of the combined total of the then independent firms subsequently absorbed by Leyland and BMC. Compared with Ford, BMC's earnings situation was extremely erratic. Despite the creation of BMC as long ago as 1952, the disastrous position in 1967 was to a large extent due to a failure to integrate completely the Austin and Nuffield empires. In terms of product, management and productive capacity, many of the opportunities presented by the 1952 merger had gone by default. Nowhere was this plainer than on the marketing side with the failure to merge the old Austin and Nuffield dealer networks. Apart from the problems presented by Standard-Triumph in 1961 and 1962, Leyland's case is one of a successful merger. Within a very short time of the completion of the merger, Leyland's earnings add up to more than the best performances of the constituent parts before merger. The larger size of the organization was taken as an opportunity to improve production methods, to integrate fully product ranges and to apply Leyland's rigorous management and cost-control techniques to the new combine. Neither unitary growth firm can be said to have suffered because of a failure to absorb other firms; the fluctuations in earnings largely reflect fluctuations in the car trade. Their growth trends in earnings are superior to BMC's but inferior to Leylands. In other words the mere fact of merging or relying on unitary growth does not save a firm from business fluctuations and neither does it mean commercial disaster or great prosperity. The key factor is clearly not the merger but what the firms do with the opportunities provided by the merger.

In the commercial vehicles sector of the industry the same general sort of picture emerges. A merged firm does not necessarily find itself either with an immediate advantage or disadvantage. This is clear if we compare Leyland's performance with that of some smaller scale commercial vehicle producers (see Table 6).

Table 6

	Dennis (1)	Leyland and Associated Commercial Vehicles (2)	Seddon (3)	ERF (4)
1957		100		
1958		87		
1959		89		
1960	100	151	100	100
1961	96·5	126	141	121
1962	145	88	48	135
1963	113	156	94	103
1964	50	260	120	139
1965	−163	297	175	146
1966	67	240	351	179
1967	129	285	436	186

The use of different base dates is necessary in order to find similar positions in the companies' earnings profiles over the period. Dennis, Seddon and ERF have largely depended on internal growth rather than acquiring subsidiaries. Seddon's relative performance was substantially better than the commercial-vehicle orientated Leyland combine between 1957 and 1967. ERF's growth was steady, if less spectacular. Dennis, on the other hand, failed to generate sufficient output to keep its large and highly-capitalized plant fully occupied. In other words, we again have the situation that a merger-intensive firm does less well than some and better than other internal-growth orientated enterprises.

Another point that emerges here is that a merger does not necessarily disrupt a company's financial and economic performance for any great length of time after the merger date. Leyland purchased the declining Standard-Triumph company in 1961 and the efficient commercial vehicle producer ACV in 1962. In 1961 Standard made a £1½ million loss and continued to lose money in 1962. However, by 1963, Leyland had made the company profitable again and in the interim, ACV had been absorbed into the combine without much disruption. In the subsequent period, Leyland's net cash flow exceeded the combined earnings of the pre-merger companies. No doubt the situation was greatly helped by a recovery in aggregate demand for motor vehicles which assisted the post-merger environment.

What we have tried to show here is that a merger of itself has no easily predictable consequences and that a merged combine does not necessarily have an advantage over unitary-growth firms in the same industry. Indeed a merger may be a case of running to keep in the same position relative to a unitary firm. The position of BMC in the post-war period certainly suggests that this could easily occur. In other instances, mergers are provoked by a determination to grow sufficiently to gain such economies and financial strength that the future of the combine is secured. During the late 1940s when Leyland was a relatively unknown firm producing 3,500 vehicles a year, it was the company's aim to become the dominant force in the UK motor industry and large enough to survive internationally. At the time this aim must have seemed unrealistic but within twenty years the combine had finally achieved its long-term goal with the *de facto* takeover of British Motor Holdings.

The major drawback to the type of analysis carried out above is that the success of a merger depends partly upon its purpose and partly upon what the individual companies would have achieved had they not merged. This information is simply unobtainable and we must conclude that the success of a merger cannot be determined in any meaningful fashion unless a case study approach is used with the full co-operation of the company.[9] One practical suggestion which would facilitate the evaluation of the success of mergers is that companies should be required to indicate in specific terms, the purpose and expected results of any mergers which they undertook. Moreover, in the light of this information, shareholders of the bidding company might be entitled to vote against a takeover. Such a requirement, however, would probably lead to the direct purchase of assets of another company rather than the purchase of its shares which would cause still more confusion for official statistics of takeover activity.

PART V

The Arguments for the Adoption of the Case-study Approach

In the earlier parts of this paper, the dangers of analysing takeover activity on an aggregate basis were stressed. In particular, the problems of defining control, defining a takeover and the lack of continuity in official statistics were stressed. It was also shown that the analysis of individual takeovers, or of selected groups of takeovers, classified by purpose or by industry, suffered from similar drawbacks if carried out solely on the basis of external data.

In either of the above types of analysis essential information, which can only be obtained from the companies involved, is completely missing and can only be obtained by direct approach to the companies. It is clear that takeover activity is just one of the many facets of a company's investment policy and that a takeover should be appraised in the same way and in competition with other available investment opportunities. For example, a company which wishes to expand may spend more on advertising or research and development, may buy more capital equipment or may buy another company. In either case the outcomes should, in theory, be forecast and compared using DCF techniques. It is surprising that considerable attention should have been paid by academics to the projects in British industry with particular reference to the extent to which DCF techniques are used, while the criteria determining the use of funds for takeover purposes have been largely ignored.

It is the conclusion of this paper that the determinants of takeover activity can only be evaluated by direct approach to the companies involved, and that we will learn far more about the takeover process by using the case-study method than we will by establishing often spurious relationships between two or more sets of imperfect data. If the case-study method were adopted, answers could be obtained to the following crucial questions:

(i) Which person or group of persons within the company is responsible for appraising each takeover opportunity and for making the decision to proceed?
(ii) What was the purpose of each takeover and how does this purpose conform with the basic objectives of the company?
(iii) How detailed an appraisal was made of each takeover and how far was each compared with competing investment opportunities?
(iv) To what extent were the assets of the company taken over integrated with those of the parent company?
(v) To what extent was the post-merger performance compared with that forecast?
(vi) How far was the merger successful in attaining its stated objectives?

It is submitted that an analysis of this sort carried out upon a relatively small sample of companies would vastly improve our understanding, not only of the takeover process but of the entire investment planning and control function. Although a single research group would need massive funds to administer such a survey, it would appear to be an area which might easily be researched in a fragmented fashion with area studies being carried out at different universities and with postgraduate dissertations being used perhaps for studies of individual companies. All that would be needed at the administrative level would be the establishment of a centre at one of the universities or within one of the government departments to co-ordinate the research and to maintain a case-study library.

Finally, we would like to express our thanks to the Houblon Norman Fund whose support has made this paper possible and will, we hope, enable us to prepare some specimen case-studies.

PART B

CASE STUDIES OF MERGERS

Chapter Seven

THREE CASE STUDIES – GUINNESS, SPILLERS AND NESTLES

K. Bhaskar

Lecturer at the University of Bristol

Editor's Introduction

In this book references are made to the need for a follow-up examination of mergers, an auditing of their performance. In the next chapter Professor Beesley refers to the monitoring procedures of government agencies and Susan Dev (in Chapter Ten) refers to the follow-up of profit forecasts. This Chapter is, to some extent, a research into the difficulties and problems of following up a merger using only public information. The information available to the public consists of the Annual Reports obtainable at Companies House and information that is from time to time published in the financial press.

The three takeovers examined in this chapter occurred sufficiently far back in time for the effects of any 'window dressing' of the accounts to have worn off. This might have been the case with the short-term profit forecasts examined by Susan Dev. One major problem that occurs when attempting to assess the financial record of a victim firm (the firm that has been taken over) is that it requires knowledge of the objectives of the firm in making the bid. It is then necessary to determine whether or not these objectives were achieved and if not how far they were from being achieved. Another problem is synergy – the marginal cash flows into and out of the firm that are attributable to economies or dis-economies following the merger. In attempting to estimate the pecuniary benefit to any firm, synergy is difficult to isolate and to quantify.

These case studies were therefore picked to fulfil two criteria. First, they were chosen where synergy was expected to be least, that is where the merger or takeover took the firm into new product and new market areas – in other words where the parent company wanted to diversify out of its existing product/market mix. It was found, however, that despite this objective it was not possible completely to abstract from the problems of estimating synergy. Second, takeovers that had occurred sufficiently far back in time – the date arbitrarily chosen was 1960 – were selected so that changes in accounting bases had been worked through.

Some of the other problems encountered were concerned with:

1. Whether or not the victim firm had remained a legal entity, with the same set of physical assets as it had owned before the takeover.

2. Whether or not there were inter-company transfers of goods. If a raw material or finished good passes from one subsidiary of a company to another subsidiary, an artificially low price may be charged and this may be reflected in a poor set of accounting results for that subsidiary.

It was found that if a subsidiary was not performing favourably, management services were transferred from the main company to the subsidiary company at a zero transfer price.

3. Special fees being charged by the parent company to the subsidiary.

Despite these problems, publicly available accounting information can be of use. The reader can examine these three cases, in particular the financial statistics, and decide whether he thinks the acquisitions were 'successful', although it should be remembered the objectives of the mergers are not known.

PART I

Guinness – A History of Diversification

Guinness has been engaged in brewing since 1759. Since 1951 the firm has been diversifying into product areas totally unrelated to its traditional product, beer.

Some possible reasons for this diversification may have been:–

1. To counteract large seasonal fluctuations

2. To develop products with a large growth potential – assuming that the management of Guinness believed that beer was a stagnating market. (However, the introduction of Harp lager in 1961 showed that the management still believed that there was some growth left in the market.)

3. To diversify into product areas that are not affected by the same variables as the brewing industry: for example, if indirect taxation is increased on beer, it might be wise to have a product that is unaffected by this increase in tax and the consequential price increase.

The areas that Guinness diversified into were:–

1951	Confectionery
1959	Pharmaceuticals
1961	Plastics and precision tools
1967	Soft drinks

None of the particular firms taken over (henceforth known as the victim firms) could be regarded as a potential challenge to Guinness. These were not defensive takeovers. The precise objectives are unknown, though the three reasons given earlier may have had some bearing on the decision. The major plausible reason must therefore be purely financial, except where Guinness took over K. G. Corfield and stated that their aim was, in part, to help the government of Northern Ireland's industrialization policy.

This section will concentrate on Guinness's diversification into the pharmaceutical field. Crookes Laboratories Limited were taken over by Guinness and Philips in

1960. Total consideration was £1.2m. with Guinness having the majority shareholding (60 per cent). Twyford Laboratories Ltd was set up by Guinness a year earlier (1959) and represents the other concern in the pharmaceutical division of Guinness.

Table 1.1 shows a summary of accounting statistics for Crookes, both before and after the takeover. Twyfords' and Guinness's profits before tax are also shown. Too much should not be read into these figures, but it is expedient to look at their general trend – which seems to be to turn a small profit into a huge loss after takeover.

In order to place these particular takeovers in their relative position in the overall strategy of Guinness, a brief outline of Guinness's other attempts at diversification is given to show that, 'As with some other major companies, Guinness has found diversification no bed of roses'. This outline will be in the form of a short historical sketch. No analysis of accounting figures has been given, although one or two are inserted to illustrate the relative importance of a particular division within the group. In general, however, not very much should be deduced from the few statistics that are shown in this table.

Table 1.1

	Crookes Laboratories Limited				Twyford	A. Guinness Son and Co. Ltd.,
	Trading profit £000	Profit before tax £000	Fixed assets* £000	Dividend (less tax) £000	Profit before tax (and before subvention receipts) £000	Profit before tax £000
1953	125	108	149	15		4906
1954	210	192	150	21		5682
1955	170	145	146	22		6371
1956	137	114	183	22		7097
1957	112	90	223	22		7461
1958	95	69	204	22		8154
1959	81	54	214	23		7420
1960	98	67	241	23	– 16	8207
1961	67	35	262	5	– 48	7989
1962	–100	–123	205	–	– 77	7768
1963	23	– 18	228	–	–151	8413
1964	–229	–365	268	–	–224	9258
1965	–316	–395	1058	–	–535	8583
1966	–216	–356	1041	–	–586	9689
1967	– 38	–171	987	–	–782	11119
1968	– 49	–180	1097	–	–462	12466

N.B. Research and development is charged against profits.
* Excluding goodwill and trade investments.

Confectionery

In 1951 Callard and Bowser, and William Nuttall were acquired. They were later followed by Lavells and Riley Brothers (Halifax). According to the *Investors Chronicle* these acquisitions 'have not been particularly good for Guinness'. Rolls Confectionery were purchased from J. Lyons (1962). Confectionery had its own problems, one being the soaring price of butter (one of the principal ingredients), another being hot weather – which has an unfavourable effect on confectionery sales.

Because of the competition one would not have thought Confectionery to be either a good growth area or even a very profitable one. Despite this Guinness announced in its Annual Report of 1961 that turnover in this area of its activities had increased by 500 per cent. This is equivalent to about 17 per cent growth compounded over the ten years since 1951. Two important points, however, are that the 17 per cent growth includes growth due to inflationary factors, and that no allowance has been made for the increase in turnover attributable to Lavells and Riley Brothers – bought after 1951.

In the sixties, profit before tax seems to have been on the decline – some examples of the group profit were:–

	1964	1965	1967	1968
Profit before tax £000,000s	0·74	0·65	0·5	0·6

Examination of the statistics of turnover (which is more difficult to juggle about with) and profits before tax of the confectionery division will perhaps show the relative strength of this product area vis-à-vis beer.

	Sales				Profit before tax			
	1968		1967		1968		1967	
	£m.	% of total	£m.	% of total	£m.	% of total	£m.	% of total
Brewing	120·2	89	116·7	89	12·2	97·6	11·4	103
Confectionery	14·0	10	12·4	9	0·6	4·8	0·5	4·5
Total of all groups	137·5		131·6		12·5		11·1	

Although profit can be a suspect statistic it is interesting to note that on the above statistics confectionery constituted about 10 per cent of the total turnover yet yields only 5 per cent of the total profit.

In so far as the three aims suggested for Guinness's diversification – seasonal fluctuation, growth markets and different variables affecting products – may have been realized, these were achieved only at some considerable cost and involved the company in a whole range of problems not envisaged at the outset. Yet despite this Guinness again expanded the confectionery division in 1961 by buying Rolls Confectionery.

Plastics and precision tools

A majority interest was acquired in K. G. Corfield in 1960–61 at the request of the Government of Northern Ireland in order to assist their economy. With great pride Guinness announced that this subsidiary was developing a new camera, the 'Corfield 66' (a 35 mm. camera). In 1963 terminal losses were reported on the closing down of the camera activities of Corfields. To have diversified into cameras and then to have closed down those activities so soon seems to indicate that Guinness thought cameras too risky. Yet if they were too risky, why go into that field in the first place?

Guinness again expanded in this area, after this not so encouraging start, by acquiring Industrial Mouldings (Warwick) Limited – an English firm and presumably acquired with no such philanthropic motive as might have been the case with Corfield.

The relative importance of this group to the group total is illustrated below:

	Sales		Profit	
	1968 £m.	1967 £m.	1968 £m.	1967 £m.
Plastics and engineering	1·3	·8	·1	–
Total of all groups	137·5	131·6	12·5	11·1

Perhaps this group was never intended to play a very important part. In the past nine years or so it seems hardly to have been of much importance at all. Even so it may be a minor irritation to the management of Guinness.

Soft drinks

Guinness, together with Showerings, bought an Irish soft drinks concern and sold its English interests to Schweppes. It might be thought that perhaps Guinness had come to an arrangement with Schweppes; this suspicion is heightened by the following comment from the 1968 Annual Report of Guinness: 'With regard to Schweppes, we are assured of the continuance of the franchise of their brands in Ireland and, furthermore, of their full technical support, which we greatly value'.

Perhaps this indicated a change in the attitude of Guinness; instead of trying to compete with the market leaders it would be better to join them and to split the profits up in some way or other.

Pharmaceuticals

This leads us to the first case study, in which the victim firm was Crookes Laboratories Limited.

In 1960 Guinness acquired a 60 per cent interest in Crookes (the remainder was bought by Philips); total consideration was £1.2m. In the Annual Report for 1960 the Chairman had this to say about the takeover: ' . . . it affords us an entry into the field of pharmaceutical and veterinary products both at home and abroad. Full development will take some years, but ultimately this business . . . should be a profitable investment with considerable scope for expansion'.

In addition Twyford Laboratories was set up in 1959.

The reasons for examining this takeover are as follows:–

1. Crookes Laboratories was an independent public company before takeover and thus published their Annual Report and Accounts.

2. Crookes had been in existence for some time and had remained comparatively free from mergers until 1959.

3. Pharmaceuticals and brewing seemed sufficiently removed from one another to avoid transfer pricing difficulties and synergy problems.

The takeover could well have been due to a growth or profitability motive. Profits in pharmaceuticals were high, or at least were reported to be high, e.g., Glaxo reported a return on capital employed of 27 per cent. This high return on capital employed in a pharmaceuticals firm (and pharmaceuticals generally) could have been a strong attraction.

Crookes Laboratories Limited

Profits were showing a downward trend until 1960. This, according to the 1960 Annual Report, was due almost entirely to the steady decline in the demand for Crookes's Halibut Oil – Crookes's best-known product. The trend of home medication had changed and Crookes could no longer expect income from that product to develop the business. However, for the first time sales of Crookes's products had more than compensated for profits lost from the reduction in sales of Halibut Oil. New ethical products were being introduced to the medical profession and in the veterinary field, but doubts were expressed as to whether such innovations would result in a higher turnover in 1961. 'The effects of increased research effort take a long time and considerable expense before they are reflected in increased turnover.' (1960 Annual Report of Crookes).

Dekraxil', a vitamin/mineral capsule, was introduced experimentally in the north of England in 1960 and it was hoped that this product would be launched nationally. The initial campaign would have been costly but if results were similar to those predicted by the experiment in the north of England and by market surveys, Dekraxil could have been quite profitable.

One wonders how Crookes would have fared without the takeover. In 1965 it moved to newer and larger premises in Basingstoke. The move would probably not have been necessary had the firm not been taken over because it seems likely that it would have been able to continue on the same scale, not increasing its profits or real value of turnover noticeably. The company would however probably have been the victim of a takeover sooner or later, since it might have been thought too small to survive on its own in the pharmaceutical industry. Only one thing would have saved Crookes from predators – some discovery that was so important as to render the firm too expensive to buy. Crookes could then have leased this discovery out.

Crookes accounting results – before and after takeover

In 1965 the shape of Crookes was altered after their move. On their own they would never have had the resources to do this.

The results of Crookes Laboratories from 1953 to 1968 are shown in Table 1.1. It must be remembered that the total investment in Crookes amounts not only to the purchase price but includes any money lent to the firm in order to counteract adverse cash flows.

Two further points emerge from an examination of the company's annual return:–

1. There are no subvention payments from the parent company to Crookes to offset tax payments for the whole group. This is because a parent company has to own three-quarters of the ordinary share capital before subvention payments are allowed.

It is interesting to speculate whether,if either Guinness or Philips had appreciated the magnitude of the losses, one of them might have wanted to offset these losses against profits and thereby reduce tax payments. However, since neither shareholder wanted to increase his shareholding to the necessary 75 per cent, one can assume that both companies failed to forecast the large losses suffered over a number of years.

2. Crookes had a substantial overdraft in 1964, before it moved to new premises. These premises seemed to be partly financed by bank overdraft and partly by a long-term, interest-free loan from Crookes's holding company (ultimately from Guinness) and another long-term, interest-free loan from an associated company. The extent of these loans is shown in Table 1.2.

Table 1.2

	Bank overdraft in £000	Long-term, interest-free loan from associated companies (in £000): Holding	Other
1962	54		
1963	188		
1964	517		
1965	750	237	158
1966	810	358	238
1967	737	617	410
1968	701	714	476
1969	794	797	531

The bank overdraft may be guaranteed by Guinness. In the 1969 Annual Report a note attached to the Balance Sheet of Arthur Guinness, Son & Company Limited reads:–

'The company has guaranteed the overdrafts of certain subsidiaries and associated companies in the aggregate sum of £9,119,000 (£9,045,000 [1968])', (square brackets indicate the editor's insertion).

More information can be gained from the holding company of Crookes and Twyford. Table 1.3 shows the principal assets and liabilities of the holding companies.

Table 1.3

	Amounts owing *by* group companies £m.	Amount owing *to* group companies £m.
1967	1·6	2·4
1968	2·0	2·1
1969	3·1	4·1

Guinness made their original investment in Crookes and since then have been lending Crookes interest-free loans and probably guaranteeing bank overdrafts. This seems to have continued from 1962 to at least 1970, even though Crookes made a small before-tax profit in 1969. Apart from these factors that emerge from the accounts there are a number of special items that depressed the profits of Crookes and Twyford. In 1964 Crookes started to move to its new premises, so that the 1964 and 1965 results include terminal losses and the costs of reorganization. The same thing applies to Twyford for 1967 and 1968.

Pharmaceutical division – late sixties

One might have thought that Guinness would have been depressed with the results from the Pharmaceutical Division; however it still continued to diversify into pharmaceuticals by acquiring, in 1968, a 47 per cent stake in J. L. Morisson, Son & Jones Holdings Limited, which is described by Guinness as owning overseas trading and manufacturing companies operating mainly in Commonwealth territories'.

The results of the Pharmaceutical Division in the late sixties are shown in Table 1.4.

Table 1.4

	Sales £m.	Profit before tax £m.
1967	1·7	−1·0
1968	2·0	−0·6
1969	9·2	−0·2

The figures for 1968/9 show the full effects of the Morisson results.

A quotation from the 1969 Annual Report echoes, in some places, phrases from the 1961 and other Reports: 'During the year the Crookes group of companies satisfactorily improved their turnover and achieved profit. Their growth continues with an enlarged product range, especially in the veterinary field. I must warn you, however, that the inevitable costs of the reorganization which the company is undergoing could initially retard the growth of profit which nevertheless we now see within our reach'. In 1969 the shareholders may have wondered how much more money and how much longer the reorganization would take.

Motives for diversification other than profits

In the 1959 Annual Report a hint is given about the motives behind the diversification: '. . . the establishment of a new research organization, Twyford Laboratories Limited . . . This subsidiary company will undertake fundamental research in fermentation and allied fields, with the aim of elucidation of the complex behaviour of yeasts and bacteria, helping our brewing interests; and we hope providing the possibility of other commerical development'.

In 1961 Twyford's activities were deemed to be '. . . basic research in the fields of microbiology and biochemistry'. If this were so, then Twyford could help Guinness's brewing interests and this help might not be reflected in the accounts of Twyford.

However, Guinness did not offer this as an explanation when Twyford was later showing big losses (see Table 1.1), and certain passages in the 1967 and 1968 Annual Reports seem to indicate that Guinness was trying to justify Twyford's existence only on pharmaceutical grounds and not on the potential help Twyford might give to Guinness. For example, the 1967 Annual Report says: '. . . Both Crookes and Twyford have several important products which are expected to be ready for marketing in the near future'. The 1968 Annual Report: 'An anti-coagulant being developed in Twyford Laboratories has aroused the interest of the medical profession in many countries; it is an entirely novel product and may prove to be of great value. It is expected that this product will be on the market in this country within the next year'. The 1969 Annual Report: 'The anti-coagulant drug "Arvin", which Twyford Laboratories is developing has aroused much interest . . . and it is unlikely that we can expect permission to market for at least eighteen months and possibly two years'.

Most of the evidence suggests that Twyford Laboratories has produced nothing as yet of any help to Guinness. However, it may do so in the future. Traditionally Guinness have been very keen on scientists helping them in their brewing interest and it may be that Guinness are keeping the secret of Twyford's potential benefit to themselves in order not to alert their rivals. (So far it has only lost Guinness money.)

There is, however, a sharp distinction between Twyford and Crookes. Crookes is wholly engaged in the pharmaceutical field and there seems little scope for Crookes to help Guinness's brewing interests at all.

A successful takeover?

Nearly ten years after the original takeover, Crookes is to be wholly owned by Guinness. The history of investment to 1969, excluding the purchase from Philips of the remaining 40 per cent of shares, is shown below:–

1960	Crookes bought	£712,000
1969	Total long-term, interest-free loans (built up over the years)..	£1,328,000
1969	Bank overdraft, possibly guaranteed	£794,000
		£2,834,000

The bank overdraft commitment is unlikely to be met by Crookes, especially in view of the obstacles quoted from the 1969 Annual Report, so it might as well be regarded as part of the investment since Guinness will probably have to pay it off eventually. Moreover Guinness are now increasing their investment in Crookes by buying the remaining 40 per cent of shares. This seems a phenomenal investment in a firm that would probably not have made much if it had continued on its own.

Guinness seem to be adamant over Crookes: they seem to want to make it pay or go bankrupt (though they are unlikely to do that) but they have never shown an ability to cut short their losses and sell this investment off; instead, they invest more and more money.

P. Sergent wrote in the *Daily Express* on 15 January 1969: 'Four years ago, when the pharmaceutical companies were losing some £600,000 [1964] Lord Boyd (then group Managing Director, now a Vice-Chairman) said that they should run into profit in the next two or three years, but profits are still thought to be that far away'. (Square brackets indicate editor's insertion.) He also suggested Guinness should sell Crookes to Boots who '. . . are looking for someone to buy'.

To tie up a large amount of funds in the Pharmaceutical Division does not seem worthwhile as far as the shareholders are concerned. Guinness perhaps, never consciously meant to invest such a large sum. It also seems possible that Crookes might have done better if it had not been taken over. One excuse that Guinness can offer is that they had no experience in pharmaceuticals and that their management, although efficient in the brewing field, could not, within the time period we have been considering, adapt themselves to the conditions of the pharmaceutical industry.

This, alas, is one of the problems encountered in any diversification, especially if the diversification involves a completely unfamiliar product and market area. It is rather surprising that Guinness did not investigate other possible areas for diversification, or at least experiment with pharmaceuticals initially on a smaller scale. Guinness probably felt safe with Philips (an established pharmaceutical firm) as a co-shareholder. Perhaps each left the central management responsibilities to the other. At least Philips had the advantage that Crookes could formulate some of its N–V Philips-Dulpher products and sell them.

The only benefit that may outweigh the capital investment is the possibility of some research into brewing by Twyford Laboratories that could enable Guinness's brewing division to operate more efficiently, produce new products or increase sales.

Editor's Conclusion

As can be seen in the Guinness case study, the acquisition by Arthur Guinness & Co. of the Twyford and Crookes Laboratories never seemed a particularly profitable venture. All attempts to make this diversification policy successful were eventually brought to an end in 1970 and 1971. The Chairman in his statement for the year ending 26 September 1970 gave details of a re-organization that had taken place within the pharmaceutical group. He pointed out that the main problem in this area of the company's activities had been the increasing cost of the research companies, in particular Twyford Laboratories. The Board had therefore decided that as it could no longer carry on with these activities on the same scale, it would 'wind up' Twyford's on 31 March 1971 and establish on a reduced scale and cost a research and development unit within Crookes's factory at Basingstoke. The hope was expressed that once this step was taken, with the growth of profitability of the pharmaceutical trading companies, this side of the company's business would move towards a modest profit.

It will never be known whether this reduction of scale and re-organization would have led to a modest profit, for on 27 July 1971 it was announced that Boots Pure Drug Co. had agreed to purchase a major part of the pharmaceutical and toiletry interests of Guinness. This sale comprised the Crookes Laboratories Group (including Twyford's) and Crookes Anestan; it did not include Guinness holdings in J. L. Morrison, Son and Jones Holdings Limited. It was announced that the sales price was in excess of £2 million in cash. The extent of the investment of Guinness in the subsidiaries is discussed in the case. Mr. Bhaskar suggests that, even ignoring the purchase from Philips of their 40 per cent of the shares in Crookes, the investment of Guinness in Crookes up to 1969 was £2.8 million. The Guinness investment in Twyford's which was also sold and is covered by the price of 'in excess of £2 million' is not known.

The Guinness Board announced, at the time of this sale to Boots, that although the pharmaceutical companies concerned had significantly improved their profitability during 1969 and 1970 and were continuing to do so, it was nevertheless thought that in light of the present requirements and conditions in the industry the growth of these subsidiaries would be slow.

The case clearly illustrates the difficulties of the diversification by a company into an industry in which it has little experience. It will be interesting to see if Boots, an organization geared mainly to the pharmaceutical industry, can make a success of these acquisitions.

PART 2

Spillers

The victim firm in this case study was Spratt's Patent Limited, which was taken over in 1960 for a consideration of about £3½m.

The accounting information about Spratt's Patent before and after takeover is shown in Table 2.1. From a preliminary glance at the figures there does not seem to be as large a change in the direction of profits as there was after Guinness took over Crookes. After the takeover, however, dividends seem to have substantially increased.

In 1964 Spratt's Patent was totally absorbed by the Spillers organization. It is impossible to arrive at a clear picture of Spratt's Patent as a separate entity. Despite the merging of identities of Spratt's Patent and Spillers, a subsidiary of Spratt's

Patent, W. G. Clarke and Sons (1929) Limited, remained a separate legal entity and was finally reorganized only after 1967. (NB. W. G. Clarke was renamed Spratt's Patent after the victim firm had been absorbed by the predator firm.)

Spillers and Spratt's, both being in the food industry and in particular in the pet foods market, are likely to have arranged intercompany transfer of goods, involving transfer pricing problems. Some attempt needs to be made to show if any potential synergy was gained. The use of public information only makes accurate results difficult to achieve and any comments made here are extremely tentative.

Spillers – the beginning of diversification

Spillers, traditionally a milling firm since 1860, branched into animal feeding stuffs during this century. Milling was still its principal activity.

The withdrawal of food rationing, and the subsequent higher standard of living, led people to seek a more varied diet, which resulted in a continuous fall in the per capita consumption of flour in England. Spillers consequently began to take over family businesses in the baking industry. This extension of its activities could be regarded as vertical integration and could be justified on purely defensive grounds:

Table 2.1

	Spratt's Patent Consolidated accounts				Spillers Limited Consolidated accounts		
	Trading profit £000	Profit before taxation before subvention receipts £000	Dividends less tax £000	Fixed assets Excluding goodwill and trade investments £000		Profit before taxation £m.	Turnover £m.
1952	206	149	36	838		2·0	49
1953	315	249	37	884		2·3	61
1954	384	311	37	941		3·1	67
1955	497	408	39	1074		3·4	65
1956	446	363	53	1261		3·8	70
1957	509[1]	387[1]	65[1]	1511[1]		4·2	78
1958	485[1]	357[1]	65[1]	1532[1]		3·8	80
1959	436	306	87	1508		4·7	83
					1960	5·0	89
1961	682[4]	498[4]	131[4]	1895[3+4]	1961	5·3	98
1961	434[2+4]	408[2+4]	131[2+4]	704[2+4]			
1962	279[2]	260[2]	125[2]	714[2]	1962	5·8	101
1963	292[2]	266[2]	149[2]	1000[2]	1963	7·6	108
					1964	8·2	118
					1965	8·9	135
					1966	7·7	141
					1967	6·9	143
					1968	9·5	160

W. G. Clarke Limited

	£000		
1950	5[2]	1961	37[1+4]
1951	18[2]	1962	21[1]
1952	20[2]	1963	26[1]
1953	7[2]	1964	4[1]
1954	11[2]	1965	26[1]
1955	−5[2]	1966	38[1]
1956	3[2]	1967	−10[1+5]
1957	26[2]		
1958	34[1]		
1959	22[1]		

[1] Accounts are part consolidated.
[2] Accounts are non-consolidated.
[3] New cannery and changed valuation basis.
[4] Accounts cover 16 months.
[5] 1967 marked a reorganization of this firm by Spillers.

1. A large proportion of the baking industry consisted of family businesses some of which, owing to taxation and estate duty, might have been unable to continue operations. If their businesses were not taken over by Spillers, they would probably become the prey of firms which were rivals to Spillers and this would make the demand for Spillers's products even more volatile.

2. The baking industry would provide 'some insulation against fluctuations in the flour trade' (Annual Report 1955).

3. The merger would enable Spillers 'to have a closer connection with the consuming public' (Annual Report 1955), and thus Spillers could gear flour milling to the current tastes of the market and promote the consumption of flour and products made with flour.

In fact their experience in the baking field may have enabled Spillers to become better suppliers to the baking trade as a whole. The process of diversification into the baking industries continued during the sixties.

Animal foods

Once the decision to expand vertically was made, cereal-based animal food was a logical extension of the flour-milling section of Spillers. The Annual Reports from the 1960s suggest that sales increased steadily during the 50s and 60s though profit margins were hit. But a profit figure would vary with the transfer price of milling products from the milling section to the animal foods section.

Pet foods

The history of the Pet Foods Division is:—

1950s	Spillers's own experimentation
1960s	Spratt's Patent Limited
1964	Robert Wilson and Sons (Food Industries) Limited

Before describing Spillers diversification into the pet food market, a brief description of the types of pet foods is given below.

Dog foods: (a) Biscuits and cereals
(b) Meat and cereal varieties
(c) All meat

Cat foods: (a) All meat
(b) Meat, fish and cereal varieties

Bird foods: Bird seeds

The flour milling section of Spillers would supply some of the principal ingredients of these varieties. With the backing of the baking and animal food divisions pet foods promised to be an easy area for diversification.

Diversification into pet foods started with a concentration on the dog biscuit and cereal market. Products were Spillers Shapes, Winalot, and Saval Puppy Meal. There was the dual advantage of using the product of the flour milling section and securing a steady market for the flour milling section. Although Spillers did produce a canned meat dog food called Wagalot, it seems to have been less successful than similar products marketed by Spratt's Patent. An interesting and unanswered question is whether or not Spillers was a supplier of flour products to Spratt's.

Canned human food

Recent developments have led Spillers into the sphere of canned (human) food. This seemed to fill a gap left by diversifying into (human) ready-to-eat foods (the baking industry) and canned meat foods for pets. Further growth is expected in this area and in the general grocery divisions of Spillers.

Spratt's patent

In 1959 the group celebrated its 75th anniversary. A new cannery had just been completed at Wisbech and Spratt's were enjoying a good reputation for all-meat canned pet foods, meat and cereals canned foods, and dog biscuits and cereals. The question was raised earlier as to who supplied Spratt's with the necessary flour. This side of the group seemed to be doing well. Not quite so happy were its major subsidiaries, Caperns Limited – packet bird seed – and Hygienic Wire Works Limited – makers of bird cages among other products. The financial trends of these two companies seemed to have weighted the group profit downwards. In the Annual Report for 1959, it was stated that competition was formidable (perhaps from Spillers). Yet further growth in pet foods was considered likely.

During the takeover bid the board of Spratt's Patent seemed to be in a strong position; first, they had £700,000 worth of quick assets; secondly, the *Investors Chronicle* and others thought that the fixed assets were possibly worth more than the book value figure of £1,507,792. However, after a one-in-four scrip issue Spratt's Patent board recommended acceptance (the offer was for £3,445,733).

It is of interest to note that two of the reasons for the directors' recommendations for accepting the offer were:

(*a*) they did not think that a revaluation would show any substantial increase in the value of the assets, and

(*b*) although improvement in trading had continued they thought that competition was very keen, and that substantial growth appeared unlikely.

The first reason is rather curious for, as has already been indicated, it had been suggested by commentators that the fixed assets might be worth more. Moreover after the takeover the fixed assets were revalued 'as a going concern' and this enhanced their value over the book value by £550,000, (a substantial increase on £1.5m?).

The second reason cannot be disputed, except on the grounds that Spillers must have thought growth was likely in order to have considered the takeover.

Spratt's major contribution in brand names consisted of:

(*a*) Canned food:

Top Dog }
Top Cat } meat and cereal varieties.

(*b*) Biscuits and cereals:

Mixed Ovals
Ovals
Bonio

(*c*) Bird seed:

Caperns

By the time of the first annual return after the takeover the quick assets were about £350,000 less. Whether the £350,000 was transferred back to Spillers is not clear. If it was used for additional investment, Spillers would have had to meet this bill out of its own pocket if Spratt's had not had the spare cash available. The fact that Spratt's paid a much higher level of dividend after the takeover is also of interest, in that it indicates the desire to transfer resources between the companies.

During the sixties the general impression given by the Annual Reports is that:–

(1) Pet foods turnover was strong and increasing
(2) Animal foods had mixed results
(3) Flour milling and baking were depressed

Pet foods were given a fillip by the takeover of Robert Wilson and Sons (Foods Industries) Limited in 1964 which brought with it increased capacity (especially in Scotland) and such brand names as Kennomeat, Kattomeat, and Jock.

Spratt's contribution

Obviously the buying and marketing of all types of pet foods could be centralized. Extra capacity was gained for cereal products. More important, the brand names of 'Top Dog' and 'Top Cat' were added, together with the techniques for the production of canned meat pet foods. Spiller's diversification appeared to have been well considered; it seemed to follow several clear steps:

(1) Produce cereal food
(2) Try producing canned food

(3) Buy Spratt's which have a good canned food business

(4) See how this investment goes: if it does well, expand (and Spillers did, by buying Robert Wilson and Sons)

'Top Dog' and 'Top Cat', being meat and cereal varieties of canned pet foods, provided an additional stable market for the flour milling section.

This process of co-ordinating the two companies started as soon as the takeover took place; the 1961 Annual Report says: ' . . . the ability to co-ordinate policy with Spratt's Patent has proved of benefit to both companies'.

Spillers's product profile

The product profile for 1968/9 was:–

	Sales %	Profits %
Flour milling	19	34
Baking	28	19
Pet foods	15	21
General grocery	10	17
Animal foods	21	1
Overseas and miscellaneous	7	8

The fact that pet foods now account for about 15 per cent of sales (about £24m. in 1968) shows the extent to which the production of pet foods has grown within the Spillers organization. The profit figures in the profile should be regarded with some scepticism because of transfer pricing problems resulting from the internal movement of goods. The type of internal organization that might occur, and the internal transfer of goods, is shown in Figure 1.

Notice that advertising, marketing, finance, and research and development can be centralized and the system by which these overhead costs are charged to various departments must, to some extent, be arbitrary. Moreover, if the transfer price of flour to the baking division is low, then the profits of the baking division may well be high in relation to the profits of the flour milling division and vice-versa. It seems that the profits of the flour milling division will vary inversely to those of the other divisions, so that higher flour milling profits imply lower profits from other divisions.

Figure 1 shows how the relationship between divisions might be organized and how, schematically, goods could pass from one division to another. Flour milling and meat divisions supply the pet foods division which passes on its end product to the grocery outlets.

Success of diversification

Some results of Spillers's penetration into the pet food market during the mid-1960s are given below. Sales can grow on account of two factors. They are related first, to the number of pets, and secondly, to the proportion of pet owners who do

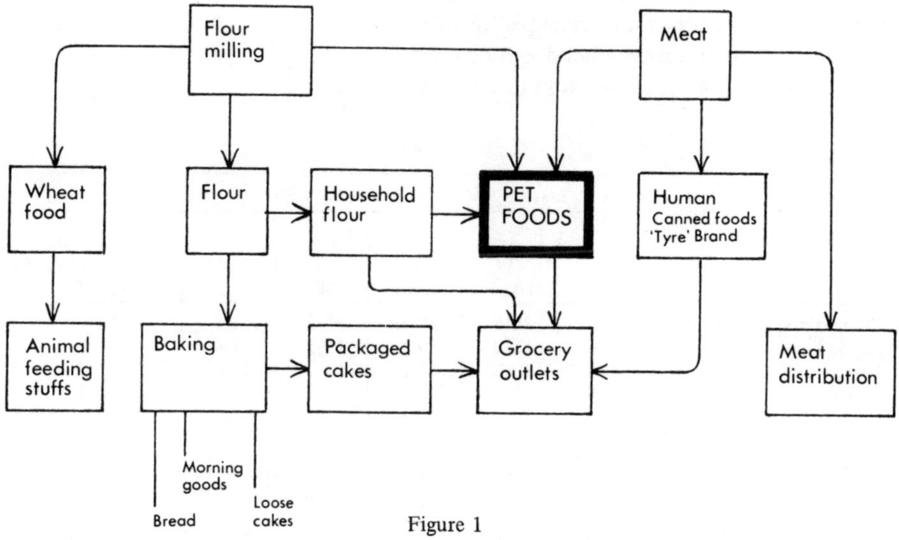

Figure 1

Table 2.3 Brand shares of leading pet foods 1968

Canned dog food by value

All meat		% of Market
'Kennomeat'	Spillers (Robert Wilsons)	18.2
'Pedigree Chum'	Petfoods	17.8
'Pal'	Petfoods	17.1
'Stamina'	Rank Hovis McDougal	7.1
Meat and cereal		
'Lassie'	Petfoods	8.8
'Chappie'	Petfoods	8.3
'Bounce'	Petfoods	6.1
'Chunky Meat'	Quaker Oats	5.5
'Top Dog'	Spillers (Spratt's)	3.3

Canned cat food by value

All meat		
'Kattomeat'	Spillers (Robert Wilsons).	22.3
'Whiskas'	Petfoods	20.4
'Paws'	Rank Hovis McDougal	6.0
Meat, fish and cereal varieties		
'Kit-E-Cat'	Petfoods	19.6
'KatKins	Petfoods	9.4
'Top Cat'	Spillers (Spratt's)	9.2
'Sam'	Petfoods	5.8
'Choosy'	Spillers (recently introduced)	2.5

not buy branded foods. For example, in 1969 only 25 per cent of dog owners did not feed their dogs on branded dog food.

The trend of the total market sales is shown in Table 2.2.

Table 2.2

Total market sales of pet foods in £M.						
	1964	1965	1966	1967	1968	Average annual compound rate of growth
Canned dog food	23·3	26·6	29·6	32·2	35·7	11·3%
Canned cat food	18·4	18·9	19·1	19·7	21·4	3·9%
Dried dog food	10·5	10·6	11·0	11·2	11·6	2·5%
Packaged bird food	2·8	3·0	3·2	3·3	3·4	5·0%

The growth rates have been higher for Spillers than for the industry as a whole. The growth rate in dog foods may be surprisingly low; however, since Spillers supply 90 per cent of the market's production, saturation might have occurred.

In Table 2.3, which shows brand shares of leading pet foods, Spillers's philosophy is perhaps illustrated best of all. This philosophy is outlined below:

1950s		1960		1964
		Spratt's		Robert Wilson
Dried dog food	→	meat and cereal canned pet foods – expansion of dried dog food	→	all-meat canned foods

Apparently, by the end of the sixties all the canned pet food plants were working at full capacity and in some areas a shortage had developed. It seems that the whole diversification into pet foods was successful with regard to the relative positions of other firms in the industry. Some attempt must be made to determine whether Spillers's £3m. investment in Spratt's was worthwhile.

Investment appraisal of the Spratt's takeover

Assume that we take £3m. as the initial outlay of this project. We then try to calculate the incremental cash flows resulting from the takeover.

The following have to be taken into consideration:

1. Net dividends of £405,000 were paid from 1961–3 inclusively. If Spratt's had remained an independent body, this total dividend could well have been higher.
2. Spratt's could provide a stable market for the flour milling section, especially if Spillers's pet food and Spratt's pet food sections could expand faster together, than independently (probable, with economies of scale in marketing – via television advertising and grocery outlets).
3. Spillers provided a stable financial backing to complement Spratt's.
4. Centralized buying could take place.

5. Management expertise was bought with Spratt's. Perhaps it was Spratt's management which suggested acquiring Robert Wilsons, etc.

6. The goodwill of the Spratt's brand names was bought with Spratt's. After Spratt's was acquired, Spillers's canned dog food 'Wagalot' seemed to fade out. Certainly the only Spillers's canned food now marketed which was not a brand name under Spratt's or Robert Wilsons is 'Choosy' and this cat food is a recent venture.

The investment in Spratt's was financed by the issue of 6 per cent debentures. In order to pay the interest on the debentures, £180,000 gross a year is required from the investment. We have seen that dividends were at a high level initially before Spratt's lost its independence (around £125,000–£149,000 net).

It seems then that the dividend and any synergy that was gained would produce more than enough to pay the interest on the debentures that were necessary to finance the acquisition of Spratt's Patent. This is not to say that their investment in Spratt's was the most efficient Spillers could have made; but the diversification certainly does seem logical and well-thought-out, especially for a firm traditionally tied to one produce – flour. The results of the takeover are not dramatic but they appear to be a success due to Spillers's realization of the potential synergy.

PART 3

Nestlé - Crosse and Blackwell

The third case study is different from the other two in that the victim firm – Crosse and Blackwell – was larger than either Crookes or Spratt's. So too in 1960 was Nestlé bigger than Guinness or Spillers. At that time Nestlé was the largest food company outside the US with sales of over £400m.

Summary of Nestlé's expansion to 1950

Nestlé was founded in the late nineteenth century and proceeded to expand its position in the milk market by acquiring Anglo-Swiss Condensed Milk (Swiss based). Later Nestlé turned to confectionery, and in particular chocolate, taking over the Peter, Cailler and Kohler companies in 1929. By 1947 Nestlé had again diversified, into the cube and concentrated forms of soup by merging with Maggi (Swiss based). In 1947 Nescafé (instant coffee) was launched.

The takeover

In 1959 Nestlé made its first offer for Crosse and Blackwell at 72s. per share (the total offer was worth £9.7m). Fisons countered with an 82s. per share bid. Nestlé, however, then offered 84s. per share and succeeded; the total offer was worth £11.3m.

Pressure on Nestlé's

The product range of Nestlé's in 1959 was as follows:

1. Milk products and baby foods
2. Confectionery, in particular chocolate
3. Nescafé and other instant drinks
4. 'Maggi' packet soups

Crosse and Blackwell's product range in 1959 was as follows:

1. Soups:
   (*a*) canned soups
   (*b*) packet soups by Crosse and Blackwell's subsidiary, Elizabeth Lazenby.
2. Confectionery:
   (*a*) wrapped sweets (by Crosse and Blackwell's subsidiary Keiller)
   (*b*) chocolate (by Crosse and Blackwell's subsidiary Tobler)
3. Canned vegetables, pickles and fish.

Notice that 1. (*b*) and 2. (*b*) are in direct competition with Nestlé's. It might be expedient to examine these two markets to see if Crosse and Blackwell was a potential threat to Nestlé's.

Packet Soups

Nestlé's product 'Maggi' had been doing well on the Continent. The £6½m. market was divided by four principal rivals: Swiss Knorr, 'Maggi'; Unilever's Batchelor; and Crosse and Blackwell (Elizabeth Lazenby). Swiss Knorr was the market leader with about 60 per cent of sales. 'Maggi' and Crosse and Blackwell had about 20 per cent of the market between them. (The figures are very approximate.)

Since packet and canned soups are competitors in the general soup market, Nestlé's purchase of Crosse and Blackwell would give Nestlé a hedge against consumer preference for canned rather than packet foods – it would also give Nestlé's added productive capacity for their packet soup if the market went the other way. But Nestlé's had a long way to go before they caught up with Knorr.

Confectionery

Nestlé's major sales are in the form of chocolate bars, and Nestlé's share of this market in 1959 is shown below:

(Figures very approximate)	Share of UK market for solid chocolate bars %
Nestlé	10
Cadbury	75
Rowntree	10

Other confectionery sales of Nestlé's amounted to less than 5 per cent. Crosse and Blackwell's subsidiary Tobler, could hardly have been a very important threat to Nestlé.

Crosse and Blackwell's position:

Crosse and Blackwell's position seems to be that of a pawn surrounded by giants. Crosse and Blackwell had the following competitors: in chocolate: (*a*) Nestlé, (*b*) Cadbury, (*c*) Rowntree; in packet soups: (*a*) Swiss Knorr, (*b*) Unilever's 'Batchelor', in canned soups: (*a*) Campbell (late 1950s), (*b*) Heinz; in canned foods: (*a*) Heinz, (*b*) General Food, (*c*) Unilever's Batchelor, and so forth. It seemed that sooner or later it would have to expand to meet the giants or become a victim of one of them.

Crosse and Blackwell in the late fifties

1955 was the 250th year of trading for Crosse and Blackwell and in the 1956 Annual Report there was heartening news for shareholders: 'Total sales increased substantially and constitute a record for the company'. It was also noted that advertising was expensive, but the 'Ten o'clock Tested' campaign seemed to be working.

In 1957 and 1958 sales were again up and thus constituted a record for the company. As Table 3.1 shows, however, profits for the holding company did not always go in the same direction as sales. In 1958 Crosse and Blackwell announced plans to expand and modernize; the Annual Report was full of confidence for the future.

Nestlé

When Nestlé took over Crosse and Blackwell, the packet soups and confectionery could be easily integrated into the Nestlé fold, but it was unexpected that Nestlé would plunge Crosse and Blackwell into the canned soups and canned food market with the enthusiasm that they did. Moreover, Nestlé further diversified into frozen foods in 1963 with Findus.

It seems strange that Nestlé suddenly felt the need to diversify into two new markets, canned foods and frozen foods (in 1960 and 1963 respectively). Either Nestlé felt that more profits could be gained in these fields or they thought that by, say, going into frozen foods and attacking Birds Eye's market (Unilever) they could relieve pressure from Batchelor (Unilever) in the packet soup market.

Later Nestlé went into tea by introducing Nestea, and perhaps did not anticipate or discounted Lyon's retaliation by going into the instant coffee market.

The accounting results of the takeover

Table 3.1 sets out the results of Crosse and Blackwell Ltd, Crosse and Blackwell Holdings Ltd and The Nestlé Co. Ltd; Crosse and Blackwell Holdings were transferred to The Nestlé Co. Ltd in 1964. Findus Ltd would have also affected The Nestlé Co. group accounts, extracts of which will appear later. A look at Crosse and Blackwell Holdings indicates a severe reversal of the trend of profit. Crosse and

Blackwell Ltd results are available for a long period of time and, apart from 1964 and 1965, do not indicate a favourable trend.

No dividends were paid from either Crosse and Blackwell Holdings or Crosse and Blackwell Ltd after 1960. Too obvious to miss is the immediate drop in pre-tax profits of The Nestlé Co. after absorption of Crosse and Blackwell Holdings; prior to this profits were stable at around £3½–4m.

Table 3.1

	Crosse and Blackwell Ltd				Crosse & Blackwell Holdings	The Nestlé Co. Ltd
	Trading Profit	Profit before tax Before subvention receipts	Debt to holding companies	Bank over-draft	Profit before Tax Before subvention receipts	Profit before Tax Consol-idated accounts
	£000	£000	£ million	£ million	£000	£ million
1953	501	466	·3	–		
1954	476	437	·4	–	989	
1955	293	253	·8	–	884	
1956	409	366	·8	–	1106	
1957	392	347	·3	–	1127	
1958	232	137	·9	–	836	
1959	277	158	3·8	–	1003	3·7
1960	158	–151	6·0	–	36	3·6
1961	–599	–817	7·6	–	–1012	3·9
1962	–559	–846	8·7	–	–1453	4·1[1]
1963	–144	–377	9·7	–	–1007	3·8
1964	301	– 22	10·6	–	Transferred	·5
1965	322	63	7·4	1·4	to Nestlés	1·5
1966	190	– 81	7·3	2·0		·2
1967	49	–239	7·5	1·5		1·4
1968	16	–359	6·1	1·4		1·9

[1] Non-consolidated figure

The large loss suffered by Crosse and Blackwell Holdings was offset by subvention payments of £1·3m. in 1962 and £0·9m. in 1963, so that the large losses were to some extent offset by a lower group tax bill, but this could not protect Nestlé from the full effects of the loss.

As with Guinness, Nestlé poured money into Crosse and Blackwell; the reorganization and development must have been expensive. In Table 3.1 we show the debt of Crosse and Blackwell Ltd (not Crosse and Blackwell Holdings) to the parent company and also its overdraft – one can only speculate that it might have been guaranteed by Nestlé.

Also of interest is the total debt of The Nestlé Co. and The Nestlé Co. Group to its holding company, which must eventually be Unilac Incorporated (Nestlé's company responsible for the western hemisphere). This is shown below in Table 3.2.

Table 3.2 in £m.

	The Nestlé Co. Group		The Nestlé Co. Ltd	
	Loans from parent company	Overdraft	Overdraft	Loans to subsidiaries
1959	3·5	–	–	– –
1960 (C & B acquired)	3·0	–	–	1·1
1961	6·5	–	–	1·4
1962	7·0	–	–	1·2
1963 Findus	14·4	1·8	–	1·2
1964 C & B integrated	16·5	8·1	5·4	10·1
1965	17·5	10·2	6·6	10·1
1966	19·0	11·3	8·1	10·7
1967	21·1	13·8	9·8	9·4
1968	23·1	14·7	12·9	9·7

As soon as Crosse and Blackwell Holdings were integrated into The Nestlé Co. accounts the effect shown in Table 3.2 seems to be fairly pronounced.

Because there are many subsidiaries and many holding companies it is difficult to know precisely what went on and what the accounts reflect, so the comments above are extremely tentative.

Integration or Diversification

It seems likely that the confectionery side of Crosse and Blackwell would be integrated and expanded or contracted as Nestlé saw fit (for example 'Toblerone' is still sold). Packet soups under Elizabeth Lazenby seem to have disappeared and their productive capacity and distribution network have been absorbed by Maggi soups.

However, in the field of canned soups and other canned and ready-to-eat foods, Crosse and Blackwell (backed by Nestlé) have launched a range of new products, for example Spaghetti rings, salad dressings, etc. So this part of Crosse and Blackwell could not be regarded an extension of Nestlé's traditional fields but an entrance by Nestlé into new fields, using the goodwill that Crosse and Blackwell had gained from its customers.

Success of diversification

The only real diversification of Nestlé was the enthusiastic entry into canned soups and canned, ready-to-eat foods. The particular company under which Nestlé continues to market these products is Crosse and Blackwell Ltd, (not the holding company) for which we have a continuous run of accounting results in Table 3.1. (In addition to these results the turnover was £18·4m. in 1967 and £20·6m. in 1968.) Before it was owned by Nestlé, Crosse and Blackwell Ltd did not give much information about the relative success of its products. Since it transferred confectionery and packet soups to its subsidiaries, however, Crosse and Blackwell Ltd results are for the canned and ready-to-eat foods.

From comparisons of the group pre-tax profit figure with Crosse and Blackwell's profit figure, it can be seen that during the 1950s, this division did less well than the rest of the group and, moreover, the resulting trend was downward.

In Table 3.3 an index of the sales trend is shown for the Nestlé group. It is unfortunate that the Crosse and Blackwell Group and the Findus Group are combined in one category. The only two significant jumps in the index apart from 1969, were in 1960 (Crosse and Blackwell acquisition) and 1963 (Findus Group). An interesting point is that if inflation is taken into account then in real terms sales have hardly increased over the years. Notice that since this sales trend is for the whole Nestlé Group, it is irrelevant that a particular product is transferred from Crosse and Blackwell to another Nestlé subsidiary.

In terms of sales, then, it seems unlikely that Nestlé substantially increased Crosse and Blackwell's market share (though it is possible that 1960 was a very much worse year than 1959). It must be remembered, however, that Nestlé has increased the range of Crosse and Blackwell's products.

Table 3.3

Index of trend of quantities sold for Nestlé Group

1959=100

	Milk dietetic specialities and cheese	Soups, bouillons, seasoning, prepared dishes, ice cream, and frozen food	Chocolate, cocoa, and confectionery	Instant drinks
1959	100	100	100	100
1960	101	308[1]	120	118
1961	100	308	130	121
1962	106	356	141	137
1963	111	510[1]	149	158
1964	117	516	155	176
1965	125	546	168	187
1966	132	581	178	196
1967	138	594	181	211
1968	145	669	184	234

[1] Includes figures for the Crosse and Blackwell Group from 1960 and Findus Group from 1963.

A successful takeover?

Financially, the profit figures available indicate a poor performance. No dividends have passed between Crosse and Blackwell and Nestlé. It is likely that Crosse and Blackwell's subsidiaries fared slightly better than Crosse and Blackwell for they could be integrated into the remainder of Nestlé more easily, whereas Crosse and Blackwell's products were in a new area for Nestlé. Not only have there been no dividends between Crosse and Blackwell and Nestlé but Nestlé has lent an enormous sum to Crosse and Blackwell. Even supposing Crosse and Blackwell can repay the debt, it still means that Nestlé has tied up a large sum of money in Crosse and Blackwell without earning any return from it. It may have been wiser for Nestlé's to cut its losses and launch into a different field.

All that has been said about profits must, of course, be qualified by reference to the transfer pricing problem and possibly pricing in order to minimize tax payments. (For example corporation tax is less in Switzerland than in the UK.) But Nestlé say in their 1968 Annual Report that in the field of soups, bouillons, seasoning and condiments, prepared dishes, etc. in the UK and Eire, production was local, and no goods were imported.

Whether this applied to the final product or to all goods and raw materials is not clear – but it does seem that transfer pricing may not be much of a problem, since Crosse and Blackwell's products were a new field for Nestlé, though there may have been some common items in the production of packet and canned soups.

The Crosse and Blackwell group cost £11·3m. and perhaps, say, another £10m. worth of loans (for the whole Group) making a total commitment of over £20m. This may be only a trifle for Nestlé and it may well be that Nestlé had planned to sustain a loss over a considerable number of years before establishing itself permanently. However, in the UK, the supermarkets' cheaper proprietary brands provide another potential threat to Crosse and Blackwell's future success.

Nestlé may have had other than financial motives for the takeover; power prestige and perhaps defensive reasons. General Food entered the instant coffee market with Maxwell House in 1954. In 1959 Nescafé's share of over 65 per cent of the market, was dropping – Maxwell House had under 25 per cent. Campbell's entry into the UK in the late 1950s may have been another worrying factor for Nestlé. This merger was, however, a compound merger, that is a mixture of horizontal integration (packet soups and confectionery) and diversification into new markets (canned food and prepared dishes).

A quote from the *Financial Times* in 1959 is relevant: 'And so far, the Nestlé Group mergers have been signally successful'. Whether the *Financial Times* would still endorse their previous view is open to question.

Conclusion to Case Studies

Some tentative conclusions have been reached concerning each of the three case studies. Two were considered to be financially unsuccessful whilst one (that of Spillers/Spratt's Patent) was considered to have been financially justifiable. However we have not examined the broader welfare effects; if Nestlé continues with Crosse and Blackwell's product range, despite C & B's losses, the public may be better off – or it may be better for Nestlé to stop and liberate their resources to a more efficient (that is lower price for the same output) producer.

In order to come to any meaningful conclusion we require more information in each case:

(*a*) the objectives of the merger and possibly a future projection of the cash flow and accounting figures;

(*b*) information about the cash flow and accounting figures as they become available;

(*c*) economic data for each industry in which the firms operate, to be able to extract unfavourable industry variables that might affect the actual figures compared with the forecast figures; and

(*d*) macro economic data for the same reason as (*c*).

Each merger or takeover should be examined on an individual basis, and it is not possible to aggregate the results and to derive any firm conclusion.

PART C

A POLICY TOWARDS MERGERS

Chapter Eight

THE CONTROL OF MERGERS IN THE UK: AN ANALYSIS OF GOVERNMENT INSTITUTIONS AND ATTITUDES.*

M. E. Beesley

Professor of Economics and Faculty Dean, London Graduate School of Business Studies

and

G. M. White

Research Officer, London Graduate School of Business Studies

SECTION I:

The Task Flow and the Structure of Control

Introduction

In this paper we are concerned with the structure of merger control and the attitude of government and its agencies towards mergers. We wish to suggest what lessons might be learned from UK experience up to June 1970 about the varying desirability of different forms of control. The analysis also provides a framework within which the tentative proposals[1] of the Conservative administration can be judged. As the work on this paper was finished before the intentions of the new government were known, and these are still uncertain, we do not comment fully here. However, where appropriate, we have inserted relevant notes on the current proposals, and we comment briefly in our concluding pages.

In the past a variety of agencies was involved, most obviously, the Monopolies Commission,[2] the Board of Trade or the Department of Employment and Productivity,[3] the IRC[4] and the NBPI.[5] The Conservative Government dissolved both the IRC and the NBPI, promised amendment and extension of the Commission, and transferred departmental responsibility for merger control policy from the DEP to the newly formed Department of Trade and Industry (DTI).[6] As far as we are aware this change of responsibility was undertaken with little alteration in the staff of the monopolies and mergers division of the Department. Consequently, we can reasonably assume that attitudes and criteria of that division would remain the

* An earlier version of this paper was presented at the Conference on Mergers and Takeovers, London, 28 and 29 May, 1970. Rewritten June 1971.

same whether under DTI, DEP or the Board. However, we do recognize that a change in departmental responsibility may well alter the constraints and freedom of action of the division. For the sake of convenience the following discussion will use 'the Board' where the past tense is appropriate (little action occurred under DEP) and DTI for present and future tenses.

One important aspect of merger control or promotion is consistency with other government policies. We are mainly concerned here with those aspects bearing on monopoly and restrictive practices. Clearly any intervention involves what we call a cost benefit analysis, explicit or implicit, of the potential trade-off between benefits flowing, and costs arising, from the intervention. Thus another aspect is the quality of the analysis, either achieved or possible to achieve, in intervening to promote or control mergers. What are the net benefits, if any, from allowing or encouraging a merger against other alternative merger propositions, or disallowing or not encouraging merger?

Now, much of the academic discussion of mergers has run in terms of what are valid forms of, and terms to enter into the cost-benefit analysis. On what is a presumption for or against increasing concentration based? For what interests precisely does one analyse? How does one weight producer or consumer benefits or disbenefits? How good can predictions of industry or firm behaviour be? These, amongst other things, have attracted comment and are important issues; but the implications of the fact that intervention is performed by a specific agency or by agencies must also be recognized and these must be distinguished from, but related to, the process of intervention itself. Thus, in any government interventionary mechanism (as in any process which sets objectives and attempts to attain them), there can be identified a task-flow system with fairly distinct stages. These stages include, but are not comprised by, the cost-benefit phase. We would argue that the effectiveness of the mechanism as a whole – the structure of control – depends on the effective functioning of *all* the phases, not simply one or two of them. The different tasks, however, may well be at any one time undertaken by different agencies (e.g., as with the Board of Trade, and the Commission). If one contemplates a change in the tasks of the agency, then a natural question to ask is how will a specific change in tasks be handled by the given organizational mix? Or, how will the task performance be affected, overall, by proposed reorganization (concentration or redistribution of the tasks)? The latter is the kind of question which, for example, confronts us at this stage of the development of merger policy.

The interventionary task flow

The first stage of any interventionary task flow may be called *the 'trigger'* mechanism; it represents the procedure by which a problem and a consequent task is recognized to exist, and it embodies a simplified set of rules to indicate whether the later stages in the task flow need to be activated. Not only must it pass on to later stages cases which cannot be adequately analysed by the simple decision rules of the 'trigger', but also cases where more information is needed. If the decision within the 'trigger' mechanism is to call for further action, the next stage, '*analysis*', follows. Here the case is analysed in depth and predictions made of its future operations with and without action by the controlling body according to the range of instruments at its command. The predictions are then compared with a set of norms or criteria comprising the evaluation of courses of action. These are set out in more detail than could be represented in the 'trigger' mechanism.

As a result of this evaluation, recommendation and a *decision* whether or not to act are made, and what form action should take. *Enforcement* of the decision must follow with sanctions, if necessary, to make enforcement operative. A final stage represents *the learning* process; it is the stage at which action is monitored to determine to what extent predictions materialize, and to what extent adaptive behaviour is required in any of the stages of the flow system. So, in summary, we distinguish the following phases of the task – the trigger, the analysis, the decision, enforcement, and the learning phases.

The effectiveness of the task flow system will be influenced by the extent to which its various stages are distributed between agencies. If the communication flow is so split up there may be lack of common awareness of (*a*) the objectives of the mechanism and the criteria to be operated (as in an organizational split between the 'trigger' and 'analysis' stages), and (*b*) the roles of each agency in respect of each other. On the other hand, a given agency may be more effective in operating any one part of the task flow than another agency. Thus any proposal to reorganize the total task will itself be associated with costs and benefits in terms of the effectiveness with which the task is performed.

A possible classification of interventionary agencies

When these notions are applied to the implementation of the government's interventionary strategies an important consideration is that of Parliamentary responsibility – i.e., the need to be accountable for actions to Parliament through a Minister. The extent to which this requirement results in a given distribution of control over stages in the system between, say, two agencies (the government department representing the Minister responsible, and the 'independent' agency established), depends on the government's philosophic approach to the task. In the interventionary field, whether for promotion or regulation, there are basically three kinds of approach, each relating to a particular government rationale.

(*a*) Where the government is clear and specific about the objectives and method of implementation of the strategy, then it is likely to be prepared to establish a mechanism and corresponding agency, independent of departmental scrutiny, but in which the frame of reference, in terms of function, criteria, and executive powers, is clearly delineated in detail by statutory directive. The restrictive practices control mechanism may be said to be such a case. The government of the day considered that the issues involved were sufficiently capable of specification to warrant judicial rather than administrative control. In this particular case, of course, the 1956 Act gave rise to debate about the question of 'justiciability'. Stevens and Yamey have identified this to be 'the ability of the legislature so to embody into a principle the policies which it intends to be effectuated by the Act, that the Courts are left with sufficiently clearly defined standards to operate the judicial process efficiently by keeping discretion within narrow limits'.[7] Over the years since, doubts on whether the Court can be effective in these terms have lessened.

(*b*) There is a second category of government agencies, where the government believes that for operational effectiveness there needs to be an independent agency incorporating within it all the stages of the task flow and relatively free from administrative supervision. In such cases only general safeguards and rules of behaviour are written into the statute. This category is associated with intervention of a promotionary nature and includes for example, the old IRC and NRDC. The IRC's brief to promote, *inter alia*, mergers, reflected the view that on balance mergers were beneficial to the economy, a view also implying that the need to prevent mergers arose in special circumstances requiring more specific supervision.

(*c*) In the third class of agency the government finds itself unable to lay down detailed criteria and rules of conduct, and sees no operational advantage in independence from administrative control. Consequently, a responsible department maintains direct control over a number of crucial stages in the flow system. Thus, in an extreme case, the independent agency is operative at the 'analysis' stage; it remains an investigatory body with no formal power of initiation and only the power of recommendation. The relevant department retains control of the 'trigger' mechanism and discretion as to which cases shall be referred for further analysis; it also operates the decision, enforcement and monitoring stages. The Monopolies Commission fitted this description at its inception and, except insofar as it may have generated informal influences, does so today. The National Board for Prices and Incomes, though it had a limited role in monitoring its own work, was another example of this category of government agency. The degree of influence which such bodies can be expected to wield is related to the extent to which the relevant department is prepared to use the resources (time as well as other resources) at the disposal of the agency. Also relevant is the personal influence of the chairman of the agency, since flows between the agency and its responsible department must operate in informal and indirect ways. (In terms of the task flow, the Conservative proposals still place the Commission in our third category of government agency, since power of 'trigger' and 'decision' is still to be formally vested in DTI.)

The significance of this categorization, we would argue, is that any substantial change in such organizational procedures would imply a change in the underlying approach of the government to the problem.

The structure of control

In terms of the task-flow, merger control consists of a 'trigger' operated by DTI;[8] an 'analysis' phase that may be operated either by DTI or the Commission; a set of recommendations by the Commission for decision and implementation by the DTI, Minister or Ministers; and a monitoring and learning process carried out by DTI.

Previous literature on merger policy has concentrated on what we term the cost-benefit analyses carried out in the relatively public forum of the Monopolies Commission. Commentators such as Rowley[9] and Sutherland[10,11] have attempted to identify how a philosophic commitment to pragmatism – i.e., a view that mergers may be on balance good, bad or neutral – is translated into criteria and analysis of the merger cases in the reports of the Commission. The commentators have unearthed some inconsistencies between merger cases and, moreover, have detected some inconsistencies between merger and monopoly references. We suggest later that it is somewhat misleading to concentrate on the most readily available manifestations of merger policy – the analyses reported by the Commission – to the relative neglect of the merger mechanism as a total system which we call the structure of control.

The question of structural control in merger policy resolves itself into two related issues; (*a*) the relationship between the responsible government department and the 'independent' agency – i.e., the Commission; and (*b*) the pressures other than analytic which may be operating to affect the outcome of the Commission's investigations. We would therefore first like to consider the relationship between department and Commission with particular reference to the nature of the flow between the 'trigger' and 'analysis' stages, and the way this has a bearing on the 'decision' stage of the mechanism.

According to the BOT's booklet,[12] up to June 1969, the Board had considered a total of 430 mergers falling under the monopoly and asset rules and the newspaper merger rules of the 1965 Monopolies and Mergers Act, and of these had only referred 12 to the Commission for further investigation. This the Board deemed to substantiate the argument that legislation had only been 'intended to provide a power of investigation for the relatively rare case which might be against the public interest'. We should note that there is a degree of circularity on this point. For example, in 1969 the President of the Board asserted that 'it is because we accept that the majority of mergers have a neutral or beneficial effect that the Board of Trade have used so sparingly their power to refer certain mergers to the Monopolies Commission . . . and in only three cases have the Commission recommended that a merger should not be allowed to proceed. So in general the merger movement has brought clear benefits'.[13] The merger movement *may* have done this, but the merger control mechanism has not shown it to do this, because it does not require that the Commission should prove net benefit to the public interest. There was a presumption by BOT, presumably inherited by DTI, that mergers are neutral or beneficial unless proved otherwise.

(*a*) *The 'trigger' decision-rule for reference*

As brief background to the discussion of the trigger rules for reference, it is worthwhile to note that the procedure involves and always involved four stages: (i) prior analysis and provisional recommendation; (ii) assessment by DTI committee which would include sponsor department officials and the secretary of the Commission;

(iii) recommendation by that committee to the Minister; and finally (iv) a Ministerial or even Cabinet, decision to refer or not to refer.

What were the decision rules in the 'trigger', in the Board's internal vetting system (which clearly itself contained a simplified form of cost-benefit assessment) which resulted in so few mergers being referred to the Commission? The central decision rule was reflected in the Board's statement that 'where preliminary enquiries reveal potential detriments, the Board will . . . consider whether there appear to be such substantial offsetting advantages as to make it virtually certain that they outweigh the detriments, in which case the Board would be free to conclude that reference to the Commission would not be justified'.[14] There is some confusion as to the implication of the Board's decisions to refer for the terms of reference to the analysis by the Commission. Both Rowley[15] and Sutherland[16] believe that a reference implies that the relevant question for the Commission 'is whether those mergers where the detriment is obvious are nevertheless, because of the benefits, actively in the public interest'.[17] This is not necessarily the implication, because the Board's decision rule only removes from further analysis those mergers which clearly are *not* likely to operate against the public interest. The Commission's interpretation of its role – 'to decide not whether the merger . . . is positively in the public interest, but only whether it may be expected to operate against the public interest'[18] – is as much in accordance with the Board's procedure as Sutherland's interpretation, but it is also closer to the spirit of the 1965 legislation.[19] Sutherland may be right in suggesting that the procedure does not allow the right question to be asked and has strong arguments to support this, but nevertheless it *is* the question implied by the Act and the Board's reference procedure, given that the presumption about mergers is adhered to.

Although the Board's booklet gives the overall decision rule for its sorting mechanism, it provides only an exhaustive list of the considerations it takes into account in particular cases. Under the four heads of 'market power', 'efficiency', 'balance of payments' and 'regional' effects, the Board poses a labyrinth of relevant questions. Now, the principle in establishing the Commission was precisely that of creating an efficient investigatory mechanism. We would agree with Sutherland's suggestion that although the Commission has up to six months to investigate a merger 'we will still look in vain [in Commission reports] for answers to many of the kinds of questions which the Board says it regards as relevant, and can answer in two or three weeks, when taking the vital decision about whether or not to make a reference in the first place'.[20] If the Commission's analysis is limited, it is difficult to believe that the Board's is more exhaustive, given the time scale. So it is a fair assumption that the Board must use rough proxies for a cost-benefit analysis, or in other words select indicators of likely behaviour and results. These are guidelines; and guidelines in dealing with mergers have been roundly castigated by the President of the Board.[21]

But, by drawing unfavourable comparisons with the American system of control, in which guidelines play a major role, the distinction between a 'trigger' and an 'analysis' stage in the mechanism was not clearly recognized by the President. Whilst the operation of the 'analysis' stage can clearly be 'empirical and pragmatic', one would expect the vetting procedure in the 'trigger' stage to be conducted according to some consistently applied, simple decision rules. Thus in the US system the initiation of proceedings invoking the Clayton Act provisions in respect of mergers is undertaken by the Department of Justice with the assistance of private litigants. 'The courts, however, are ultimately responsible for the definitive interpretation and application of the anti-trust laws'.[22] The rigid guidelines of the US system, so often referred to, are the decision rules operating within the Department of Justice to determine whether civil or criminal action against a merger should be triggered. The outcome of the court case is not necessarily determined by the guidelines, though as these are amended to reflect case-law decisions, this will increasingly be so.

The relevant objection to the US system from the UK government's point of view is not the existence of guidelines in themselves, but the nature of the guidelines. The US system has a different task orientation. The laws do not ask whether in a particular case the maintenance of competition will promote or retard welfare, but whether the conduct that has been called into question promotes or retards competition from which effective performance is expected to flow. The Department of Justice asserts that it 'will not accept as a justification for an acquisition normally subject to challenge under its . . . merger standards the claim that the merger will produce economies',[23] whereas UK merger policy recognizes economies as a justification. So guidelines for the reference procedure should not be dismissed *per se*, and, indeed, should be explicitly recognized if, as we suggest above, they already implicitly exist. We later consider the 'analysis' stage of the task-flow.

(*b*) *'Assurances' as a method of control*

Meanwhile, the question of information in the analysis of mergers (and particularly, of their benefits) by the Board takes on added significance in the light of the stated intention of the President: 'to seek assurances somewhat more freely in major merger cases'.[24] The Board reports in its booklet that in eight major cases[25] the decision not to refer to the Commission was conditional upon the companies undertaking certain assurances about future behaviour (e.g., Ross/Associated Fisheries April 1969*). To that list may now be added the mergers of BIMC/National Bus Company, BICC/AEI Cables* (also an arrangement between Pirelli General/ Enfield-Standard Power Cables)*, Leasco/Pergamon, and Reed/IPC.[26] It is clear that the 'intention' of the President is already operative, and that the 'analysis' stage of the flow mechanism as embodied in the Commission, is being by-passed perhaps more regularly than was the intention of the original legislation. Sutherland has already indicated some of the dangers of the assurances approach. Assurances may be ineffective either because they are so vaguely framed that a breach of them might not be recognized, or because 'there is no effective sanction even if a breach is recognized, unless a government, previously reluctant even to refer a merger, would now be prepared to contemplate the much more difficult task of breaking up a

*In these cases, where assurances were secured, the IRC was involved in support of the merger.

completed merger'.[27] There are additional criticisms to make from the point of view of the process through which the decision is formulated to extract assurances, and the process through which the nature of the assurances is negotiated.

'Assurances' or 'undertakings' are negotiated with companies by the Board of Trade (now DTI) with or without the report of the Commission. If the Commission does report it will sometimes suggest undertakings which will then set the scope and direction of the negotiations the DTI conducts, though there is of course no formal requirement that DTI follows the Commission's line or indeed exacts assurances even when the Commission calls for them. We have to consider the problem of assurances in two situations – when the Commission is not brought in and where it is. First, and generally, we must note that although assurances betoken the existence of potential deteriments, there is no necessary existence of substantial economies which may be lost if the merger is not allowed to proceed. Neither are such economies necessarily thought to exist. This arises from the 'presumption' about mergers which we have already noted (see p. 129). So it seems that if the DTI can see its way to extracting 'practical' undertakings safeguarding the public interest from the exploitation of monopoly power, it might well rest its analysis there.

Without a Commission Report, of course, the Department's only sanction in the event of a breach of 'assurances' would be reference to the Commission, and this it cannot do in merger cases once six months have lapsed from the time of merger. Reference after the six months would only be possible if the merged companies fell within the monopoly rules of the 1965 Act.[28] There were signs, however, that the Board was having some doubts about the 'presumption', as noticed by Sutherland.[29] This suggests that, at least recently, the government may itself have raised more often the question of identifying positive benefits when deciding whether to extract assurances or to refer to the Commission. But this again raises the question of information. It seems very doubtful if DTI is to retain a 'trigger' role whether it would be able to satisfy itself about the offsetting nature of benefits, when the Commission, with much more time, has become increasingly exasperated at the lack of willingness or ability of companies to produce quantification of any expected economies. Also, the Commission has sometimes discounted economies claimed on the grounds that their realization was not dependent on the merger. How able is the DTI, with less information, in judging on this matter? Once the question of positive benefit is raised, it is logical to ask whether the merger is a *necessary* as well as a *sufficient* condition for their realization. This implies the need to study alternative means to the same end, complicates the task and sharply increases the needed information. These issues are discussed more fully later.

In Commission investigations, too, a decision about whether assurances are an adequate method of control has to be made. Of the ten non-newspaper mergers it has investigated to date, assurances were sought in eight, extracted in five, and instrumental in the merger being accepted in three cases.[30] In these last three cases the Board did not use its delaying powers and the mergers were completed either before or during the process of investigation. In one particular case – that of BICC/ Pyrotenax – this factor must have impeded the Commission in its investigations, as

Sutherland suggests.[31] Substantial benefits were not expected to arise from the merger, and the potential public detriment in the created monopoly position in the production and distribution of mineral insulated cable was implicitly recognized from the extensive general and particular assurances undertaken by BICC[32] and accepted by the Commission.[33] But less critical consideration was paid by the Commission to the practicability of these assurances than in any other report where assurances were an issue. For example, the Ross/Associated Fisheries merger was disallowed after the practicability and relevance of the suggested assurances were carefully analysed and rejected by the Commission. Thus the following somewhat paradoxical effect of the system of control can be noted: in the Ross/Associated case, the Commission speculated about the likely effectiveness of assurances after the merger and counted this into the general assessment of the merger; in the BICC/ Pyrotenax case no such stipulations were made – possibly because this was an *ex-post facto* case. But the potential detriments were very probably greater in the BICC than in the Ross case. So, failure to use delaying powers has its costs in a restriction of the Commission's analysis.

Even in cases in which merger *was* delayed during investigation, the Commission reports reflect a lower commitment to assurances than do the activities and declared intentions of the Board.[34] This may be due to their opportunity for deeper analysis. A Commission investigation provides a focus for the expression of views of interested parties to the merger. The Board was less effective here. In a number of cases the Commission had used statements of opposition to the merger to spot-light relevant areas for investigation. Such a definition is only available to the DTI to a much lesser degree. Now, were cost-benefit analyses of potential benefits, sufficient to offset the risks attached to assurances, to be systematically applied, the Commission would be better placed to do this, by reason of a greater initial scepticism and opportunity than DTI.

However, how well or badly the analysis of assurances is done, now or in the future, in the present type of control system, it only acts as a premise to negotiations with companies. The latter may, and do, object to the assurances demanded. The first stage at which this may occur is before the DTI decides to refer to the Commission. The extent to which companies are likely to object to assurances, or to consent to modified demands, depends on a balance of considerations, among them the probability that DTI will refer the merger to the Commission. If, to take an extreme case, a main motivation for merger is the acquisition of dominant market power and/or special competitive advantage with zero possible economies in view, then the companies might be expected to attempt to avoid giving assurances that constrained the exploitation of market power. (In this connection it must be remarked that, at least with the amendments of the 1964 and 1968 Acts, we have a relatively stringent law on restrictive practices, which may be a substantial motive for a merger.) But in deciding this, the companies have to weigh up the probability of a reference to the Commission, known to be less sympathetic about assurances, and costing, directly or indirectly, a great deal in terms of executive time, possible unwelcome publicity, and delay in the merger. This possibility may reduce companies' resistance to accepting assurances – and must stiffen the determination of companies to negotiate reduced assurances. And they may well rate the possibilities of effective monitoring[35] of such assurances as are given as low as some commentators, ourselves included, do. We fear that this might result in the Department being more successful in the extraction of practicable and realistic assurances from companies little concerned with the market power implications of their merger, and less successful in those cases where the prime motive is increased market power. In other words, we suggest that there is a possibility that inadequate assurances may be undertaken in just those merger cases where detailed assurances and rigorous monitoring are most necessary in safeguarding the public interest, and securing net benefit (if any).

The evidence for this hypothesis from past merger cases is necessarily slight and circumstantial, because the reports from the Board on merger cases and the assurances undertaken give little information about the details of the assurances, or the circumstances in which they were requested and undertaken.

SECTION II

The Cost-Benefit Phases in Merger Control

O. E. Williamson[36] has suggested that the anti-trust mechanism in the US should incorporate an explicit welfare trade-off between the costs and benefits to be expected from a merger. British commentators have analysed the operation of UK merger regulation from the same cost-benefit point of view. The Board, DTI and the Commission have also recognized this conceptual framework. We have suggested that the nature of the control mechanism may supplement or even over-ride any cost-benefit trade-off that is attempted. But let us first define what is involved in a cost-benefit analysis here. As will be seen, a major question of consistency of government attitudes arises.

The nature of the cost-benefit analysis

A cost-benefit analysis of merger proposals in principle involves the prediction of effects with or without any given form of intervention, be it prohibition of the merger or acceptance with extraction of assurances of various kinds. These expected states of affairs are compared by:

(i) specifying the parties or interests relevant to the analysis (e.g., consumers, producers, workers, and the nation at large as represented by the foreign trade balance);

(ii) specifying the effects on the parties (e.g., state A results in higher profits for producers, greater innovation – new consumers – and X000 more redundancies compared with state B);

(iii) specifying whether the effects are 'good' (benefit) or 'bad' (cost) (e.g., high price is 'bad', high profits 'bad', greater innovation 'good', redundancy 'bad'); and

(iv) specifying the relative weights to be attached to these effects (e.g., £1's worth of 'good' or 'bad' is the same to whomsoever it accrues).

In a fully consistent government policy, alternative proposals to promote mergers (what used to be IRC's function) would be analysed in the same framework; moreover, all government departments having an interest in mergers – the Treasury, DTI, etc., would agree in the constituency of analysis (i) and the direction and weights to be attached to outcomes (iii) and (iv). In fact many sources of conflict among the agencies appear.[37]

Sources of conflict between agencies

Fundamental disputes of principle between the agencies could arise from at least two main sources – the addition of further items of benefit and cost to the trade-off analysis; and disagreement about the weights to be accorded to the interests of the parties concerned. For example, the NBPI probably attached more weight to the macro (inflationary) implications of a price rise than would the (Monopolies) Commission, even though the latter might include as an ancillary consideration other macro effects (e.g., the balance of payments effect). Time horizons and hence discount rates probably diverged between NBPI and Commission analyses. The definition of the 'society' for which the analysis is held to apply may differ between agencies; e.g., the Commission, with its general commitment to the interests of domestic consumers, regards import duty changes as a valid instrument in monopoly control, whereas DTI has international trading agreements to observe which imply greater concern, at the least, for the foreign consumer.

The major source of divergence, however, relates to the different weights attached to consumer and producer gains from mergers. The Commission, if it attempted the welfare trade-off explicitly would undoubtedly weight the direct consumer interests very highly. Consumers must not, at least on balance, be seen directly to lose; and price falls tend to be regarded as a good thing. The Commission is fairly certain to look with disfavour on a merger whose outcome is pure producer gain and its acceptance of a merger whose outcome is a mix of consumer and producer gains is likely to be dependent on the extent of profit increase. 'Too high' a rate of profit, measured against some norm derived from average industry experience, runs firms into the risk of being condemned for consumer exploitation; in general high profit rates can only be justified, it seems, by their specific use to promote innovation in the firm or industry concerned (e.g., the Pilkington's case). In terms of public welfare as a whole it does not seem necessary that agencies should concern themselves with who gains and who loses (i.e., transfers) nor with the specific purposes to which gains are devoted. The IRC, it seemed, took this kind of view of prospective merger outcomes.

These potential and actual conflicts of view can only be resolved ultimately, if they *are* to be resolved, by an explicit clarification of policy by the government, that is by resolving its own doubts about the tasks of the various agencies, and by bestowing the appropriate weights in the cost-benefit analysis. We cannot but feel pessimistic about the possibility of such a resolution.

Another dimension (and a very important one) to the problem of sources of conflict within government, is that which relates to the role of the sponsor department, and, in particular, the sponsor division within that department. To some extent, where we have criticized the Board we have implicitly criticized the monopolies and mergers division of the department. This is too simplified a view because it fails to recognize the constraints within which that division had to operate. As we have already indicated, the procedure on reference may have to involve a Cabinet decision. When the division was within the Board (and as it is now under DTI) it had to argue for a reference against opposition from other divisions within the department who had responsibility for certain industries and who were defensive about them, because a reference to the Commission would make its working relations with that industry much more difficult. This was the main source of difference and conflict, and it could often reach a pitch such that the merger division was cautious about requesting information from an industry's sponsor division because this would reveal its line of investigation and might cause the sponsor division to reject or qualify its provision of information. It might be said that within the Board the merger control division had too many pressures operating against it, whereas in the DEP (which had little commitment to a division, which it regarded as a temporary burden) there were too few pressures working for it.[38]

We would suspect that conflicts of the two general kinds described above tended to bring Ministers and the Cabinet more regularly into the reference and decision procedure than one might have anticipated. This strengthens our plea for greater explicit clarification of the grounds upon which references are decided, or for some debate on the grounds that should be used.

Information requirements of the cost-benefit analyses

If the cost-benefit analysis of mergers were to be as extensive as academic commentators would clearly like it to be, and the regulatory agencies hopefully assert it is, the information to fit the specification outlines above would be formidable. There is first the gap between the information apparently made available to the Commission and the information requirements suggested by the Board in its booklet as necessary for its appraisal (even though the information needs of the latter are less than that of the former). The Commission itself has become increasingly aware of the lack of sufficient information and expressed its dissatisfaction in the Unilever/Allied Breweries Report where the claimed benefits were not only small but also were not demonstrated. It is perhaps significant that after the two latest reports the Commission published the same appendix in which it commented that 'mergers now play so important a part in the reorganization of British industry that it seems to us desirable . . . that more should be known about their effects . . . it would be in the public interest if more information were given by companies about the reasons for acquisitions, their real cost, and, subsequently, the growth and earnings of the acquiring company and each of its major divisions or acquisitions'.[39,40]

Thus there is a real lack of sufficient information for the needs of the cost-benefit analysis. This is despite the fact that, in contrast to other aspects of monopoly control (such as restrictive practices), the regulation of mergers *should* have an inherent advantage since there is likely to be an overlap of the information requirements of the regulatory body, and the needs of a company in its acquisition strategy or those of companies entering an 'agreed' merger. The evidence needed for rational private decisions and for social appraisal overlap. The congruency of information requirements becomes apparent if the Board's list of considerations and questions[41] for appraisal are compared with the considerations, which, say, Ansoff[42] or Allen[43] regard as a necessary part of an acquisition strategy. In the process of 'industry search' as part of the diversification strategy, for example, companies will wish to know the growth trends in the industry, its product and market characteristics, its level of technology, and the structure of competition within it. In the 'company search' part of such a strategy the acquiring company will require to know the product, market, profitability, and liquidity characteristics of the companies, their methods of distribution, their cost structures, their management expertise, and their rates of return on investment. It would then have to compare such industry and company profiles with its own 'competitive and competence' profiles in order to see how various industries and the various companies within them might strengthen weaknesses or exploit strengths revealed from its own profiles. As can be seen from the Board's booklet these are the same considerations the regulatory body needs to make in identifying the economies or market power detriments likely to arise from a merger. True, however congruent the items of information required may be, the weights attached by the government to the information will not be the same as those attached by the companies, and consequently particular issues will be pressed further by one of the two parties (e.g., it is an essential part of the Board's appraisal to consider regional and balance of payments effects, but companies would probably not weight these factors as highly). But there is a substantial degree of overlap of information flows, which, if the cost-benefit analysis is to be adequate, should be fully exploited. Could it be so exploited?

It seems reasonable to assume that companies will be unlikely to volunteer information unless the context is such that it would be to their advantage to do so. The presumption in the current mechanism that mergers tend to be neutral or beneficial to the public interest means that companies will not feel that the onus is on them to prove the benefits of a merger. The reports of the Commission seem to indicate that companies are unlikely to quantify their claims of benefit unless one or some combination of the following factors exists:

(i) it seems to be necessary that the merger was the outcome of a deliberate acquisition strategy by at least one of the companies (e.g., the contrast between the Dental Manufacturing Company's evidence in its bid for the Amalgamated Dental Co., and the evidence put by the Dentists' Supply Co., of New York whose bid was a spontaneous counter to the DM Co., bid);

(ii) if the merger was delayed during the investigation, quantification of benefits is more likely than if the merger was completed before or during the investigation, in which case it seems that the merger is inevitably accepted, albeit with assurances;

(iii) where, depending on the pressures brought to bear, there was extensive and significant opposition to the merger, quantification is more likely (e.g., in the Ross/AF and Thorn/Radio Rental cases extensive opposition was met from trade associations, customers, competitors, and this was associated with fairly extensive quantification of cost savings etc.); and finally

(iv) where detriment was identified which could not be offset by assurances – i.e., where offsetting economies would have to be shown before the merger could be permitted – this seemed to be a stimulus to quantification (e.g., Ross/AF). Conglomerate mergers (i.e., Unilever/Allied; Rank/De la Rue) do not fit this analysis of variables explaining quantification very well, but then they do not lend themselves to quantification, for no specific horizontal or vertical relationships exist; if like is not merged with like a common currency for measurement is lacking.

Companies will not be prepared to quantify benefits in a Commission analysis unless they are able to do so (i) and unless it is in their interest to do so (ii), (iii), and (iv). Therefore if the government wishes to take advantage of the overlapping information flows inherent in mergers and their control, it seems to be necessary to make it to the companies' benefit to do so as well. If adequate information is to be forthcoming these inducements have to be greatly strengthened – particularly in the case of 'agreed' mergers. Nothing short of changing the onus of proof of showing benefit to the companies concerned seems likely to succeed, so that once a merger has been referred, the inducement is simply that permission depends on producing the evidence. The cost to the companies might often be negative i.e., their analysis of merger prospects would improve. This shifting of the onus is often coupled with the suggestion of a shift in the presumption from being for, to against merger. We suggest later that this is not a necessary connection.

Even, if, however, companies could be induced to give more information, a competent analysis would still require, it seems to us, simplification of the issues to be determined, and, since the volume of mergers promises to remain large, economy in the use of the analysts, which we identify as the experts, the Commission members and support staff.

The commentators who propose a shift in the presumption imply a very substantial increase in both the quantity and quality of the Commission's analysis of mergers. The Commission has already been soundly criticized for its 'failure' to analyse issues such as present and future cross-elasticities for the reference goods, potential competition, and relation to the shifting strategies of firms.[44] Add to this the requirement that substantial net benefit should be a necessary as well as sufficient condition for merger, and the analysis task would indeed be greatly enlarged. The need for simplification of the analysis is *a fortiori* higher if this line of development is followed.

By simplification we mean both the narrowing down of the interests to be considered (redundancies, for example, should, we believe, not be dealt with in the context of merger policy), and the according of explicit weights to those considered (thus, for example, a simple rule might be that producer and consumer interests might be regarded as equally worthy). What further can be done to make the task more manageable depends on the stage of the mechanism. Let us comment on each, bearing in mind that in the current mechanism a cost-benefit analysis is undertaken at the 'decision' as well as the 'trigger' and 'analysis' stages, with no guarantee of consistency between them.

(*a*) *The 'trigger' stage*

(i) We shall argue that the general decision rule within the 'trigger' mechanism should remain as it is – i.e., that a merger should not be referred to the Commission where it is clearly not against the public interest, either from lack of detriment or from substantially offsetting benefits. There is one necessary qualification, however. Assurances should not we think, be used by the DTI as a method of offsetting detriment and hence employed as an alternative to reference to the Commission. Analysis of their justification, relevance and practicability, should be dealt with by the expert analysts, the Commission; neither can the sanctions at the power of the DTI be, we think, adequate. Thus, assurances should only be the outcome of a Commission cost-benefit analysis. But this will of itself automatically have the effect of increasing the load on the Commission.

(ii) The directive to the Commission on a reference of a merger to it should remain as it is – i.e., to determine whether the merger is likely to operate against the public interest, implying an acceptance of mergers being neutral or beneficial to the public interest. The only alternative directive would be for the Commission to approve a merger only on the demonstration of net benefit. The reasons against this are discussed later.

(iii) As in the US system (see p. 131) we think that the 'trigger' mechanism can be simplified by making an explicit statement of some rules of thumb, since, as we argued earlier, these must in practice already be operated in deciding whether or not a merger should be referred for further investigation – i.e., to the courts in the US, to the Commission in the UK. This would be to make explicit what has hitherto been implicit in the UK mechanism. A given rule of thumb is more efficient than another the greater its predictive power about market structure-conduct relationships. There is clearly great scope for increasing understanding of the implications for behaviour of a particular market structure, and increasing awareness of the economies necessary substantially to offset the identified market detriment. The remarkable upsurge in American empirical studies in relating performance to structure in the last ten years has yet to find its reflection in the UK studies. Much could be done through research to make rules of thumb more sophisticated than simple concentration ratios, existing market shares, etc.

(*b*) *The 'analysis' stage*

At this point we would like to contrast our proposals with those made by Alister Sutherland.[45] He suggests that the 'trigger' should include a mechanism of automatic reference of all mergers involving companies above a certain absolute size, and that mergers amongst companies of very large size should only be justified on the demonstration of substantial net benefit. The principle of automatic reference in particular cases is reflected in our proposal that the rules of thumb implicitly operated by DTI should be made explicit, although we would hope, as we have just argued, that DTI methods go beyond the absolute size rules suggested by Sutherland.

He has also suggested that all mergers before the Commission should only be approved on the demonstration of positive net benefit. Our criticisms of this suggested re-emphasis of the task of the Commission flow from the required change in the 'trigger' decision rule. Sutherland sees this as an advantage: 'in deciding whether *prima facie* they (mergers) should be referred, the Board would then in future . . . give much more weight to the presence of potential benefit, and less to the apparent absence of detriment'.[46] Let us put the implication more realistically; for net benefit to be the *only* justification of a merger before the Commission, would require that only *substantial* net benefit could prevent a merger from being referred. We have three related objections to this:–

(i) Such a change in the 'trigger' decision rule would increase the load of work of the departmental staff considerably, since it would not be sufficient for them to approve a merger by demonstrating absence of detriment. In all the merger cases coming before them under the rules of the 1965 Act (there were 430 of these between the time of Royal Assent to the Act, and June, 1969) they would have to satisfy themselves that there existed substantial potential net benefit before they could decide not to refer to the Commission.

(ii) Given the lack of time, information and resources at DTI disposal and given that DTI abided by this decision rule for reference, it seems dubious that it could satisfy itself in this way in many cases. The Commission would consequently, in turn, become much more loaded with merger references.

(iii) Such over-loading of both DTI and the Commission would arise essentially from the presumption that would exist in Sutherland's proposed mechanism that mergers neutral from the public interest point of view (or at least marginally beneficial or detrimental) should not be permitted. We are reluctant to accept, *a priori*, that there is any good reason for finding a merger unacceptable in the absence of identified detriment (i.e., at worst, neutral to the public interest). Our suggested retention of the present tasks of both Commission and DTI would tend to avoid what we would regard as a threatened over-load of the Commission, since absence of detriment is easier to identify and demonstrate than the existence of potential net benefit.

Therefore Sutherland's proposals would involve the Commission in an increased work-load. It seems unlikely that the Commission could be given much of an extension in the time permitted for its merger analysis, and consequently an increase in the number of staff could be the only possible way in which the Commission could cope. But Sutherland's rephasing of the tasks of the Commission imply that more has to be proved (i.e., net benefit in all cases) and the analysis has to be of higher quality than at present. This extra burden can only be carried, not by increasing staff, but by increasing the time and information available, and these, we suggest, are subject to constraints. Moreover, an increase in the number of references would tend to cause a deterioration in the analysis of individual cases, given the time and information constraints. We see little prospect of the Commission's satisfying the standards of critics of its analysis; the task is too complicated. But we have a suggestion to make, more compatible in our view with this and the work-load capability of the Commission.

This is to make the Commission analysis focus particularly on the detriment aspects of merger proposals, and to shift the burden of proof of *offsetting* economies onto the companies concerned. This would have a number of desirable consequences:

(i) It would help to resolve the two conflicting requirements of cogency and certainty in the law and practice on mergers. The Commission could concentrate on evolving more sophisticated rules about the desirability of certain market structures and behaviour. These could become part of an explicit Commission view such that companies would be deterred from merging unless they knew and could prove that their merger would have desirable consequences sufficient to offset the detriment identified by the Commission's recognized rules. Companies might then be deterred from 'mergers designed merely or largely to buy the assets and/or profits of the acquired company cheaply and without reasonable expectations, on the basis of positive plans, that they can use the acquired assets more effectively'.[47]

(ii) The companies would find it to their advantage to make full co-operative use of the information at their disposal. To quote from US experience – the companies 'possess the basic data as to costs and are in a position to analyse the data more quickly and effectively than the government. Because the burden of proof is upon them in considering cost, they interpose no obstacles to the submission of cost information and are willing to supply it in the form and degree of detail which the Commission believe to be necessary'.[48]

(iii) It would be more practical in terms of the demands of the Commission, since the latter need not set itself impracticable comparisons of the alternative means of securing the economies claimed for the merger, via competition, internal expansion, etc. Such comparisons involve complications of projecting time spans for the alternative realization of economies, discount rates, etc. These are avoided where the issue is the benefit, if any, of the specific merger under consideration. The question would be whether the merger benefits are sufficient to offset detriment, not whether the benefits are a necessary concomitant of the merger.

We suggest one further amendment to the Commission analysis stage, namely, that only the Commission should have the right to ask for assurances, where it thinks on the basis of its cost-benefit analysis, that they are relevant and practicable in the safeguard against exploitation of monopoly power.

(*c*) *The 'decision' stage*

In the current mechanism this stage is a function of the DTI and is undertaken in a merger case in one of two ways. The DTI can by-pass the Commission's analysis by the exacting of assurances, according to its own criteria as to relevance and practicability or it can refer the merger to the Commission, and negotiate with the company in the light of the recommendations of a Commission report. In making its recommendations the Commission ought to be aware that certain instruments for control are more acceptable to the DTI and other departments than others (e.g., tariff reductions are probably not a very acceptable method of monopoly control), but within that framework ought to be confident that its recommendations will be implemented. In other words, the 'decision' stage ought to be a direct consequence of the 'analysis' and 'trigger' stages as long as the recommendations stemming from the latter are made with full awareness of what are acceptable 'decisions'. We understand that in this respect there is closer informal relation between the Commission and the DTI as to whether the Commission recommendations are likely to find acceptance by DTI.

The NBPI, whose role in the overall structure of control closely corresponded to that of the Commission, and which was far more explicit about structure of control issues, had recognized the potential dilemma in having an investigatory body whose recommendations have no executive authority – 'in so far as the Board adheres reasonably to the rules laid down for it and the government fails to ensure the execution of our recommendations, then one of two things must follow; either the Board must frame its recommendations in the light of a possible failure of action by the government, in which case the government's own rules could prove to have little meaning; or the Board sticks to the rules, in which case the government is shown to be either unwilling or alternatively powerless to carry out its own requirements'.[49]

An example of this point is DTI's power of divestiture and its willingness to use it. Either it is a real power or it is not; if it is not, or as long as it is not shown to be a real power, then all mergers should be delayed during the process of Commission investigation. From the past record failure to delay appears to have had the effect of reducing the likelihood of quantification of benefits, reducing the probability of prohibition (i.e., divestiture in such a case), and consequently increasing the likelihood of impractical assurances being extracted. (There is of course the additional point that it is fairly certain that even were a merger to be unscrambled on the recommendations of the Commission, the competitive *status quo ante* would not be restored, after the interchange of information and views between the companies involved, particularly if the merger was 'agreed' between the parties.)

(*d*) *Feedback*

It is essential in the interests of minimizing uncertainty faced by firms on the one hand, and of improving the quality of the analysis in the control mechanism on the other, that inconsistency between the principles operated at different phases of the mechanism should be minimized. This can only be ensured between the 'analysis', the recommendations flowing from it and the 'decision' phase by making the latter have a more formal relation to the former. Between 'analysis' and 'trigger' phases there has to be a learning process, such that decision rules operated in the 'trigger' are amended and made more sophisticated in the light of judgements made at the 'analysis' stage. 'The Department [of Justice] anticipates that it will amend the guidelines from time to time . . . to reflect changes in enforcement policy that might result from subsequent court decisions, comments of interested parties, or Department re-evaluations.'[50] Again the American system provides an example which the British system could do well to emulate.

SECTION 3

Conclusions and some Organizational Implications

In the second section we made a number of suggestions involving certain changes in the current merger control mechanism. The first section arguments require us to consider whether the proposed alterations suggest any organizational restructuring – any changes in the roles of the agencies concerned – to facilitate the most effective functioning of the total structure of control.

Summary of Proposals

Within the 'trigger' mechanism we see no need to change the *general* decision rule employed to determine what mergers should be referred to the later stages of the mechanism. Hence the rule should be *not* to refer mergers where there is no detriment (i.e., at worst neutral) nor mergers where detriment is predicted substantially to be offset by benefit (i.e., substantial net benefit). This calculation would be made, not with any elaborate cost-benefit analysis, but by applying explicit rules of thumb representing expectations about detriments and benefits. No assurances should be extracted at this stage of the mechanism.

Within the 'analysis' phase of the mechanism we think that the Commission's task should remain the investigation of whether or not a merger is likely to operate *against* the public interest. The onus of proof of benefits, however, should be transferred to the companies involved. We also consider that the formulation and negotiation of assurances, insofar as they are regarded as a valid method of control should become the responsibility of the Commission alone. In our proposals assurances become relevant where identified detriments exceed identified benefits. The assurances may therefore be used to reduce the potential detriment to an acceptable level (i.e., where benefits accrue, and detriment to the public interest is safeguarded).

The Commission would have to take a view on the probability of the assurances being effective, counting this into its assessment.

At the 'decision' stage of the task-flow, which we accept to be the legitimate function of the DTI, there should be a closer formal relation between the recommendations of the Commission and the implementation of such by the DTI. The government clearly should have the right to over-rule the recommendations of an 'independent' agency, but both it and the other interests involved ought to be aware of the costs of so doing. In other words, the agency concerned ought to be aware that certain recommendations are more likely to be acceptable to the government than others, and on the basis of this expectation, should perhaps undertake some contingency planning in its recommendations (e.g., by proposing second-best solutions). Our proposal here implies a formal process rather than the informal dialogue which, we understand, is beginning (as envisaged in the Conservative proposals). At the 'feedback' phase there should be some process of monitoring the effects of an accepted merger to determine how far predictions at the time of the merger have in fact materialized, and, in the event of their failure to materialize, how far this alters the agency's view of the desirability of the merger. There should also be a more general learning process leading to increased sophistication of 'trigger' and 'analysis' decision rules.

The present structure of control

We have already argued that the system as it operated under the Board & DEP did not maximize the effective operation of the tasks. Our recommended respecification of the tasks are likely, of themselves, to improve its effectiveness, and we would suggest that the main fault of the mechanism lay mainly in the inadequate specification of organizational roles and relations, and the tasks at each stage of the mechanism. However, the respecification we have attempted here does have some implications for tasks and for organizational structure.

Thus, our proposals for shifting the onus of proof of merger benefits onto the companies concerned, as a method of improving information flows, also introduces a note of scepticism about the value of mergers which is absent from the current presumption. Similarly, our proposals to set up explicit guide-lines for the 'trigger' mechanism, and our suggestion that it is the Commission that is a more suitable forum than the DTI for the extraction of assurances, both imply that the executive power of the DTI in the reference procedure is reduced sharply. Consequently, the 'trigger' mechanism could be placed within an independent agency, such as a Registrar of Monopolies. How far would this improve the effectiveness of the mechanism?

The original notion of a Registrar of Monopolies and Mergers with self-referencing powers came from the Conservative Party as early as 1964. Since June, 1970, Mr. Davies has indicated that this notion had been abandoned because of certain constitutional difficulties in that the Registrar would neither be within the framework of law, nor be responsible in any conventional administrative and parliamentary sense. Self-referencing powers, apart from constitutional problems such as their source of legitimacy, would not of themselves solve the main problems, since we have advocated that, whatever system of reference one employs, the essential element (and, in the past and at the moment, lacking) is that the rules of reference should be explicitly recognized. We are broadly in sympathy with the Conservative proposal to place greater authority and legitimacy in the role of the Commission, to give it power to make public recommendations to the Minister as to possible subjects for inquiry (with the Minister retaining the formal power of reference), and to direct the Commission's attentions to more specific issues in the interests of increased brevity of investigation. However, we must hold reservations at the time of writing because the issues with which we have mainly been concerned – institutional and procedural matters – have not yet been specified in sufficient detail for comment. We know nothing of intentions in respect of the use of assurances, of the criteria to be employed in triggering a reference or in the evaluation stage, of the relationship between Commission recommendations and DTI action, nor of the onus to be placed on the companies involved, nor of the 'presumption' about merger effects that will rest behind the legislation.

Assuming that the system will remain broadly similar to its present form, we emphasize that improvements can only be made by specifying precisely the tasks of each stage in the task-flow, perhaps by reorientating those tasks along the lines we have suggested, and most important by clearly outlining the nature of the flows between the stages, and the respective organizational responsibilities, relations and functions.

A legal solution

Our analysis of the difficulties surrounding the prediction of the effect of mergers and exacting, and monitoring, assurances have led us to believe that they are so great as to raise doubts about whether any pragmatic, cost-benefit system can ever be made to work satisfactorily. If the possibility of detriment in merger is accepted, and it is the aim of public policy to prevent detriment, action has to be taken to counter it. The problem is compounded by the fact that in many, perhaps most merger cases, detriment will not occur; but it is extremely difficult to predict and control for it, and thus to take effective action concomitantly with the licensing of a merger. An obvious, and in principle, attractive alternative is to focus on *actual* detriment after a merger, should it occur, and deal with it entirely within the framework of the courts. This is essentially what the original Sherman anti-trust Act, as it is now interpreted in the USA, sets out to do. The offence is monopolization, and it is inferred from a course of action, by the defendant. Thus, for example, instead of binding a company to avoid predatory competitive behaviour – i.e., action directed at one competitor, as opposed to competition in general – such behaviour, if shown to have occurred, would attract severe legal penalties. In terms of an effective total interventionary process there is little doubt that this would work far better: the issues are perfectly justiciable (inferring behaviour from a course of action is the prime expertise of the courts); enforcement and monitoring belong to the same general system; and triggering is done via aggrieved parties. It would integrate merger policy with that of the larger firm in general. It would be credible in the eyes of the companies and, once in action, would become part of the usual decision making process surrounding company practices, including merger, particularly once a body of case law had been established; one would tend to avoid behaviour – or perhaps even a merger itself – doubtful in the eyes of the law. It is attractive perhaps most of all, for the greater equity of treatment between companies than now occurs – the element of lottery, though by no means eliminated, would be lessened. It could be combined, or not, with control over the actual process of merger. Our own judgement is that it would be important to adopt such a dual control.

But all this, desirable as it may be, requires a radical change in our methods of dealing with monopoly, perhaps too radical to be seriously entertained yet. We have therefore presented reforms in the current broad framework, dealing with the assurances problems as best we can; but we suspect that better legal solutions can be found.

APPENDIX

An example of assurances, reflecting the kinds of detrimental behaviour potential in some merger situations.

BICC/PYROTENAX;[51] *May, 1967.*

BICC were very co-operative in undertaking extensive assurances which were accepted by the Monopolies Commission.

Two general assurances were extracted:

Para. 146 'that the future commercial development (including the necessary research) and exploitation of mineral insulated cable in the UK and overseas would not be hampered by other BICC interests.'

Para. 149 'that the cost reductions achieved as a result of the merger will be used to promote the use of and expand the sale of mineral insulated cable, and to reduce net selling prices to customers (or to avoid increases that would otherwise have been necessary).'

Particular assurances were requested by interested parties who feared the market power created by the merger in the production and distribution of mineral insulated cable (mic). Most of these were accepted in more specific terms by both the Commission and BICC:

Para. 150 'that BICC will continue to supply wholesale distributors with mic on normal commercial terms*'.

Para. 157 '(i) that BICC will continue to supply other cable makers with mic, and will do so at prices and on terms*, and with service and continuity of supply, which will make it commercially practicable for them to participate in sales of mic.

'(ii) that BICC will not give its own electrical contracting organization more favourable prices, terms*, service or continuity of supply for mic than it gives to other comparable electrical contractors.

'(iii) that BICC will not offer specially favourable prices or terms* for mic to customers for the purpose of winning business in other types of cable

'(iv) that BICC will not offer uneconomic prices or terms* for mic to customers calculated to drive competitors out of the business of supplying mic.

'(v) that BICC will publish its list prices and will make available to each category of customers its terms* for mic appropriate to that category.

'(vi) that, if at any time the Board of Trade should so request, BICC will grant licences under any patents relating to mic, including accessories, on reasonable terms.'[52]

* 'The word 'terms' here includes terms and conditions as to discounts, rebates, and credit.'

Chapter Nine

THE TRADE UNION RESPONSE TO MERGERS*

John Hughes

Vice-Principal, Ruskin College, Oxford

Surprisingly, this is a subject barely touched upon in the extensive literature on mergers. There are, it is true, especial problems in identifying patterns of trade union response, given the elements of diversity both in mergers themselves and in trade union organization and policies. Besides, given the time-lags involved in adjusting trade union organization and bargaining perspectives, these are early days to judge the whole range of trade union reactions generated by recent merger movements. Nevertheless, the subject appears important enough to merit far more attention, and above all many more research enquiries,[1] than it has yet secured. The treatment that follows is in many ways superficial and incomplete, but if it stirs some interest and controversy it will have justified itself.

My approach falls into three parts:

(1) Initially, it is important to indicate specific and diverse aspects of mergers which are significant in shaping subsequent trade union response. Here, my analytical distinctions involve basic assumptions that I should make explicit. I see mergers as only one aspect of a wider shift to an economy dominated by giant firms; both the shift and its association with mergers operate in both sectors of our mixed economy. My other assumption is that powerful elements of uncertainty, risk and dynamic upheaval persist in the wake of many mergers. Even if the merger set out to ensure some degree of stabilization for the long-run development of the enterprise it cannot in fact guarantee such stability. This is not merely to say that the biter can subsequently be the one that is bitten.

(2) The main part of this paper examines the patterns of response to mergers so far exhibited by trade unions and by the TUC. It is concerned with policy response quite as much as organization.

(3) Something should be said about the *future* pattern of response; this is partly a matter of projection, partly of advocacy on my part. There are in particular a number of unresolved organizational tensions we should be conscious of.

---

*Paper presented at the Conference on Mergers and Takeovers, London, May 28 and 29, 1970.

Mergers: The Characteristics that Influence Trade Union Response

This discussion is partly concerned with *why* the mergers are taking place, *what* kinds of merger are involved, and *whose* mergers, since management attitudes to unionization may differ.

Why mergers? There are obvious problems in identifying the main causal elements in the enormous range and extent of mergers that took place in Britain in the 1960s.

(*a*) In many cases it is possible to identify the pressures exerted by dynamic competition, linked with the need for major effort in research and development. The combination thus produced, of increased risk and insecurity, and a rising threshold size of research and development effort to stay in the race, has been powerful in certain sectors. These include aircraft, electrical goods, chemicals, machinery and instruments, and vehicles.[2]

(*b*) In other cases the pursuit of 'efficiency' and cost reduction – for instance through exploiting the more obvious economies of scale – become entangled with the pursuit of greater security through market domination. A Board of Trade survey found over 80 per cent of the mergers falling within the scope of the 1965 Monopolies and Mergers Act were mergers involving firms in the same industry or product field ('horizontal'), and nearly 40 per cent of all mergers subject to review either created or strengthened a technical monopoly situation as defined by successive Monopolies Acts.[3] Of course, the strengthening of such market domination is no more than an element of stability in a wider Schumpeter-type process of 'creative destruction'; large multi-product, multi-national companies pursuing concentration within the 'parent' country at the same time as further development of subsidiaries abroad.[4]

(*c*) Large-scale takeovers, and accompanying regrouping of resources, by *some* firms have altered the whole balance of markets and relative market shares. Such destabilization and the prospect of more to come has driven other firms to seek protective alliances, defensive mergers. We are looking at a chain reaction; it is not the sort of process major firms can stand aside from.

(*d*) All these motives for mergers are to an important extent influenced in their timing and in their success or failure by financial management of the takeover. This requires careful timing of bids, and some element of stage management of share prices. These considerations play an important role in the subsequent early stages of management of the merged firm. It is clear that there is excessive concern to achieve short-run results, such as increased profitability, since there is continuing manoeuvering for position in the stock market. Thus, bunching of takeovers, generated by financial considerations as to timing, may be carried over into a bunching of hastily contrived post-merger 'rationalization' measures.

In all this, there are at least risks from the 'bounded rationality' of those managing the new industrial and commercial aggregates. Directors caught up in the complexities of new organizational patterns and a revision of production requirements and market expectations, caught up, too, in a continuing concern for financial manipulation (whether the firm is being aggressive or defensive about further takeovers), such directors may not think through rationally the new industrial relations situation they are creating. They may not fully consider short-term implications, let alone longer run issues. This is, I suppose, simply to say that when you study why mergers have occurred, you become very conscious of the number of loose ends involved – for all the talk there may be of corporate planning. And labour relations are likely to feature among the loose ends.

What mergers? The impact of mergers on labour utilization, plant loading, and the whole range of industrial relations procedures is partly a question of what kind of merger. Has it further *diversified* the activities of the company? Or are there wide areas of overlap of the range of products or services, so that the combined range is capable of standardization and simplification? We know all too little about this, though the high proportion of mergers classified as predominantly 'horizontal' suggests there has often been potential scope for such simplification. Nor do we know enough about post-merger experience of the pursuit of more coherent organization.

Thus, even if the product range ('industry') of merging firms is the same, the merged firm may not inherit an industrial relations pattern of a consistent kind, or methods of wage payment that have been systematized. *Successive* mergers may add to the complexity, while not producing enough organizational stability to encourage management to grasp the nettle of fragmented industrial relations and pay systems. One might take the complex series of mergers that led up to the formation of British Leyland Motors as an example.

Perhaps at this point one can offer the simple generalization that if major re-grouping and mergers can be foreseen, and the pay system *is* standardized, this is not exactly the time to de-stabilize and fragment it. Yet that unlikely behaviour is what has been experienced in the local government world, since the Prices and Incomes Board increased the pressure on local authorities to develop fragmented incentive-schemes (not based on any standard measures of performance). Assuming we proceed to a major re-grouping of local authorities into the large ones envisaged in the *Maud Report,* they will have some difficulty in resolving these newly-created problems of pay systems and variations in standards within the new authorities.

Whose mergers? There is a simple but important point here. Mergers may be between firms whose labour forces are largely or almost entirely unionized, or there may be a much lower level of unionization, in part or the whole of the new enterprise. These shifts, and the accompanying question of higher management's attitudes to unionization, may turn out to be of major importance.

Two examples may be used. Steel nationalization (the largest horizontal merger of any in the 1960s) meant that the merger was handled by a higher management required to accept unionization at all occupational levels. This replaced the various restraints on white collar unionization in the constituent steel companies, which up to then had left white collar grades only partly unionized. As we know, subsequently there was an awkward, and awkwardly handled, issue as to which trade unions should be recognized as competent to recruit such workers into membership and represent them.[5]

The second example is one where the management of the firm taking over others was hostile to unionism. The details emerge in the Commission on Industrial Relations investigation of General Accident Assurance.[6] In this case the unionization that had been built up in a firm taken over (Yorkshire Insurance) was swamped, the base for recognition and collective bargaining undermined. 'Almost certain recognition', said the union concerned, 'had been snatched out of its hands'.

It is important to recognize the diversity in levels of unionization of the labour force involved in major mergers in recent years, even when the merger does not involve as dramatic a reversal of the previous industrial relations pattern as in the two cases mentioned. If we take the sectors most affected by the merger waves of the 1960s, we could group them as follows:

High level of unionization: paper and publishing; vehicles; steel.
Intermediate level of unionization: electrical engineering; textiles; chemicals.
Lower level of unionization: clothing; distributive trades; banking and insurance; food and drink.

Now, even where there is a high level of unionization, and union representation of the labour force is fully accepted and effective, mergers may have significant effects. For they may alter the relative size and influence of particular unions within the new combine. This may de-stabilize the balance of inter-union relationships; it may precipitate more active or more competitive organizational efforts on the part of some unions, it may lead some to support and some to oppose attempts at re-shaping collective bargaining units and wage systems within the merged enterprise. But in addition, where mergers are taking place in sectors where unionism is weak, the interest of trade unions embraces an even wider field. Is the merger a threat to what recognition and organization exists, or an opportunity for union growth? Since mergers may bring with them the imposition of a particular firm's labour management approach on other firms taken over, there may be a great deal at stake besides short-period concern at employment security.

How the Trade Unions have Responded

It is necessary to distinguish two levels of response. One of these is concerned with detailed adjustment to particular merger proposals or situations. The other is concerned with a wider response to the process of mergers, taken as a whole. If anything, the wider response has been the more significant so far. But to grasp the nature of both levels of response we have to recognize some relevant elements in the nature of trade unionism.

In the first place it is far too narrow an approach to view trade unions simply as 'bargaining agents'. They *are* that, and consequently mergers and post-merger rationalization produce challenges to them as bargainers as well as longer run potential advantages. But they are also more than collective bargainers. Especially where their industrial bargaining position is weak, or bargaining cannot readily reach through to the main decision-making process that is relevant, trade unions have been and remain interested in reinforcing their industrial bargaining pressure by protective legislation, by securing the operation of state agencies in a supporting role. There are, too, palpable institutional interests; the direct interest in unionization of a particular labour force connects with a more complex interest in the power and authority of particular unions, and their further growth. Finally, the trade union provides a system of linkages; however imperfectly, unions ensure access from the shopfloor to a wider regulatory, co-ordinated mechanism of protection and policy formation. The system of linkages, in the widest sense of self-government, is concerned with bargaining – but also with much else. Mergers intrude new sets of relationships. The unions have to add these to the complex linkages that already operate; what pattern of group representation develops, how are new connections formed and for what functions? These are matters that affect power relationships within the union, as well as inter-union relations and more narrow bargaining responses.

Amalgamations

One of the most striking aspects of the wider response of trade unions to the pace and scale of company mergers was the formation in the 1960s of major trade union amalgamations.

The amalgamations are not *simply* a response to mergers and the increasing dominance of giant firms in the economy. Trade unions, like many companies, are caught up in competitive pressures and are conscious of the need to formulate a viable growth policy. In much the same way as companies there is an obvious impetus to 'integration'; the union has to determine its attitude to non-unionized (or under-unionized) groups of workers with whom its members are brought into contact through the ramifications of production processes. Thus unions may increasingly become 'open' in the recruitment that marks their growth path; in this sense 'general' unions may be seen as equivalent to conglomerates, but many other unions retain a more distinct sense of linkage (either vertically to 'allied' industries, or to other occupational groups in their original industry).[7] 'Open' unions may find themselves in wider competition for membership, or in a network of contacts with other unions, as a result. One constructive solution may be that of amalgamation. Thus the amalgamation of NATSOPA and the Paperworkers' to form SOGAT was an exercise in vertical integration in print and paper that anticipated by several years the Reed-IPC merger. Indeed, it may be that the Reed-IPC merger will help to create a stronger sense of the relevance of SOGAT since its two constituent unions had hardly gone very far in the consummation of their marriage and the amalgamation was being questioned from within. Such an example serves to remind us that amalgamation is not simply a mechanical response to an antecedent merger; both may be seen as relevant responses to much the same complex production system and related questions of market and growth.

There is much that is analogous in the structural pattern of the large firm and the large trade union. But the *constitutional* principles and power relationships involved in a successful trade union merger are distinctly different from those attached to company mergers. The similarities in structural pattern might be set down somewhat crudely as follows:

Large trade union	*Large firm*
An established membership *base,* or *bases* (often connected by processes of production and distribution).	Internal 'integration' of processes.
Likely to play predominant role in bargaining etc., for its main membership base.	Interest in establishing element of market domination, or leadership in certain product range.
Leading role of the union diminishing in wider range of industries or occupations in which it has pockets of membership; this shading off of its power often regional in character.	Market power shading off in wider product range, or in other regional or national markets in main product range.
External links with other unions (joint industrial councils etc.; 'workers' sides'), but also elements of competition (modified by inter-union agreements, and by 'Bridlington Rules' of TUC).	External relations through market remain significant over wide range of functions and products; competitiveness modified by elements of co-operation (e.g., trade associations, employers' federations), but of pervasive importance in longer run (via innovations etc.).

At least there are enough similarities between the two for it to be understandable that both the forces making for company mergers, and the mergers themselves and their industrial impact, should also operate to drive trade unions towards structural re-organization. But trade union amalgamations have other requirements.

In essence, in order to attract major unions into an amalgamation a *federal* pattern of trade union government has been necessary – that is a significant and continuing degree of group identity, elements of autonomy, and specific representation and servicing for the main groups involved. The attractive appeal has to be felt by both membership and the union hierarchy of officers if it is to succeed. The pattern is exhibited of old by the Transport and General Workers Union, but more recently has been an important requirement for unions as diverse as NALGO, the Boilermakers', SOGAT, and most recently of all the new Amalgamated Union of Engineering Workers (which has now brought the AEU, Foundryworkers', Draughtsmen, and Constructional Engineers' within a federal framework). There are a number of comments to make on this basic pattern.

First, we should not expect a large trade union of this kind to operate as a 'unitary' form of organization. There seems to be some tendency to accept that we need to abandon a 'unitary' concept of industrial relations in the business enterprise in favour of a 'pluralistic' framework of reference.[8] But we should not then go on to assume that trade unionism should operate in the tidy way that 'unitary' assumptions might suggest. In fact there are, persistently, group interests that need to be adequately represented and it is one function of trade union leadership to reconcile. The federal structure of large 'open' trade unions has meant the development of industrial and occupational groupings within the multi-industrial and multi-occupational straddle. Trade union leadership is concerned with problem solving, therefore, within two pluralistic frameworks; that generated by the necessary complexity of representation within and between trade unions, and that caught up in the disputes and discussions with management (and beyond that, the state).

Secondly, because of these features, there is not normally a single act of creation involved in the formation of a new amalgamated trade union. Instead there are initial 'bridging' rules producing joint decision-making over agreed subject areas, but the constitutional practices and practical autonomy of internal government of the merging unions may largely continue. Subsequently, the successful unions exhibit a further shift towards rationalization of the work of full-time officers and extension of common services – that is, a slower modification of the federal pattern. The benefit of combination is found most of all where there is enhanced power in trade union councils, a greater capacity to lead in multi-union situations, reinforced recruitment strength in 'open' recruitment areas accessible to the amalgamated union. If these characteristic features of government are distinct from those of the merging business enterprise, the ones that follow are more obviously similar.

Thirdly, there is no guarantee that the direction the amalgamation movement takes represents an adequately 'planned' development. Instead, what may emerge may be a more disturbing pattern than ever. The building and construction unions can be cited as a painful example. What had been anticipated in the early 1960s was a series of amalgamations to produce three groupings, one round woodworking, one involving the building 'trowel' trades, and one metal-using. Instead, the metal-using unions concerned have linked with different unions outside building and construction (the Plumbers' with the Electrical Union; the Constructional Engineers' with the AEU; the Heating and Ventilating Engineers' with the Sheetmetal Workers'). One of the building craft unions has joined the TGWU. The main building trades union (AUBTW) is discussing a merger with the Woodworkers', but the resistance of the latter to a federal solution is an obstacle (although it has absorbed the Painters'). The other main woodworking unions are still standing aside (perhaps partly because of the uncertainty as to the autonomy they would preserve in a woodworking amalgamation and partly because of their wealth). The whole sector is one of weak unionization and inadequate union organization, but it hardly looks as if the structural upheaval is resolving the main problems and tensions involved – in some ways it may add to them.

Fourthly, the process of trade union amalgamation may still have far to go. There are many genuine possibilities, and a wide range of continuing discussions. In the last year (1969/70) there have been extensive talks between the EETU (Electricians) and the General and Municipal, though these involve real problems as to the distribution of power. NALGO has obvious possibilities of growth through amalgamation both within the public sector and possibly beyond it. The Clerical Workers' (for whom incidentally company mergers and concentration of office administration provides an expanding base of readily organizable membership) are talking with a number of suitors. There is an enormously strong case for a powerful federal union covering finance, banking and insurance. In other words, the situation is as dynamic, and the process as incomplete as is the case with company mergers.

The outcome of all this is not necessarily to produce a more unified pattern of trade union organization within the giant firm (although the Engineering amalgamation represents a major step forward in that sector). Suppose we try to think of a typical multi-plant combine formed out of a series of mergers. For a large trade union, before or after amalgamation, grouping of its members within the new combine is only one of the networks of communication, representation, and internal and external comparison, that it is caught up in. We can hardly ask trade union organization to correspond with any exactness to the shifting frontier of large business enterprise, merging at one point and 'hiving off' at another. A trade union's organizational reactions can only be *ad hoc,* and need to retain flexibility. There may after all be more significant identity between similar product departments in different enterprises than between the far flung extremes of product range that may carry the name of a single corporate enterprise. Moreover, it is difficult for the trade unions through amalgamation alone to tidy the system of worker representation. This needs both machinery for and experience of planned exchange of membership, and orderly re-grouping of spheres of influence. This is quite as difficult to come by in the trade union movement as it is over in business itself.

Interventionism and the Trade Union Movement

If amalgamations merely connect with and to some extent mirror the merger process, at least the policy responses of the trades union movement have been more direct. What has happened is of considerable significance. For, faced with the rising tempo and scale of mergers, the TUC – as representative of the trade unions collectively – has demanded more state intervention and more public accountability.

Considering that in the later 1960s the trade union experience of incomes policy was leading them to resist state intervention and dictation in the incomes field, and that in 1969 there was a major confrontation as a result of the state reaching for a 'punitive' interventionist role in disputes, their response to mergers is important. It is a somewhat surprising tailpiece to trade union suspicion over the coercive role that the state appeared to be assuming in industrial relations, to find the TUC using the merger process to recreate a recognizably socialist series of demands as to the role of an interventionist state in industrial organization.

One aspect of this has been concerned with the extent to which public agencies involved in the merger process may take account of the employment and other interests of employees affected, and recognize, too, trade union concern about organizational rights. This is not mainly a question of the extent to which the Monopolies Commission may have paid attention to trade union representations, if only because only about three out of each hundred mergers falling within the scope of the 1965 Act have been referred to the Commission. It is rather more concerned with the practice of the Industrial Re-organization Corporation, and with the criteria used by the inter-departmental Mergers Panel that scrutinizes takeovers falling within the legislation. In fact, it is one of the surprises of the work of an ostensibly social democratic government that these agencies showed minimal interest in the industrial relations aspects of mergers until brought under more pressure by the TUC's growing interest in the subject.

The TUC used the medium of its annual *Economic Reviews* – and the departmental discussions associated with those documents – to press for a widening of the notion of public interest that these agencies were using to embrace general principles safeguarding both employee and trade union interests. When discussions were held with the IRC, that body pointed out that its statute had not explicitly raised the question of the public interest in terms of industrial relations practice, but 'increasing attention' was being given. The IRC undertook to have full consultation with the unions on all matters affecting the work force in the firms it controlled.[9] If anything, it looks as if the IRC has been more sympathetic to the TUC proposal that state agencies should back a 'code' of good industrial relations practice in mergers than has the government. For ministers in their discussions with the TUC talked of 'encouraging rather than compelling' companies involved in mergers to accept the need for good industrial relations, and in their practice have largely limited themselves to urging on companies the practices outlined in the DEP booklet *Dealing with Redundancies* – which is itself a weak approach and particularly ambiguous about the degree of trade union recognition required and the role of collective bargaining in handling manpower planning.[10]

The TUC chose to set out its views on a 'code' of industrial relations practice in Chapter 4 of the 1969 TUC *Economic Review* and Chapter 3 of the 1970 *Review*. Thus although it did not succeed in its demand that government agencies should 'require' companies to accept the code 'as a condition of the receipt of government assistance for . . . re-organization and as a condition of approval of proposed mergers', at least its exposition helped to educate member unions of the TUC and to co-ordinate their pressures on companies involved in mergers.

The general objective expressed by the TUC is that 'adequate guarantees must be provided to employees to safeguard their interests, and that standards of industrial relations must be raised to the level of the best practices, in procedures and facilities as well as in substantive agreements'. That may well stand as a clear and significant statement of the potential that trade unions may seek to exploit in the merger process – a levelling up to the best standards. More specifically the TUC argue for negotiation of agreements covering five main areas:–

(i) Recognition of *bona fide* trade unions, and facilities for workplace representatives to deal with members' problems and for trade union officials to recruit.

(ii) Machinery for negotiation and consultation, with procedures for avoidance of disputes and for appeals against dismissals.

(iii) Information to unions about the manpower plans of the merging firms, including information about structural changes, production policies, and employment policies (including recruitment, training, redeployment and redundancy). The TUC argue for joint examination of marketing and manpower projections and joint arrangements about manpower allocation, recruitment, transfers and training opportunities.

(iv) Procedures for dealing with redundancies.

(v) Agreement by the company to negotiate adequate compensation not only to redundant workers but also to those whose income, promotion prospects or seniority are affected by re-organization.

It is difficult to judge as yet the significance of the TUC efforts to identify guidelines for agreements that would fit merger situations. Certainly the state agencies concerned with mergers have been made more alert to industrial relations aspects. But in practice the watch on impending mergers by the trade unions and the TUC does not appear to have been a very exacting one. It is possible that at the level of particular trade unions there simply are not the specialized services that could analyse and identify the likely implications and consequences of specific mergers. The TUC has expressed its willingness to help co-ordinate trade union response ('bringing together the unions involved . . . providing information and initial servicing'), but it has to step delicately in areas of specific trade union interest. Besides, in the years of most hectic merger activity, its own departments were under-strength and struggling to cope with the work load generated by incomes policy, increased intervention in disputes, and extensive consultations and arguments on wider questions of industrial relations policy in the aftermath of the *Donovan Report.*

The TUC used the *Economic Reviews* also to express a wider view as to the need for a more pervasive scrutiny of the merger process, more accountability over merged firms and over giant companies in general. Thus it argued for more explicit guarantees from companies when the Merger Panel is examining proposed mergers, stronger informational requirements, post-merger examination, public directors where the firm achieves a dominant market position, and the application of such principles of accountability to all large firms including multi-nationals. Both the Labour Government's Industrial Relations Bill and its proposals for a Commission on Industry and Manpower fitted in with this approach, at least in adopting definitions of size of firm which brought companies within an extensive network of public accountability. By 1970, however, the TUC had already moved beyond what the Labour Government was contemplating to pursue the idea of linking such a system of accountability with the process of planning economic development.

It is not difficult to see how the demands of the TUC – the code of conduct, the informational demands, the link with forward planning – over mergers connect comprehensively with trade union interests in dealing with giant firms. But we should not ignore the overtones of interventionist socialism, reworked to fit a modern context. If private sector industry does not like the new-found programmatic socialism of the TUC, it should note how far the felt insecurity – of jobs and of trade union organizational rights – generated by mergers has drawn the trade unions on. Within the merger process, development of stronger state agencies and the further expansion of the public sector may have appeared to offer firmer guarantees of effective unionization and trade union influence.

There is besides one further aspect of these general policy directions in which the trade unions have been moving. At the very moment when statutorily backed intervention in incomes determination, and the PIB as its main probe, were repudiated by Congress, the trade union concern over mergers offered an alternative mode of operation. What was unpalatable on its own was accepted and indeed welcomed by the TUC as part of a re-working of state intervention on mergers. The new Conservative administration if it merely repudiates the notion of a Commission on Industry and Manpower will find it difficult to maintain a serious scrutiny of wage and salary claims and settlements able to command some degree of trade union consent.

Trade Union Response: The Detail

To come down from these exalted heights to specific problems of detail, trade union response may be usefully viewed under three headings.

(*a*) *The defensive*

In the first place, defensiveness may be a matter of trade union anxiety as to the organizational rights that may be recognized by the new combine. This is particularly in evidence in sectors where unionization is patchy. Thus, the evidence presented by the Union of Shop Distributive and Allied Workers to the Monopolies Commission was opposed to the proposed takeover by United Drapery of Burton's. The fear was that the degree of organization and recognition secured within Burton's would be in jeopardy in the merged company, since the United Drapery management was expected to be the dominant force had the merger gone through. Similarly, in the case already mentioned earlier, the unionization achieved in the smaller Yorkshire Insurance Company was diluted by the takeover by General Accident, with its management ideology resistant to trade union recognition. The check to trade union growth created by a higher management denying recognition and discouraging recruitment is evident in this case. The trade union concerned claimed that even the mere knowledge that the Commission on Industrial Relations was considering the recognition question in this case led to a considerable rise in membership.

More widespread and more publicized has been trade union concern that post-merger re-organization could affect income and job security. This is not simply a question of the handling of closures, but also the problems involved in transfers of work and of workers. The variety of possible combinations of re-grouping and transfer of resources in the case of a large multi-plant, multi-product, merger gives management very considerable initiative. It is palpably difficult for trade unions to co-ordinate their response across the whole combine since some areas and plants will gain what others lose; this certainly appeared to be the case in the major re-organizations and outright closures following the GEC/AEI takeover.[11]

Where the trade union side in such situations is made up of a number of unions, such a situation may nevertheless act as a unifying force, encouraging a joint trade union response. Thus GEC/AEI/EEC in combination have produced a standing joint council of the trade unions concerned which the combine uses as a channel of consultation. But the diversity of industrial and product range within the combine makes the linkages established even by individual unions complicated to handle.[12]

In the case of the mammoth 'merger' that created the nationalized British Steel Corporation, the trade union response was to establish a joint committee that works within the framework of the TUC and is serviced by its departments. (It seems strange that it has occurred to no-one to use the same basis for something as important as trade union co-ordination within the electrical engineering sector.) This joint trade union Steel Committee has in fact succeeded much more than equivalent organizations in the private sector in securing understandings on post-merger re-organization and the way it is handled. Thus, discussions with the Steel Corporation produced an 'early warning' system on plant closures giving six months prior notice, and a joint corporation/trade union working party has been established on security of employment and continuity of income.

(*b*) *Competitive*

The normal post-merger pattern appears to have been some wider definition of organizational and recruitment interests within the new combines by specific trade unions, rather than any jointly planned trade union exercise. Earlier post-war experience of the response to the organizational upheavals of nationalization suggested that this would be the case. (That, for instance, was when the Railway Clerks broadened out to become the Transport Salaried Staffs, and when NALGO followed the members who found their local government enterprises and hospitals being taken over into national services and thereby became a public sector instead of merely a local government union.) Where a firm base for membership has been provided by recognition, specific bargaining arrangements, and those limits on inter-union competition known as the 'Bridlington rules', there is little likelihood of major re-grouping of members between unions except through amalgamation. But there may be considerable rivalry in seeking to recruit in only partly-unionized sectors of the combine. The example of white collar recruitment in the Steel Corporation is notorious and has been mentioned already. The CIR investigation of industrial relations at Birmid Qualcast provides a recent private sector case study. In this case, the merged firm found itself caught up in a series of damaging disputes. The fragmentation of bargaining units within the company which had recently been created out of mergers provided a series of platforms for competing multi-unionism. The Transport and General Workers' Union in particular had been actively recruiting in what had previously been under-unionized sections, and was using what one might call the demonstration effect of a militant pursuit of collective bargaining as an aid to recruitment. The company through its mergers had inherited a sectionalized bargaining system that lent itself to this pressure, but lacked any managerial policies that would resolve these tensions.

With this recognition that with overlapping multi-unionism a post-merger system of industrial relations may offer a dispute-strewn path to fuller unionization, we should turn to the more positive aspect for trade unions – that is, the scope for 'levelling-up'.

(c) *Potential improvement*

Empirical studies relating the degree of unionization to size of economic units have dealt with 'establishment', size rather than firms as such. Nevertheless, there is little doubt that the organizational changes stemming from mergers are likely to strengthen the position of trade unions in many cases where not only production but also administration and research are concentrated into larger units. Official surveys carried out at the time of the Royal Commission on Trade Unions showed clearly the contrast between large and small establishments. So far as adult full-time workers were concerned, establishments with 100 or more workers accounted for 63 per cent of all trade unionists but only 36 per cent of all non-unionists (one only has to apply the residual percentages to the establishments with under 100 workers to sense the contrast). As a further indicator of effective 'shop-floor' organization, it was also estimated that 78 per cent of the shop stewards surveyed were working in the 100+ establishments. It is at least worthy of note that 1969–70 represented a new break-through in terms of trade union membership. At a time when total employment has, if anything, been contracting slowly, trade union membership has begun to rise quite significantly, notably (but not exclusively) in the white collar field. Clearly, such factors as increased official trade union militancy – and in money wage terms 'success' – and the shift in attitude to white collar unionization notably since the *Donovan Report* have contributed to this rise. But it would seem reasonable to suggest also that the cumulative effect of the mergers of the 1960s is here also apparent, creating both some of the motives for joining a union and some of the increased organizational opportunities required if the new areas of unionization are to be firmly based.

The post-merger environment is obviously a suitable one for pressure, perhaps over a long period of time, for 'levelling up'. Of course, so far as wages and conditions are concerned, the force of new internal comparisons within the merged firm will depend on how far the merger involved a combination of similar rather than diverse industrial and commercial operations. (It will depend, too, on the pace at which union communications – official or unofficial – and 'combine' organization turn the raw material for bargaining and agitational comparisons into actual bargaining strategy.) But even where wage systems and job requirements are diversified, there is considerable scope for recognition and the practical facilities afforded trade unions, that is for the characteristics of procedures in their widest sense, to be levelled up to the best practices in the pre-merger firms. The same may be true of bargaining over aspects of manpower planning, such as transfers and compensation. All in all, there is considerable leverage for trade unions where the pre-requisites of established recognition and an adequate degree of unionization to ensure bargaining strength are already present in the merging firms. It need hardly be said that there may be significant elements of long-run cost to the firm in such a process, which it may not have fully accounted for when the pros and cons of merger were examined.

It is interesting to take an example where the process discussed above took place very swiftly, and where the management of the merged firm clearly recognized what was involved and took a rational view of the advantages to them of establishing for the new merger a basis of 'good' – albeit more unionized – staff relations. The National Union of Bank Employees went to the 1968 TUC to express anxiety as to the lack of recognition they had secured and the threat to members' security and prospects in view of pending mergers in commercial banking. But in fact, in the months that followed the National Westminster merger NUBE were afforded recognition, new agreements were negotiated based on levelling up to the best conditions in the constituent banks, and in a further happy touch £1 million was distributed as a merger bonus to staff in recognition of the post-merger adaptation required from them.[13] At the 1969 TUC, NUBE re-appears holding this up as a model and demanding pressure on other commercial banks to handle recognition in the same way. Meanwhile back in the National Westminster:

'[The National Westminster's] attitude has been most co-operative, and as a responsible trade union we have ourselves responded with serious and co-operative attitudes. In this newly merged bank all the staff, through their chosen representatives, are consulted in the many problems that mergers bring. This makes good industrial sense . . .'[14]

And the Future?

Where a single union operates in the merged firm no serious problems of trade union organizational response arise. It is simply a matter of how far, within the union, 'combine' servicing is pushed, e.g., employment based branches, officer specialization, conferences of 'combine' stewards, analysis of 'combine' agreements held, and so on.

But in many cases the approach required is made more complex by multi-unionism within the combine – and indeed, within Britain we may be concerned only with one part of a multi-national corporation. Among the difficulties that might be listed are the following:

there may be competitive constraints on the development of the combine co-ordination and servicing required; sectionalism of approach may only be consolidated if each union attempts to develop the democratic participation of its members on a combine basis;

joint committees of stewards may cut across this pattern and establish combine-wide links; but these are not easy to maintain beyond a fairly limited range of functions; besides they may create new areas of tension. (Are they recognized and given any role within the established bargaining procedures? And how does their decision-making connect with that of 'official' unionism?);

a particular union may have the majority in specific collective bargaining units within the merged firm, and this may be an important rallying element in that union's recruitment appeal; particular unions may therefore resist co-ordination of bargaining within the combine if this reduces the leading role exercised in specific areas of the merged firm.

This suggests there may be a case for the TUC, at least with the largest and most complex merged firms, showing more interest in co-ordinating the future work of unions within specific combines. Data and analytical services, and some initiative in handling inter-union contacts and their agendas would be obvious starting points. Unions might be more willing to see such functions in the hands of the TUC than to hand them over to one of their number. At several points such a servicing role on the part of the TUC would link with other processes that they handle; for instance, the largest firms are likely to find themselves subject to some degree of public accountability (if only over the agreements they may have to register with the Commission on Industrial Relations). Arguments about alternatives to company policy on closures or the location of development require liaison with planning agencies. The TUC could use the experience of such servicing to connect up with a wider process of co-ordination of trade union interests and policies in major sectors of the economy. At the very least, the TUC should be reviewing the experience of post-merger adaptation of trade union organization and policy in different sectors of the economy, and using such an analysis to create a more adequate awareness among its constituent trade unions of both the potentialities and the problems that mergers and their aftermath produce.

Editor's note

The SOGAT amalgamation, which is referred to on page 152, has since broken up and has reverted to the two constituent unions.

There has been an amalgamation of the Woodworkers' Union with the AUBTW, the possibility of which is referred to on page 154. Further, the TGWU have secured the amalgamation of both the Chemical Workers' Union and the Vehicle Builders' Union.

Chapter Ten

MERGERS AND SHAREHOLDERS *

Susan Dev

Lecturer in Accounting at the London School of Economics and Political Science

Outline of the Paper

The first section of this paper discusses the information needs of the shareholder.[1] It examines the nature of the information normally made available to help him with investment decisions. It then suggests that detailed forecasts published by the directors should, in theory, prove to be of considerable use for this purpose, not only at the time of a specific offer for his shares.

The second section gives some of the results of a study of bid[2] forecasts, the object of which was to assess the usefulness of published forecasts to the shareholder in evaluating the alternatives open to him. The methods of attack and defence used in these cases are discussed in the third section, in so far as they are relevant to the theme of the paper. The paper concludes with some further observations on the relevance of profit forecasts.

1. INFORMATION FOR THE SHAREHOLDER

The Basic Information Needs of the Shareholder

The shareholder, *qua* investor, in appraising his investment always needs to be forward-looking. In a routine investment appraisal, for example, he requires information to assist him in forecasting the size, timing and risk of the cash flow that is likely to come to him as a result of his continued ownership of the shares. To make a rational decision on whether to retain, increase or dispose of his holding he will compare this stream with the net cash flow from other investment possibilities. In many cases the benefits of ownership will be in the form of periodic cash dividends. Less often the expected benefit may be a liquidation dividend. The market price provides an alternative cash flow should the shareholder decide to sell at any time, thereby transferring the right to the future dividend stream to a buyer.

In the case of an offer for his holding, the shareholder's information needs are basically no different. He needs data to help him assess the relative financial merits,

* Paper presented at the Conference on Mergers and Takeovers, London, May 29 1970.

from his point of view, of the consequences of accepting or rejecting the offer, of taking no action and of selling his shares.

From the reasoning above, it appears that the rational shareholder ought to concern himself with an estimation of the future dividend stream and its associated risk. Hence, as the market price of a share reflects the value of a company to the investing public, it would seem rational that it ought to be determined by the expected dividend stream. Others would argue that the prospective earnings of a company ought to be, and are, a more important determinant of share prices.[3]

It is not proposed to pursue the argument here and it will be assumed that the shareholder is interested in assessing both the future dividend stream and earnings prospects when making an investment decision.

The Information Normally made Available to the Shareholder

The annual report and accounts and notification of half-yearly results are normally the only communications from the directors of a company to its shareholders. It is to be expected that the information they contain is used – at least to some extent – by the shareholder, or his adviser, in evaluating the prospects of a company. It is, therefore, useful at this stage to consider the purpose of the accounting report and to discuss how well the figures it contains fulfil their aim.

In its report into Company Law reform, the Jenkins' Committee[4] agreed with the *Recommendations on Accounting Principles* issued by The Institute of Chartered Accountants in England and Wales[5] that 'the primary purpose of the annual accounts of a business is to present information to the proprietors, showing how their funds have been utilized and the profits derived from such use. It has long been accepted in accounting practice that a balance sheet prepared for this purpose is an historical record and not a statement of current worth'.[6]

The historical cost basis has been defended on the grounds that it reduces to a minimum the amount of subjective opinion required in the preparation of accounts for shareholders. As is well known, when price levels are not stable, its continued use makes the interpretation of profit and loss accounts and balance sheets less significant, particularly where fixed assets are concerned. For example, the shareholder may try to assess managerial efficiency by comparing profit earned with assets employed. When figures are based on original cost the answer will vary according to when the assets were acquired. A better guide to the success of management may be to relate profit – with depreciation adjusted to current levels – to the current market value of the assets employed, a figure which may not be provided. This difficulty may, to some extent, be met by adjusting the historical figures by applying a general price index.[7]

Although the element of personal opinion may be reduced by using the historical – or adjusted historical – cost basis, the attempt to measure profit annually means that the directors of a company are forced to exercise judgement in valuing transactions that are expected to benefit both current and future years. As a result, a multiplicity of balance sheet valuations is possible each giving rise to a different yearly profit, even disregarding the price level problem. If the valuation methods all come within the bounds of accepted accounting principles, and are applied consistently, the resulting accounts could all be certified by a competent auditor as displaying a 'true and fair' view.

Not only are comparisons between companies affected by the use of different accounting conventions.[8] The apparent trend of profitability within a particular company can be varied according to the conventions chosen. Consequently, accounting reports are an imperfect tool for the shareholder to use in gauging how his company has fared financially as compared with earlier years and relative to other companies. The Institute recently announced that it intends to recommend standard accounting practices wherever possible in order to narrow the areas of differences and variety in accounting usage.[9] If a company departs from these standards, it is proposed that it should disclose the fact. It also intends to recommend that, when the accounts include significant items which depend substantially on judgements of value by directors, the accounting bases used should be disclosed. These are interesting suggestions which should enable more meaningful historical comparisons to be made.

However, even if accounting conventions were standardized, the accounting report would still provide information relating to past achievements. There seems to be no *a priori* reason why this is necessarily the best information that the directors can provide to assist the shareholder in his forward-looking task of investment appraisal.

The Need for Forecasts

Pursuing the argument further, it would appear that forecasts would be of considerable use to the shareholder in his investment decisions. From the earlier discussion, the directors' forecast of the expected future dividend stream for as far ahead as possible would seem to be the best information for the shareholder. However, it is unlikely that he would be entirely satisfied with a schedule of estimated future dividends unless this were accompanied by additional information from the company to enable him to assess their riskiness. Profit forecasts may be seen to be helpful here but the limitations of the conventional profit calculation, already mentioned, must be borne in mind when interpreting the figures. An alternative suggestion is that companies might disclose their long-run cash budgets[10] and state the assumptions upon which they are based. This would seem to be the type of supporting information that would be helpful to the shareholder and others interested in prospective company performance[11] since, in the end, profits depend on cash flows.

For the purpose of this paper, I shall consider the less radical proposition that the financial community would like to have, at least, profit forecasts – backed up by information on such matters as sales and cost forecasts, proposed capital expenditure and future financing requirements – in addition to dividend forecasts. To assist in interpreting the profit calculation, details of the methods and assumptions used in valuing stocks, calculating depreciation and dealing with other expenditure likely to benefit later years, such as research and development costs, would also be required.

There seems to be considerable merit in the directors' providing a range of forecasts rather than a single point estimate. For example, a cautious, an optimistic and the most likely projections might be given with an indication of the circumstances that were expected to affect the figures one way or the other. This would give the shareholder some idea of the range of possible results and the riskiness of the dividend stream. He could then make his own judgement of what the results would be. This would not necessarily coincide with a point estimate given by the directors.

For a forecasting system to be of real use, a detailed report and analysis of differences between actual results and forecast should, in due course, be given. This would add to the reader's knowledge of the unforeseen factors affecting the company and would enable him to form an opinion on the efficiency of management and its forecasting ability and attitude. This would help him in interpreting forecasts for future periods and especially in judging management quality.

The Usefulness of Forecasts

One of the main criticisms levelled against the publication of forecasts for any purpose relates to the difficulties of making accurate predictions when the future is uncertain. Unexpected events are bound to occur and results are unlikely to match the forecasts exactly. However, the true test of the usefulness of such a forecast is whether it leads to better decisions by the shareholder than he might otherwise have made and consequently better operation of the financial markets.

On the assumption that the public is motivated to make the most profitable use of the funds it has available for investment, its collective actions, if successful, should result in share prices reflecting their relative expected returns and risks. However, the market's expectations of these returns may well differ from those of the directors due to a disparity of information. An ill-informed investing public may place an 'incorrect' valuation on one company's shares relative to another's. At the margin, this may deny new funds to a company that, on economic grounds, should have them, thereby frustrating the efficient allocation of resources.

It is to be expected that directors are in the possession of more and better information on the details and likely financial effects of the plans they have made for the future of the company than the shareholder who is forced to rely on published accounts and other snippets of information to form his estimate of the future dividend stream. If the directors were to publish their forecasts, fewer investment mistakes might be made and this would be to the economic advantage of the community.

The Case for Compulsory Forecasts

Owing to the alleged apathy of the small shareholder and the apparent reluctance of the institutional investor to interfere too much in the internal affairs of a company, there is generally little pressure on directors to publish much detail on the future prospects of the company. In his annual statement, a chairman may give specific dividend and/or profit forecasts but they are normally only for the current year, part of which has already elapsed by the time the forecasts are made known. The fear that competitors will learn of their plans and the uncertainties involved in long-term forecasting (with the fear of criticism by the financial press if forecasts turn out to be over-optimistic) normally act as disincentives to the directors to publish forecasts further ahead than the current year, even if they believe that the company's shares are grossly undervalued by the market. That these arguments are not conclusive can be shown by the fact that there are four situations where the directors have good reason to dislike undervalued shares and in which they may be prepared to disclose further information – including forecasts – in the hope that the market will raise its valuation. First, a body of shareholders may overcome its indifference and agitate for changes in the Board in view of the latter's apparent inefficiency. Secondly, a company may require new share or loan capital and, in the absence of more detailed disclosure, this may be unobtainable or more expensive than it ought to be. Thirdly, the directors may attempt to make a takeover bid for another company and may therefore wish to reduce the cost or risk of failure by improving its market rating. Lastly, a company may find itself the unwilling target of a takeover bidder.

In recent years, a number of forecasts have been made in connection with takeover bids, sometimes for two or three years ahead. As is well known, this practice has attracted the attention of the authors of *The City Code on Take-overs and Mergers*[12] as well as the Institute whose Council has issued a statement of guidance concerning the accountants' report on forecasts required by the Code.[13] The President of the Institute stated in 1969[14] that, 'In takeover situations I believe it is desirable for directors to give forecasts if they can, otherwise shareholders would be at a disadvantage in trying to judge the value of their shares and the merits of the offer'.

To recognize the benefits of forecasts in a takeover situation is certainly a step in the right direction. But it would seem to be in the interests of the community and the shareholder (whose guardians the directors are supposed to be) that forecasts should be disclosed as a normal course of events and not only when the company is faced with a crisis. The efficient company should have nothing to fear from this practice. It could be argued that firms would adjust their plans for consistency and that this might reduce the risk of economic bottlenecks or waste of resources, hence better satisfying the wants of the community. The publication of detailed forecasts could also reveal areas where industry output was planned to be at a non-optimal level. This could enable the situation to be remedied in time, thus improving economic efficiency.

It is interesting to speculate whether directors would be motivated to scale their profit forecasts up or down for publication. In the past, the financial press has tended to be scornful of companies whose actual results have fallen short of forecast. Rather irrationally, it has often praised a company which has exceeded its forecast, rather than to suggest that its forecasting ability was poor. For this reason, in a contested bid situation, it may well be that the Board of a company being bid for[15] would be motivated to forecast a level of profit that it believed was just high enough for the bid to fail, even if it really believed a higher figure would be achieved. There could also be a tendency to conservatism if regular forecasts were made compulsory. However, one would expect Boards to gain reputations for being under- or over-optimistic in their forecasting and the market would presumably adjust for this.

2. A STUDY OF BID FORECASTS

Outline of the Study

Due to the recent interest shown in forecasts, and their theoretical appeal, it was decided to examine takeover and merger situations where specific earnings or dividend forecasts had been made for at least twelve months ahead. The object of the study was to assess the usefulness of these forecasts in specific cases to the shareholder who was interested in knowing what future profits and dividends were likely to be.

The study was restricted to forecasts made in 1967, a period long enough ago to allow a post-audit to be made. A list of quoted companies that made forecasts in 1967 for at least twelve months ahead was obtained by reading the 'Bids and Deals' section of the *Investors' Chronicle* for 1967. These are listed, and some details given, in Table 1.[16] Further information, particularly relating to the forecast and actual results, is given in the Appendix to this paper.

As the cases were examined from the shareholder's point of view, information that would have been readily available to him was used in the study. Where possible, the following data was obtained for each of the companies listed in Table 1:

(*a*) Annual report and accounts from five years prior to the bid to the present time.

(*b*) Moody Cards.

(*c*) All circulars sent to shareholders by both parties to the bid, and their advisers, including those containing the forecasts.

(*d*) Comment on the companies by the *Financial Times* and the *Investors' Chronicle* from 1966 to date.

(i) The Circumstances of the Forecasts and the Detail they Contained

In 1967, the *Investors' Chronicle* reported nearly two hundred bids and deals, yet in only six cases does it appear that specific forecasts for more than a year ahead were made. In many more cases, forecasts for a shorter period were published but the shorter the forecast the less use it would presumably be to the shareholder concerned with a more distant future.

Not surprisingly, all the forecasts were made during contested bids when the directors were under pressure. Only one company seemed eager to publish its forecasts and the figures were included in its offer document. As it had just had an unsatisfactory year, it may have considered that the bids would have more chance

Table 1

Quoted companies publishing forecasts in 1967 for more than twelve months ahead in bid situations

Date of forecast 1967		Company making forecast	Details of bid: Other party: Co. bid for	Bidder	Was bid successful?	Extent of forecast (to nearest month): Profits	Dividends	Equity Capitalization[1] (prior to bid) £ (millions)
February	4	Telephone Rentals ('TR')		GEC	No	22	10	18
July	12	International Distillers and Vintners ('IDV')		Showerings	No	35	–	23
	20	Crofts Engineers (Holdings)		Renold	Yes	17	5	16
October	21	Associated Electrical Industries ('AEI')		GEC	Yes	26	26	94
	30	General Electric Company ('GEC')	AEI		Yes	17	5	178
December	16	Allen West & Company	Electrical Apparatus		Yes	14	14	6
			Contactor Switchgear		No			
	20	Midland Aluminium ('Midland')		Central Wagon	No	18	18	2
	29	Central Wagon Company ('Central')	Midland Aluminium	–	No	13	1	1

[1] Given as an indicator of the size of the companies studied.

of succeeding if its forecasts, which showed a great improvement in profits, were published. In some cases, forecasts were virtually forced out by the bidder and, in the two cases where both sides produced forecasts, it appears that the bidder published forecasts because the biddee had already done so.

An examination of the chairmen's statements immediately prior to the bids (from which some extracts are included in the Appendix) shows that none of the companies gave specific forecasts a few months earlier when there was no pressure on them to do so. One chairman, probably the least helpful in his statement on future prospects, was prepared only two months after the Annual General Meeting to forecast profits for seventeen months ahead.

From published information made available at the time, it was apparent that the three companies which forecast furthest ahead already had systems of long-term forecasting in operation for internal use, so it must have been a simple matter for them to publish their forecasts. The largest company, GEC, was, it seems, not in the habit of forecasting results beyond the end of the current operating year and, in response to AEI's forecasts, the Board requested the operating units to prepare 'forward estimates' for the following year.

All the forecasts were prepared before the current Code was published so an accountant's report was not expected. However, it was made known at the time that two of the companies' forecasts had been examined by auditing firms. In Midland's case, the chairman reported that auditors acting for its merchant bankers 'have reported that in their opinion the forecasts of sales and profits have been prepared in a competent manner and on a fair and reasonable basis'.[17] To support his company's forecasts, IDV's chairman reported that its auditors had 'confirmed that over the past three years the Board's annual internal forecasts have, in each year, been exceeded by the results, which I suggest shows a commendable caution on the part of the Board'.

This notion that cautious forecasts are good seems widespread and, of the eight companies examined, five implied that their forecasts would be exceeded. However, none gave any indication of the extent of the conservatism, thereby making interpretation difficult, particularly for the shareholder who could find little to choose between the alternatives open to him. Even the directors who forecast a profit of a specific amount for their company were really no more helpful unless they believed that only one outcome was possible, which would be unlikely in an uncertain world.

This weakness may not be so important if the forecaster provides adequate supporting information to assist with interpretation of the figures. However, of the eight companies, six gave only forecast profit figures with no additional quantitative information. One exception was Midland which, when announcing its forecasts, gave an analysis of turnover and profits before tax for each of its five divisions for the previous five years and for the two years covered by the forecasts. It also provided an analysis of the book value of capital employed by each division at June 30, 1967. The other exception was AEI: when advising rejection of the second offer from GEC, it gave a breakdown of its forecast profits between product groupings but not for earlier years. In the absence of information to the contrary, one can only assume that in all cases the forecast profits were calculated using the companies' normal accounting conventions.[18]

In three cases, the forecasts were said to be 'subject to unforeseen circumstances'. Interpretation and comparison become very difficult when no information is given on what circumstances have been allowed for in preparing a profit forecast. As EAC's chairman said in his reply to Allen West's forecasts, 'unforeseen circumstances to the management of Allen West are not necessarily unforeseen by us'.

(ii) The New Information Conveyed by the Forecasts

The information available at any time to the various shareholders, and their advisers, may well differ. Consequently, it is difficult to say whether the information relating to future prospects released during the bid (and quantified in the forecasts) was new to the shareholder.

The purpose of considering this point is to pursue the matter of the general relevance of forecasts. If the bid – and, hence, the forecast – had not been made the shareholder may have had to rely on data such as past accounts, the chairman's statement, press comment and interim results in order to estimate the future prospects of the company. If the directors' bid forecasts could not reasonably have been predicted prior to the bid, one can suggest that they improved the shareholder's knowledge of the future, provided they proved to be nearer actual results than his pre-bid predictions.

Some would argue that, because the directors are under special pressures during a takeover bid, their forecasts can be expected to differ from those they would publish if called upon to do so in the normal course of events. This argument ignores the necessity now of an auditor's, or consultant accountant's, report on the forecasts.[19] One would expect the auditor to ask many searching questions of the officers of a company whose bid forecasts differed from those prepared for internal use prior to the bid. One would also expect him to take especial care in examining the bid forecasts of a company which, hitherto, had no budgeting or forecasting system in operation.

Using information publicly available prior to the bid, my subjective forecasts differed – often quite considerably – from the directors' forecasts. Information arising during the bids often caused me to revise my forecasts but, in all cases, I found that the directors' forecasts conveyed information to me that I could not have predicted beforehand. Provided I believed their forecasts, if I were a shareholder I would, therefore, have found them useful in the decision facing me, as they conveyed information which was otherwise not available to me. People with more information or using more sophisticated tools for prediction or whose temperaments differed from mine may have found prediction much simpler. If they were able to predict the figures fairly accurately, one could still say that the directors' forecasts were useful, as they would have confirmed their own predictions.

Two major sources of information available to any shareholder who wishes to estimate future profits are the chairman's customary annual statement and the annual accounts. It has already been mentioned that, in the cases examined, the chairmen's statements all lacked clear indications of what future profits would be. One alternative is for the shareholder to use past profits as a guide to the future despite the uneasiness he may feel that the future may not be like the past.[20] However, two major stumbling-blocks were met in the cases examined. Firstly, the chairmen of the majority of the companies explained that in certain years profits were low because of some exceptional, non-recurring event such as labour disturbances or removal to new premises. However, the effect on the profit was never quantified hence making it virtually impossible to establish what the profit would otherwise have been. This distorts any extrapolation of past figures. Secondly, five of the companies examined had had major Board changes in the few years prior to the bids. Consequently, one can expect recent profits to include exceptional gains – or losses – from reorganization and also to be affected by new management policies, again making extrapolation difficult. For example, GEC's rate of growth in profits from the time of its reorganization in the early 1960s up to the time of its bid for AEI would probably not have been expected to continue if the company were to remain in its existing form. Midland's case is especially relevant in this context as major Board changes had taken place a few months before the bid and a new chairman appointed less than a month beforehand. Past results would seem to be of very limited use in this case.

Probably of all the cases examined, TR's profit should have been the easiest to forecast as the chairman had been helpful in his statement on prospects and past profits had shown a fairly linear trend. However, this is the one case where the chairman openly stated that the internal forecasts had been revised upwards to meet the bid situation. Consequently, in the absence of the bid, the forecasts of the directors (and any good forecaster who did not anticipate the bid) would have been lower than the bid forecasts.

(iii) The Credibility of the Forecasts

For forecasts to be of use, they must be believed. Belief is subjective and can be expected to be influenced by the information available to a person and the use he makes of it, as well as his temperament and attitudes to risk and uncertainty. To assess whether others believed the forecasts, financial press comment, the reaction of the other party to the bid and share price movements were all examined.

The only forecasts about which the two press sources were openly sceptical were Midland's for 1968/9 and AEI's,[21] a scepticism apparently shared by respective bidders for these companies. Renold expressed no opinion on Croft's forecasts at the time of the bid yet, in the subsequent Annual Report, its chairman stated that the figure for 1967 was higher than should have been expected at the time of the bid.

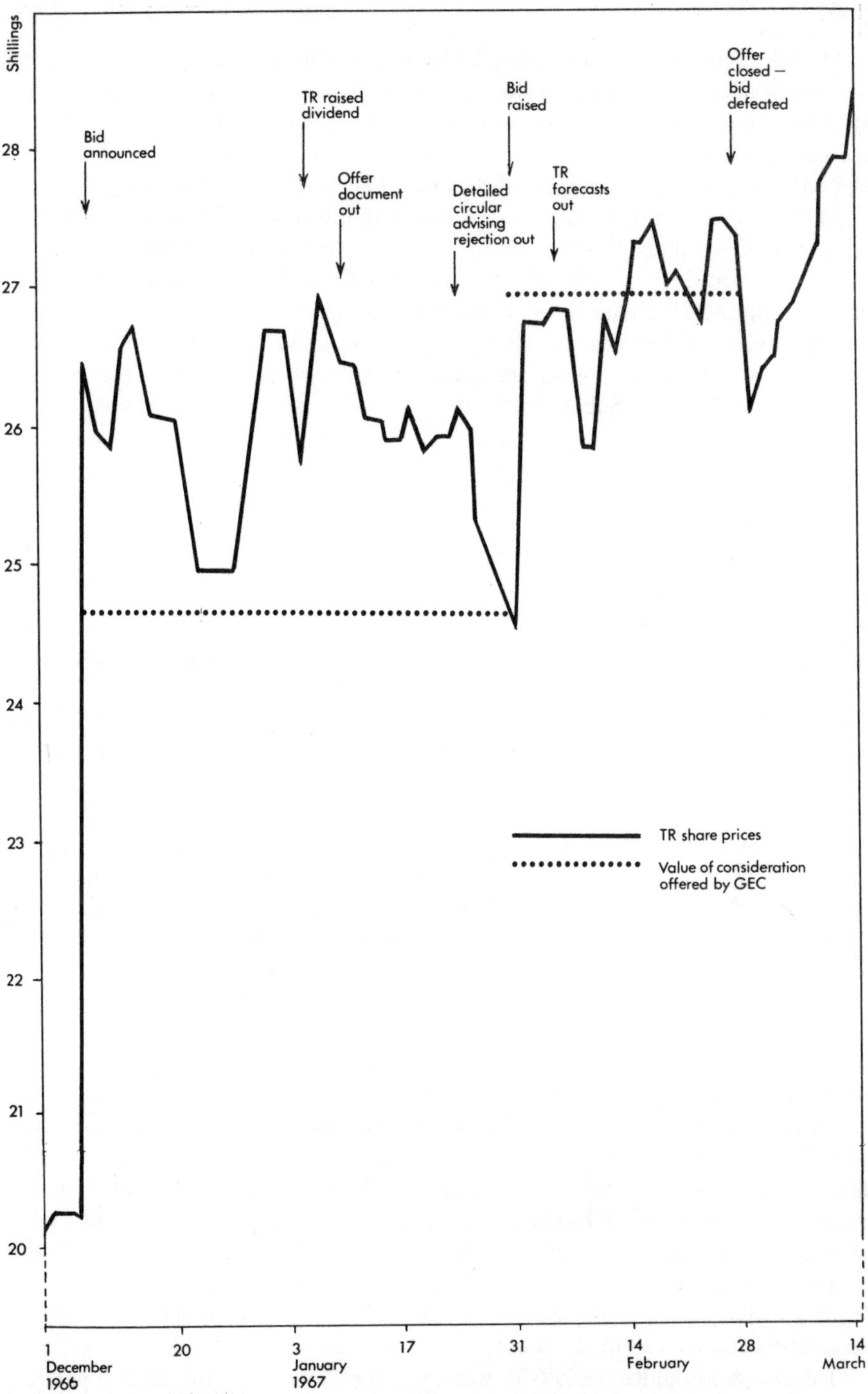

Diagram 1. Telephone Rentals Ltd – share price movements during the bid from GEC

On the assumption that a company's share price is some function of the market's estimation of its future dividend stream, one would suppose that new information affecting the expected dividend stream – such as profit forecasts – would cause the share price to alter. If the price remained unchanged after a directors' forecast was released, one may conclude that the market chose to ignore it as being unreliable, or irrelevant, or that it was in line with previous expectations so did not affect the expected dividend stream. In a non-bid situation, observation of share price movements may be a useful indicator of the belief in a forecast by the market. However, during a bid there are so many things happening at once that it is very difficult to isolate the effect of one piece of information on the share price. Typically, in the cases examined, the market price of the biddee rose at the time the bid was announced. Subsequently, it fluctuated as new information was released and as the bid terms altered. TR's share price movements are shown in Diagram 1, as an example. It was expected that the bidder's share price would also be affected by the bid but, in no case, was a noticeable reaction to the forecasts observed.

(iv) Post-audit of the Forecasts

A measure of the forecasting ability of the directors is to compare the forecasts with subsequent actual results and to examine the reasons for the divergencies. Table 2 shows actual profits as a percentage of forecast in those cases where they are comparable. In the Appendix to this paper the results are graphed and extracts from the chairmen's statements, indicating some of the reasons for the divergencies, are given.

In several cases, forecast and actual results were not readily comparable. For example, the bids for AEI and EAC both succeeded and both sides issued forecasts.[22] As the control of these companies changed, one would not expect the new managements to adopt forecasts of the managements they had supplanted and neither bidder forecast the profits it expected from the biddee. A simple addition of GEC's and AEI's separate forecasts gives a figure close to the combined actual results, but the combined profit for Allen West and EAC was below the forecast for Allen West alone. It is possible that part of the shortfall was due to rationalization and reorganization expenses charged against profits which offset the initial gains from the merger. But one can only guess as no reason at all was given for the divergence.

TR substantially exceeded its 'conservative' forecasts, yet little explanation was given for the divergence. It is possible that the shareholder who parted with his shares on the strength of the forecasts might not have done so if information on the extent of the conservatism had been disclosed. IDV also exceeded its forecast by a wide margin, but part of the difference was said to be at the expense of the following year whose results are not comparable because of a subsequent association with Watney's which was not allowed for in the forecasts as talks were only at an early stage when Showering's made its bid.

The profits for Midland and GEC were very close to forecast for the first period. However, both admitted that results in the individual divisions were off target

Table 2
Actual pre-tax profits compared with forecast

Company making forecast	Extent of profit forecast		Actual profit for year compared with forecast
Telephone Rentals	1967	(10 months)	114%
	1968		122%
International Distillers and Vintners	1967/8	(11 months)	125%
	1968/9		Not comparable
	1969/70		Not comparable
Crofts Engineers (Holdings)	1967	(5 months)	83%
	1968		Not comparable
Associated Electrical Industries	1967	(2 months)	50%
	1968		Not comparable
	1969		Not comparable
General Electric Company	1967/8	(5 months)	101%
	1968/9		Not comparable
Allen West and Company	1967/8	(2 months)	117%
	1968/9		Not comparable
Midland Aluminium	1967/8	(6 months)	102%
	1968/9		33%
Central Wagon Company	1966/7	(1 month)	104%
	1968		86%

implying a 'swings and roundabouts' effect that one might expect a diversified organization to experience.

The effect on the profit calculation of a change in control of a company received much publicity when AEI's results for 1967, prepared by GEC's staff, revealed a loss of £4·5 million instead of the forecast profit of £10 million. Of the shortfall, £9·5 million was said to be due to 'adjustments which remain matters substantially of judgement'. One place where judgement would have been used was in calculating stock obsolescence and contract provisions of £10·7 million at the end of 1967 which compared with only £2·8 million in 1966. Valuation depends on expectations and intentions and it may well be that the policies of GEC justified the greatly increased provision. In two other cases, profits were lower after a change in control than might otherwise have been expected. Croft's results after the takeover by Renold indicated a profit lower than forecast and, in Midland's case, the accounts immediately prior to the bid – which showed a sizeable loss – were prepared under the direction of the newly-constituted Board. In neither case is there any indication whether the shortfall was due to the new management taking a more severe look at the assets it had inherited than the previous management would have done. If this were a contributing factor, the effect would be to enhance the profit performance of the new management in the next, or later, years.

3. METHODS OF ATTACK AND DEFENCE

In this section, the methods of attack and defence used in the cases studied will be examined in so far as they are relevant to the theme of the paper.

(i) The Terms of the Bid

Of the six defending chairmen, the initial reaction of five was to announce that the terms of the offer made to his company's shareholders were inadequate, sometimes in form as well as amount in spite of the bidder having offered more than the pre-bid share price. This is tantamount to saying that, in the chairman's opinion, the market under-valued the future prospects of the company under the control of the existing Board. Subsequently, in each case, more and more information was released to substantiate the chairman's initial remark. In the absence of the bid, it is a matter of speculation whether any of the chairmen would have been prepared to disclose further information to enable the market to revise its assessment of the share value to a more 'correct' level if it had wished.

For example, prior to the bid from GEC, TR's share price had hovered around 20s/3d. GEC initially offered loan stock worth about 24s/9d which was said to be 'completely inadequate'. Later the consideration was raised to 27s/0d after which TR's chairman published figures said to indicate that the shares were worth 30s/0d. – almost 50 per cent above the pre-bid price.

(ii) Dividend Increases

Table 3 shows the dividends that each company had paid on its ordinary shares in the few years prior to the bid; the dividends forecast during the bid and subsequent payments for comparison with the forecasts. In each case, the forecast dividends were in excess of the most recent payment. Taking into account the previous dividend pattern, the forecast profits and the cover, it seems that in some cases the forecast dividend increase was a bid tactic. In other words, if the bid had not been made, dividends would not have been as high as those forecast during the bid.[23] It is interesting to examine why a company may decide to increase its dividend unexpectedly.

First, one can consider the information that the increase may be perceived to convey. Frequently, companies do not raise their dividends unless they expect to be able to pay at least the revised amount in later years.[24] Thus an increased dividend may imply that future dividends will not be less than this sum. If the market was not anticipating this revised dividend stream, one would expect the share price to rise or, in a bid situation, at least to have a favourable impression on the shareholders' estimation of the potential financial benefits that will accrue to them under existing control.

In bid circulars, it is customary to show the potential income to the shareholder from accepting or rejecting the bid, the comparison being based on the most recent dividends unless forecasts have been made. Hence, in a bid situation, another explanation for an increased dividend is to make the alternative look relatively more attractive purely from a short-term income point of view.

However, to increase dividends means that less cash is retained in the company to earn future profits and, hence, enable future dividends to be increased. Whether a company is acting in the best interests of its existing shareholders by raising its

Table 3

Ordinary share dividends forecast and paid

Year in which financial period ended	Telephone Rentals %	IDV %	Crofts %	AEI %	GEC %	Allen West %	Midland Aluminium %	Central Wagon %
1959	8·7							
1960	8·7		14·2					
1961	10·4		16·7	10·0				
1962	11·1		18·3	10·0	4·1			
1963	14·6	12·1	20·0	10·0	4·1	11·0	18·0	7·5
1964	17·5	12·1	22·0	12·0	6·0	11·0	20·0	7·5
1965	17·5	13·0	22·0	13·0	8·5	11·0	20·0	10·0
	*							
1966	25·0 (F)							
	25·0	13·0	22·0	13·0	10·0	11·0	20·0	12·0
		*	*	*				*
1967	30·0 (F)		30·0 (F)	13·0 (F)				22·0 (F) (1)
	31·2	19·0		15·0 (F)	10·5	8·0	3·0	22·0
					*	*	*	
1968				15·0 (F)	13·5 (F)	10·0 (F)	6·0 (F)	17·75 (F)
		19·6			13·5	10·0	6·0	18·2
1969				19·0 (F)		12·0 (F)	20·0 (F)	
		20·0				12·0	10·0	

(1) Central's forecast was for a 15 month period.
* indicates when the bid was made.
(F) Dividend forecasts during the bid – AEI revised its forecast for 1967 at a later stage during the bid.

dividend is a complex matter, the relative rates of return on the reinvestment opportunities of the company and its shareholders being an important factor in determining the point.

(iii) **Information on the Advantages of the Proposed Merger**

When a shareholder is faced with an offer for his shares, he needs to weigh up the financial consequences of accepting or rejecting the offer. Assuming he finds profit forecasts helpful in this choice, he will in all cases want to know the expected profit of the company of which he is already a shareholder. If the alternative offered is to become a shareholder or creditor of the bidding company, he will also want to know what the profits of the combined enterprise will be.

Consequently, in circulars from the bidding company, or its advisers, one would hope to find a clear indication of the benefits to be derived from a change in control. In all the cases examined, both parties to the bids were in the same industry. The bidders stressed the areas of overlap and indicated where economies and rationalization measures could be put into effect if the two companies were to combine. In not one of the cases, however, were the expected benefits from the merger quantified in any precise way. Three of the bids failed and the fact that each bidder was prepared to raise the terms of its offer up to a certain limit, and no more, suggests that some arithmetic on the benefits had previously been done. Publication of the figures might well have made the shareholder's decision less difficult and could possibly have helped the bid to succeed.

(iv) **Alternative Proposals by the Biddee**

AEI announced details of its own rationalization proposals during the bid so shareholders were, in effect, being asked to weigh up AEI's scheme against GEC's. However, AEI's forecasts specifically excluded the additional profits expected to accrue to existing shareholders from the rationalization scheme it proposed to put into effect if the bid failed. It can be argued, therefore, that the forecasts published were not those most relevant to AEI's defence. In the document advising rejection of GEC's bid, the chairman of AEI announced that Lord Beeching was to join the Board in January 1968 with a view to becoming chairman in the first half of the year although the present chairman would not reach retiring age until late 1969. To announce the appointment during the bid can also be viewed as a defence tactic designed to support AEI's case.

In three cases, defending companies announced that talks were in progress with other companies. In two of these the talks were said to be at too early a stage for the possible benefits to be given and, in the third, the chairman announced during the bid period that agreement had been reached to acquire another company's equity for cash. The purchase was seen to be a logical extension of the business and would come into effect if the bidder's offer lapsed or was withdrawn.

(v) Appeals to History

History produces evidence which may or may not be helpful in predicting the future course of events. Successes or failures achieved in the past will not necessarily be repeated in the future if the circumstances and environment are quite different. In the cases examined, recent management achievements and accounting results were frequently referred to in bid circulars.

For example, Showering's chairman stressed the economies and profits derived from his company's acquisition of Harvey's of Bristol eighteen months before the bid for IDV. He was confident that similar benefits would arise from the proposed amalgamation with IDV. The chairman of GEC emphasized his company's recent profit growth and compared it with AEI's less successful record. He also pointed out that AEI's forecasts should 'be treated with considerable caution, particularly in the light of constantly confounded forecasts and statements made by the Board of AEI in the last six years'. It should, however, be noted that AEI had had major Board and management changes at the beginning of 1967 which had not yet had time to show results.

Book values of assets, even as approximations of current values, are of little relevance if their earning power gives them a greater value as management's intentions would presumably be to continue the business as opposed to selling off the assets. Yet two of the defending companies compared the relative book values of the two parties in support of their claims that their shareholders were being offered an insufficient proportion of the equity of the combined enterprise. In two cases, the bidders compared the value of the consideration offered with the asset values, one stating that 'the increased offer is substantially in excess of the asset value'.

The Electrical Apparatus Company was reluctant to forecast in reply to Allen West's bid because, in the chairman's opinion, 'the only reliable guide to future profits is the experience gained over many years of trading in the industry and historical profits which reflect the ups and downs of trading over a reasonable period are the appropriate measure of profitability for any well-managed company in our industry'. That may have been EAC's experience and its subsequent forecasts showed a cyclical pattern similar to what it had experienced in the past. However, to criticize Allen West for making a forecast ignores the fact that the company had undergone a number of management and policy changes in the few years prior to the bid. These culminated in new major Board appointments early in 1967. In these circumstances, it would appear unreasonable to expect the past profit level to be repeated in the future.

4. FURTHER OBSERVATIONS ON PROFIT FORECASTS

When a shareholder is faced with an offer for his holding he is, in effect, being asked whether he approves of the transfer of the assets of his company – which may be worth many millions of pounds – to the control of another party. This is an important economic decision which will not only affect his future wealth but will also have an impact on other members of the community as workers, suppliers or customers. Yet this decision is often based on very limited information concerning the future. Vague statements would seem to be inadequate substitutes for detailed calculations on the merits of the alternatives under consideration from those who should be in the best position to supply them – the directors of the companies concerned.

The 1967 evidence indicates that in very few merger and takeover situations were directors prepared to publish forecasts for more than one year ahead. Forecasts for a lesser period were common but these would appear to be of limited use in predicting the future course of events.[25] Since the introduction of the current Code, the Institute has advised its members who are requested to report on the bases of profit forecasts to confine their review to forecasts for the current year. This seems to be an unfortunate move which may well deter companies from publishing forecasts for a longer period.

It would be presumptuous to make sweeping generalizations on the usefulness of bid forecasts following a detailed study of only eight cases. However, one point that stands out in particular is the absence of quantitative information accompanying the profit forecasts to assess the uncertainties involved. One would be very naïve to expect a forecast to be achieved exactly but, if no information is given on the likely range of results, interpretation becomes extremely difficult. Another point is the lack of quantitative information on the benefits expected from the change in control. A defending board, for example, which truly believes that the community is better served by the company remaining under its control has every reason to disclose as much relevant information as possible.[26]

It was argued in the first section of the paper that there is good reason why forecasts should be made obligatory. The growing use of budgetary control and long-term planning techniques by companies means that many could produce forecasts for publication if called upon to do so. If they do not use modern management control techniques, they may well be leaving events to chance, in which case the shareholders should be made aware of the fact.

The argument that the dissemination of further information is unnecessary because the large institutional shareholders and stockbrokers can get the information they require from informal contacts, company visits and private briefings is indefensible. Information available to one shareholder should be made available to all existing and potential shareholders, and that includes the entire community. Alternatively, one can argue that, even if they do not intend to become shareholders, other members of the community – such as employees – have an interest in the future prospects of a company and that this is an added justification for the publication of detailed forecasts. Some would say that members of the public, including the private shareholder, are not capable of assimilating and interpreting more information than they already receive. This argument ignores the fact that there are intelligent members of the public and also that professional advisers, many of whom do not have inside information, exist to help the inexperienced.

APPENDIX

Further Information Relating to the Profits of the Companies Studied

Telephone Rentals Ltd

1966

23 May	Date of Annual Report for 1965. Extract from chairman's comment on future outlook: 'We shall do everything in our power to ensure that the profits continue to rise each year, though it must be appreciated that the rate of increase during the next two years or so is likely to be less than it has been during the last three or four.'[27]
28 September	Results for the half-year to 30 June 1966 9 per cent up on those for the first half of 1965.
7 December	Bid from The General Electric Company Ltd.

1967

23 January	Detailed circular from chairman advising rejection: 'The accounts for 1966 now in course of preparation will show an encouraging improvement in profits before tax over those for 1965. As to the future your directors are confident, on the basis of the projections before them, that the past record of satisfactory growth in profits will continue.'
4 February	'Conservative' forecasts for 1967 and 1968 published.
18 May	Date of Annual Report for 1966. Extract from chairman's statement: 'On the basis of our trading results so far there is every indication that our forecast profits for 1967 will be achieved.'

1968

16 May	Date of Annual Report for 1967. Extracts from chairman's statement: (*a*) Relating to forecasts – 'During the early part of the year, it was necessary for us to revise our targets for new rental business, in order to obtain a volume of business high enough to achieve the profit forecasts we had been called upon to make, whilst at the same time ensuring that we would have sufficient cash resources to finance our commitments, including the increased dividends for which Treasury consent had been obtained.'

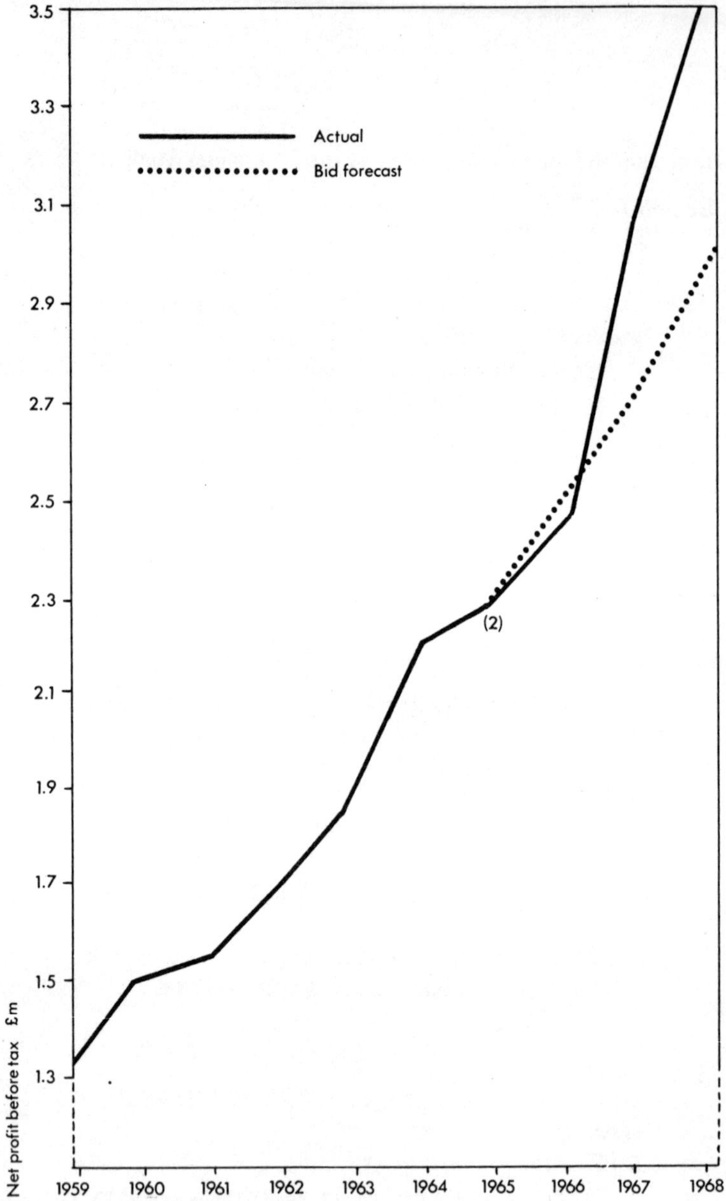

Diagram 2. Telephone Rentals Ltd. Net profits before tax[1] 1959–68

[1] Both forecast and subsequent actual figures have been adjusted to make them comparable with the pre-bid figures.

[2] Profit said to be adversely affected by certain exceptional and non-recurring items, the effect of which was not quantified by the chairman.

(*b*) Reasons for divergence of actual from forecast profit for 1967:
None given except for the effect of the sterling devaluation of November 1967:

'Devaluation . . . enables our [overseas] companies to buy equipment from us at lower rates, though this advantage is to an extent offset by unavoidable price increases from our own suppliers.'

1969

15 May	Date of Annual Report for 1968. No reasons given for divergence of actual from forecast profit for 1968.

International Distillers and Vintners Ltd

1966

1 December — Date of Annual Report in respect of the year ended 31 May 1966. Chairman's comment on prospects:

'It is too early in the year . . . to foresee what the current year will bring. On the export and overseas side . . . we can expect higher profits than last year. This and the expected reduction in the cost of bank borrowing should more than offset other adverse factors.'

1967

5 May — Profit for the eight months to 31 January 1967 showed an 8 per cent increase over the equivalent figure for the previous year. It was reported that the directors considered the figure to give a 'balanced picture' of the position.

22 June — Bid reported from Showerings, Vine Products and Whiteways Ltd.

4 July — Detailed letter from IDV's chairman advising rejection. His comments included:

'The Directors are of the opinion that the results for the full year ended 31st May 1967 will be in excess of £3,200,000 . . . Present estimates for the current year indicate a significant increase in the level of profitability throughout the group . . . present forecasts indicate that [profits further ahead] will be far in excess of their current level.'

12 July — 'Conservative' profit forecasts published.

4 December — Date of Annual Report for 1966/7. The Chairman stated:

'Provided there are no totally unexpected twists of fate, we believe the forecast made for those three years will be achieved.'

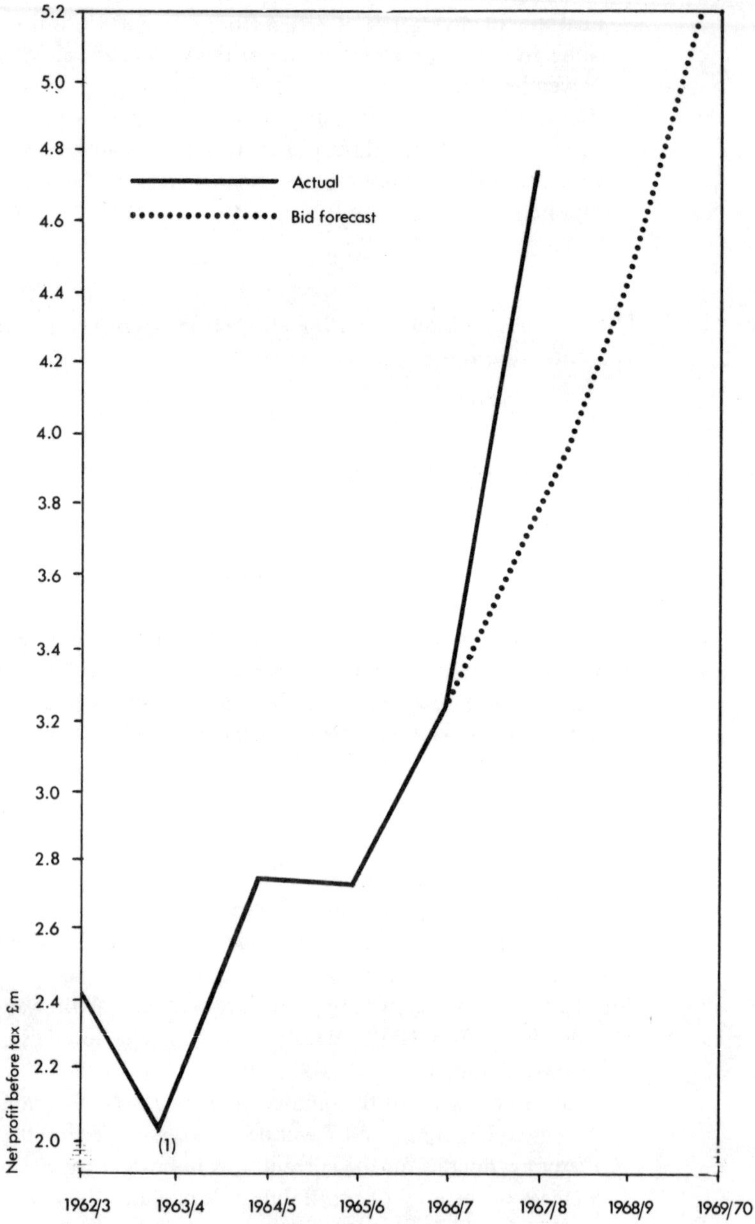

Diagram 3. International Distillers and Vintners Ltd. Net profits before tax.

(1) Profit said to be adversely affected by 'temporary difficulties', of which the precise effect was not stated.

1968

26 November	Date of Annual Report for 1967/8. The Chairman indicated that targets were exceeded, at the expense of 1968/9, by the bunching of whisky shipments to the USA at the end of the year. This was done in anticipation of a threatened long-shoremen's strike on the eastern seaboard. No mention was made of the effect of devaluation on profits. As the majority of cases produced are exported, one would expect there to be a substantial favourable effect.

1969

20 November	Date of Annual Report for 1968/9. Chairman's remark: 'With the integration of Brown and Pank into our overall home trade activities, it would serve no useful comparative purpose to show sales and profit contributions separately.'

Crofts Engineers (Holdings) Ltd.

1967

29 March	Date of Annual Report for 1966. On prospects the chairman stated: 'Were the economy more buoyant, I would feel happier in my forecast for 1967. As things are at the moment I am reasonably confident of another satisfactory year for the Group. When the there is an upsurge in trade it will find us well placed to take advantage of the position, as we have not yet reaped the full benefit of our recent capital expansion.'
30 June	Bid from Renold Ltd. announced.
20 July	Detailed letter advising rejection which included profit forecasts. The wording was: 'We feel that for 1968 a profit of £2,250,000 could well be achieved.'

1968

27 June	Date of Renold's Annual Report for the year ended 31 March 1968. Extract from the chairman's statement: '[The results] of the Crofts' companies (whilst unsatisfactory compared with their estimate of £1,900,000 for the 12 months ended 31st December 1967 – made more than half-way through that year – with which they countered our offer) were nevertheless in line with what should have been expected

in the light of their position and prospects at that time. In the event the estimate of £1,900,000 was not reached even taking into account 15 months' profit of Crofts' UK companies. As we have already stated, we are satisfied that the benefits attainable from the merger fully justify the terms of the acquisition.'

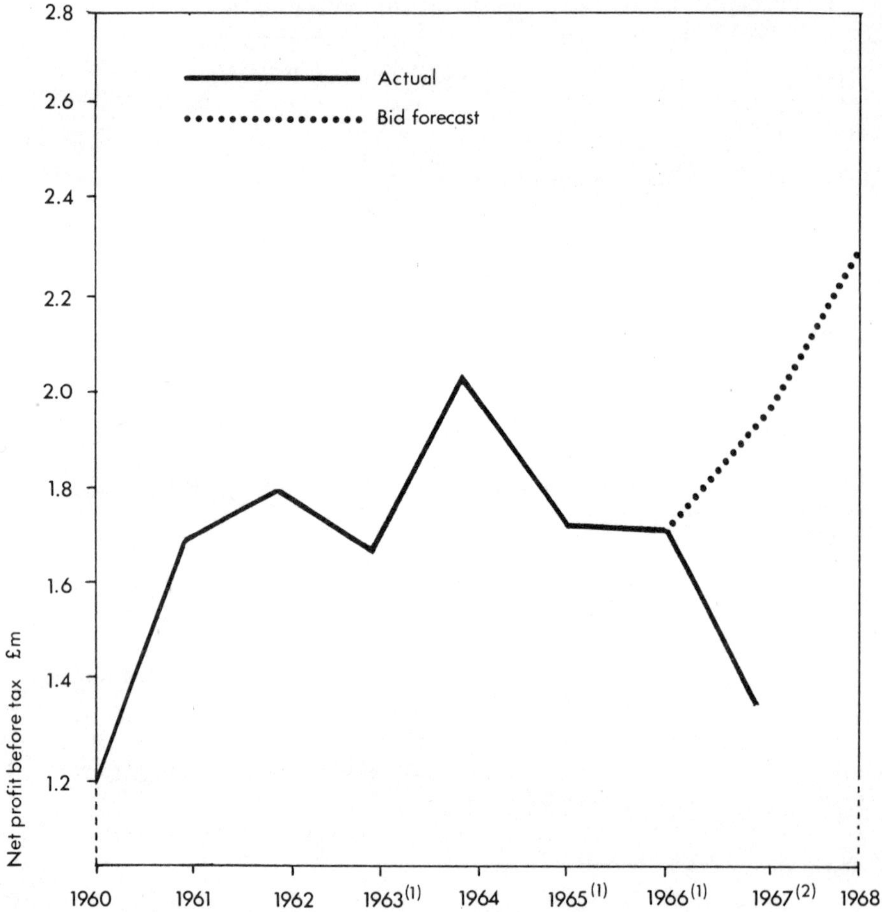

Diagram 4. Crofts Engineers (Holdings) Ltd. Net profits before tax.

(1) Profits said to be affected by various exceptional circumstances, the effects of which were not quantified.
(2) The accounts for the fifteen months to 31 March 1968 were prepared by Renold Ltd., who won control. 12/15ths of the profit has been taken to make it comparable with the other figures shown above.

1969

26 June	Date of Renold's Annual Report for 1968/9. Extract from the chairman's statement: 'Integration with Crofts at home is proceeding but, as forecast last year, completion will take a little time.' No remark on Crofts' forecast for 1968.

Associated Electrical Industries Ltd.

1967

8 March	Date of Annual Report for 1966. Extract from chairman's statement: 'The overall profits of the company will not represent a satisfactory return in 1967, but we expect them to be higher than in 1966.'
15 September	Results for first half of 1967 showed a pre-tax profit of £3·7m. (£6·88m. in 1966). Forecast profit and dividend same as 1966 actuals – £9·2m. and 13 per cent respectively.
28 September	Bid from The General Electric Company Ltd.
20 October	Forecasts published in letter advising rejection – £10m.; about £16m. and in excess of £20m. respectively for the years 1967, 1968 and 1969.

1968

30 July	GEC's results for the year ended 31 March 1968 announced and various documents relating to AEI's results published. (*a*) Extracts from auditors' report on the profit forecasts addressed to AEI's directors and dated 20 October 1967: 'In the time available to us . . . we had necessarily to restrict our view to inquiring into the bases adopted and the procedures followed in compiling the forecasts . . . On the basis of our inquiries we have formed the view that the forecast profits . . . have been prepared on a fair and reasonable basis and in a manner consistent with the principles followed by the company in preparing recent published annual accounts.' (*b*) Extracts from the auditors' report on the forecast and actual results of AEI for 1967 requested by GEC's chairman and dated 29 July 1968: 'You will appreciate that the appraisals of stocks, contracts and a number of other matters involve the exercise of judgement; they are not matters of precision. Broadly speaking, of the total shortfall of £14·5m. we would attribute roughly

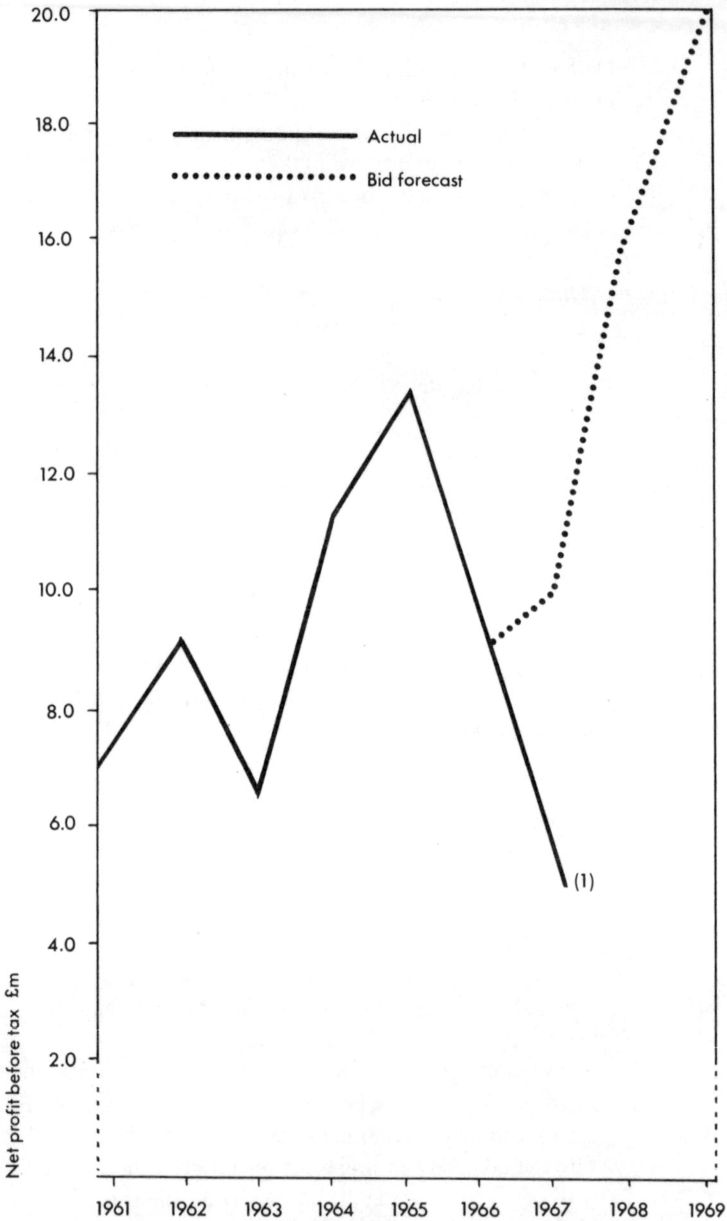

Diagram 5. Associated Electrical Industries Ltd. Net profits before tax.

(1) Accounts prepared by the staff of GEC who won control. Profit figure adjusted by £9·5m. to eliminate effect of judgemental differences (see page 189).

£5m. to adverse differences which are matters substantially of fact rather than of judgement and the balance of some £9·5m. to adjustments which remain matters substantially of judgement.

'We have not found it possible to judge the extent to which these adjustments reflect a difference of approach on the part of management under GEC control and therefore contribute an element which would not have been in the expectations of the former AEI Board.'

(*c*) Extract from the statement made by twelve former directors of AEI on 29 July 1968:

'The AEI monthly accounts for the eleven months to November, 1967 (prepared in the customary way), showed a profit before tax of £7·8m. The budgeted profit for the month of December was £2·2m.; profits in some parts of the company were expected to be below budget, but there were known to be year-end credits.'

(*d*) Extract from the chairman's statement:

for the three months ended 31st March 1968, AEI and its subsidiaries 'show a loss of £1·4 million . . . the period . . . was one of transition from the old patterns of AEI to the adoption of GEC concepts.'

1969

20 August — GEC's results for the year ended 31 March 1969 published. Results of AEI merged with those of GEC (see page 190).

The General Electric Company Ltd.

1967

4 July — Date of the Annual Report for the year ended 31 March 1967. Extract from the chairman's statement:

'All in all, we are looking forward to a better result in the current financial year.'

28 September — Bid for Associated Electrical Industries Ltd., announced.

28 October — In announcing a revised offer for AEI, the chairman expected 'profits for the year ending 31st March 1968, to be of the order of £21 million'. (1966/7 £17·7m. actual). For the following year, the estimated profit was 'more than £24 million'.

1968

30 July

Results for the year ended 31 March 1968 published. Extracts from chairman's statement:

(*a*) Relating to forecasts:

'At the time of the merger we estimated GEC's profit would grow in the past year to around £21 million and in the current year to £24 million. The latter figure was estimated some nine months ago but events since then, including trading up to 30th June, 1968 support the view that it was realistically based.

'Although we did not accept the forecast of the then AEI Board, we did believe that the combined Group should achieve fairly quickly a profit of about £40 million before taxation and the interest on the convertible loan stock which was to be issued, and that this would provide a base for further growth thereafter. It would not be prudent to predict that this figure can be achieved in this first full year of operation, but we hope for a result not too far short of it.'

(*b*) Comparison of forecast with actual profit for 1967/8:

'In the course of our bid for AEI, we forecast profits for 1967/68 of the order of £21 million. Although in total the actual result was better than this, the content of the final figure differed from the detailed forecasts. We made better profits from higher sales of consumer durables, and costs worked out slightly better than expected in switchgear and telecommunications. Several of our overseas companies fared worse than forecast. At home, neither Osram nor Woods of Colchester could maintain their profit margins. There were also some other less significant variations from predictions, but the figures were not enhanced by devaluation.'

1969

20 August

Results for the year ended 31 March 1969 published. Extract from chairman's statement:

'The year ended 31st March 1969 was one of great achievement, and the profit of £39·9 million before taxation and Convertible Loan Stock interest exceeds the aggregate of best profits of GEC and AEI (£21·25 million by GEC in 1967/1968 and £15·6 million by AEI in 1955).

'Apart from a major setback in India, where the profit was considerably lower than last year and well below forecast, the other results were in line with our expectations.'

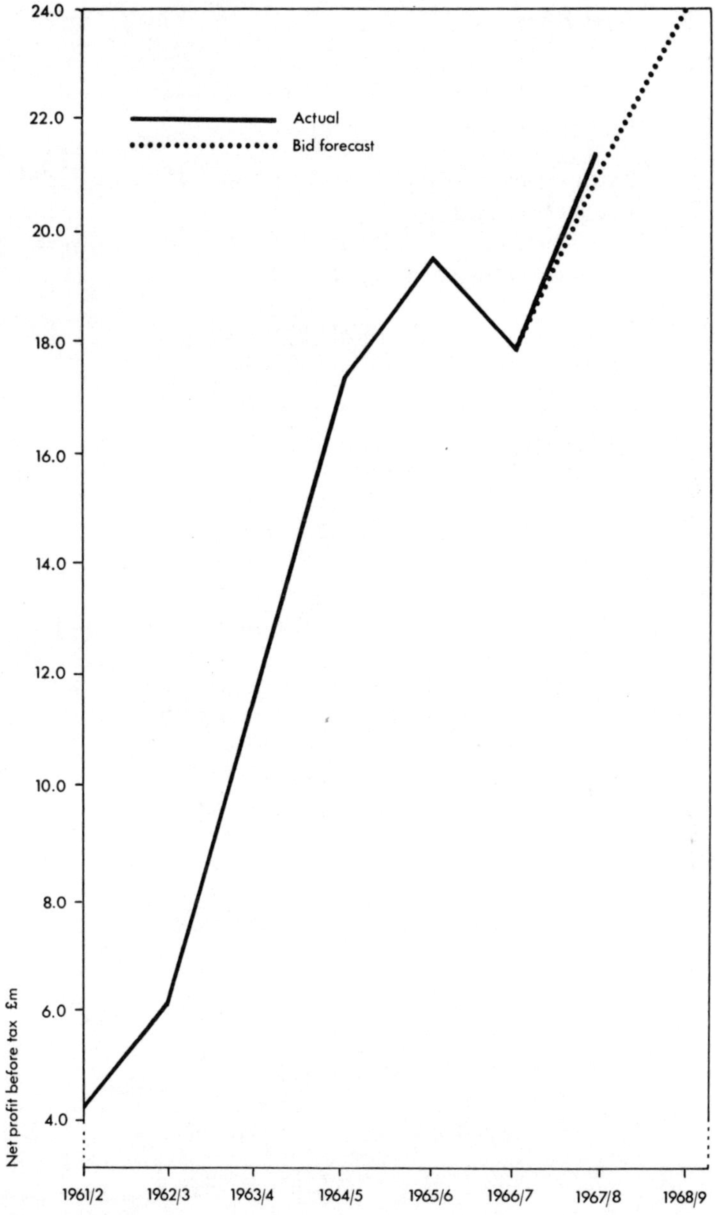

Diagram 6. The General Electrical Co. Ltd. Net profits before tax.

Allen West and Company Ltd

1967

26 May	Date of Annual Report for the year ended 31 January 1967. Extract from chairman's statement: 'I believe our prospects are good and the results this year will show some improvement over those of last year.'
2 December	Bids for The Electrical Apparatus Company Ltd., and Contactor Switchgear Ltd., announced.
15 December	Forecasts included in offer documents: 'The present Group's profit before taxation should exceed £800,000 for 1968/9.'

1969

23 May

Date of Annual Report for 1968/9. Extract from chairman's statement:

'These results, although lower than those forecast at the time of the EAC negotiations, were substantially better than those for the previous year.'

No mention was made of the reason for the shortfall. The actual pre-tax profit of £795,000 was derived from the following companies whose forecasts were:

Company	*Forecast*	
	£	
Allen West	800,000	Forecast by Allen West during bid for EAC.
Electrical Apparatus Co.	310,000	Forecast by EAC during bid from Allen West
Hackbridge-Faraday	90,000	Press estimate (acquired by Allen West on 13.2.68)
	1,200,000[28]	

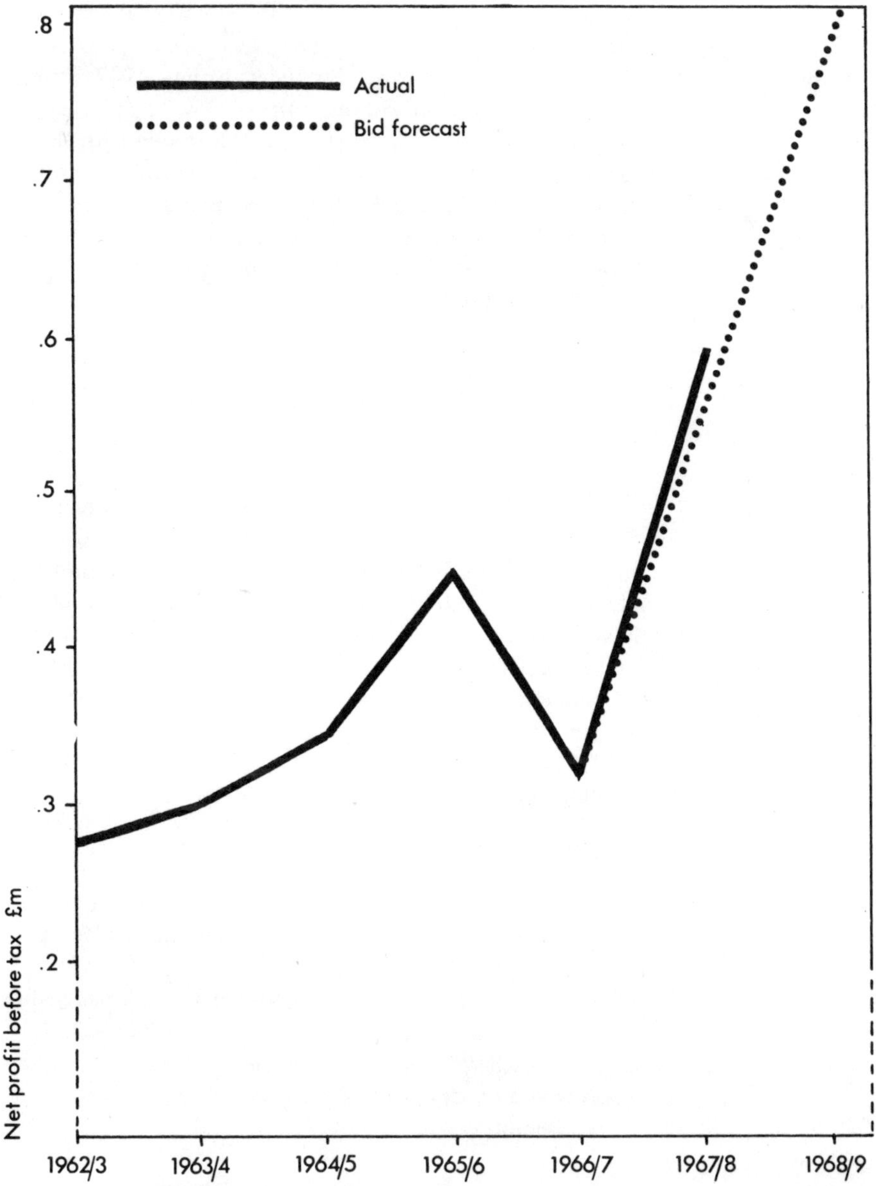

Diagram 7. Allen West and Company Ltd. Net profits before tax.

Midland Aluminium Ltd.

1967

2 November	Announcement in the *Financial Times* that a new chairman had been appointed.
22 November	Date of Annual Report for the year ended 30 June 1967. Extract from the chairman's statement on prospects: 'I am assured by the management that the accounts for the year to 30th June 1968, will show an overall profit. I believe that adequate profits can be made. Your Board and I are determined to see that they are. I cannot however at this stage make any firm forecast as to the amount of them.'
28 November	Bid from Central Wagon Company Ltd.
20 December	Midland's forecasts published in the circular advising rejection. Chairman's comment: 'Your Board is confident that they will be met.'

1968

18 November	Date of Annual Report for 1967/8. On prospects, the Directors' Report said: 'Forecasts were made last December which envisaged profits before tax of £675,000 in the year ending 30th June 1969. Since then there has been a substantial reduction in consumers' purchasing power and an overall increase in operating costs. It is probable that the original forecast will not be achieved. However, the Board considers that the Group should still make profits . . . sufficient to recommend payment of dividends totalling 20 per cent for the year as forecast.'[29]

1969

2 May	Interim results announced. Forecast profit for the year to 30 June 1969 revised down to £216,000 before tax and the dividend to a total of 10 per cent.
25 July	The *Investors' Chronicle* reported that Midland's chairman had had to produce the forecast for 1968/9 swiftly 'before he had fully acquainted himself with the potential. He admits that he mistimed the recovery and the company is only now running at the forecast rate of profitability.'
26 November	Date of Annual Report for 1968/9. An analysis of sales and the net profit of £224,000 between divisions was given (see Table 4 on page 196 which compares the figures with those forecast in November 1967). Reasons for the poor results were given. For example, the Holloware division's

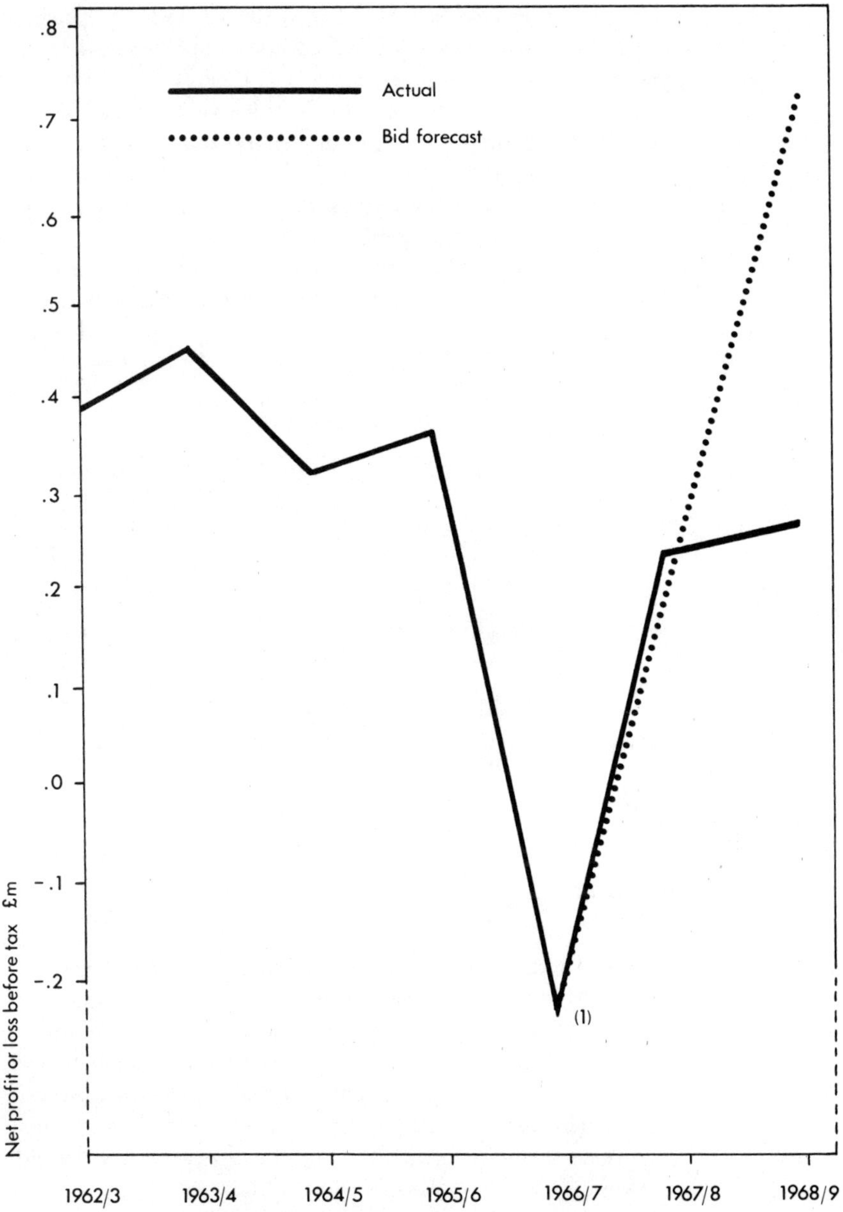

Diagram 8. Midland Aluminium Ltd. Net profits before tax.

(1) First accounts produced by a reconstructed Board in respect of the financial year prior to its appointment.

results had been adversely affected by the disruption of production caused by faults in new equipment installed in November 1968. The major engineering subsidiary – The London Aluminium Company Ltd. – was sold shortly after the year end and, in 1968/9, it had 'suffered a series of setbacks due to strikes among its major customers in the motor industry and to the production cuts by domestic appliance manufacturers after the hire purchase restrictions in November 1968'.

The directors reaffirmed the forecast they had made in August of a pre-tax profit of £589,000 for the year to 30 June 1970.[30]

Table 4

Midland Aluminium Ltd.

Comparison of forecasts made in November 1967 and actual results for the year to 30 June 1969

Division	*Actual*		*Forecast*		*Actual/Forecast*	
	Sales £'000s	Profit £'000s	Sales £'000s	Profit £'000s	Sales %	Profit %
Holloware	4539	185	4175	253	+ 8·7	– 26·9
Engineering	2193	(71)	3078	89	–28·8	–179·8
Glow-Worm	2926	181	3422	347	–14·5	– 47·8
Aerosols	874	13	1137	26	–23·1	– 50·0
Overseas	1346	32	906	39	+48·6	– 17·9
	11878	340	12718	754	– 6·6	– 54·9
Less Holding Co., expenses		116		79		+ 46·8
Net profit before deducting taxation and minority interests		224		675		– 66·8

Central Wagon Company Ltd.

1967

7 March — Date of Annual Report for the year ended 1 October 1966. Extract from Chairman's statement:

> 'This result fully justifies the considerable re-organization which was carried through during the year and which, indeed, is still continuing. Our current financial year has opened well . . . and profits to date are running ahead of last year. I am sure we shall give a good account of overselves in the current year.'

28 November — Bid for Midland Aluminium Ltd., announced.

29 December — Forecast for 1968 published. Profits before tax were expected to be 'not less than £525,000 for the 12 months to 31st December 1968.'

1968

23 September — Forecast for 1968 revised downwards.

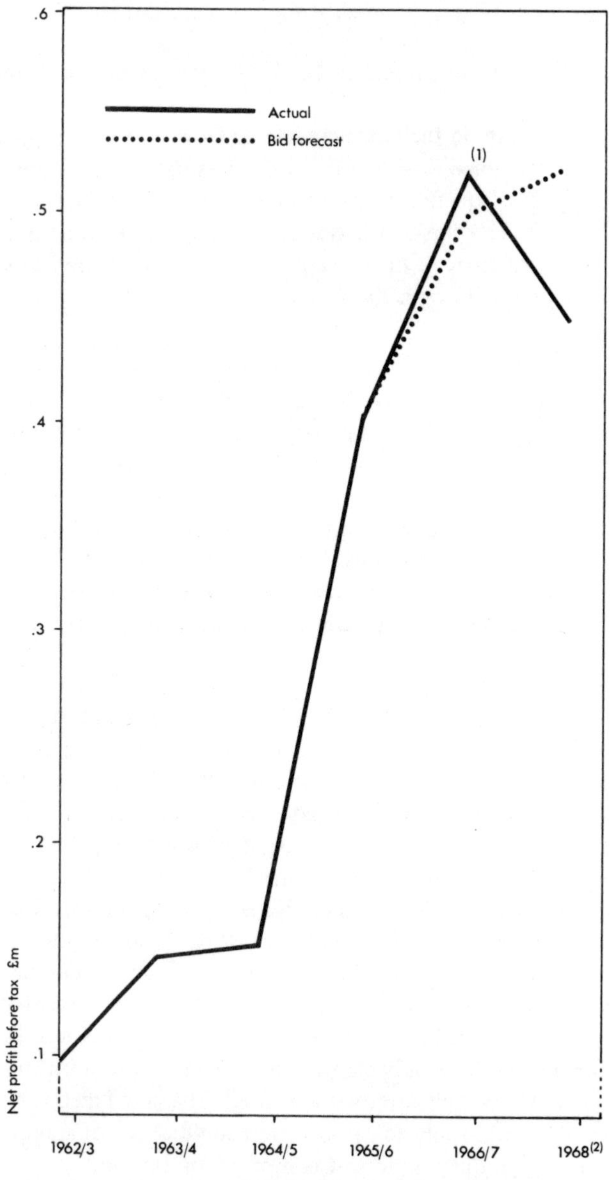

Diagram 9. Central Wagon Company Ltd. Net profits before tax.

(1) Fifteen month period to 30 December 1967.
(2) Actual and forecast profits for 1968 exclude the contribution from Epco Ltd, acquired in 1968.

1969

18 April Date of Annual Report for 1968. Extract from chairman's statement:

> 'Early in the year we suffered from severe cuts made by the National Coal Board in its orders for mining equipment. In consequence, we had to reduce our profit forecast. The integration of Tangyes Ltd., took somewhat longer than anticipated, the company is now reaching the rate of profit growth originally planned.'

Editor's note

The Panel on Takeovers and Mergers (details of which are given in Chapter 11) have become very concerned with the profit forecasts made by companies at the time of a merger or takeover. As is explained by Mrs. Dev these forecasts are often crucial to the outcome of any bargaining or bid, for it can be on the basis of these forecasts that the shareholder decides whether or not to sell his shares. The Panel have been keeping records of such forecasts since 1 May 1969. Up to 30 September 1970 they have been able to compare the forecasts with the actual outcome in 210 cases. They report that in 170 of these cases, with a margin of 10% on either side, the forecasts were achieved.

Of the 40 bad forecasts, 31 were made by offeree companies (that is, the company defending itself against a bid), but in only one case did the forecast form part of a successful defence. In the 9 bad forecasts by the bidding company, 4 were under forecasts. Since the operations of the Panel began, therefore, it does not seem as if companies on a large scale have deliberately been influenced in their forecasting by the takeover or merger negotiations in hand.

The Panel published a Practice Note in June 1971, concerned with clarifying the position on the disclosure of the assumptions on which a profit forecast is based. Any forecast is the result of judgement. Listing the assumptions on which a forecast is based should enable the shareholder to form an opinion on the 'reasonableness and reliability' of the forecast. The City Code states that these assumptions must be disclosed in any document sent to shareholders. In the past however some companies have only shown a minimal amount of information on the assumptions on which their forecasts are based. The new Practice Note offers general rules which should apply to the selection and drafting of assumptions; it is aimed at tightening up the practices of companies on this point.

It is essential that the position with regard to forecasts should be clarified so that all know the standards of honesty and disclosure involved. The content of a Prospectus, a document inviting people to subscribe for shares, is covered by Company Law, and the type of statement that can and cannot be made is clearly defined and rigidly enforced. It is just as important that any document issued to induce people to sell shares or retain them has equally high standards of accuracy and disclosure and that it is just as strongly enforced.

Chapter Eleven

THE CITY REGULATIONS ON MERGERS AND TAKEOVERS*

Michael Blanden

INTRODUCTION

It is perhaps slightly ironical that the debate on the subject of takeovers and mergers should apparently be reaching its peak at a time when the merger movement has lost a good deal of its impetus. For a number of reasons, the takeover business is not just now very active, and it is not a matter, as it was a year ago, of major public controversy.

Yet it may be all to the good that the debate should be getting under way at a time when there is no great public pressure for action to control the City's activities. For in some ways it was a pity that the Takeover Panel was established in the heat of great public controversy over the City's tactics and behaviour. The Panel has, so far, been successful in bringing a measure of restraint into a particularly conspicuous area of the City's behaviour where things had been going badly wrong. Yet the problems which the Panel was established to solve in the specific area of takeovers are of far wider significance. Seen against the background of the much more general debate which is beginning to get under way in almost every country of the western world, over the nature of capitalism, the proper behaviour of securities markets in general, and the place and character of the company in a modern society, the specific argument about takeovers raised many fundamental points and problems. The action taken to deal with these problems so far has been superficial. It is as well that they can be considered anew rather more calmly, and they may provide one starting point for the argument which will be going on for years to come over the fundamental problems of the western economic system.

The Background to the Code

It is not necessary for the purpose of this discussion to look in detail into the events which led up to the creation of the present Takeover Panel and Code. It is, however, illuminating to consider briefly the nature of the problems which the system has been designed to solve and the circumstances which formed the background to current thinking.

---

*Paper presented at the Conference on Mergers and Takeovers, London, May 29, 1970.

The first general point which stands out is that it was a remarkably long time before the City felt the need to establish any kind of organized and active control over takeover tactics. In the US the disastrous experience of the late 1920s led directly to the establishment of the SEC as a separate authority as early as 1934. In London, the Stock Exchange had established a long tradition of supervising the market and of using its influence over the companies which required a market quotation for their shares to press for an ever greater degree of disclosure of information to shareholders, and has for a long time been able to boast that in this aspect of the securities market it has been in advance of the standards of disclosure required by the law. But it was not until the late 1960s, after the post-war merger boom was well under way, that the City felt it necessary to begin the creation of rules to govern its own activities in the context specifically of takeover bids, and recognized the need for specific rules to control its own members.

The reasons for this long delay lie deep in the psychology of the City itself. At its extreme, this took the form of firm resistance to any interference in the activities of the City, the resentment of any publicity given to its operations, and the conviction that what the City does is its business and its business alone. This attitude is by now largely dead, and even the most traditional merchant banks, for example, have accepted external scrutiny and, in the interests of their clients, have recognized the need to create and maintain good relations with the press and other outsiders.

More rationally, however, the traditions of the City encouraged the belief that within the gentlemanly traditions of the City establishment no regulation apart from self-regulation could be needed. Beyond providing the minimum of protection against fraud and against the unavoidable mishaps which were bound to happen in a competitive climate, the City's professional ethics should leave no room for the kind of sharp dealing which would require strict control. Against this background it has taken the City a long time to understand that the problem, not of honesty but of protecting outsiders – specifically shareholders – against the effects of the City's own activities, was an issue of quite a different nature which would require its institutions to subject themselves to a strictly enforced code of practice.

The second main point is that it has been only a very small number of major cases which have brought the issue to a head. Perhaps half a dozen major takeover battles, fought out in the full glare of publicity, established the need for regulation. Out of all the merger and takeover activity which has been seen in recent years, only in these few cases did the scandal – that is not too strong a word – reach proportions which attracted public attention. How many other minor affairs there were which would have offended against present thinking it is hard to recall. In these few major arguments, however, the issues became too clear to be ignored. They were enough to make the City itself, in the first instance, realize that some kind of rules would be necessary to govern its conduct in bid situations, and finally to bring the Labour Government into the ring with the realization that confidence in the City required not merely a set of rules, but in spite of the City's traditions somebody to put them into effect and power to ensure they were observed.

Finally, from this experience it is possible to identify the nature of the problem which the present system is designed to cope with. It is this background – and the general experience of the merchant bankers who have taken the main responsibility for writing and enforcing the code of conduct – which has determined the nature of the Code and the form of the operations of the Takeover Panel.

The problem of the securities market is not confined to the control of takeover bids. But it is in the context of a hard-fought battle, where large amounts of money and personal reputations are at stake, that the issues are raised in their starkest form. Winning and losing – as well as the particular merits of one offer or another – are important; decisions which may vitally affect the outcome are taken at white heat. And in these few outstanding cases, the issue raised itself largely as one of tactics, the manoeuvres adopted in takeover situations which could win or lose the battle without apparent reference to the merits or demerits of a particular proposal. The arguments brought out the fact that the City, in spite of its gentlemanly approach to business, could in the heat of a battle reach a point where the combatants were at each other's throats. Taking advantage of the City's traditional freedom of competition, actions could be taken which simply offended against a general sense of fair play. More particularly – and this was the basic issue as presented in these arguments – takeover contests could be decided apparently without reference to the main body of shareholders.

The Big Scandals

This was already clear in the first of the big upsets, the famous British Aluminium affair in 1958. It began with substantial buying of the company's shares under nominee names by the Reynolds Metals-Tube Investments partnership. It developed into a bitter fight, with Warburgs – then very much still an 'upstart' in City merchant banking circles – ranged with Tubes and Reynolds against the British Aluminium Board with its alternative proposals for a link with Alcoa and the support of Lazards and Hambros at the head of a powerful group of City interests. And apart from exposing hostilities within the City, it brought out the major issue which has run through all these arguments – tactics which leave shareholders in a company without a clear choice between opposing proposals and without the information on which they might base a rational decision.

As Christopher Marley observed in his recent book *Accounting Principles and the City Code* (written in collaboration with Professor Stamp), this marked a turning point for the City. On one hand, from this time on the merchant banks developed their professional skill in the conduct of takeover situations to a point of finesse demonstrated again and again in subsequent events. On the other hand, the affair led directly to the creation for the first time – by the main City institutions under the leadership of the Bank of England – of the Notes on Amalgamations. Vague in expression, reflecting a determination not to interfere with the freedom of the market, the Rules nevertheless for the first time marked the recognition that take-over tactics required guidance and that shareholders had a right to justice.

The second major theme which has run through the recent arguments – that all shareholders should be treated alike – was also brought out early in the Richard Thomas and Baldwin bid for Whitehead Iron and Steel in 1963. RTB, advised by Rothschilds, assured its success against Stewarts & Lloyds through a market operation which guaranteed the big institutional shareholders the full value of RTB's subsequent bid but left the minor shareholders to their own devices. This led directly to a revision of the Notes which for the first time established the enduring principle that a bidder who buys shares in the market or through a deal with a large holder is bound to offer similar terms to all shareholders.

The Code of conduct was finally written in 1968 after an increasing number of incidents in the City and with the backing of the Bank of England. It was – and is after the 1969 revisions – a thoroughly professional job. It had, and still has, weaknesses; some of them will be cured in time as experience of the control of takeovers is applied to the Rules. By 1968 the City's battles had become so conspicuous as to attract the attention of the Prime Minister as well as of the City authorities themselves. And a clear pattern of problems had emerged, which, with variations, lay behind the public scandals which led up to the establishment of the Code and behind those too which followed during the experimental period of the Takeover Panel's first year. The nature of the Code was determined by these, guided by the experience of the group of merchant bankers who took the direct responsibility for writing it.

The Main Problems

Three or four major problems had emerged, which the Code should have been capable of dealing with. In the first place, simply by existing, the Code was designed to reduce the bitterness and acrimony between competing companies which it had been shown could arise in bid situations – and which, to the City's own great concern, could be carried over to their merchant bank advisers and destroy the carefully cultivated image of the City's civilized aristocracy. It had been seen in the first battle, for British Aluminium. It reached its peak after the new Code went into operation in 1968 with the outburst which Sir Frank Kearton – now Lord Kearton – let fly at the City in general, several of its leading institutions in particular, and the press. His complaint arose directly out of one of the first public efforts made by the newly established Panel on takeovers under the leadership of Sir Humphrey Mynors, which criticized Courtaulds and its advisers Hill Samuel for its conduct in the battle for control of International Paints. Sir Frank had not been consulted before the Panel published its arguments. But his anger, while immediately prompted by this incident, followed a series of three particularly acrimonious battles. His disillusion with the City reflected his personal experience; but it also reflected the City's real problems.

Of the more specific issues which have repeatedly arisen in takeover situations perhaps the most conspicuous has been the technique, pioneered in the British Aluminium case, of a company frustrating an unwelcome bidder simply by issuing new shares to a favoured third party. That case provided the simple form of this manoeuvre, where without reference to shareholders the Board was able to propose the issue of enough shares to give Alcoa a one-third interest and block the Reynolds-Tubes approach. Variations on this theme have repeatedly stirred the City, and the technique is one which has again and again required close watching. It happened between Courtaulds and Cook & Watts in 1967, when to counter a bid from Macanie, Cook & Watts arranged to buy a Courtaulds' subsidiary by issuing shares which would give Courtaulds 28 per cent of the Cook equity. The technique reached its pinnacle in 1967 in the battle for control of Metal Industries, which was the last straw and which led to the creation of the Code and Panel. In this case, Aberdare Holdings had already established control of Metal Industries, with the help of a friendly market operation; but this control was destroyed in one stroke by Metal Industries' agreement to buy a subsidiary of Thorn Electrical in exchange for a substantial share issue – and the deal, conditional on the success of a Thorn bid for MI, was self-evidently only a paper transaction.

Finally, this type of operation again played a part in the uncommonly bitter fight for control of the *News of the World* late in 1968, the fight which completed the demise of the City's first attempt at creating a workable system of control through the Mynors Panel. Again, it was a case of a company, faced with an unwelcome bid – in this case, from Pergamon Press – finding an ally – in the form of Rupert Murdoch's News Ltd of Australia. Again it involved a purchase of assets from News in exchange for a large proportion of the increased News of the World equity.

Another specific issue, which is being refined by the present Panel to cover situations unforeseen in the early attempts at control, is the fundamental question of equal treatment for all shareholders. It covers both the now outlawed practice of paying special terms to gain control of large single blocks of shares and the question of the price paid for normal purchases through the market. It was an issue, as I have mentioned, in the early case of Whitehead Iron. It arose in the Courtaulds-Wilkinson and Riddell incident, where prices way above the value of the rival bids were paid in the market for the last few shares. And it was right at the centre of the other of the three major cases during the reign of the Mynors Panel in 1968, the American Tobacco partial bid for Gallaher. American Tobacco had offered for half the Gallaher capital; it acquired a large number of shares in one of the fastest buying operations in history, in which important institutional holders of shares were able to unload the whole of their holdings at the bid price. Other shareholders could sell only half. The incident resulted in public criticism of the merchant bankers and the brokers involved, Morgan Grenfell and Cazenove, by the Panel. It brought direct intervention by the Governor of the Bank of England. But neither of the City participants suffered any punishment.

Finally, there has been the issue which is perhaps central to the problem of control in the wider context of the securities market as well as takeovers, which is still exercising the Panel and which perhaps will never be brought under complete control; the problems associated with market dealings during a bid. It would go right against the grain for the City to stop dealings during a bid situation – although in some cases such as the struggle for control of the *News of the World* it has proved necessary – yet by leaving the market deliberately unfettered the Rules leave the way open to activities which are the most difficult to subject to control. Again and again – in Cook & Watts, in Wilkinson & Riddell, in the bid by Aberdare Industries for Metal Industries, in the buying which helped Philips to gain control of Pye in 1966, and finally in the *News of the World* case where, by the time the Panel stepped in to stop dealings, the *News of the World* Board and its allies had already secured enough votes to ensure success for their case – dealings during a bid have created major difficulties.

These, then, were some of the main aspects of City activities which lay behind the creation of the City Code. Much more, however, went into the Code. It was created by a group of merchant bankers, and all their experience in the takeover business contributed to the drafting of the Code. It is designed not merely to cover the market tactics of companies and their advisers during bid situations, but to cover virtually every aspect of their dealings with shareholders. It includes, for example, detailed provisions to govern the techniques of profits' forecasts – an aspect of the takeover problem which in fact had not been particularly conspicuous in the particular battles which had forced the City to take itself in hand, but which had repeatedly caused retrospective trouble through the over-enthusiasm of company boards in the course of numerous less obviously troublesome battles.

There is no need to go in detail through the provisions of the Code. In its twelve general principles, and the series of detailed rules which follow them, it provides the basic guidance needed for all participants in takeover situations, the companies, their advisers, the stockbrokers concerned directly or indirectly, and the associates of all these. It is, I think, accepted by the City as being by and large a fair and reasonable document. And because it is accepted in this way, and because most of the City knows perfectly well anyway how it ought to behave, the Code should work. It is not, of course, a binding document in the legal sense. But its nature is perhaps best indicated by the important first general principle, which enjoins all participants in bids to observe the spirit, as well as the letter, of the principles and the rules. The City, which created the Code, understands quite clearly what this means.

The 1968 Panel

This is true of the present Code; it was also true of the Code as it was set up first in 1968 – none of the revisions incorporated in April 1969, although extensive, were fundamental. Given the obviously sensible nature of most of the rules, therefore, and their general acceptance, it perhaps seems strange that even after the Code had been set up, with a Panel under the leadership of Sir Humphrey Mynors to run it, it did not work. It would be unfair to Sir Humphrey to suggest that the 1968 Panel and Code were complete failures. A great deal of valuable work was done during that period which formed the foundation for later efforts at control, and many decisions were made which influenced City thinking. But it is not unfair to say that on two or three occasions the system was found to be lacking – in the sense of being unable still to control powerful City and industrial interests.

The reasons for this may have lain partly in the character of the Panel itself. But much more fundamentally, they lay still in the nature of the City. What is extraordinary is that even at this late stage, after the City had accepted the need for a Code of conduct and somebody to put it into effect, it still basically rejected the idea of its activities being controlled in this way.

The constitution of the Panel was widely criticized during that trying period because it gave the Panel no 'sanctions' – no power to punish transgressors. In my view, this aspect of the problem was less important than the sheer failure of the City institutions and their various representative bodies to give whole-hearted support to the thing they had created. If the Panel was weak and indecisive, the reason was partly because its position was weak.

This made it possible for the Panel's decisions to be openly questioned and its authority to be put in doubt during the Gallaher affair. The Panel used its main weapon, of public censure, on Morgan Grenfell and Cazenove, over their handling of the American Tobacco purchases of Gallaher shares which clinched the bid. But these powerful City companies were able to say publicly that they did not agree with the Panel, and neither the Stock Exchange nor the Issuing Houses Association, the two professional bodies concerned, showed complete conviction in their support of the Panel. This incident brought a public statement from Sir Leslie O'Brien, Governor of the Bank of England: 'The Panel's rulings have been questioned and even their general authority has not always been acknowledged. It is in no one's interest that this state of affairs should continue'.

The same sort of weakness also lay behind the Panel's own hesitancy in dealing with the later problem of the Pergamon-News of the World-News Ltd battle; the Panel, in this case, simply acted too late. By the time it stepped in to stop market operations, the alliance between the News of the World and Mr. Murdoch's News Ltd of Australia was already in a position to block the Pergamon bid. The Panel decided to neutralize the votes which had been bought during the course of the bid; but the damage had been done, and within a few days the President of the Board of Trade, Mr. Crosland, was heard threatening yet again that statutory control would be introduced if the City could not reorganize its affairs.

1968 and 1969: Contrasts

It is interesting at this point to draw a contrast between these incidents, which were the major causes of the early reconstitution of the 1968 Panel, and the two important cases which during 1969 determined the reputation of the revitalized Panel. Above all else that happened during 1969, it was the Leasco bid for Pergamon which established the authority of the new Panel and its executive. It was the first, and so far the only, instance in which the Panel has been called on to adjudicate in an issue which attracted constant publicity, which involved important and sometimes difficult personalities as well as vital and utterly opposed interests. The contrast, at least as far as the Panel's reputation was concerned, could hardly be more complete with the previous case involving Pergamon.

In fact, the affair has to be seen in retrospect still as a failure for the City in the protection of shareholders' interests. For the Panel itself, the compromise solutions which it painstakingly evolved with the two parties concerned in day and night sessions quickly broke down. And in spite of the Panel's efforts, shareholders were left with a share quote suspended for months and their hopes of eventually receiving a bid dependent on the outcome of lengthy investigations.

It was, in fact, an impossible situation for the Panel. A price had been named in what had started off as a perfectly friendly merger, which was to all intents and purposes already sewn up. The bidder, Leasco, had paid a price approaching that level in the purchase of a large number of shares in the market. When Leasco found that its intended purchase was not what it had expected, it pulled out of the deal. The Panel had no sensible grounds for stopping Leasco from what was in fact on at least two grounds a technical breach of the Code. It could not reasonably force the bidder to continue. It could only try to arrange a reconciliation to keep the bid going, and set up, through the Board of Trade, an investigation to discover precisely what was the state of Pergamon, part of the problem which was outside its own area of responsibility.

Yet for all this, the Panel came out of the situation with its own reputation enormously enhanced. Whatever the outcome, it had left no doubt in anybody's mind that it had the will and the power to make its authority felt, the strength to stand no nonsense from the personalities involved, the ability to make quick decisions and at the same time to persevere with a course of action even if it meant working half the night, and the complete support of the authorities including the Board of Trade. The Leasco-Pergamon battle was very far from providing a typical problem in the takeover business, and for the development of the Code and the Panel's thinking it was a good deal less important than the very large number of less publicized but more normal cases in which the Panel was involved during the year. Yet at the time it was seen clearly as the Panel's first big test, one which it passed with flying colours.

Perhaps more indicative of the change in the atmosphere in the City as a result of the new Panel's activities, however, was the case early in 1970 involving Kleinwort Benson acting on behalf of Trafalgar House in the battle with Bovis for control of Cementation. This was a far more straightforward problem, of interpretation of one aspect of the Code, which provided a complete contrast again with the experience of the Panel in 1968 when it was put in the position of having to criticize a merchant bank. The problem arose out of Kleinwort's purchase for cash of a block of shares in Cementation which had been built up by aggressive buying in the market by Samuel Montagu acting for Bovis. When Bovis finally pulled out of the battle, Kleinwort bought Montagu out on behalf of Trafalgar House. The Panel executive, ruled that there was all the difference in the world between buying shares in dribs and drabs through the market as Montagu had done, when the opportunity to sell was available to all holders of Cementation shares, and buying a single critical block from a single holder, as Kleinwort had done. Under General Principle 8 of the Code the executive ruled that Kleinwort should make a similar cash offer to the rest of the Cementation shareholders. Kleinwort disagreed, and appealed to the full Panel against this ruling. The Panel supported the executive, and – in absolute contrast to the arguments which had followed the Panel's censure of Morgan Grenfell in 1968 – Kleinwort accepted the decision. It was quite clear that Kleinwort, or at least the executive directly involved, felt the Panel might be wrong. But it accepted the Panel's authority without question, and took upon itself the cost of providing the required cash alternative.

1969: The Strengthened Panel

The transformation in the control of takeovers has to be attributed to the changes which were made early in 1969. These removed, it seems, the weaknesses which afflicted the City's first attempt at policing takeovers through the City Panel. The main developments fell into three main groups. First there was the revision of the Code itself. This did not for the most part involve any fundamental changes in either the theory or the practice of the takeover rules, except perhaps in one area: control over the problematical business of profits' forecasts in bid situations was greatly strengthened. The Panel, with the full support of the City, has consistently argued that it would be wrong to ban profits' forecasts altogether, since on the one hand this would remove one of the main weapons in the hand of a board of directors fighting an unwelcome bid, and on the other, as American experience has shown, it would simply encourage the circulation of unofficial and unsupported forecasts to a limited number of shareholders.

At the same time, the Panel has recognized the problem which has repeatedly occurred in the past of over-enthusiastic forecasting, and limited the scope for company boards. The period for which forecasts could be made has been sensibly restricted to one year. The accounting profession in its manifestation as auditors to companies, and the merchant banks who act as their financial advisers, were persuaded to put their names to the bases on which forecasts were prepared by the companies concerned, and it was made obligatory that these bases, and the assumptions involved in making the forecasts, should be published at the same time.

Secondly, there were the changes made to the constitution and methods of operation of the Panel itself. The Panel ceased to be the body responsible for the day-to-day administration of the Code, and this function was passed over to a newly established full-time director general. This was of vital importance for the success of the reconstituted Panel. It was this that made it possible for the Panel to build up its reputation for being able to deal extremely quickly with enquiries, and by the same token to step in rapidly and decisively where it saw the need for action to avert an impending problem. Simply, having a full-time and experienced executive available made it possible for the Panel to match the merchant banks themselves in speed of decision and action and in tenacity. And the personalities involved have been important too. In Mr. Ian Fraser, himself a merchant banker, the Panel has had a director general who is familiar with all the details of merger negotiations and with all the tricks of the trade; it has also, I think, had a man who has shown a strong sense of diplomacy, knowing the need to convince the City that the Panel was fair as well as strong, knowing when to persuade and when to threaten. Behind him as chairman of the Panel Lord Shawcross has brought his prestige and his forensic skill – shown in the Panel's cross-examination of the contestants in the Pergamon-Leasco case – to bear in the City's interests.

Thirdly, there were the changes made in the relationship between the Panel and its sponsoring bodies, the City institutions. The changes included for the first time giving the Panel the sanctions which were required. The Panel is able to use against any offending bank or broker or other institution whatever disciplinary powers are available to the appropriate professional body – the Stock Exchange Council, the Issuing Houses Association or whatever, and the Board of Trade. The result is that it has at its command strong weapons. This has been important in itself. Mr. Fraser told me that, although it was not necessary to invoke the sanctions during 1969, the threat was an extremely useful stick to wave in the fairly frequent situations where the Panel executive had to find a way of dealing with utterly opposed and apparently irreconcilable points of view in takeovers. More than this, though, it also required for the first time a whole-hearted public commitment to the principles of the Code and the functions of the Panel by the whole City – by the merchant bankers and brokers, but also by the unit trusts, the big institutional investors like the insurance companies and pension funds and, in effect, by the whole of industry and commerce. Responsibility for enforcing the Code was seen to rest with the whole of these groups, not just with the Panel; it was made absolutely clear that the Panel's authority – subject to the newly established appeals procedure – was absolute and final.

1969: Aspects of the Panel's Operations

Again, little purpose would be served by going in detail through the events of 1969; the main points, including details of a number of important decisions which have been made by the Panel executive affecting the interpretation of certain parts of the Code, have already been set out in the annual report. But the experience of this year confirmed the Panel in its position as the chief arbiter of City takeover tactics, and I would like to pick out two, perhaps three, aspects of its operations during this period which seem important to the future development of the voluntary system of control.

First, its method of operation. The really striking thing about the activities of 1969 were not the one or two major cases like Pergamon-Leasco where the Panel operated in the full light of publicity, but the very large number of less conspicuous bids where it was called upon to give judgments. It was in the context of this mass of mundane work that its authority was firmly established and its views became respected.

The annual report drew attention to the scale of these operations. The full Panel met only eight times during the year 1969; five of these meetings were routine occasions; three were *ad hoc* meetings called to consider specific problems – the

Pergamon-Leasco affair, an appeal on behalf of the 'C' shareholders in Swears and Wells (this concerned the problem of the relative prices which should be paid for voting and non-voting shares in a bid) and an appeal in the Trafalgar House-Cementation situation. On these three occasions full reports were issued by the Panel, and they were the only three occasions in which the decision of the executive was not finally accepted.

The report also showed, however, that in one way or another some 80 per cent of the total number of bid proposals were the subject of consultations or Panel enquiries – and this is not taking into account the further hundred or so cases where the executive was consulted but where no published proposals materialized, and a similar number where the Panel was asked for advice without being told the names of the companies involved.

Of course, the great bulk of these activities involved only minor points; many of these 'consultations' would have meant only a brief telephone call, or at most a short meeting at the Panel's offices. But this is really the point of the operation. The Panel was involved in a very high proportion of the bid activity, and it is in this way that its presence was most strongly felt. As a result of these operations, the principle has been firmly established that the Panel executive should be asked in advance whenever a company or its advisers are in any doubt at all about their plans. It has become an accepted part of the City's way of life to put in a quick call to the Panel; and for its part the executive has made certain that it is available for consultation at all times. Similarly, the executive has used its own initiative to intervene in cases where it foresees that there might be trouble. Its members know well by now the kind of problems that are likely to arise, and the circumstances which are likely to give rise to them; they know, for instance, that as soon as a bid proposal involving a company with a complex or odd capital structure comes up – like Swears and Wells – it is liable to cause trouble, and they will approach the companies and their advisers to make this point. Again, the executive has repeatedly stepped in off its own bat to press points which it regards as important – for instance, it has made an issue of the habit of holding special meetings of large institutional shareholders during bid situations to present the case of one or other of the contestants; where it heard of plans to hold such meetings, which it felt went right against the principle that all shareholders should be given equal information, it has either prevented them from happening or warned the participants not to disclose any information which was not made available to the rest of the shareholders.

The Panel, this is to say, worked in the way it is best designed to work – by prevention. It acted habitually in the early stages of bid situations to anticipate trouble. It is impossible to tell how many problems might have arisen during the year if the Panel had not been in existence; but it can be said that the takeovers proceeded smoothly, and it is reasonable to suppose that the Panel had something to do with this.

The second point I would bring out is the extent to which in 1969 the Panel and the executive carried out a continuing development of the principles enshrined in the Code as a result of its experience in interpreting those principles in relation to actual situations. As Lord Shawcross foresaw, by 1970 it had already built up a substantial body of case law – although the Panel, which is not bound by precedent, would probably prefer to call it merely experience of certain typical situations – which developed and extended its ideas of the Code's meaning. In its annual report for 1969 the Panel said that it had drawn a number of points to the attention of the Issuing Houses Association to be considered when the next revision of the Code is undertaken, although it also indicated that no radical changes in the present rules would be involved. But the report also includes sufficient evidence of the way in which the Panel's thinking has already been refined as a result of experience, in the list of important rulings appended to the report. One of the main complaints against the Panel during the later months of 1969 was that it was hard for a banker to anticipate how the Panel would react to a problem; the rules are written down in the Code, but around them there had already grown up a whole range of interpretations which were not published.

The incident involving Kleinwort and Cementation provided an example of this; in making its decision, the Panel indicated that it was drawing on experience it had already gained in two previous similar cases in insisting that Kleinworts should provide a full cash alternative for Cementation shareholders. The irony of this was that Kleinworts had actually been involved in one of these previous cases, though on the other side, and had not known about the Panel's decision.

By setting out with its report these decisions affecting the Code, the Panel went some way in answering this criticism. Fifteen of these decisions were included, some involving fairly substantial developments of the Code. The Kleinwort decision, for example, meant a significant extension of General Principle 8 of the Code, requiring all shareholders of the same class to be treated similarly, through the Panel's gloss that this also means that where a 'critical' block of shares (a term itself open to different interpretations) is bought for cash by an offeror with a paper bid, the cash alternative has to be extended to all shareholders. The Swears and Wells decision involved an interpretation of the Code's rule number 10, which requires a 'comparable' offer to be made to holders of all classes of capital, whether voting or or not, if voting control is transferred; it is now made clear that 'comparable' is to be interpreted in relation to market prices over a period. Rule 31, concerning share purchase in the market during a bid situation, is again significantly amended by the clarification of its definitions included in these judgments.

All this, moreover, is quite apart from the more formal developments incorporated in the publication of the Panel's 'practice notes', setting out its thinking on certain aspects of the Code. Three of these have been published so far [1970]; one covered the position, in the light of the Code, of private and unquoted public companies; one was concerned with the details of directors' emoluments and service contracts which have to be included in bid documents; and one set out the Panel's thinking on the subject I have already mentioned, the publication of information, the holding of special meetings of privileged shareholders, and the related question of the publication of special surveys and profits' estimates by stockbrokers who have a close relationship with certain companies. Three more are on the way; one is to deal with the particular problem of the frustration of bids by a third party; one is to take further the Panel's thinking on the still problematical area of the publication of details of share transactions during bid situations, and is expected to extend even more widely the definition of an 'associate' to make sure that nothing escapes the net; and one is to be concerned yet again with the recurring problem of profits' forecasts, and among other points is likely to consider the situation of companies which make profits' forecasts outside the context of a bid – when there is no effective restriction on what they may say – and may in effect avoid the strict control over forecasts imposed when they are made in a bid document.

These examples are indicative of the development of thinking about the control of takeovers even in a relatively short period, and of the Panel's ability within a voluntary system of control to adapt and change its attitudes to suit changing circumstances.

Finally, I would select a point worth emphasizing from the 1969 experience, the Panel's ability, when it chooses, to undertake what might be called more fundamental research into specific problem areas. The obvious example of this was the investigation into merchant banks, and specifically into the relationship between their corporate finance divisions, which in the course of advising companies in bid situations may frequently acquire privileged information which would be very valuable in making investment decisions, and their investment advice departments.

The summary of the Panel's conclusions from its investigation which was included with the annual report for 1969 gave a general clearance on this point for the merchant banking community as a whole. Nevertheless, it was clear that the Panel, while generally happy about the standards of ethics observed by the established merchant banking community, and about the arrangements they all make to avoid a conflict of interest, was more concerned about the increasing number of newcomers to the business who provide financial advice and who might be less aware of the potential dangers. To help them, it set out a series of nine guidelines to the best practice of the merchant banks in this area.

This type of general investigation, given the Panel's standing and authority, may well provide in the future a valuable forum for the discussions and elucidation of the City's problems.

The Present State of Takeover Control [1970]

This, then, is in outline the present state of the Panel and the Code after the first effective year of operation since the major revisions. Whatever the remaining weaknesses and faults of the City's voluntary system of control, at least the 1969 operation appears to have answered the previous main criticism; that the system was too weak to exercise any effective control. So far at least, the Panel has been a strong force. For this reason alone, it is fair to say that the heart has been taken out of the problem; as long as the Panel succeeds in operating as it did during 1969, the pressure for the government to intervene with a statutory system of controlling the stock market is unlikely to be renewed with any strength. This is not to say, of course, that the Panel may not fail yet.

At the same time, the Panel has demonstrated the advantages claimed for a voluntary as opposed to a statutory system, which in all fairness to the City have to be admitted to go beyond the mere fact that the voluntary system is more palatable to the City institutions and more in tune with British traditions. Lord Shawcross has drawn a sharp contrast with the way in which the Americans have tackled the problem through the SEC, an example which has frequently been held up for the City to follow by the critics of the present system. He argues that statutory methods of control, whether of takeover tactics in general or of specific issues such as the merchant banks and their conflict of interest, has two major drawbacks. They are far slower in operation than the voluntary system – imposing long delays on the operations of the capital market which may greatly hinder its effective operation. And they are less flexible; on one hand, setting out rigid rules simply invites people to find ways round them, and on the other hand, it would be impossible in a statutory system to carry out the kind of development and extension of thinking about takeover tactics which has been a feature of the Panel's operations in London.

The Panel has shown the benefits of its informality of operation, the speed with which it can reach a decision in the course of a rapidly developing takeover situation, and the flexibility it can bring to its approach to the problem. The 'spirit of the code' is the overriding principle of operation; the City knows what this means in general terms, and usually in any specific context. And because of the nature of its authority, grounded in the support of the same institutions it is set up to control, the Panel has the ability to interpret this principle freely to fit different circumstances.

Is Legislation Needed?

It is precisely because of the voluntary nature of the system, however, that it also contains drawbacks which have not so far been obvious but which, if eventually a more formal system is found to be needed, are likely to provide the basis for criticism of the operations of the Panel in its present form. There are, to begin with, weaknesses in the Code itself. There are parts which appear to be unworkable. There are areas such as profits' forecasting and the general question of dealings during bid situations which are likely to be a constant source of trouble and where the rules are certain to require constant change and refinement. But it is not in the Code that the real problems are likely to lie. These weaknesses can be gradually eliminated or at least reduced, and the Panel has already done much to refine the Code as a result of its experience in enforcing the rules. In any case, it is by no means clear that the situation would be improved if the Code were turned into law; the proponents of the voluntary system surely have much on their side in arguing that a statutory system of control would be much less able to adapt its principles to changing circumstances and to cope with the continuing development of City techniques. Replacing flexible rules with rigid laws would hardly make things better.

It is the character of the system itself which could in the end bring about its own replacement with more formal techniques. For however powerful it may appear to be, the Panel is in fact a very curious animal. It has no real standing except in relation to the goodwill of the City. And it depends for its effectiveness on retaining that goodwill and above all on the personal contact of its executive with the City.

This means, to begin with, that while it remains effective the voluntary system concentrates a very great deal of power in the hands of the small number of men who sit on the executive. This may be acceptable to the City while the alternative is understood to be direct intervention by the Government. Its success, however, must depend on those men and their successors keeping the confidence of the City.

It is necessary to be clear about the nature of the power the Panel wields. It affects much more than merely the City itself. The concern of the Panel, even in its inception, was far wider than merely keeping control over the market tactics of merchant bankers and stockbrokers and included responsibility for exercising restraints over the companies involved and their boards. During 1969, even while holding to its brief of looking after takeover situations, the Panel more than once found itself drawn into pronouncements which have implications far beyond its prescribed range of operations. It was on the grounds that the Panel had exceeded its brief in its comments on the Pergamon-Leasco situation (which unavoidably involved the whole question of Pergamon's reporting standards and its past profits) that Mr. Robert Maxwell went to the Panel's Appeals Committee. He lost the argument, but the point he was making was real enough. To work, the voluntary system has to carry the support of industry and commerce in its widest sense as well as just that of the City institutions.

Moreover the power of the Panel is in the ultimate analysis neither clearly defined nor directly answerable to any single authority. It is also, within the general confines of the Code, arbitrary.

The general point has been put most strongly by Mr. J. A. Franks, in a deliberately provocative article in the *Solicitors' Journal* in 1970. Criticizing the Panel for having no real legal basis, for greatly enhancing the status and power of the merchant banks, and for failing to operate in the real interests of shareholders or with a proper understanding of the duties of a board of directors, he argued that 'if left as it stands, there is a case for legislation on the subject of takeovers far better than if there were no Code and Panel at all'.

I would not put it as strongly as this. But it does seem possible that the nature of the present system contains the seeds of its own supersession by a more formal method of control. The basic point is this; however strong the sanctions apparently available to the Panel may be the Panel would find it very difficult actually to use them to enforce a decision which was generally unpopular in the City. The sanctions are a useful stick to wield, but the day that they actually have to be invoked will be a day of failure for the Panel. It works best, as I have indicated, through prevention; it is not in a strong position to act retrospectively once the damage has been done, and may in fact be quite unable to undo the harm. If there were again a major boom in merger activity, and if the Panel were faced with a number of really tricky cases to handle publicly, there is no certainty that it would be able to cope. And one bad error, or one act which lost it the confidence of the City, would do harm to the system which would be hard if not impossible to repair.

This is not to say that there is any sign at the moment that there is any pressure for legislative action. This is a step that the Labour Government at least has shown it would be most unwilling to take.

The Securities Market

Nevertheless, there are some signs that the present stage of development is really only the beginning of what may eventually turn out to be a major step towards much closer, and perhaps finally legislative control of the City and of the securities market in particular. This is so not specifically because of the nature of the Code and the Panel as it applies to takeover and merger situations. It is so because the takeover Code and Panel cover only one aspect of a far wider problem which is only now beginning to be grasped. It is the newest and the most conspicuous body dealing with the securities market, and it is concerned with that aspect of share dealings, the takeover, which has been most prominent in recent years and which has caused the most trouble. But the problems which have cropped up in the context of takeovers are only the symptoms of a much deeper malaise which we are a long way from solving.

If anything, the activities of the Panel have served simply to highlight this more general problem. The obvious aspect of this is perhaps the convulsions through which the accounting profession is now going. The Pergamon-Leasco affair, as the Panel admitted itself, involved issues beyond the scope of its authority, concerned with the whole basis of company accounting, its purpose and its accuracy and its usefulness as a guide to investors. It is as a result of this and other similar cases that the profession, under the leadership of Sir Ronald Leach, of the Institute of Chartered Accountants in England and Wales, began the great heart-searching through which it is now going. Accounting has been the subject of a great deal of criticism; the Institute has virtually acknowledged that the critics were right. It has admitted in effect that the principles followed in the creation and presentation of company accounts have allowed far too great a latitude to company directors and far too wide a choice of alternative methods of presenting the same figures. The result is that company accounts, while they may fulfil the traditional function of reporting to the owners of a company – the shareholders – on the stewardship of the directors during the year and the way in which they have handled shareholders' funds, are not far short of useless as an instrument for comparing one company with another and therefore as the foundation on which to base investment decisions.

The Institute is tackling the urgent problem of getting more sense into accounting methods. But by implication it has recognized the more basic point that the whole purpose of accounting has to be rethought. It realizes that stricter accounting principles will require the members of the profession, in their capacity as auditors of company accounts, to be prepared to lay down the law to company directors. It is prepared to insist that company boards give much more information about the bases on which their accounts are prepared. And it has even, by entertaining the idea of setting up a group to undertake fundamental research into the philosophy of accounting, including representatives of the academic section of the profession, recognized that the whole basis of accounting techniques needs to be reviewed. The present reforms could take the profession much further away from its traditional approach to the job than it perhaps realizes itself.

The accountants are only one of the bodies concerned with what may be defined as the general problem of the securities market. The Board of Trade has the responsibility for controlling and guiding legislation on companies and their disclosure of information. It is not a subject which recently has greatly interested the presidents of the Board of Trade who might have been in a position to put a new impetus behind the Board. And it is not unfair to say that the civil servants who have carried the main responsibility in this area, while strict in their application of the law and insistent on the proper disclosure of information by companies, have taken an approach which is defined in terms of the law and is not directly related to the needs of investors. It is the Board of Trade's task to regulate companies, to prevent fraud, to ensure that the company Acts are observed; it is not its job, except incidentally, to protect shareholders or to ensure a proper market in company shares.

Even the Stock Exchange Council, much closer to the market and much more intimately involved with the shareholder, has not, I feel, quite touched the centre of the issue. It can claim to have been in advance of the law in the degree of disclosure of information it has required of companies, it can claim to have been assiduous in exercising control over its own members and in maintaining an orderly stock market. Yet still its interests, as a City institution representative of City companies, have not, I would argue, lain ultimately with encouraging the development of capitalism in the United Kingdom or of ensuring in the broadest sense that a proper basis is available on which to make investment decisions.

For this is the issue which I think is being raised. Britain presents a contrast with the US in that the stock market does not occupy here, as Wall Street can be said to do in the US, a central position in the economic and social philosophy of the country. Historically, Americans have been concerned both to make the stock markets run properly and to encourage the population at large to take an interest in it.

The implication of the government's interest in the proper regulation of takeovers, of the activities of the Takeover Panel itself, of the revolution in the accounting profession, seems to be that in future the securities market here is going to be taken more seriously. Regarded as the place which determines the marginal cost of capital to industry, the stock market should occupy a higher place in official economic planning; and even under a Labour Government there was no indication of a will to remove this function from the City. The implication ought to be that a greater effort will be needed to build, and not merely to regulate, the securities market.

Quite what form this will take is not at all clear. It will happen, if at all, against a background of new thinking in many other related areas – we are likely, for instance, to see over the next few years a new approach to the institution of the limited company evolving to combine some form of social responsibility – already widely acknowledged by industry – with a greater accountability to employees – possibly in the form of worker representatives on the board. This will inevitably imply a change in the traditional and legal concepts of the relationship between the company and its owners, the shareholders. However it ends, nevertheless, it seems probable that a process of revision has been started which still has a very long way to go.

The point I want to stress has two aspects. First, at present the job of controlling and regulating the stock market, and the related function of regulating companies and governing the information they release for public consumption, is divided up among a number of bodies. None of these bodies is in a position to take an overall view of the problem. Second, there is nowhere in this country a body or a centre of opinion which is charged with the basic function of ensuring that the securities market operates efficiently, not merely in the limited City sense but in the context of the economy as a whole. That there is real and growing concern about this problem seems to be evident from the anxiety which has been demonstrated from various sources to improve the operations of the market as they bear on the efficiency of industry – for instance, Sir Brandon Rhys Williams' efforts, on the one hand, to provide a greater role and greater power to control company boards for the small private shareholders, and on the other the pressure from people like Mr. Fred Catherwood for the large institutional shareholders to play a more active part in advising companies and forcing them to improve their efficiency.

At the moment, the Takeover Panel is the nearest approach Britain has to a body whose main aim is to protect shareholders and to ensure that the stock market is efficient. But its brief is limited and, without criticism, concerned essentially with the more superficial aspects of stock market operations (although many of its decisions, as I have remarked, have far wider implications).

I do not believe that at the moment there is any real pressure for the voluntary system of takeover discipline to be replaced by a statutory form of control, although eventually a more formal constitution may be necessary. But out of the more general problem, which is only just beginning to be analysed and discussed, it seems likely that the need will eventually emerge for a new central body to collate and inform the various and diverse efforts of the more specialized organizations – an authoritative Panel for the City, if you like, with the task of organizing the whole effort and inspiring it with an ideology, if that can be taken to signify fundamental principles.

This is not likely to happen yet; there is as yet neither the will nor probably the understanding of the problem to make it happen. And if eventually it does happen, it would probably be a mistake to follow too closely the pattern of the American SEC, which after all was designed to meet conditions in another country and in another time. It may grow out of the Panel, which is at least the one organization which represents a united effort by all the various sections of the City and of the government involved with the problem to get to grips with one aspect of the securities market. Certainly the experience of the Takeover Panel will be invaluable; it is no criticism to say that it may need to be superseded.

Editor's note

As Mr Blanden explains, when the Panel on Takeovers and Mergers was first set up there was considerable opposition to the idea of a voluntary code. There was a body of opinion that thought the rules of behaviour should be legally enforceable. It soon became obvious however that the City Code did have an effect, and certainly brought to an end the worst practices of the takeover raids of the mid 1960s. The Code as administered by the Panel was flexible and in its early days decisions were required on situations that could not have been legislated for in advance. Perhaps the biggest asset in favour of the Panel was its speed of action; it was able to make a decision within a few days, whereas a legislative body, similar say to the Restrictive Practices Court, would have taken very much longer.

Perhaps one of the most surprising facts about the Panel is the amount of work it is still required to do. In the year ending 31 March 1971, a year in which takeover activity was on the decline, the Panel at its executive level was called upon to examine, to advise upon, and to intervene at an average rate of eight cases a week. The Panel in its short life has produced a number of Notes to guide companies when involved in Takeover and Merger situations, and it has adapted and clarified the Code as circumstances dictate. As the Panel itself says, it has silenced much of the opposition to a voluntary system.

The Panel has helped to reduce one obstacle in the way of fair, workable competition. A company can now feel that its position is more secure, and that if it is acquired by another company the acquisition will be the result of a contest in which it has had a reasonable opportunity to defend itself and it has not lost because of some trick. The worrying factor now regarding the influence of the capital market on the degree of competition in the economy concerns the position of the small company. There are virtues in having small companies competing in the market place. These are dealt with in numerous chapters in this book. But the relative importance of the small company is declining. This has been well documented by the Bolton Committee.

One of the reasons for the decline in the number and importance of small companies is the growth of the financial institution. The institutions are usually only interested in investing in the shares of a company if they can buy and sell large numbers of the shares without affecting the price of the share by more than a few pennies. They are reluctant to hold a large proportion of the shares of any particular company, because they are not investing in it with the object of controlling the company but purely to obtain a balanced portfolio. They therefore concentrate the bulk of their investment in the shares of large companies.

Because an increasing proportion of the savings of the country are being placed in the hands of the institutions, an increasing proportion of the investment of the country is going into the shares of large companies. If the City, or the Government, is interested in preserving the small company something needs to be done to halt and perhaps reverse this trend. This would seem to be the problem of the 1970s.

Chapter Twelve

TAMING AND CONTROLLING POWER*

R. Goodman

Vice-Chairman of the Acton Society Trust

Different societies in different historical epochs bestow power on their leaders in different forms; priestly power, kingly power, military power and economic power are some of the types.[1] In western society at the present time, the typical form is economic. It is achieved through three kinds of organization: commercial companies or corporations, trade unions and governments. The economic organizations that are characteristic of our age are consciously developed by their leaders so that they themselves may derive from them, and through them, the maximum power which those belonging to them and working for them will tolerate.

The strategy of economic power is similar in many respects[2] to that of military power. Attack is the best form of defence. To expand one's territory is the most certain means of preserving one's base. Thus, size of organization becomes the all-important consideration. It is both a measure of triumph and a proof of the security of one's own organization. Moreover, size itself creates the resources of further expansion. These are maintained in a pool of reserves that can be switched across internal lines of communication from one part of the organization to another. Rapid expansion can be obtained by two methods: successful aggression with one's own resources or in combination with an ally's. In this way takeover bids and mergers are, in the terminology of financial journalism, what battles and alliances are to military historians. Successful aggression leading to the conquest of territory and eventual empire, regardless of consequences in terms of real benefit to the home population, is the common goal that military and economic leaders share.

The industrial leader is not so much concerned with maximizing his profits, or with his workers' wages or even his own and co-directors' salaries, as he is with increasing the availability of capital and credit that will enable him to increase the size of the organization which he commands and the share of the market that it aims to dominate. Similarly national politicians, in their roles as economic generalissimos, are concerned first and foremost with the cash flow resulting from their country's foreign trading. Hence their favours and privileges are bestowed on the largest commercial employers who are likely to be the strongest and most aggressive forces in

*Based on material in *The Impact of Size,* The Acton Society Trust, 1969.

the export field. But if exports are insufficient, they will not hesitate to sanction the sale to a foreign competitor of some of their country's best firms at a sufficiently high price.

The politician has, therefore, been as anxious as the industrial leader to promote mergers and takeovers and to increase the size of economic units. But it is important to see that, whether Labour or Conservative, he has been brainwashed into believing this to be necessary. Only a few years before he was equally busy preaching the necessity of competition or of restraining the growth of monopolistic practices. A few years hence, in a different climate of 'informed opinion', he may be advocating something quite different. The politician has not the knowledge, nor indeed, except in outstanding instances, the philosophy to follow a consistent policy. He is dependent, as are also an increasing number of people who wish to form opinions without going to the trouble of acquiring fundamental knowledge, upon professional opinion formers: upon mass-media pundits, economic journalists and writers of specialized books who claim to have the 'one-off' answer. It is they who have prepared the ground for the Cult of Bigness, it is they who proclaim its inevitability.

Although economic power is the characteristic form of power in our age, it is not true to say that political power has become overtly subordinate to it. The relationship is more subtle. The successful holder of economic power is the one who knows how to play the political machine. He insinuates himself into the politicians' confidence, forms pressure groups, anticipates political situations and has his case considered well before time. He employs experts to advise him how to avoid the worst consequences of legislation or to turn it to his advantage. Above all he works through public relations officers and the mass-media pundits themselves, so that the climate of opinion is nearly always favourable to his long term interests. The most successful of all is one whose power base is not located under any one political sovereignty. He can shift his own throne from one country to another according to political and economic circumstances. Thus, the international company is in a position not only to allocate its greatest profits to those of its subsidiary companies sited in the lowest tax-paying areas, but also to move its cash resources from country to country so that they always stand the best chance of being revalued in terms of the strongest currency of the moment.

The most thorough-going apostle of bigness is, however, the successful trade union leader. Whatever the situation – business merger, local authority amalgamation, creation of new *ad hoc* authority or nationalized industry – he is always on the side of size writ large. For, the larger the unit in which his followers are employed, the greater is the power he wields through the strike weapon. Moreover in his own union affairs, he is every bit as much an amalgamationist as any industrialist or financier. The empires of the few really adept trade union despots are made up of as many disparate and unlikely entities as any conglomerate or financial empire.

'The power impulse', says Bertrand Russell, 'has two forms: explicit, in leaders; implicit, in followers. When men willingly follow a leader, they do so with a view to the acquisition of power by the group which he commands, and they feel that his triumphs are theirs.'[3] In combating economic power, in trying to tame it and to bring it under control, both aspects have to be considered: the gratifications experienced by leaders and by followers. Leaders enjoy its thrills, and followers the senses of security and vicarious prestige that stem from belonging to large aggressive organizations.

Neither love of power by the strong nor the dependence on it by the weak can be abolished from society. However, both can be reduced and, in being reduced, put to good purposes. This has been the constant theme of liberal democracy. A leader can acquire a sense of responsibility towards those he governs and develop an awareness of the multitude of independent aims which his followers wish to realize. For their part, followers can develop the initiatives, skills and abilities to do for themselves much that they would otherwise want to be done for them. Education, a secure broadly based political system and the widespread distribution of opportunity have been some of the many important traditional ways of attempting to achieve these ends. But the most important and certain of all have been the liberal policies of decentralizing power, dividing it and multiplying checks upon its use and enjoyment. 'Power follows property' and no rebellion against its concentrated exercise can be successful that fails to redistribute its property base.[4] Decentralized units of initiative competing against each other tend to cancel out and balance the power of each other; their existence also ensures that the state is never dependent upon a single source of leadership. It is absolute power that corrupts absolutely and concentrated power that tyrannizes.

How may these principles, gathered from centuries of liberal political development, be applied to the large-scale structures of economic power that now dominate society, cripple the initiatives of individuals and destroy their expectations of a fuller life?

The liberal aim has been to secure its policies by strong laws and by broadly based constitutions. Acton often referred in his essays to the liberal procedure being one of 'revolution towards constitution'. Conscience dictated the nature of the changes there should be; reason and a long tradition of tried principles, the forms they should take. These ideas were of universal application so that leaders of liberal revolution never legislated for particular cases nor created single classes of interest to give its policies expression. Thus, they recognized no authority but the authority of the law itself, and their ideal of constitution was for the law to hold in check and to control the exercise of decentralized power.

Belief in these principles gave to the leaders of liberal revolution in western countries a formula for devising new political institutions and altering old ones. Their need for such a formula arose from the fact that they faced an apparent contradiction: the reduction of the powers of the privileged and the raising of the liberties of the masses of people bespoke a decentralized society, whilst the need for formal institutions and a vigilant system of laws bespoke a centralized one. From this contradiction they developed their formula of liberal revolution, which was to separate into two elements rights that had hitherto been considered indivisible: the first set, the private, they declared the inalienable possession of the individual to do with as he wished and to enjoy as he wished, either alone or in association with his fellows; the other they declared to be a public right, the no less inalienable function of central bodies of society to administer. All rights, all liberties were individual until, in the exercising of them, the point was reached when either they conflicted with each other or they threatened a larger good.

At that point the court's, the policeman's or the central government's function began. The line between the two was arbitrary and not always clear in advance; nevertheless in practice it was always discoverable. There was a public aspect to every private right and advantage. Moreover, both the private and the public were enforceable. And so, under the umbrella of public protection and public qualification, private rights, thus limited, grew; personal liberties flourished and the masses of people began to enjoy initiatives not open to them before. In these ways institutions were given negative and restraining functions, in order to promote the positive and widespread enjoyment of individual initiatives and liberties. An example may be given: landed property rights were qualified both by general laws and by restrictions in deeds of ownership and tenancy agreements as between different owners and classes of owners, and between tenants and sub-tenants. Death duties and taxes were devised to restrict the amounts of capital and income the owners might possess. The law also made it possible for very many different rights to be created out of the same area of land, and most of these survive to the present day. There are ground landlords, leaseholders of buildings, tenants and sub-tenants, estate owners, farming tenants and owners of fishing rights, shooting rights and mineral rights; there are also rights of way, public footpaths, commons. Superior to all these, there is the right of the public to acquire land for roads and other public purposes, and, in recent times, town-planning legislation enabling the community to control development and to place yet further limitations upon personal ownership. Other liberties, such as freedom of association and of publishing, were similarly qualified by legislation in the interest both of individuals and of the community.

It is important to appreciate, however, that this formula of liberal revolution was not applied to the industrial and commercial realm in the same way that it was to others. In the first part of the 19th century, it is true, ancient monopolies and privileged corporations were broken and the decentralization of economic activity was achieved. But fewer limitations were placed on the enjoyment of rights arising from the corporate ownership of industrial and commercial property than there were upon other classes of ownership and other forms of right.

The public limited company itself was a mid-century creation of utilitarian-liberal policies. It possesses now, as it did then, rights in perpetuity: it never has death duties to pay; it can accumulate massive reserves of money, taxed at very much lower rates than individuals with similar incomes; it has no leaseholders or sub-tenants with whom to share its enjoyment of what it owns, and there are fewer restrictions placed on the use to which it can put its capital; it may buy out other companies and eventually, contrary to general liberal principles, achieve a dominance of its particular market or markets.

Another aspect of the ownership of industrial property which 19th-century utilitarian-liberal policy neglected was the distribution of new wealth. It assumed, often uncritically, that profits should belong exclusively to shareholders. In this way all new wealth tended to flow back into the hands of the privileged wealth-owning minority. Very little thought was given to increasing the abilities of wage-earners to own the means whereby they could seek their fulfilment or to purchase a greater proportion of the goods they had helped to produce.

In a short period the freedom given by utilitarian-liberal policies to the limited liability company enabled it to establish a kingdom within a kingdom. The consequences are well known; for example, the slums and ugly town centres bequeathed by industrialism. Today most people of liberal sympathies would be closer to Marx in condemning that 'kingdom's' treatment of its workers and the roles it assigned to them, than would their liberal forefathers who tolerated its autonomous development.

The 20th century has, of course, seen great changes. Collective bargaining has gained higher wage-levels and improved conditions of work. The welfare state has intervened to provide security and benefits in kind, if not of effective choice. Nevertheless, in at least three very important respects there has been significant deterioration. First, technological innovations and mass-production methods have sub-divided the processes of 'detail work' into tens of thousands more minute parts than ever Marx foresaw. Secondly, the small industrial firm and the decentralized units of initiative typical of the 19th century have given way to the vast concentration of economic power typical of this. In a country such as Britain, whose share of international trade is decreasing and where inflation continues unabated, the needs and values of the large corporation increasingly dictate the nature of most social and political actions. Thirdly, materialistic standards have permeated nearly all departments of life; work and leisure have become wholly involved in the money form and few activities remain to be pursued for their own sake or for the intrinsic pleasures they give. Aesthetically, but not perhaps physiologically, the gin-palace was superior to the bingo hall: at least people talked to each other. The economic realm now dominates every other.

The problems neglected by mid-19th-century liberals, therefore, have become crucial: how should corporate rights derived from industrial and commercial activity be qualified in the same way as other rights; how should the workers' role in industry be defined so as to allow them to participate, as their individual abilities and inclinations warrant, in controlling the processes they perform and in the wealth they help create? How can corporate sovereignty and the rights of capital ownership be limited within a broader political framework established according to liberal and human values; and how within such a framework can the advantages of large-scale organization and small-scale initiative combine?

The Tendency Towards Large Political Units

Similar questions to these arise if we turn from the problem of industrial structure to those of government. Is it possible for a common answer to be found to both sets of questions?

Rights of national sovereignty, no less than those of the public limited liability company, are in need of qualification and sub-division. They are altogether inappropriate to contemporary circumstances. Nowhere is this more apparent than in the case of those new nations which have been created out of the former British, French, Belgian and Dutch empires. Not only are their boundaries artificial ones, often cutting through the territories of the indigenous peoples, drawn by the negotiators of the colonial powers in the 19th century and at the end of the 1914–18 war, but a substantial proportion of their very limited resources is spent on armies to maintain them. All too often the army officers are the only people capable of exercising power, so that the civil authorities have continually to look over their shoulders to see that they are in step with the troops behind them. In an atmosphere of continuing crisis, the natural spontaneity of the governed people is repressed, and the life of liberty to which they looked forward on independence is denied them. Age-long patterns of culture have been put in a melting-pot to be re-forged in new imported moulds which they do not know whether they want or not.

Those responsible for the development of the new nations are bedevilled by the confusion created by the overlapping of three considerations – economic, cultural and political. Economically, the need of their states is often to cover larger territories than they do at present; culturally, their problem is often to discover what is the right emphasis and degree of self-government to give to peoples of different traditions and languages contained within their borders, as, for example, in Kenya and Nigeria; whilst politically, their *raison d'être* is to build up a strong centralized administration in order to maintain the boundaries allotted to them on independence and to create a lively sense of one nation. It is impossible within the framework of national sovereignty as at present understood for these three sets of desiderata to be fully or even partially reconciled.

The highly developed nations of the world face similar issues. The smaller units, of which larger entities are constituted, count for less and less. The small local authority, for instance, has to yield to central government directions; amalgamations of different urban and rural councils, sometimes even of county councils, are forced upon them, so that the functions of the one-time significant parish council and the small rural or urban district council, which served a useful cultural purpose in the community, as well as being an efficient, small 'face-to-face' unit of self-government, are being lost in amalgamations and schemes of reorganization. Regionalism, it is true, has become a fashionable concept; but one, it is suspected, that will be used to extract power from local authorities and to establish listening posts and local out-stations for central government.

The tendencies towards centralization in national government and industry converge. Each time an independent local business is taken over by a larger national company, a significant number of independent local men are lost to the community. Managers replace owners, and travelling specialists replace the hitherto indispensable 'characters' around whom the affairs of the firm once revolved. What is worse, the new men do not come to stay: they move from one of the new larger firm's subsidiaries to another and from one branch town to another. No one of importance or of potential influence any longer stays in one place, except at the headquarters – and the headquarters are synonymous with four or five large cities, the new 'headquarter towns' which industry shares with the most important departments of government. The local community thus loses both its independence and the men who, once foremost in its life, might have been able to restore its vitality.

Movement of men of ability from one place to another is neither new nor deplorable in itself. Everybody has the right to move or not to move, as he wishes. But what is new and deplorable is that large corporations move men and women around solely to satisfy company needs. Moreover, the satisfaction of these needs takes them from the places where their roots are established to one impermanency after another, or else to the inorganic communities that surround the headquarter cities. For most, home is where the suitcase is; therefore promotion in these large impersonal corporations often means that people of superior ability cease to have the opportunities of social leadership that come to those long known and respected in one place.

Problems of national sovereignty and of the large industrial or financial corporation have, therefore, much in common. Both the nation and the typical large modern corporation embrace a number of entities which, for many purposes, can be separated from them: nations can be subdivided into provinces, different ethnic and cultural groups, and separate areas of local government; corporations into separate firms and quasi-independent 'divisions' or separate factories belonging to the same parent company. These distinctive entities can be broken down until finally the significant responsible group of individuals is reached. It is these units to which significance should be restored and new vitality injected. But no sooner do we recognize this need than we have to admit that the tendencies towards large units and centralized administration, both in government and in industry, stem from the technology of modern society that bestows on us all the advantages of sciences required to fight poverty, disease and necessity.

Whatever excuses oligarchies have needed to justify their gaining control over very wide areas in both economic and political fields have been provided for them by those who study modern techniques and point out that their most successful, their optimum, exploitation can be enjoyed only by the very largest units of organization. Modern communication-media, automation, applied electronics and all the many ingenious machines that have been devised in this century are so large and expensive that they can only be afforded, economically developed and utilized by the largest conceivable units employing mass techniques. Similarly it is argued that in the course of a hundred years management and administrative techniques and decision-making procedures have been improved out of all recognition. Whereas at the Battle of Solferino in 1859 Napoleon III and Franz Josef of Austria found it impossible to control armies of no more than 140,000 men, in the second world war the German and Russian chiefs of staff each had forces of more than 10,000,000 men under well-organized control. The same system of command and administration which they used is now available, it is argued, in civilian life, to industry and to central and local government. Therefore, rather than envisaging the sub-division of existing industrial empires and political entities into smaller units, the apologist's of large-scale organizations advocate still more amalgamations and still greater extensions of centralized control. 'Maximum efficiency in production and marketing', reads an advertisement in *The Times* newspaper of July 4, 1965, 'increasingly calls for larger units in modern industry. Takeovers and amalgamations bring the advantages of rationalization to all concerned.' Given the industrial structures and strategies we have at present, the claims of this advertisement are more than half-truths.

Notwithstanding these developments, the traditional advantages of small and medium-sized suitably equipped units remain and continue to be recognized. Large armies find it difficult to beat small efficient forces, as the limited wars of the 50s and 60s have shown. Defence ministries, looking ahead to the nuclear and biological wars of the future and to the need to disperse their forces, are once again thinking in terms of small highly mobile forces and decentralized posts of command. Smaller business firms make larger profits relative to their size and assets than larger ones. It has recently been shown,[5] for example, that in Britain firms with assets of over £65,000,000 yield an average return of only 13·93 per cent; those with assets of between £500,000 and £1,000,00, 20·39 per cent and small firms of less than £250,000 assets, 18·70 per cent. In the United States, another survey showed 'that independent investors and small technologically based companies are responsible for a remarkable percentage of the important inventions and innovations of this century'.[6] The overwhelming majority of industrial psychological and sociological opinion is that small groups and small-sized firms are the most happy and creative environment for the normal person.

A Possible Solution

We can now put forward the guide lines of a possible solution to the problems that have been raised. The problem of scale in the international sphere, it is recognized, is that of finding the right kind of organizations which will guarantee the integrity of small national units, yet at the same time provide them with the advantages of belonging to large-scale international bodies. The answer will probably be found in two ways: first, in the creation of supra-national agencies to carry out certain specific functions and, secondly, in the coming together of independent nations within the same geographical area or within areas sharing the same cultural and political aims, into some kind of confederation. Examples of supra-national *ad hoc* bodies are the International Monetary Fund and the various organizations set up by the European Economic Community. But there are no examples in the present-day world of the type of confederation that seem likely to come about, although possibly the Austro-Hungarian Empire that existed until 1919 and the organization of Switzerland into cantons, which survive to the present day, may be considered in some respects prototypes.

If this be the pattern for the solution of the problem of scale in the international sphere, is it possible for the same pattern to be applied in the economic and national? Can supra-sovereign bodies be created in different industries to administer some of the benefits of rationalization, the advantages of scale, on behalf of the independent firms in them? Can some of the subsidiaries of economic empires regain some of their independence within such a structure? Can autonomous legal institutions be created to exercise watchfulness over these bodies on behalf of the community? Similarly, can joint bodies be set up to administer some of the economies of scale in government, so that instead of, for example, local authorities and county councils being amalgamated they can be given renewed vigour and efficiency? Can restrictions be placed on the new wealth created by industry so that the community can benefit and those creating it can earn their just entitlements and use their increased earnings to pursue aims of their own choosing?

These questions point to the possibility of umbrella-like confederal structures being the answer both to the problems of scale and to the dilemma caused by the tension between liberal, political and economic thought. Semi-autonomous bodies, neutral as between state and private ownership, it is proposed, should exist to provide services for a multitude of independent units. The chapters that follow[7] will argue the case for such institutions and will suggest some of the functions that they should perform. Meanwhile, a generous selection of quotations from Keynes's essay, 'The End of Laissez-Faire',[8] will make clear the general intention of these proposals and illuminate the standpoint of value from which they are addressed.

'It is not true that individuals possess a prescriptive "natural liberty" in their economic activities. There is no "compact" conferring perpetual rights on those who Have or on those who Acquire. The world is not so governed from above that private and social interest always coincide. It is not so managed here below that in practice they coincide. It is not a correct deduction from the Principles of Economics that enlightened self-interest always operates in the public interest. . . . Experience does not show that individuals, when they make up a social unit, are always less clear-sighted than when they act separately. . . .

'We cannot, therefore, settle on abstract grounds, but must handle on its merits in detail, what Burke termed "one of the finest problems in legislation, namely, to determine what the State ought to take upon itself to direct by the public wisdom, and what it ought to leave, with as little interference as possible, to individual exertion". We have to discriminate between what Bentham, in his forgotten but useful nomenclature, used to term Agenda and Non-Agenda, and to do this without Bentham's prior presumption that interference is, at the same time, "generally needless" and "generally pernicious". Perhaps the chief task of Economists at this hour is to distinguish afresh the Agenda of Government from the Non-Agenda; and the companion task of Politics is to devise forms of Government within a Democracy which shall be capable of accomplishing the Agenda. . . .

'(1) I believe that in many cases the ideal size for the unit of control and organization lies somewhere between the individual and the modern State. I suggest, therefore, that progress lies in the growth and the recognition of semi-autonomous bodies within the State . . . bodies which in the ordinary course of affairs are mainly autonomous within their prescribed limitations, but are subject in the last resort to the sovereignty of the democracy expressed through Parliament. . . .

'(2) We must aim at separating those services which are technically social from those which are technically individual.'

Whenever the problems of company size and future industrial structures are considered, it will be useful to bear in mind, therefore, the importance of separating those problems which are technically social from those which are in Keynes' terminology technically individual; those which are technically appropriate to be performed by semi-autonomous bodies and those which are best carried out by individual firms or spontaneous groups of like-minded individuals; then, having so separated the functions appropriate to each, to consider the two further problems: first, of how the semi-autonomous bodies, on the one side, and individual firms and groups, on the other, may be best enabled to carry them out; secondly, of how government departments and even Parliament itself may be adapted so as to limit the abuses of power by leaders in the economic realm and to provide the material opportunities for relatively small firms and groups of like-minded individuals to fulfil the projects which their members have formulated.

The essays collected in this volume will do much to illuminate these problems from the very practical standpoint provided by the merger and takeover movement of the 50s and 60s. Nevertheless, before the inquiry suggested by Keynes over 45 years ago can be regarded as completed, there are other questions to investigate which these essays explore rather than answer. It will be appropriate to name a few of them:

1. If there is such a thing as an optimum-sized firm in industry?
   (*a*) Does it matter whether this size is achieved by internal growth or by merger?
   (*b*) Does it vary from industry to industry?
2. (*a*) Can the growth of some highly successful firms be explained by the idea of replicative extension; e.g., banks, retail stores and perhaps some mines?
   (*b*) Can the growth of others be explained by the possibility of delegating the functions of control to the operating unit, except only for contact between top management and management of subsidiary about such items as finance, marketing and technical developments?
   (*c*) Either as an alternative or complementary hypothesis: is firm-size affected by the 'think-content' or lack of 'think-content' in the work done?
3. If it is important on grounds of value, as the present writer believes, to encourage firms of the size where people working in them can participate intelligently and imaginatively in all the processes carried out, as well as themselves having absorbing work to do:
   (*a*) What is the desirable form of inter-dependence between various types of 'think-work'
   (*b*) Does such work require more or less co-ordination than 'non-think' work; and what form ought this co-ordination to take?

These and similar questions have been taxing the minds of some of the writers of the essays collected here.

PART D

THE INTERNATIONAL ASPECTS OF MERGERS

Chapter Thirteen

MERGERS AND TAKEOVERS: PROBLEMS OF THE MULTI-NATIONAL COMPANY*

Michael Z. Brooke

Lecturer in Management Sciences, University of Manchester Institute of Science and Technology

SUMMARY

This paper begins by discussing 'straws in the wind' which indicate problems in the merger process, a process whose advantages were virtually taken for granted until recently. These 'straws' consist partly of publicly expressed doubts about this process by an increasing number of people, and partly of discoveries made during the study of international concerns. Some of the difficulties are concerned with vertical integration; others include the use and misuse of managerial talent.

The problems here considered are mainly of a behavioural nature. They have been isolated in the course of studies of management and its activities in multi-national companies involving interviews with nearly 500 managers in 80 firms. Their frustrations alone, however, are hardly likely to produce a move to unmerger, but will lend additional support to national attitudes that are building up. These particularly involve an unusual consensus between the financial establishment and the trade unions in countries which receive a large amount of foreign investment. In spite of bringing in capital, know-how, employment and other advantages, the foreign firm threatens national aspirations in significant ways – for instance by removing from the money market some of the growth areas of the economy.

Countries will not want to forego the advantages of foreign investment, but there is bound to be a tolerance limit somewhere. Hence government action against monopoly, as well as in defence of national sovereignty, will bring a move towards the break-up of large concerns. But the real trend to unmerger will come when someone finds a formula for making money by it. It is suggested that a formula, whereby the benefits of internationalism can be combined with the advantages of smallness, can be found.

---

*Based on a paper presented at the Conference on Mergers and Takeovers, London, May 29,

1. Straws in the Wind

'It doesn't do any of this maliciously, to be sure, any more than an elephant feels malice when it rubs up against a sapling and breaks it in two. An elephant must behave like an elephant, . . .' This comment from a recent American book is on United States investment abroad.[1] The author says, in effect, that the policies as well as the reputation of his country are being determined in many fields by the American investor; he adds that neither the official organs of government nor the companies themselves often realize what is happening until it is too late. Activities are mentioned as frustrating 'the government in various proceedings that have full public endorsement'. This statement represents one aspect of current questioning about the multi-national firm, alongside powerful arguments about the benefactions it is bringing to mankind.

My professional acquaintance with this type of organization goes back seven years to the start of a research project which still continues as a joint venture between the University of Manchester Institute of Science and Technology and the European Institute of Business Administration at Fontainebleau. The project was started with a grant from OECD. In 1963 the subject was a fairly esoteric area of study in Europe, and all the literature was American, that is the literature which looked at the multi-national company in its own right, and the development of theories and concepts relevant to the total management process. Naturally there has always been considerable interest in specific aspects of the subject, such as investment abroad; but widespread general interest has grown only recently. A managing director of Shell has referred to this growing interest in the following words:

'The multi-national corporations have recently become the darling of the management sociologists, economic columnists and a pet subject for seminars and conferences. Five years ago they were a favourite target of left-wing politicians. Today they have achieved moderate respectability, and research grants are being made to study them.'[2] He also said that all this research is putting a burden on senior managers.

One change in recent years that has odd political implications is the mounting onslaught on the activities of such firms from inside the capitalist system, by the financial establishments in many countries. A consequence of this onslaught has been the publication of major government reports in countries like Canada and Australia.[3] There are a number of important reasons for this development: one of them is that by insisting on 100 per cent ownership of local subsidiaries, companies are removing from national money markets businesses which may well form the most dynamic part of the local economy.

One suspects that it is this two-pronged attack – from the socialists and the trade unions on the one hand, and from the financial establishment on the other – that has made the subject so topical.

The picture of the multi-national firm presented in the literature on the subject available in the mid-sixties was very different from that provided by the critics of the left or the right. Innumerable articles in American business (and particularly business school) journals painted a glowing picture of the rise of the multi-national corporation. This was enhanced by company handouts and press articles. Rich rewards, it was asserted, were available to those who invested as far and as fast as possible. By a happy dispensation of providence, the argument continued, what is profitable for the parent company is also enormously to the advantage of its foreign subsidiary, of its country of origin and of the foreign states in which it operates. All four benefit at the same time; and everybody enjoys a higher standard of living thanks to these universal providers. One American professor was so infected by all this enthusiasm that he forecast that world business would be dominated by three hundred super-firms by the end of the century, as we are constantly being reminded.

No doubt the cult of bigness further promoted the whole idea of the multi-national firm. For this type of concern was the ultimate in the optimum use of resources according to the prevalent theory. The merger across frontiers enabled the fullest advantage to be taken of the developing techniques of global planning in finance, marketing, production, personnel and every other function. This is really where this subject fits into this book. My briefing was to bring out some ascertainable problems of the multi-national firm which relate to the pros and cons of mergers.

Interviews with many hundreds of company executives, and the investigation of correspondence, reports and other documents, have brought together detailed evidence of how the international company works. Out of all this material much precise information is available, so are two definite but unprovable impressions:

(1) the amount of managerial talent there is at the disposal of these companies.
(2) the difficulties of realizing the alleged advantages of the international operation in practice, and how easily the expectations at the time of a merger turn sour.

The talented manager is often the critical one; and the nature of his criticisms suggests that there may be other organizational forms, in at least some industry groups, that will achieve business objectives more efficiently than the all-absorbing, large firm as we know it. Changes may happen within the present corporate framework: indeed one of the fascinations of studying the multi-national company is that one is walking around in what are in effect the most advanced laboratories of organizational experiment in the world. On the other hand the established framework may not suit, and the experiments may fail. In this case progress will come through the break-up of companies into their component parts, with some contractual arrangements replacing the organizational.

My interest in merger problems developed as a by-product of the study of the multi-national firm. Naturally any method of expansion has its difficulties; but those most frequently mentioned by company executives were connected with mergers, and especially with those designed to achieve vertical integration. The evidence for this statement has gained a new significance in the last year or two, as what may be called 'straws in the wind' have accumulated, showing doubts about the uncritical acceptance of the merger process in general. Thus, in significant particulars, mergers within countries and across frontiers, as well as the general cult of bigness, are all being questioned at the same time. No one doubts the need for rationalization in some businesses; it is the uncritical use of the same prescription which is being questioned.

These 'straws' included:

1. A speech by the director-general of the NEDC in December 1969 suggesting an examination of the trend to bigger businesses.
2. A speech in the same month by the President of the Board of Trade which emphasized that small firms were more than pulling their weight in the export drive.
3. A leading article in the *Financial Times* on 8 December 1969 which was headed 'Controlling the Giants', and emphasized the new-found agreement between left and right by quoting a Fabian pamphlet.
4. A Unit Trust[4] advertisement series under the new slogan: 'Do you know that small, successful companies tend to provide a better return on investment and grow faster on average than large companies?'
5. An article in the *Harvard Business Review* for January 1970 entitled: 'Bigness versus Profitability', which showed how the smallest firms are now more profitable than the largest, and how this is a recent development. The article has been widely quoted, and the air has since become thick with these straws.

The most relevant problems that are actually reported by executives of multinational firms are the problems of vertical integration already mentioned, together with those of activating and retaining managerial talents and those of relationships with local countries and their governments. In the rest of this paper, each of these will be examined in turn. In my examination an attempt is made to present the case for a fresh approach. At the same time this case rests, as does any possible alternative, on certain assumptions. These need to be exposed to the light of day for public inspection, and this also will be briefly attempted.

2. Vertical Integration

A characteristic goal of mergers is vertical integration, the purchase of suppliers or customers or both. This has great attractions for the domestic firm, including the improved use of under-employed resources and other common motives for expansion. Special advantages are also expected from this particular route of growth, such as a better control over the quality of material and components, and guaranteed outlets for products. Once the expansion strategy becomes global, these attractions are increased, and others become apparent. Effectively, the advantages of vertical integration are added to those of multi-national operations, and the sum is increased still further by the extra benefits of vertical integration across frontiers. The whole proposition is so obviously attractive that it can hardly fail to break through all the caution and inertia of any Board that has the resources available.

The particular advantages that are relevant to this paper can be summarized as follows:

> Vertical integration across frontiers makes possible standard specifications, and the more effective use of the firm's technical advantages internationally. It also enables production units to be sited where capital and labour are available and relatively cheap. The company is further enabled to use the transfer price mechanism (pricing of goods sold within the group) to minimize taxes and avoid possible exchange losses.
>
> The company has assured outlets in a number of markets, and is thus cushioned against a recession in any one of them.

In practice these attractions often prove illusory, and have accompanying disadvantages.

Take, for instance, two firms in different countries which have come within the same group as a result of a vertical merger. Firm A is the principal supplier of an essential component to firm B, and has been bought for that reason. Although firm B has taken over firm A, a production manager in the former concern can no longer shop around; his relations with his supplier have ceased to be those of a customer, and have come within the sphere of company politics.

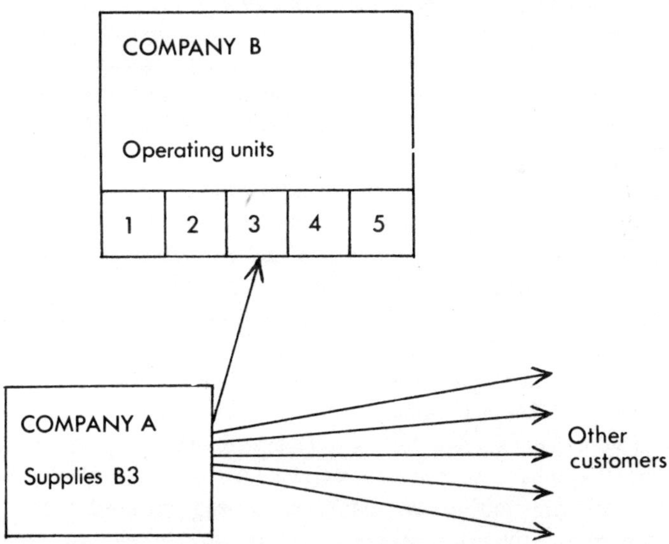

Figure 1. Vertical integration across frontiers.

On the other hand the manager of firm A, we will further assume, has other customers and needs these for his unit to remain viable. From now on these customers are likely to have priority if any difficulties arise, because firm B cannot cancel its order. It is open, naturally, to the manager of firm B to bring every form of pressure at his disposal to bear on the manager of firm A. But now that he is within the group, firm A's manager has a number of possible alibis which would cut no ice with an outside customer. He may, for instance, be able to argue that the problems have arisen because the last capital budget he submitted was severely cut at group level, on the grounds that available finance was being committed this year to another part of the company.

The international frontier will strengthen the position of the manager of firm A. For, even if firm B succeeds in convincing group executives that the supplier is at fault, there are few convincing sanctions. With the domestic company, the manager of the defaulting firm may lose his job; with the multi-national company he may have the protection of the local directors and even the local law. Tough words but not tough deeds summarize the results of much of our investigation of the handling of difficulties across frontiers.

In the case on which the above description is based, the frustrated management in firm B naturally performed badly; and in this instance they were held responsible. Their superiors argued that they were entitled to change their suppliers if this situation arose. This is often said by firms, and is doubtless the letter of the regulation; but few managers do go outside a group for supplies which can be obtained at whatever inconvenience inside. In spite of the outcome of this particular case, they regard such an action as too risky for their careers; they may also be mindful of the chance of being moved to firm A. They also assume that they will not be held accountable for problems incurred with internal suppliers; whereas they would clearly be in trouble if they insisted on going outside the group and still failed to produce the expected results. The fact that the managers of firm B were wrong in this particular assumption does not alter the widely held belief just described; as a matter of fact they took it for granted that they were held accountable because they had the misfortune to be on the domestic side of the international frontier.

The managerial problem just described can be made worse by a normal difficulty of vertical integration, that of increasing the group's exposure to slump on that particular side of the business. If the company is multi-product, this may well lead to the commitment of capital to other product groups, a natural safeguard which increases the problems of those affected.

Other expected advantages of vertical mergers may also turn sour when mixed with the realities of the management process. A case of this was discovered in discussions on a company's research policy. This particular firm was one of the minority which did have substantial research departments in its larger foreign subsidiaries. Attempts to find out what research was being done in one particular affiliate showed that the main activity in fact was making the local product fit the group global specifications. The difficulty was that the mandatory raw material was not available locally, and yet the parent company insisted on sticking to global requirements instead of sanctioning a local adaptation; hence expensive research into a non-existent problem. This was obviously an unusual situation, but there are numerous parallels. Specifications or operating instructions laid down by some central services division with worldwide responsibilities produced expensive distortions in a local subsidiary somewhere in over half the firms investigated in depth.

This sort of experience suggests that there is room for a much closer examination of the expenses of vertical integration as against the costs and difficulties of contractual relationships, or other means of handling business between a customer and a supplier. To these expenses must be added the frustration of managers and the effects of this on their efforts. This last consideration raises issues which will be explored in the next section.

3. Human Resources

A merger may be undertaken to make a more economical use of material and financial resources involved. The true costs of management have been more closely examined since Drucker first began to point them out,[5] and these costs are now rising in any case. We shall see later that the most significant argument in the case for unmerger is that there should be a profit to be made out of using managers more effectively. In connection with its use of talent, the multi-national firm enjoys some advantages of a rather intangible but noticeable kind. There is, for instance, the prestige of working for a company that is a household name throughout the world; there is the travel involved, a considerable attraction to the more enterprising executive; there are other fringe benefits as well. There is the possibility of glittering prizes in the future. These are benefits of the sort that tarnish easily. As against them, there are disadvantages which arise from the size of the firm, from the merger itself, and from the nature of international operations.

A number of writers on the theory of the firm[6] in the last ten years or so have pointed to the strong pressures on the manager in the large company to avoid risks and to promote growth rather than profits. The penalties for failure may be severe, whereas the benefits of success may be limited; hence the executive is disinclined to take risks. But growth can be achieved slowly and safely. The increasing size leads to fresh opportunities for promotion for the manager and his colleagues, who thereby become his supporters. As a matter of fact the pressure against risk in the foreign subsidiary may be less, for the manager there has a secure position. In spite of statements to the contrary we found, for instance, very few examples of foreign chief executives who left because their plans had not succeeded. On the contrary, it was the successful ones who left, because they were frustrated with their positions. The evidence suggests that managerial turnover in the subsidiaries results from success rather than failure. But it still remains true that a high proportion of the subsidiaries examined had been notably successful; it could be that the security is part of the reason for the success, an unanticipated by-product of the realities of multi-national organization.

In the case of mergers, a particularly ironical situation arises. Asked why they buy another company instead of establishing a fresh unit of the parent body, most firms will reply that one important reason is that their present management is overstretched. In effect they are buying management. In view of this, they will naturally go on to say that they bought a particular company because of the 'proven qualities' of its management. Sometimes this works; there are famous examples of men brought into a large organization after a takeover who have been outstandingly successful there. In a considerable proportion of the cases examined in our studies, however, this has not worked. The man who was successful when managing his own business did not succeed when brought into the security of the large organization. His main spur seemed to have gone. This common experience illustrates how another supposed advantage of a merger can turn out to be illusory.

Another of the alleged advantages to which this can happen is that of increased specialization. The argument here is that the large firm makes a better use of talents by allowing managers to concentrate on areas which they have the greatest expertise. But salary and career structures, in fact, often cause the opposite to happen. The really able specialist is promoted to a senior post in general management, and ceases to use his specialization. Thus we have the situation whereby the UK is short of engineers, while many of the most able members of the profession have given up engineering.[7] In the small specialist firm this does not happen, and the rewards are often greater for practising one's skill.

Many of these problems are exacerbated in the large company, as is the problem of promotion. The large organization can offer the greatest prizes of all, but they are available only to the very few. On the other hand it can offer great frustrations, in particular freakish changes of authority. The international firm has two additional frustrations to offer its foreign managers in this connection. One is the need to get along with expatriates who may be brought in to fill coveted positions merely to give them experience abroad. Along with this contemporary brand of nepotism, the other is that promotion often stops at the frontier, which can mean at a comparatively junior position.

International promotion is examined later; meanwhile a digression into the forms of organization used in multi-national firms will illustrate how managers find themselves demoted through no fault of their own. There are four main types of organization available to the company which operates in different countries; these are normally discrete categories, but some firms are naturally 'in transition' at any particular time. First is the simple type when the chief executive abroad reports directly to a member of the main Board of the company, and his specialist managers have close links with their opposite numbers at head office, in the *central services* departments there. This is the traditional form, and it still exists in some firms. Two pressures have led to changes. One is the growing importance of foreign operations in companies that yet have a strong home base; this leads to the development of a specialist department with the necessary expertise to handle the activities abroad. The other is increasing emphasis, strongly reinforced by influential consultants, on reorganizing multi-product companies along product group lines. These two pressures produce the characteristic features of the second and third types of organization – the *geographical* where local companies report to managers with responsibility for some country or part of the world, and the *product group* where managers abroad report to executives with overall product responsibility. For completeness, the fourth type of organization is the *mixed,* where the same managers report along more than one line. Multi-reporting systems are interesting and important in their own right, but are not relevant to the current discussion. The problems which arise are discussed at length elsewhere.[8]

What is relevant here is that any departure from the first type effectively moves the subsidiary management down the hierarchy, and blocks promotion channels unless the company facilitates moves across frontiers. For the subsidiary manager finds himself no longer a direct subordinate of the Board of the group, but reporting to a divisional officer who may even be in a regional headquarters. This is certainly regarded as demotion in the subsidiary. Figure 2 shows the situation described.

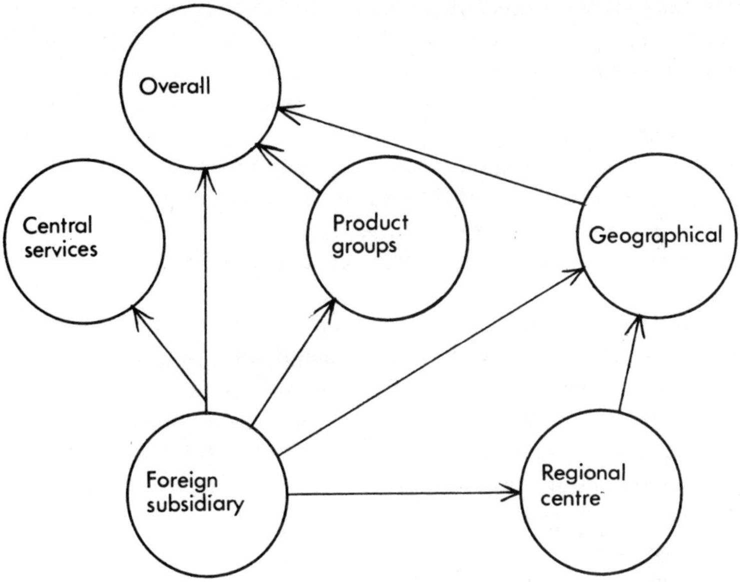

Figure 2. The four projections of management in the parent company of the multi-national group.

The foreign subsidiary can report along any of the lines, but this figure demonstrates how the management there is effectively demoted as the system becomes more complex.

Another problem is that management development policies frequently produce a strong resistance to change within a group. This may occur in a number of ways. For instance men join the company with certain expectations, and if they are nationals of the home country these may include a spell of duty abroad. Under these circumstances the withdrawal of expatriates may lose for the company its most enterprising recruits. One company, that has been in the habit of planning succession up to twenty years ahead, has discovered that this has produced rigidity where flexibility was needed. Many companies reported efforts to internationalize their management development programmes; but up to now these efforts should be treated with some scepticism.

A further problem of the large company, which is considerably increased when it becomes multi-national, is that of the amount of effort put into co-ordination rather than more constructive activities. The complexities of co-ordinating along all the three projections – the central services, the product group and the geographical link – at once are considerable. A variety of executives may be concerned, for instance, with the marketing policies of one product group in one particular country, or the personnel considerations of another product group in another country. All this co-ordination adds up to more frustrations for those at the receiving end, and often the co-ordinators are wasting their talents anyway.

In view of these problems it is not surprising that much thought and effort goes into the discovery of fresh means of motivating managers. But these efforts all point to the possibilities of breaking up companies; for they rest on the assumption that independence and personal responsibility are the strongest spurs to more effective management. One company even uses the phrase 'owner-manager concept'. This surely provokes the question, why not the 'owner-manager'? For a nominally independent position in a highly centralized organization, backed by a few shares in a huge company which are anyway only negotiable on a foreign stock market, comes nowhere near to ownership. Yet the evidence continues to show that for most people, independence is a strong incentive. To quote an interview published in *The Times*: 'Managing a division is just not the same as managing your own business and that is the crux of it'.[9]

This assumption is clearly crucial to the present argument, but there are powerful reasons for supposing that any moves to unmerger will come by a different route. For the decision-makers involved are in positions of considerable power. They are unlikely to abdicate this willingly unless the evidence becomes much more decisive. On the other hand changes are likely to be enforced by law, formulated as a result of public opinion. In the formation of this opinion, we have already suggested, there is a union of normally opposing interests; and the next section will examine this aspect of the subject.

4. National Opinion

The influence of national public opinion on multi-national firms is being very widely discussed at the moment. (Some aspects of this are examined in another chapter, see page 248). In country after country foreign investment, both inward and outward, is becoming more topical. Among issues discussed are: the taking of decisions outside a country which significantly affect its well-being, the removal from the local money market of high-potential stock, the threat to labour of moving operations from one country to another, the limitation of career opportunities, the blocking of the national research effort, and a more general and vague, but none the less real, feeling of hostility to the foreigner and to the foreign organization. As against these social implications, we have the economic benefits and liabilities discussed elsewhere.

The limitation of career opportunities is an issue that arouses strong feelings inside firms; it is, however, an issue on which some action is being taken. Several companies report that they are increasingly able to recruit foreign executives for posts at headquarters. One such firm keeps all senior management records on a head office computer. When a suitable post is available anywhere in the world, the specification is fed into the computer which then produces a short list. Those named are flown to head office for interview if they wish to apply. Another company claims to have more foreign executives in the headquarters than expatriates abroad. Yet another withdrew foreign managers from one South American subsidiary when it found that able local nationals were leaving. The performance of the locals improved to such a degree that this policy was then adopted elsewhere.

Discussions with firms, on the other hand, which do retain expatriate managers brought out two points. There is a problem of career structure for the home country[10] national, the problem mentioned earlier, which is especially acute when the firm has most of its investment abroad. How does he get sufficient scope, and above all the chance of experience within the company? In such a firm, it is argued, the chance of a post abroad is essential. The other point companies make is the need for certain functions to be filled by executives with experience of head office because this is a cheap and efficient means of co-ordination. In some companies a majority of the foreign chief executives are from head office; this rule may apply to men in charge of operating units as well as of subsidiaries. Some companies still insist on appointing expatriate finance managers because their main job is to get money out of the country, a job at which the patriotic local might be less than whole-hearted.

Some ingenious ways have been devised to overcome the problems of staffing across frontiers. These include bringing potential foreign executives to the home country for a substantial period for training and experience. This reduces the problems of co-ordination produced by the withdrawal of expatriates. One company has a staff college in the home country for this purpose. Other firms have developed an international grade. Once appointed to this, a man is theoretically available for service anywhere in the world, whatever his country of origin. Naturally there are political limitations on this, as one company discovered when they promoted a man from one country to another just before war broke out between the two. Further, more and more countries are imposing limits on the issue of work permits to foreign nationals; there may be special difficulties here, but in general it is easier to gain a work permit where it can be said that movement both to and from a country is possible. Ultimately there can be little doubt that firms are going to adopt some form of international grading scheme.

The problem for the operative in the multi-national firm is the opposite of that for the manager. He wants to maintain stability of employment, and one of his fears is that the firms are too footloose, able to move from one country to another to avoid pressure from labour organizations. This problem is currently being investigated by the International Confederation of Free Trade Unions, and is clearly one that concerns officers in the labour movement. The reaction of the rank and file is more unpredictable. They certainly show no more sustained hostility to foreign bosses than they do to native ones, although naturally the foreignness of the firm will be mentioned if there is a row. Such firms also have some advantages. A report on the building of the refinery at Fawley published twenty years ago gives an example of a remarkably successful handling of a difficult labour force by foreign supervisors, in spite of confident predictions to the contrary.[11] Texas Instruments is an example of a firm in the UK that has used unconventional methods of handling labour with great success. Warnings have been given that similar methods of handling labour do not always make a favourable impact;[12] nevertheless it would seem that dissatisfaction with the personnel policies of multi-national firms is more common among managers than among operatives.

That there should be difficulties between companies and countries should only surprise those who believe that there can be an identity of interest here. There is no doubt that multi-national companies do bring many advantages both for their home countries and for their host countries, but clearly their objectives are company biased and, more, they are head-office biased. This is only to say that the international firm benefits from its internationalism. Nevertheless there are snags both for the foreign subsidiaries and for the host countries. Our studies have shown that there are four main ways in which funds are moved around in multi-national firms:[13] charges against income (interest, royalties, fees), dividends, capital transfers (including loans and trade credits), transfer prices. Within the limits imposed by the taxation and exchange-control authorities these can all be used to the advantage of the group. Among the beneficial ways of using them are: moving money out of countries whose currency is under threat and ensuring that larger profits are made by subsidiaries in low tax countries. To these should be added the points that foreign companies bring little money into a country after the initial investment, and that net inflows to the home countries exceed net outflows by a substantial margin (up to 3½ : 1 in our data). All these facts represent disadvantages to the host country.[14]

The second type of problem that a company sets its host country is the fact that decisions are taken outside that country on matters of importance to the national economy. One example is when the trading policies of the country of origin and the host country conflict. In the past examples have mainly concerned American companies operating in countries which foster trade with communist countries; more recently controversies have occurred over the foreign subsidiaries of British firms trading with Rhodesia, Mozambique and elsewhere.

Cases frequently appear in the press, but one especially interesting example was that of Fruehauf France. This company, the French subsidiary of the Fruehauf Corporation of Detroit, won a sub-contract from Berliet for lorries destined for China. Just before delivery was due a telegram from Detroit ordered cancellation. In this case a strong-minded local management resigned and put the case before the courts. The result was the installation of an administrator with instructions to fulfil the order, and this was upheld on appeal. In a lengthy verdict, the higher court expressed its reluctance to interfere in the internal affairs of a private concern, but thought it right to intervene in this case to prevent French trading policies from being frustrated by instructions which really came from a foreign government. French economic well-being could not be made dependent on American politics.

Other problems posed for various sections of the population of the host country include the damage that is done to the money markets. Among the more general ways in which these problems gain strength and significantly influence the policies of companies themselves is patriotic and anti-foreigner feeling. While fervour is sometimes aroused on specific issues, nationalism is by no means a simple matter; indeed internationalism, plainly, is also an important factor, and an advantage to the multi-national firm. One of the odder paradoxes that results from the complex inter-relationship of national and international attitudes is illustrated by one company with interests in both consumer and capital goods. With their consumer goods, international brand names sell best; but with their capital goods they are seeking government contracts, and for these a local alias is required. Electors are assumed to want their governments to buy national, while they themselves increasingly buy international.

Another paradox is that, in spite of what was said earlier about company-biased objectives, *some* foreign investment would appear to be easier to justify to the host country than to the shareholders – if the company felt under any obligation to justify it to either. This applies, for example, to small investments by large companies in developing countries. The local economy may benefit considerably, but the profits to the company may be absorbed in a disproportionate amount of head office time devoted to it. Of course the investment may be one of those that will produce eventually rich rewards.

It would be possible to argue at length about the factors which do, as well as those which should, influence the climate of opinion within the countries where companies operate. It would seem, however, that the present trend towards encouraging foreign investment while developing legislation to ensure that this does not threaten national sovereignty will continue. This is likely to lead to different forms of ownership, for instance more joint ventures, and to new patterns of control in international business. It is not impossible that the future will see a trend towards small countries, as well as smaller companies, combining into larger trading blocks; and that business organizations may develop to match this trend.

5. The Alternative is Already There

One fascinating aspect of the multi-national company is the contrast between statement and reality on questions of local autonomy.[15] Ask senior executives at a head office what is the policy on this, and they unanimously reply decentralization. They may even strengthen this by saying that the main problem is to get the local operations to stand on their own feet. At the same time an examination as to where decisions are taken will show an exactly opposite trend in many firms. Decisions are being moved to head office and away from the local subsidiary.

No doubt there are several reasons for the discrepancy. Senior management may be bemused by their own propaganda, or may not realize the implications of some of their decisions; but one reason appears especially significant – that different groups of managers are involved. In this connection head office may be said to comprise the four types of managerial responsibility mentioned earlier (see Fig. 2). Members of the overall projection are interested in fostering local autonomy and initiative, and the same may be true of the geographical one; but the central services and the product group managers are likely to have the opposite influence whatever the intention.

Indeed this may be necessary, so as not to lose the advantages of global planning. The appropriate functional department at head office will clearly exercise strong pressure to ensure that the techniques it has so expensively developed – be they in planning, operations research, marketing, computer usage or what – are used throughout the group. Similarly a strong product group organization at the centre is usually found to be incompatible with independence for the local unit. Indeed, one significant organizational problem for the multi-national group has been this incompatibility. For some years now there has been a trend in business, fostered by well-known consultants, towards autonomy by product group. There are now signs that this trend is changing, meanwhile increasing problems for the foreign subsidiary have resulted.

Most of these problems exist in a similar form for the domestic unit as well, except that international frontiers increase the difficulties disproportionately. The problem can be stated in the form of two assumptions which are widely made: that independent, personal responsibility makes a manager more effective, and that modern techniques limit the discretion of the individual decision-maker. If these two propositions are accepted, then the logical response is for more independent organizational units with less discretion. And these already exist. Another assumption, less widely made but implicit in much of the argument, is that the supplier-customer or adviser-client relationship is more suitable in modern conditions and for certain types of business than that of employer-employee.

This is recognized in organizational experiments, which have been pioneered by the multi-national firm. Some efforts to produce different relationships within a large organizational framework, such as the owner-manager concept, have already been mentioned. These usually take the form of efforts to secure greater managerial independence, but there are also moves towards smaller units within the large corporation. Some companies prefer the small feeder factory, on a separate site, to the large complex.

Further, there is now an increasing interest in patterns of organization which involve separate ownership, including sub-contracting and franchising. Both of these have had chequered careers, but both have been coming back into fashion and increasing rapidly in recent years. It is estimated that new franchise businesses are opening at the rate of 40,000 a year in the United States. Although it is generally assumed that franchising is only suitable for certain types of business, notions about which types are changing all the time. The case of sub-contracting is similar. Firms are already hiving off more and more ancillary tasks to smaller independent businesses; and again ideas about what are suitable for different sizes of unit are changing.[15] This process is also increasing, and will increase whatever the outcome of the current debate on mergers. Office-cleaning, security and the provision of company cars are just three of the functions being moved out of the company. The leasing of property or equipment is another parallel tendency.

6. Towards an Age of Unmerger

To look ahead, it would seem that a number of changes are likely to occur, some initiated by business and some by government. Most governments will not want their countries to be deprived of the benefits that the foreign firm brings, but at the same time there is bound to be a tolerance limit somewhere to the outside control of important parts of the national economy. At least, the reaching of this tolerance level is likely to make more countries insist on local participation in the national subsidiary; it may also involve a government-appointed director with some specific powers to ensure that the company's trading policies are not incompatible with those of the host country. It should be remembered that such action would be restrictive in Europe, although in most countries enabling legislation does exist; elsewhere it could be liberalizing. Japan, for instance, has traditionally been inhospitable to foreign capital, but her policies are changing as Japanese businessmen increasingly desire the right to invest abroad themselves. As other countries have found, the principle of reciprocity is a strong restraint here. And this suggests the other likely trend. In addition to limits on the big company, at least to the extent of increasing local participation, there will be many more companies in the field. Some of these will come into international business, like the Japanese, through their own efforts; others will have the active support of governments in countries anxious to develop into trading nations.

If governments are likely to activate legislation to limit foreign ownership, they are even more likely to activate restrictions on monopolies and large aggregates of economic power in general. Again the laws already exist, although it must not be forgotten that the country which has the most anti-trust suits also has the world's largest companies. Legislation has been largely inactive in European countries in recent years because of the belief in the efficiency of the large unit, and its greater competitive power in world markets. In view of this belief it has seemed crazy to operate legislation which, by limiting corporate growth, could do more harm than good to the national economy. If, on the other hand, the large company is demonstrated to be inefficient and wasteful of resources, the climate of opinion can be expected to change. Dormant legislation will surely be brought into use.

Along with likely government action, possible business moves should be considered. The merger movement of the sixties came not by theories of the economies of scale, nor by the desire to fight off foreign competition. These theories came from the spectators, usually after the event. Nor were company amalgamations often fostered by government intervention; where this has happened, as in the UK, the political action often came later. Mergers became fashionable because some entrepreneurs learnt by and demonstrated how to make money out of them.

The reverse process is likely to come the same way. This means that someone will devise a method of making money out of buying companies and selling or leasing their component parts as separate entities to owner-managers. This implies, to use an all too fashionable phrase, the devising of a package. For no one is going to make a fortune out of selling off a creaky empire in job lots.

If there is money to be made here it is because an independent businessman, with adequate training and resources, can produce substantially better results than the dependent manager. This assumes also that adequate skills are available. Managers, like other professional people, have been at pains to convince us that they possess a rare talent. The extraordinarily flimsy arguments used to support this view, reaching down into the realms of animal psychology, are enough to arouse suspicions even if there were not observable evidence the other way. The calibre and competence of managers have increased as their numbers have grown. As in other spheres of activity more is being found to mean better.

Given these assumptions, the 'package' suggests itself. A company is first broken down into suitable parts: including service, sales and production units. The optimum size for each will depend on a number of calculations about the technology, the market and so on. Each segment will be leased or sold, either outright or by hire purchase, to a suitable applicant. The conditions of sale will include a thorough selection and training, as well as the provision of services and possibly a trial period during which the sale can be revoked. These conditions are necessary because naturally the unit will remain closely interlocked with others spun off the same company. Similarly a system of contractual arrangements will have to be devised with other interdependent businesses.

Skilfully drafted, the contracts could retain the advantages of the large concern while shedding its liabilities. Since the agreements could be terminated, there would be flexibility; but where a unified approach was beneficial, the contracts would provide for it. These arrangements would also apply internationally, where a consultancy firm drawn from the old company's planning department could help make the best use of global opportunities. For what has been said about tolerance limits is not to be taken to mean that business should surrender to a primitive nationalism which spurns contemporary opportunities.

This paper started by suggesting that there were a number of 'straws in the wind' indicating a swing away from the merger fashion. We have seen that these consist of numerous indicators, many of them small; put together they must at least be taken seriously. Frustration with the big organization in all its forms is, after all, a powerful force in contemporary civilization without the problems here identified. These include employee attitudes, suspicions about the efficiency of the large unit, tolerance levels for the organization which cuts across national frontiers.

We have seen that these indications are strongly reinforced when relationships other than those of employer-employee are taken into account; we have also suggested that there may be a profit to be made out of turning managers into independent businessmen. Another factor, not mentioned here but indicated in the chapter in this book concerned with shareholders' interests (Chapter Ten), is the possibility of a shareholders' revolt. If there are increasing signs of an unmerger movement, there is surely also going to be among shareholders an awakening strong enough to force complacent boards into greater sensitivity to their interests.

Finally we have suggested how an unscrambling programme could be mounted, and mounted in such a way as not to destroy the advantages of the present system.

It is important not to lose the advantages of internationalism in tackling the problems. All this adds up to a strong presumption that the age of unmerger is not far away. Did we say 'straws in the wind'? Perhaps a gale in the hayrick may soon be the phrase.

Chapter Fourteen

EUROPE'S LOVE AFFAIR WITH BIGNESS*

Philip Siekman

A fascination with giantism, a mania for mergers, call it what you will, but Europe's leading businessmen are infected with it. They are merging companies with such haste and sweep that no label seems quite adequate. If the trend continues – and it may not abate until all potential partners are wedded and bedded – the European industrial landscape will soon be dominated by a small number of very large companies, each with a near monopoly in its national market, or what *would* be a monopoly save for imports and the presence of American and other foreign-owned subsidiaries.

Created with the encouragement of their respective governments and, in some cases, with direct financial assistance from the state, these giants are wrapped in clouds of national pride and prestige, employ tens of thousands of workers, have privileged access to government orders, and are, in effect if not in fact, nationalized institutions – their policies a matter of parliamentary debate, their health a matter of government concern.

It's fear that fuels the trend. During the sixties, Europeans slowly and painfully awoke to the sight of large US corporations gobbling up their venerable companies by the dozen and marauding through their markets almost at will. The concern was intensified when Jean-Jacques Servan-Schreiber brought out his celebrated book, *The American Challenge*, in 1967. If something wasn't done quickly, he warned, the Continent would become ward and colony of US industrialists. Ever since then, a gaggle of academics and journalists have been pontificating about 'gaps' between the US and Europe – in technology, management, and education – and proposing ways to head off the Americans at the pass.

The Perils in Concentration

Some would like simply to erect barricades. France, for instance, recently blocked an attempt by Westinghouse to take over an electrical-equipment company, Jeumont-Schneider, even though its Belgian owner was anxious to sell. But by and large, the favoured way to fend off the Americans has been to create countervailing

*Reprinted from *Fortune*, March 1970, by special permission; © 1970 Time Inc.

powers, to put together European goliaths that can take advantage of large-scale production, research, finance, and management. Within the last several years the concentration trend has swept through coal and steel, automobiles and trucks, computers and aircraft. Other industries – from chemicals to electrical apparatus to home appliances – seem certain to be added soon to that list.

The European giant builders may, however, be creating problems rather than solving them. They are surely correct in their conviction that many industries are fragmented and overpopulated by small family companies with limited managerial and financial resources. It would be a mistake, however, to ascribe all the weaknesses of European industry to this one affliction. To do so would be to ignore a point made by the head of a small Italian chemical company. 'Historically', he observed, 'it is the small that have survived. It was the dinosaurs that failed to adapt'. Many of the new corporate monsters may find it very difficult to adapt and, in the end, may become flabby nationalized companies that will offer even weaker competition to US – and Japanese – corporations.

A Merchant Banker Wields the Shotgun

These developments in European industry differ greatly from the recent wave of mergers in the US. First, most of the European mergers have taken place within single industries; very few of the new giants are conglomerates. Next, in sharp contrast to the US government, with its vigorous antitrust enforcement, European governments have smiled encouragingly on concentration and, in many cases, have played an active matchmaker's role. Some of these governments, as well as the European Economic Commission, have antitrust powers. But the intent has been to curb only flagrant abuses of monopoly power, such as price fixing, rather than concentration as such.

This sharp difference in government attitudes is most clearly seen in Britain, the country where merger fever has raged most fiercely and where industrial reorganization has received the strongest overt governmental support. When the Labour Party took over the British government in 1964, it inherited several well-consolidated industrial sectors, including such nationalized industries as the railways, coal mines, and electric power. Later, for political more than economic reasons, Labour renationalized the steel industry, putting 90 per cent of Britain's steel capacity in one ungainly and still unprofitable lump.

In other industries, the Wilson government stopped short of nationalization but has used the power and influence of the government to reorganize private enterprises. Its chief tool has been the Industrial Reorganization Corporation, created in late 1966. Now run by Charles Villiers, a former merchant banker, the IRC has spent the last three years loping through one industry after another, shotgun in hand, pushing sometimes reluctant, sometimes eager, companies to the altar; at other times it has acted like a Victorian parent breaking up a love match in order to wed the bride to a more suitable mate. In its effort to reorganize industries in the manner it deems best, the IRC shoves companies together, persuades one company

The genealogy of two British giants

Table 1

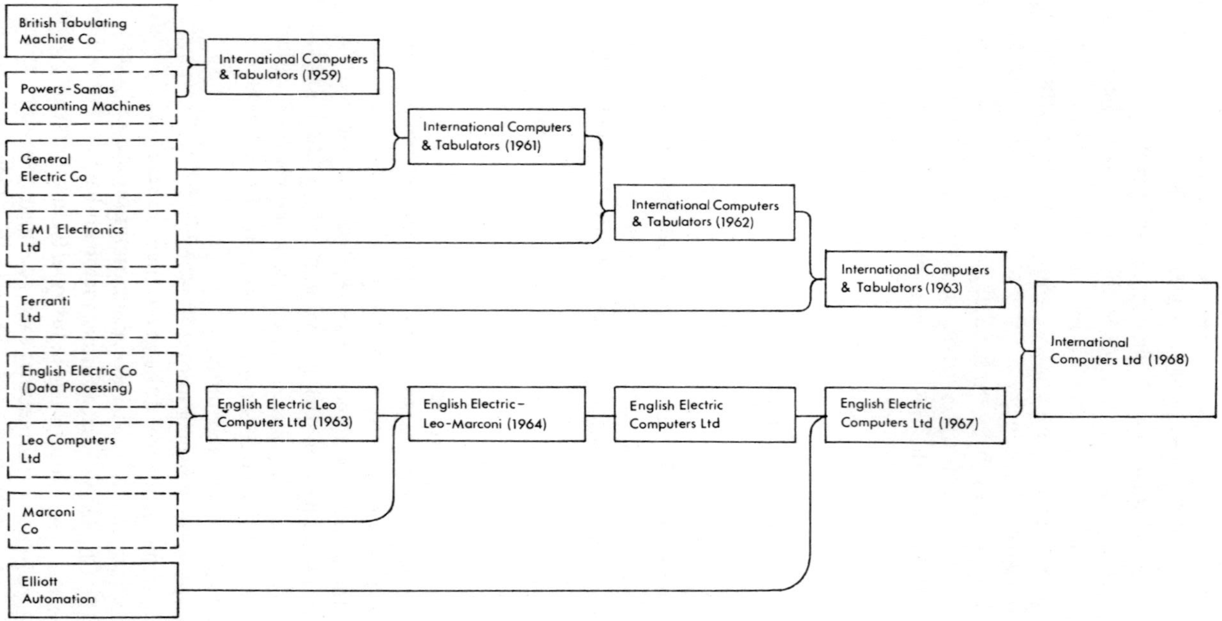

Britain's flag-bearing computer company, International Computers Ltd, is the sole survivor of a series of mergers involving a total of nine British-owned companies or divisions of companies (the latter indicated by boxes with broken lines) that made computers in the late 1950s. With 1969 sales of $276 million, ICL is now the only British-owned manufacturer of commercial and scientific computers.

Table 2

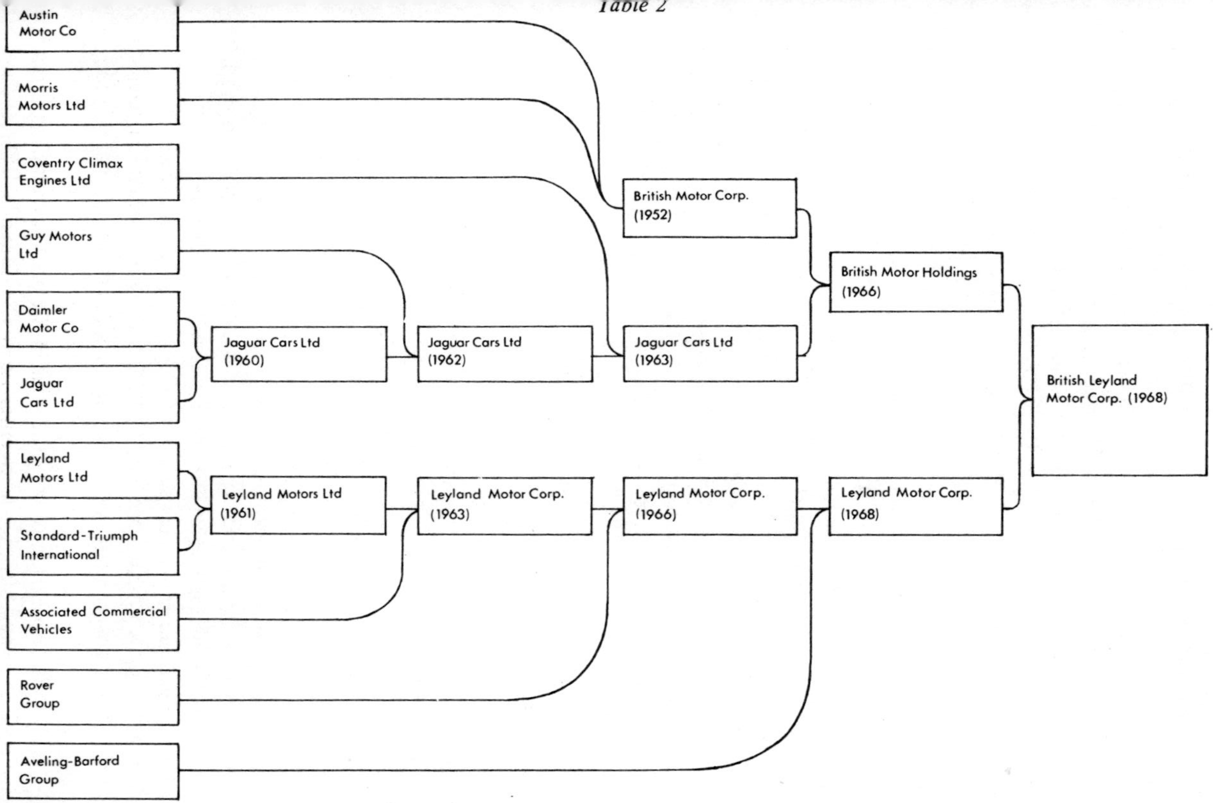

British Leyland Motor Corporation, now the only major British-owned manufacturer of cars and trucks and the second-largest European maker after Volkswagen, has eleven automotive ancestors, some of which were the result of prior combinations. Its 1969 sales were $2·3 billion. As in the case of computers, consolidation of the auto industry was actively promoted by the British government.

to sell a part of its operations to another, supports the new ventures with infusions of debt and equity capital (it can draw up to $360 million in government funds) and, frequently, puts its own watchdog on the board.

Although the IRC has helped to block attempts by General Foods and SKF, the Swedish ball-bearing company, to acquire British firms, Villiers insists that he is not opposed to foreign investment in Britain. But he does believe that one of his prime missions is to create British companies large enough to resist the battering onslaught of US subsidiaries. Two of the IRC's most dramatic adventures have been in automobiles and computers, industries in which the British-owned units are up against brutal US competition. In both cases British hopes and aspirations now ride heavily on single corporations: British Leyland Motor Corporation and International Computers Ltd (see Tables 1 and 2).

In its short, active life, the IRC has been involved in more than twenty industries, and some British businessmen are ready to cry 'enough'. A former head of the Confederation of British Industries says the only job left for the IRC is to preside over its own demise. But Villiers believes that work remains to be done in many medium-size industries such as machine tools, speciality steel, and footwear. Moreover, he thinks the time has come to look across the English Channel, to search for ways to correct what he has called the 'surprising failure' of European companies to join forces across national boundaries. On the Continent, Villiers and his associates are trying to drum up interest in a version of the IRC that would be funded by a number of governments and would guide and encourage inter-European mergers.

Each in His Own Fashion

Thus far, anyway, Villiers's idea for a European IRC has not received an enthusiastic reception on the Continent. In general, businessmen and bureaucrats there are much more interested in copying the IRC's national approach – that is, consolidating their own industries.

This year [1970] the French government is setting up its own version of the IRC, the Institut de Développement Industriel. The new organization will be mainly concerned with medium-size companies. The government has already made use of the state planning agency to encourage concentration of most of France's largest industries. Two companies, Usinor and Wendel-Sidelor, now account for two-thirds of France's crude steel production. Renault and Peugeot, the only surviving all-French carmakers, are as much partners as competitors. Three nationalized companies, Sud-Aviation, Nord-Aviation, and SEREB (missiles and rockets), have just been merged. And a government-inspired reorganization of the electrical-equipment and chemical industries has been almost completed.

Companies accounting for 60 per cent of the sales in the electrical and electronics industries have been absorbed into two large enterprises, Cie Générale d'Electricité and Thomson Houston-Hotchkiss Brandt, and these two seem headed for some sort of merger. They already jointly own a number of companies, including Compagnie

Internationale pour l'Informatique (CII), the flag-bearing computer company created as part of the government's *Plan Calcul*, which is designed to strengthen the French-owned computer industry. A regrouping of the chemical industry culminated last summer in the creation of a combine that includes Rhone-Poulenc, the industry leader, plus Progil, Naphtachimie, and Pechiney-Saint-Gobain. It had consolidated sales of $2·1 billion last year and accounted for about a third of French-controlled chemical production.

Consolidation in the rest of Europe has been less deliberate and less a matter of formal government policy. But in its own fashion, each country has been similarly nudging together major corporations. There were forty-six sizable mergers in Germany last year [1969], including fusion of the conventional and nuclear power-plant businesses of Siemens and AEG, and the creation by Mannesmann and the Thyssen group of a jointly owned subsidiary that will account for about two-thirds of the national production of steel tubes.

In Italy, the state-owned holding company, IRI, which already controls companies accounting for at least 15 per cent of the nation's total industrial output, is spreading ever outward like a blob of tomato sauce on the industrial tablecloth. Among other things, it is now merging all its electronics companies and also is tying the operations of its airframe company, Aerfer, to those of Fiat. In 1968, IRI and ENL, the state-owned petroleum company, carried out a raid that in effect gave them control over Montecatini Edison, a chemical giant formed by a merger only four years ago.

Sweden meanwhile, is conglomerating its nationalized companies. The two largest steel companies in Belgium have decided to merge. In Austria two state-owned petroleum and chemical companies, OeMV and OeSW, are joining forces to form that nation's second-biggest industrial enterprise. And the Swiss chemical giants, CIBA and Geigy, hesitate to consummate their romance mainly because of doubts about whether the Justice Department would bless the union of their sizable US interests.

'Pooling Inefficiencies'

None of the new European industrial giants has been around long enough for a fair assessment of whether it will, in fact, be more efficient and competitive than its components were individually. Certainly, size is no guarantee of improved profits. A recent French study, for example, revealed that smaller European companies tend to get a better return on investment than bigger ones. For example, the three German chemical companies, Bayer, BASF, and Hoechst, get a better return than either Imperial Chemical Industries or Montecatini Edison, even though the British and Italian companies are much larger and are substantially unopposed by other locally owned companies within their home markets.

Nor is bigness a cure for a lack of good management or a panacea for dying industries. Some of the European mergers have been marriages of desperation between weak companies that lack technical or managerial sophistication. 'Pooling inefficiencies' is the way a Common Market official describes the process.

Even when one of the partners is healthy and well run, there is a clear risk. In Britain for example, one important reason why the Industrial Reorganization Corporation encouraged the series of mergers that ultimately combined Associated Electrical Industries, Elliott-Automation, English Electric, and General Electric Co., (GEC) was to bring all of them under the command of Arnold Weinstock, forty-five, a tough, shrewd manager who earned a considerable reputation in the early sixties by turning around GEC. (It is not related to its US namesake.) But although the new company with sales last year of $2·1 billion, is four times larger than GEC was in 1966, Weinstock's style and very small staff remain almost unchanged. He has yet to show that he can nurture as well as prune, that he can lead the company into new markets *and* train the men needed to run it in the future. 'As often as not,' says a US businessman who keeps a close eye on European mergers, 'you can quadruple your short and medium term problems when you merely double in size'

European government officials are aware of the abuses of dominant market positions that could result from the recent wave of mergers, but they profess to be unworried. Most would agree with an OECD official who contends, 'The international market has obsoleted the concept of monopolies'. Even where the process of consolidation has left only one flag-carrying producer in a country, these officials argue, that giant will still face sharp competition. Not only do most European corporations rely heavily on export sales these days, but at home they must compete with imports and with US and other foreign-owned subsidiaries already firmly established on their own soil. Within the Common Market, of course, there are no longer any tariffs to impede the free movement of industrial products across the member countries' frontiers.

Nevertheless, some of the giants, especially in the nationalized basic industries, are protected to a considerable degree from outside competition. If necessary, they could keep covering their inefficiency with higher prices, thus raising the costs of other industries. The German government, for example, has just helped create Ruhrkohle AG, an amalgamation of twenty-five coal companies that together account for 75 per cent of the national output. As part of the deal, Ruhrkohle received twenty-year contracts to supply the coal needed by most of the German steel companies. In Britain the process is carried a step further. Industry has only one major source of steel, the nationalized British Steel Corporation. In turn, BSC has one source of coal and coke, the National Coal Board. In December 1969, a few days after the government approved a rise in coal prices, BSC filed for permission to increase the price of steel.

Most of the new giants have a monopoly on government research-and-development contracts, and on procurement orders from national and local authorities, including the school system and the state-owned corporations. Whenever possible, government agencies buy only locally made computers. Public power companies order generation and transmission equipment from national suppliers. Police departments buy cars made in the country.

This is, of course, the custom in the US too. But the US government, while following the 'Buy American' rule, parcels out its orders among a number of companies, and government business tends to be even less profitable than private sales. In Europe, the respective governments already are, or soon will be, dealing with single suppliers that will have no incentive to figure costs very closely. A French Deputy in the National Assembly recently complained that CII had a monopoly on government computer orders and 'feels neither threatened nor stimulated by European and world competition'.

Preferential treatment by government buyers can have the perverse effect of weakening the domestic industry it is intended to protect. Such a consequence was cited not long ago in a report by the Society of British Aero-space Companies. A series of consolidations had left Britain with only two major manufacturers of airplanes, British Aircraft Corporation and Hawker-Siddeley. Her Majesty's Government helped underwrite the development costs of BAC's long-range VC-10 and Hawker-Siddeley's medium-range Trident. But as a result of government pressure, the Society's report states, the planes were 'tailored so closely to national airline requirements that their overseas sales suffered'. The Society could have added that the nationalized airlines, BOAC and BEA, might not have purchased British planes at all if they had been allowed to order US equipment.

That one British example underlines two flaws in the way much of European industry is being restructured. First, US-size companies are being erected on national markets much smaller than the American market. Next, the government usually takes a direct or indirect role in the venture, yet its aims and goals – the needs of nationalized corporations, the desire for regional development, the political and social attractions of full employment – are not always synonymous with industrial efficiency.

Indeed, inefficiency can beget further inefficiency. If the new giants begin to stumble, they are likely to be wrapped even more tightly in the government's smothering embrace, fed with subsidies, and protected from the harsh elements. As this happens, there will be increased demands to nationalize the companies in fact as well as in practice and then to shield them as much as possible from outside competition.

The 'European' Solution

Some Europeans have believed all along that the only real answer to American competition is to create 'European' giants rather than French or British or German giants. Building 'European' companies means still more consolidation; a reduction from eleven to, say, three major auto makers, from a dozen aircraft companies to two, and so on. That would leave unanswered the question whether bigger and bigger really *is* better and better. The outcome of transnational mergers, however, would be companies with continental-size markets. If the various governments consolidated their research support and their purchasing, the new combines would also have access to a single big 'customer' capable of supporting high-technology products through development and the early stages of production, as the Defense Department and NASA do in the US.

Common Market officials believe that joint government research support and purchasing could be a way of encouraging the formation of European-wide companies. They have proposed a number of scientific and high-technology projects that they think could be jointly undertaken by companies not only from the six Common Market countries but from Britain and elsewhere. They have, for example, proposed that Britain's International Computers Ltd join with several European companies to construct a giant computer. Collaboration of this type, the men in Brussels say, could lead to a more formal consolidation later on.

'A Most Unpleasant Choice'

The main barrier to such trans-European mergers is the lingering notion of national prestige. These days, only a very secure or a very small nation is willing to concede that maybe it really does not need a stake in all the prestige industries – and no European country seems ready to make that concession. Moreover, the larger a company becomes, and the larger its role in a given industry becomes, the more the company itself becomes a matter of national pride. When that happens, cross-border mergers become difficult to imagine. Would France, for instance, now permit a company that represents nearly its entire electric-appliance and electronics industry to merge with Siemens or with GEC-English Electric? Would it be politically possible in Italy to permit the Montecatini Edison chemical complex to merge with Imperial Chemical? Could British Leyland merge with Volkswagen? How would anybody go about merging two legally nationalized companies?

Other problems might be raised by political or diplomatic considerations that have nothing to do with business. Britain, for example, could not merge its flag-bearing International Computers Ltd with Siemens's computer division without taking into consideration the extremely damaging effect this might have on France's CII and thus, indirectly, on the attitudes of the French government toward co-operation with the British on other matters.

But if CII were brought into the deal, what would happen to the other weak European computer makers? The solution that might appeal to politicians would be to put them *all* together. But while this would result in an enlarged market for the surviving company, the new super-giant – freed from worries about European competitors – would be even more likely to prove inefficient, Indeed, it is possible that even with a continent-wide market a European producer of high-technology equipment, such as computers or aircraft, would still not be able to compete effectively with US corporations like IBM.

In a recent book entitled *European Advanced Technology,* Christopher Layton, a British academic and industrial consultant, warns, 'Concentration into large national units could face Europe with a most unpleasant choice between an industry divided up into separate national monopolies or a single European monopoly'. The way to avoid this, Layton suggests, is to move now toward international mergers of companies that do not represent the whole of a given national industry – to create, for example, three nuclear-power equipment groups each containing what were formerly independent British, German and other national companies. Even these will be difficult to arrange in prestige industries. But that hurdle might be taken if neither the management nor the owners of one of the predecessor national companies appeared to dominate the new combine.

Appealing as this solution sounds, it will be difficult to put into practice. As has been pointed out, most of the major industries have been or soon will be boiled down to what is, in effect, one company per country. Moreover, perfectly balanced mergers in which no partner would dominate will be hard to arrange. Any automobile company in Europe (except Volkswagen or British Leyland) would be overwhelmed if it joined with Fiat. Any one of the three German chemical makers might be overshadowed by Imperial Chemical Industries. Paired deals in which, say, France accepted a minority position in one venture in return for a major role in some other industry might be more practical – and would result in an industrial structure closer to the one that would result in a free market. But such continental wheeling and dealing is about as unlikely as a concerted agreement by the governments to let the industrialists work it out for themselves.

Meeting on the Rhine

There are a few, admittedly feeble, signs that the US competition that set off the wave of national mergers may finally push the Europeans into transnational ventures. There have been only two cross-border mergers in postwar Europe, and each has taken place in an industry where the Europeans are being battered fiercely by US corporations. These industries are photographic materials and aircraft.

The first was the creation, in 1964, of Agfa-Gevaert by a merger of Belgium's Gevaert Photo-Producten with Agfa, a subsidiary of Germany's Bayer. It was an ideal marriage. Gevaert was well known in the professional photography business; Agfa was strongest in photographic materials for amateurs. And both were being trounced by Kodak. Today the company is carefully half German, half Belgian. One month the management board meets near Antwerp under the chairmanship of a Belgian; the following month it gathers on the Rhine in Leverkusen with a German at the head of the table. There is only one thing wrong: profits have declined. Company executives insist that the situation would have been worse if Agfa and Gevaert had remained independent companies.

This January the honeymoon began for another effort at an evenly balanced, transnational marriage: Zentralgesell-schaft VFW-Fokker mbH, a combination of Royal Netherlands Aircraft Factories Fokker and Germany's Vereinigte Flugtechnische Werke. Fokker and VFW are old friends that have worked together on a number of projects. VFW, for example, makes tail sections for Fokker's F.28 Fellowship short-haul passenger jet, and Fokker is developing wings for the VFW 614, a new short-haul jet. Nevertheless, merger discussions still took five years, broke down once, and, near the end, became heated over a minor point – the location of the central office. Düsseldorf, roughly halfway between VFW headquarters in Bremen and the Fokker offices in Amsterdam, was the final choice.

VFW-Fokker could be a nucleus for a full-scale European airframe company. Joint projects and consortia already connect the company with almost every other European aircraft manufacturer. Fokker and France's Dassault, for instance, share ownership of SA Belge de Constructions Aéronautiques (SABCA). It will probably sadden trans-European enthusiasts to learn that United Aircraft has a minority interest in VFW and Northrop has a small interest in Fokker.

To describe European efforts at industrial integration solely in terms of the Agfa-Gevaert and VFW-Fokker arrangements understates what has been achieved by other means. A large number of subsidiaries are owned by companies based in different countries. In the last six months, for example, Unilever and Nestlé have combined their German, Austrian, and Italian ventures in ice cream and frozen food. And Philips, which since 1962 has had an equal share with Siemens in Deutsche Grammophon, joins forces with Ignis, the second-largest Italian company in the home-appliance business.

There also have been a few sizable cross-border acquisitions. Hoechst, the West German chemical concern, which already has a 22 per cent interest in a French chemical maker, Roussel-Uclaf, recently purchased control of a leading British paint company. Last year a Dutch synthetic-fiber and chemical company, Algemene Kunstzijde Unie (AKU), bought up Belgium's Fabelta, further strengthening the position as the Common Market's leading synthetic-fiber company. AKU later merged with KZO, a Dutch chemical and pharmaceutical producer, to form a new group with annual sales of some $1·7 billion (and a controlling interest in two US corporations, International Salt and American Enka).

The growing number of industrial interconnections leads some Europeans to conclude that cross-border mergers may not be necessary, and that the variety of less formal arrangements will grow and compound, slowly integrating industry, not necessarily in a predictable pattern. 'Most things that happen in the world of economies and industry', says an OECD official, 'are never planned, never thought out, and yet turn out to be very good'.

Clearing the Bramble Patch

Such echoes of *laissez-faire* are rare in Europe. Younger businessmen and economists, especially, believe that some sort of positive action must be taken. Christopher Layton, for example, suggests setting up a European IRC and establishing a program of common government purchasing, joint scientific and development projects, and 'Buy European' policies to replace the 'buy national' policies. (He would use the last to bargain away similar protectionism in the US.)

Such suggestions are greeted sympathetically by Common Market officials, who also are actively promoting their idea of joint R. and D. projects that would get European companies accustomed to working together. Despite some disheartening experiences in nuclear power and earth satellites, the men in Brussels would like to see trans-European collaboration in such fields as telecommunications, oceanography, and pollution control, as well as computers. However, their enthusiasm is tempered by a decade of trying to get six countries to collaborate, and they would be willing to start on a more prosaic level by clearing away the bramble patch of different national tax and corporate laws that seems to hamper cross-border mergers.

The legal obstacles are not insurmountable. Agfa-Gevaert and VFW-Fokker get around them, as do US corporations. But harmonizing legislation would make things easier. In fact, some Europeans fear it would make things a bit too easy for Americans; they would like to exempt subsidiaries owned by companies based outside the EEC from the benefits inherent in a uniform European company law. Even then, US corporations would retain a major advantage in making acquisitions: typically they have more cash, or can borrow it more easily, or can offer the seller a packet of parent-company shares and debentures far more attractive than anything most European companies can assemble. A healthy Europe-wide capital market might be the strongest stimulant to continental mergers that could be devised.

The Real Barrier

In the end, as an official in the French government said recently, 'the real obstruction to integration of Europe's industries is national egoism'. No matter how willing industrialists and financiers might be to think in terms of a continent rather than a nation, that barrier will be overcome only by a surge of political effort.

For some years the will to exert that effort has been lacking. The Common Market has been bogged down. And national negotiators have approached discussions of trans-European projects seemingly intent only on extracting the maximum national gain. Since the leaders of the six Common Market countries met at the Hague in early December 1969, there have been signs of change. The most newsworthy result of that session was an agreement to begin negotiations this year with four applicants for admission to the EEC – Britain, Ireland, Norway, and Denmark. Yet that was only a symptom of the most important event – an apparent commitment by France and the other EEC member states to get on with the job of putting together a unified Europe.

By coincidence or not, two developments followed shortly after the Hague meeting: an agreement between Britain, Germany, and the Netherlands to co-operate in the construction of uranium-enrichment plants, and the formation of a consortium of companies from six countries to develop a gas-cooled breeder reactor. Neither depended directly on what happened at the Hague. But the agreements would not have been made without an atmosphere of co-operation, and a general willingness to put the needs and future of Europe ahead of nationalistic pride. If that atmosphere can be maintained and nurtured, the rush of national mergers and industrial consolidation may indeed prove only another step toward European unity. But the seventies will be filled with opportunities to procrastinate, to put national needs before all others. If Europe succumbs to nationalism, today's trend will be tomorrow's obstacle.

Editor's Note: The Changing Policy Towards Mergers in Britain and the European Economic Community

The article by Philip Siekman was written in March 1970 when a Labour Government was in office in Britain. In June 1970 a Conservative Government was elected, after a period of five years in opposition, and one of its first acts was to wind up the Industrial Reorganization Corporation and to announce plans to strengthen the Monopolies Commission and to extend its powers.[2]

Siekman here emphasizes the fact that the IRC were preoccupied with size, that they encouraged mergers and in so doing increased the market power of certain companies. As a number of the papers in this book point out, the evidence to support the advantages of size is not always as clear as is usually assumed. Having encouraged the increase in size of companies and so market power, it became necessary to control this power in the public interest, and this, under the Labour Government, was the role of the Monopolies Commission. There was obviously a paradox in having one body that sought to maintain competition and another that acted to reduce it. This possible conflict was recognized and so the Commission was instructed to be concerned with the situation 'where the domination of so many industries by a small number of firms means that it is increasingly difficult to rely on traditional market forces alone to protect consumers'.

The Labour Government had less faith in the idea that the workings of the market mechanism would bring about firms of an optimal size and would ensure that they acted in the public interest, and so they took actions to stimulate efficiency and to protect the public. It appears that the Conservative Government have a greater belief in the power of the market mechanism and so wish to create conditions in which competition can flourish. They intend to introduce legislation in the 1971/2 Parliamentary session which will have the objective of stimulating competition.

Certain steps have already been taken and statements have been made indicating future action.[3] The IRC has been disbanded, the Monopolies Commission will be strengthened and its powers extended to cover the nationalized industries and the service sector of the economy. The Commission has been asked to become expert on situations of imperfect competition and to provide the government with information on this subject. The staff will be enlarged and the Commission can itself suggest matters that it thinks should be investigated, rather than waiting for cases to be referred to it. Attempts will be made to speed up enquiries. The law relating to restrictive practices and cartels is also to be strengthened, ensuring that more anti-competitive practices are registered. Mergers will only be referred to the Monopolies Commission if it appears that they will lead to a reduction of competition without compensating advantages.

The Conservative attitude towards mergers therefore reflects their attitude towards all aspects of competition. They will rely as much as possible on the workings of the market mechanism, but will take action where necessary to prevent interference with the free workings of the market. Mergers will not be actively encouraged by a government agency, nor will they be opposed, except where competition is reduced without any compensating advantages. The rule, which continued through at least the first year of the Conservative Government's term of office, whereby all mergers involving assets worth £5 million or more are automatically referred to the Commission, may be brought to an end.

The Conservative Government wish to develop a system of workable competition, but because some industries can only be organized with a few large companies competing in a world market, it is in these cases necessary to think of workable competition on a world scale and not just competition within a country. There is however a danger that companies in most industries would like to think of themselves as operating in this context and would thus attempt to use this as a justification for any merger. The government therefore intend to depart from the old definition of a monopoly: that is where one company controls one third or more of the national market. The government will be flexible on the percentage market share that suggests a monopoly (that is a situation that might require investigation); in some industries it could be a market share as high as 50 per cent and in other industries as low as 25 per cent.

This means that in some industries a merger of two comparatively small firms may require investigation, whereas in another industry the merger of two large firms could be justified, either because it does not create a unit which fits within the the market share definition of a monopoly or because although it reduces competition it has sufficient compensating advantages. A difficulty with this more flexible policy arises, of course, in deciding what is the optimal size of a company which has to face the competitive market of a particular industry.

British industry can no longer be considered in isolation. Competition will be increased as tariffs are reduced upon Britain's entry into the European Economic Community. The Monopolies Commission will therefore have to examine proposed mergers with reference to the enlarged European market.

The EEC has rules on what is regarded as market dominance. These rules will become relevant to British firms. At the moment the commission have not attempted to prevent a merger, let alone to investigate a merger, before it has been allowed to proceed. The Director-General for Industrial, Technological and Scientific Affairs in the EEC Commission, has stated however that, 'We encourage co-operation, especially between companies in different member states, but within certain limits, and the time may come when we shall have to carry out prior vetting of proposed amalgamations between the largest companies'.[4] Upon entry to the EEC British companies will not, under the present practices, have to fear the investigation of a proposed merger by an EEC body, only by the Monopolies Commission.

Article 86 of the Treaty of Rome deals with the abuse of dominant positions by companies in the Community. Until comparatively recently very little action had been taken by the Commission against firms holding dominant positions – an expression the EEC prefer to the term 'monopoly position' which is more often used in Britain. The Commission concentrated its attention in the early years on the problem of restrictive agreements between companies. Recently, however, it challenged the dominant position of two companies, one of which was the result of a newly created merger, the other of existing and proven domination.

The first case concerns the takeover in 1970 of the leading Dutch packaging company, Thomassen and Drijver Verblifa, by the American Continental Can Company. The Commission was not happy with the situation that resulted from this merger. Continental Can had previously purchased the leading German canning company, and it announced plans to integrate its two subsidiaries. The Commission is empowered by Article 86 to prohibit any dominant position abusive to competition or consumers' interests in the Community; the Article states that 'action by one or more enterprises to take improper advantage of a dominant position within the Common Market or within a substantial part of it shall be deemed to be incompatible with the Common Market and shall hereby be prohibited'. The question is whether or not the integration of Continental Can's Dutch and German subsidiaries would result in the abuse of a dominant position.[5]

The problem revolves around defining a market sector, both with regard to product and geographical region. If a sector is defined very narrowly many companies would find themselves in a dominant position; if it is defined broadly enough, there would be hardly any companies that could be classed as dominant. Continental Can claim that within the overall EEC market for cans they only control about 10 to 20 per cent of production; the EEC Commission claims however that for certain regions and for particular industries using the product, Continental Can control perhaps 60 to 70 per cent of the market. On the question of the regions that should be considered as markets, the crucial issue is the transport cost of the product.

These issues affecting market dominance have still to be resolved. They are basic to the whole question of monopoly control and the examination of mergers. The result of this case is expected to set a precedent for the Commission's future policy towards mergers and takeovers and the Commission are taking a tough line.

In the second case currently being considered under the market dominance provisions, the Commission have condemned the practices of the German GEMA company, a company that, amongst other things, controls performing rights on musical compositions. The complaint is that the practices adopted by the company militate against the interests of non-German composers seeking to promote their works in that country.

Since the Commission turned its attention to market dominance it has shown that it intends to deal severely with companies that do not provide sufficient information on which it can make a decision. In its investigation of the Community's sugar industry, and in particular the market for this product in Belgium, it was decided that the dominant company had failed to provide the Commission's investigators with the data they required, and the company was fined.

It appears that the EEC is now beginning to enforce its rules of competition with regard to monopolies, which will have an immediate impact on companies contemplating mergers.

Since Mr. Siekman's article appeared in March 1970, the number of industrial interconnections has continued at an ever increasing pace. The types of arrangements that have been arrived at between companies within a country and in different countries have become more involved. If management is as ingenious in running the companies as it is in bringing them together, either through joint trading arrangements or under common ownership, the future for the companies should be bright indeed.

In this note certain of the developments that have taken place since 1970 in the cases discussed in the chapter should be mentioned. The strengthening of links between Rhône-Poulenc SA and the Saint-Gobain-Point-A-Mousson SA group continues apace. The former company will purchase most of Saint-Gobain's 39 per cent stake in the Produits Chimiques Pechiney-Saint-Gobain SA company, to give it a 90 per cent share of this company. This near outright control will remove any obstacles in the way of merging Pechiney-Saint-Gobain with Progil, another subsidiary of Rhône-Poulenc SA.

Also in Mr. Siekman's chapter there was reference to a possible link between Cie Générale D'Electricité with Thomson Houston-Hotchkiss Brandt. At the end of 1971 this had not taken place, but CGE have continued to expand through acquisition. A French electrical engineering company, Jeumont-Schneider has been a subject of interest to the US company, Westinghouse Electrical. The French Government have been reluctant to let this company be taken over by an American company. It appears as if the turbo-alternators and power station plant interests of Jeumont-Schneider will be taken over by CGE, with Westinghouse only being allowed to acquire an interest in the rest of the company's activities. The French Government will have ensured a continuing French ownership in the area of the company's activities with which they were particularly concerned.

Developments between companies connected with the motor industry have continued. At first the mergers or trading arrangements were between companies in the same country, but the new pattern seems to be the linking of companies across national boundaries. Dunlop of Britain and Pirelli of Italy have brought together their interests. Citroen of France and Fiat of Italy have entered into certain co-operation agreements. In this industry there undoubtedly are advantages in size, and so this trend of merging or making trading arrangements can be expected to continue.

The takeover activities of companies within the EEC have been dealt with by Siekman. To obtain a balanced picture of the changing competitive situation the actions taken by the Commission to prohibit restrictive agreements and to limit the abuse of dominant positions needs to be considered. Although they have only recently taken action in the latter situations, they have been very active for a number number of years against restrictive agreements. Many have been terminated because they resulted in restraint of trade. One of the more recent test cases arose out of a decision taken by the Commission in 1969 which resulted in heavy fines being imposed on six European chemical companies found to be operating a cartel. Three of the six companies involved appealed against the decision to the European Court of Justice. The Court ruling in 1970 supported most of the Commission's actions on this matter; it only failed to uphold two minor judgements. This has set a precedent for the future treatment of firms involved in price fixing arrangements.[6]

To conclude; although firms in Europe still show a definite leaning towards mergers, or at least an urge to come together in some form of arrangement, the EEC Commission, having in the past been active in the pursuit of cartels, are now beginning to act against monopolies. Therefore, although certain governments in Europe may not do very much to investigate the advantages or otherwise of mergers and takeovers, the Commission is beginning to enforce certain standards. As has been shown in the detailed account of the changing British legislation the attitude regarding acceptable competitive practices at any one time within a country can depend on the political party in power. Once an agency such as the EEC Commission has power to investigate and takes action on unfair practices the position from the point of view of the company will be a lot clearer, not necessarily more favourable, but less likely to change over time.

PART E

THE EVIDENCE

Chapter Fifteen

THE INTERNATIONALIZATION OF CAPITAL AND THE BRITISH ECONOMY*

R. Murray

Institute of Development Studies, University of Sussex

One of the principal issues raised by the growth in the number and scale of international-firm operations in the post-second-world-war period has been the potential incompatibility between the continued growth of these firms and the relevance of the nation-state as an economic unit. Raymond Vernon has recently written that 'international corporate groups . . . growing in strength and importance in response to modern needs, are not congruent in all respects with the national sovereignty concept'.[1] Charles Kindleberger goes further in saying that 'the nation state is just about through as an economic unit'.[2]

This concern is not new. In the first two decades of this century, the effect of the internationalization of capital on nation-states was an item of major debate among socialist writers on the international economy. Did not the spread of capital overseas, the development of international cartels, trusts and banking networks undermine the significance of nation-states? Most writers on the subject, with the notable exception of Kautsky, denied the proposition. They acknowledged the importance of international corporate networks, but saw them as inherently unstable. The 'fortress' of the nation-state still remained the dominant international economic category. In Bukharin's words, 'significant as this process [of internationalization] may be in itself, it is, however, counteracted by a still stronger tendency of capital towards nationalization, and towards remaining secluded within state boundaries'.[3]

In the second quarter of the century the spread of international cartels led to a revival of the issue in liberal as well as socialist writings. For some, the cartels were the dominant force in the world economy, and this dominance was used abusively, particularly in the armaments industry. For others, this very power over individual nation-states was seen as a progressive force. Louis Koucheur advocated international cartels as the only way of eliminating national trade barriers. Edouard Herriot and Gustav Straseman saw cartels as a means for European unification, and as models for international political co-operation.[4]

*An earlier version of this paper was presented at the Conference on Mergers and Takeovers, May 27, 28, 1970, and subsequently rewritten.

Since the second world war, international cartels have been reduced in extent. Rather it is the growth in the number of firms with an international spread of productive operations which has raised again the issue of the 'robustness' of nation-states. Modern international firms are certainly more consolidated than the consortia and cartels of the earlier period. They are more stable, less likely to turn back to seclusion within state boundaries. But it still does not follow that nation-states are, as a consequence, outmoded. Most international firms are still strongly identified with one country, politically, economically and financially in terms of ownership. The 'fortress' may be as much a base for attack as a shelter for defence. We cannot assume that the growth of international firms implies the decline of nation-states, any more than we can assume that some quasi-Galbraithian social conscience on the part of the international firms (what Val Duncan of RTZ recently called a corporate 'soul'[5]) can mitigate the inherent conflicts between firms and states.

For an analysis of the effects of the internationalization of capital on nation-states, two aspects of the problem seem to me of particular importance. First what are the interests of the international firms themselves with respect to the continuing performance, throughout their international operating space, of economic functions traditionally performed for their home operations by their mother state (property protection, liberalization/standardization, macro-orchestration, the provision of generalized inputs, intervention for social concensus, and support against foreign competitors)? Will these functions be performed for the firms by other states when they move abroad; and if not, who will perform them? This brings us to the second point, which is the capability of the mother state to continue to perform its traditional functions not only for its capital expanding abroad, but for its domestic capital when this is threatened by foreign competition. These two points are the ones I would wish to emphasize in any analysis of the international firm and the state: the interests of private capital, and the power of the state.[6]

The present paper is concerned with the latter of these points, and only a part of it at that: how far does the internationalization of capital diminish the power of British governments to perform one of its traditional functions, the management of the domestic economy? The question we have to answer is not simply whether or not this power has been diminished: it is difficult to deny that it has. Rather the question is, how far has it been diminished, what are the consequences of this diminution, who stands to gain and lose, to what extent can these effects be counteracted by government policy?

The paper is in four parts: some introductory remarks on the extent of the internationalization of capital as it affects the British economy; and then, in sequence, a discussion of the effects of internationalization on monetary, fiscal and balance of payments policies.

PART 1

In this section I want to suggest (*a*) that international firms are a significant macro-economic category in the British economy – to do this it is necessary to show that foreign firms have a significant stake in the British economy, and that major British firms have substantial international operations; and (*b*) that the significance of both foreign-owned and British-based international firms in the British economy has been growing over time. Both points are disputed.

Figures from Britain's overall international capital involvement are given in Table 1. Most items speak for themselves. The external claims and liabilities of UK banks in foreign currencies is principally made up of Eurocurrencies, and the large rise in these items reflects the central role that London has played in the growth of this international money market.[7] The doubling in value of portfolio assets and liabilities is mainly the result of capital appreciation: the figures are probably a good deal lower now as the result of the decline in stock exchange prices. Direct investment is the item with the next largest growth: though it is not clear whether this also entails a growth in its significance *vis à vis* the British economy.

Table 1

UK external assets and liabilities 1962 and 1968
(£ million)

Item	Assets		% change	Liabilities		% change
	1962	1968		1962	1968	
Monetary						
1. Official	2060	2016	– 2	3045	6125	101
2. Private:						
UK banks external claims and liabilities in:						
sterling	634	1252	97	1419	1602	13
foreign currencies	996	7051	608	1028	7098	590
Other private	747	1197	60	319	313	– 2
Long Term						
3. Official	710	1115	57	2670	2995	13
4. Private:						
portfolio[1]	3000	5800	93	1050	2200	110
direct investment[2]	4885	7755	59	2130	3720	75
extra-sterling area borrowing by UK companies (excl. oil cos)				5	165	. . .
Total	13030	26195	101	11665	24220	209

[1] At estimated market value.
[2] At estimated book value of net assets. Figures for assets exclude the direct investments of UK banks; those for liabilities exclude the direct investments of overseas banks and insurance companies in the UK.

Source: *Bank of England Quarterly Bulletin*, December 1969, pp. 444–5.

John Dunning has estimated that foreign direct investment in the UK constituted over 10 per cent of the net capital stock of companies in the UK and that foreign companies accounted for 27 per cent of net fixed capital formation in the UK in 1965.[8] If this relationship between new capital formation and the existing stock of capital holds over time (and the rate of growth of new foreign direct investment in the UK between 1962 and 1968 compared to the overall growth of capital formation in the UK over the same period suggests that it does) then it follows that the foreign proportion of the net capital stock of companies in the UK is rising. This conclusion is supported by figures recently prepared by the Monopolies Commission. They calculate that for those quoted companies with assets over 0·5m. in 1961 and mainly engaged in the UK, the growth rate of assets was 95 per cent over the period 1957–67. On a slightly different basis of evaluation, they also calculated that the 1,253 companies still surviving from their original sample in 1968 showed a growth of net assets between end 1957 and 1968 of 165 per cent, of which 48 per cent was growth by acquisition (centralization) and 117 per cent internal growth (concentration). Table 2 below gives gross data over a comparable period for 19 foreign subsidiaries in the UK. Their overall growth in net assets was 174 per cent, only a small proportion of which was accounted for by acquisition.[9] If we assume that the Monopolies Commission sample of British firms, and the sample of 19 foreign subsidiaries are representative of their respective classes, then we can take these results as further evidence of the growing foreign stake in the UK economy.

Table 2

Growth of foreign-owned firms in the UK, 1957–68

Company	Parent Country	Business	Net assets £s. m.		
			1957	1968	% inc.
Esso	USA	Petroleum	116	257	122
Ford	USA	Motors	82	240	193
Vauxhall	USA	Motors	55	120	118
American Tobacco	USA	Tobacco	41	114	178
Philips	Holland	Electrical	24	85	254
Standard Telephone	USA	Telecommunications	17	74	318
Chrysler	USA	Motors	21	60	186
Mobil Oil	USA	Petroleum	26	58	123
Massey-Ferguson	Canada	Agric. machinery	5	56	920
Nestlé	Switzerland	Food	12	48	300
Heinz	USA	Food	14	41	193
Goodyear	USA	Tyres	15	38	153
Burroughs	USA	Office Machinery	5	25	400
Monsanto	USA	Chemicals	19	25	32
International Harvester	USA	Agric. machinery	9	20	122
May and Baker	France	Pharmaceuticals	11	19	73
Proctor and Gamble	USA	Soap products	8	18	125
Firestone	USA	Tyres	4	18	350
British Enkalon	Holland	Man-made fibres	3	17	467
Total			487	1333	174

Source: Department of Trade and Industry: *A Survey of Mergers 1958–68*, HMSO, 1970, Appendix 13.

Table 3

The degree of international involvement of major British corporations, 1969 – all figures in percentages

Rank in Times 1000	Company	Sales Abroad			Profit from overseas opns.	Taxes paid abroad	Net assets abroad	Employment abroad
		Total	Overseas subsid.	Exports				
35	Union International	–	–	2	–	99	–	–
43	Burmah Oil[1]	–	–	5	98	97	–	75
17	Dalgety	91	91	0	97	100	–	84
3	BAT	90[2]	89	2	87	95	85	94
2	BP	90	–	–	–	100	–	63
27	RTZ	86[4]	81	5	96	98	82	–
5	Unilever	–	–	2[5]	–	79	–	69
25	Con. Tin Smelters	–	–	7	72	62	–	–
38	Coats Paton	67	59	8	80	90	57	48
49	Tate and Lyle	–	–	9	–	67	–	–
14	Dunlop	65	57	8	72	89	–	48
19	Hawker Siddeley	57	37	20	–	29	34	21
48	Ranks	–	–	17	–	57	–	23
39	Bowater[6]	53	51	2	62	68	69	58
4	ICI	52	34	18	27	23	–	26
18	BICC[7]	49	34	15	58	68	30	26
8	British Leyland	49	–	–	40	35	–	10
10	Courtaulds[8]	39	23	16	–	31	–	16
12	GKN	38	30	8	29	30	26	27
9	GEC[8]	38	22	16	10	17	15	–
36	C T Bowring[9]	35	–	–	–	8	–	–
30	Reed Paper	33	30	3	29	25	–	23
33	Rolls Royce	–	–	33[10]	–	6	–	3
40	Amalgamated Metals	–	–	5	33	40	–	–
42	Cadbury Schweppes[11]	32	28	4	36	35	–	30
13	Associated British Foods[8]	30	29	1	40	40	–	–
44	Lucas	26	12	14	–	22	–	12
34	Tube Investments[12]	24	10	15	17	27	9	7
21	Distillers[8,13]	–	–	23	–	10	–	–
45	Allied Suppliers	19	18	2	32[14]	30	–	–
37	Sears Holdings[8]	19	9	10	7	9	–	–
22	GUS[8]	15	12	2	10	11	–	–
26	Allied Breweries	10	9	1	–	5	–	–
24	Rank Hovis McDougall	9	8	1	–	9	–	6
41	Thorn	–	–	9	5	8	–	–
50	Boots Pure Drug[8]	5	2	2	4[15]	3	–	–
32	Unigate[8]	3	2	1	7	5	4	5
6	Imperial Tobacco	–	–	–	–	3	–	–
23	Marks & Spencer[8]	2	0	2	0	0	0	0
29	Bass Charrington	–	–	1	–	1	–	–
47	Tesco	0	0	0	0	0	0	0

Notes to Table 3

The firms covered are the top 50 from the 1970/1 *Times* 1,000 with the exception of four private companies, Shell Mex & BP (7), Metal Traders (20), Shipping Industrial Holdings (28) and Czarnikow (46); four companies controlled from abroad, Esso (11), Ford (15), Gallaher (16), Woolworths (31), and finally Shell Transport and Trading (1) for whom we could obtain none of the relevant breakdowns.

Figures are for 1968/9 or 1969 except where specified.

A dash indicates that the figures were not available.

[1] Burmah Oil derives 50 per cent of its profits from franked income from Shell and BP; the figures in the table exclude this holding.
[2] Figures for sales abroad are estimated from 1968 data.
[3] BP figures exclude Sohio.
[4] Sales figures include intra-group sales comprising 9 per cent of total turnover.
[5] Export figures are assumed to include intra-firm exports, and have therefore been compared to total sales including intra-firm sales.
[6] Sales figures for 1967, and net asset figures for 1960.
[7] Net asset figures for 1965, employment figures for 1966.
[8] Figures for year 1969/70, save GEC net asset figures (1968/9).
[9] The figure of 35 per cent sales abroad represents almost entirely premium income in foreign currency: it excludes shipping income, foreign commodity sales, and foreign investment income.
[10] Export figures are for proportion of total revenue from all foreign sources, almost all of which is from exports; exports and total sales figures include indirect exports.
[11] Sales figures include intra-firm exports.
[12] Figures are for the 17 months to 31 December 1969, save for profits which are for the calendar year 1969.
[13] Distillers have 47 per cent of their turnover outside the UK and Europe.
[14] Profits abroad include profits on exports.
[15] Estimated for 1967/8.

If we turn now to the significance of the international economy to UK firms, we estimate that in 1965 overseas direct investments made up approximately 20 per cent of the net capital stock owned by UK companies internationally, and that nearly one-third of all net fixed capital formation by British companies took place abroad.[10] We also know, from a study undertaken by Dunning and Morgan for the Committee on Invisible Exports that approximately 30 per cent of total profits of British companies are derived from their overseas operations and that firms with substantial overseas interests show a higher growth rate than others.[11] Recently Robert Rowthorn has confirmed these orders of magnitude by virtue of an ingenious calculation. Between 1957 and 1965 he estimates that 32 per cent of the increase in sales of British manufacturing firms was accounted for by exports (12 per cent) and the sales of overseas subsidiaries (20 per cent), although this last figure he regards as an underestimate since he was working with figures which excluded petroleum companies.[12]

These figures suggest both a substantial stake by UK companies abroad, and a growth in that stake. Both points are confirmed if we look at individual data for major British firms. In Table 3 we have calculated the degree of international involvement, under various definitions, of 41 of the top 50 firms from *The Times* 500. The table is divided into quartiles: 14 of less than 25 per cent involvement; 12 of from 25 per cent–49 per cent; 8 of from 50 per cent–74 per cent; and 7 of 75 per cent or over. In all, 27 or 66 per cent of the sample have foreign involvement of over 25 per cent. From what we know of those nine companies that have been excluded from the table, their inclusion would raise not only the percentage of those firms of over 25 per cent involvement, but the share of those in the top quartiles as well.[13]

For comparison, we have constructed from data compiled by Bruck and Lees a similar table (Table 4) for the top US firms, covering only those with 25 per cent or over foreign involvement in the top 50 of the *Fortune* list. There are no companies in the top quartile, and only two in the second, compared to 15 with 50 per cent or over in the British list. In the third quartile there are 15; giving 17 in all as against the British 27.

Table 3 gives current international involvement and supports the general indications given by the macro-figures. Those firms in the bottom quartile are manifestly from sectors traditionally linked to the home market (food, distribution, and brewing); the brewing firms in particular have recently shown an increased trend towards internationalization.[14] However, we still lack satisfactory data on the overall change in the degree of international involvement. From circumstantial evidence we would expect a similar table compiled in 1959 to show the firms currently in the top and bottom quartile to be in the same position. The marked change would be likely to be seen in the second and third quartiles, many of whose current members are those who have been increasing their degree of overseas involvement over the last decade. BICC, for example, with 49 per cent sales abroad in 1969, had a figure of 31 per cent in 1960, and 41 per cent in 1964. Glaxo, not in our sample but 76 in the 1969 *Times* 500, increased its sales abroad from 60 per cent to 70 per cent of all sales during the decade 1960–70. British Leyland, GEC, Reed Paper, Cadbury Schweppes, and Associated British Foods have all shown similar trends. We may suggest, indeed, a distinction between the old imperial internationals (the oil companies, Unilever, Tate and Lyle, BAT and Coats Paton) and the new (BICC, British Leyland, GEC).

The major British firms dominate overseas investment. The Board of Trade has estimated that the top 50 British overseas investors (including some firms not in our sample) account for 80 per cent of UK overseas direct investment, with companies owning less than £½m. foreign assets directly accounting for only 5 per cent of the total. In exports the Board of Trade estimated that in 1965 the top 30 firms accounted for one-third of all British exports, and the top 120 firms for half.[15] For 1969 *The Times* 1000 published a list of the 20 largest exporters from the UK (12 of whom are included in Table 3) in that year who between them accounted for 30 per cent of total British exports,[16] so that control if anything appears to be becoming more concentrated. On the basis of these figures we may justifiably link the arguments derived from the firm data with the overall conclusions from the macro-evidence.

One part of the argument remains to be filled in. I have suggested that two-thirds of the major UK firms have significant international involvement, with over one-third selling more abroad than in the British market. It remains to be shown that these same firms also constitute a significant part of the British macro-economy. We have no up-to-date figures on this, but from the Census of Production and from Inland Revenue data we know that:

(1) In 1951–2 the 100 largest industrial and commercial companies accounted for 20 per cent of the aggregate profit of all trading concerns;

(2) in 1958 the 180 manufacturing firms with more than 5,000 employees each accounted for more than a third of total manufacturing employment and 38 per cent of net output, while the top 95 firms in mining, quarrying and construction accounted for approximately 20 per cent of the total output and employment of those sectors; and

(3) in 1963 the top 95 manufacturing firms ranked by assets controlled 65 per cent of aggregate net assets in manufacturing.[17]

Table 4

The degree of international involvement of major American corporations – all figures in percentages

Rank in *Fortune* 500	Company	Sales Abroad	Earnings from overseas opns.	Assets Abroad	Emplymt. Abroad	Prodn. Abroad
3	Standard Oil (NJ)	68	60	52	–	81
30	International Telephone & Telegraph	59	60	61	72	–
6	Socony Mobil Oil	49	52	43	51	76
39	Caterpillar Tractor	43	–	19	17	–
36	Phillips Petroleum	–	–	–	–	42
17	Standard Oil (California)	35	43	9	29	69
8	Texaco	35	25	–	–	65
20	Goodyear Tyre & Rubber	–	34	40	–	–
9	IBM	30	30	32	36	–
35	Eastman Kodak	30	15	28	37	–
49	United States Rubber	–	–	30	–	–
10	Gulf Oil	–	29	33	–	76
21	Union Carbide	29	22	17	43	–
46	Sperry Rand	28	–	42	–	–
19	International Harvester	28	19	26	32	–
31	Firestone Tire & Rubber	–	26	–	–	–
5	Chrysler	25	–	26	24	22

Source: Bruck & Lees, *Foreign Investment, Capital Controls, and the Balance of Payments,* N.Y. University, 1968, pp. 83–5.

Notes: 1. Data is given for those firms in the top 50 of the *Fortune* 500 list with foreign investment of 25 per cent or over.
2. We have excluded the one foreign company in the US top 50, namely Shell.

Finally we know that the period since 1957 has been one of great merger activity; the top 40 companies ranked by assets which owned 35 per cent of the total assets of the Monopolies Commission's sample in 1957 controlled 49 per cent of the total by 1968, while the figures for the top 80 firms rose from 44–63 per cent.[18] We would accordingly expect the concentration percentages given above to be by now significantly higher.[19]

PART 2

Monetary Policy

The internationalization of capital in the form of international companies might be expected to blunt domestic monetary policy because such companies have a privileged access to funds that remain relatively unaffected by changes in British monetary policy. Such funds might be of two kinds: internal or external. In terms of internal funds international companies, like large national firms, certainly have available large amounts of internally generated surplus. Prior to the Johnson restrictions on direct investment, US firms provided the majority of their financial needs from internal sources: of total funds of $14·8b. raised for US overseas business in 1965, 22 per cent came from US sources (in part from funds internal to the firm in the US), 46 per cent came from re-invested earnings (net income plus depreciation and depletion minus income paid out) and 32 per cent came from external foreign sources.[20] Since the tightening of restrictions, flows from the US have fallen and those from external foreign sources have risen, but it still appears that internal funds compose the major part of overseas financing. Brooke and Remmers have shown that the American companies in their sample of 115 foreign subsidiaries in the UK provided three-quarters of their total financial requirements from cash flow (net profits after tax and depreciation) over the period 1960–7, compared to a figure of 69 per cent for British quoted manufacturing companies over the same period.[21]

British firms similarly have access for their British investment not only to undistributed earnings and depreciation provisions on their British operations, but surplus funds generated from their overseas affiliates. Net earnings on UK foreign investment amounted to £568m. in 1968 with depreciation provisions coming to £229m. A large part of this total is re-invested overseas, but a proportion is returned either as remitted profits, or as disinvestment from the sale of share and loan capital, the receipt of dividends in excess of profits, the repayment of credit previously extended on UK exports and the repatriation of working balances. In 1968 remitted profits plus other net receipts came to £348m. (though much of this was remitted only on paper), while gross disinvestment totalled £197m. (as against a gross investment of £607m).[22]

It should be made clear that as far as internal sources of finance are concerned it is the size of the international firms rather than their international nature that is important. Were the internal market large enough to accommodate national firms of a similar scale, there would be no question of distinction. But as far as Britain is concerned, the size of the internal market cannot accommodate such size in most sectors: firms are driven abroad for markets and raw materials; accumulation leads to extra-territorial extension. It is in this way that international firms operating in Britain can be said to have a privileged access to one form of capital more or less insulated from domestic monetary policy (i.e., internally generated funds).[23]

The second source of capital to which international firms, and particularly American firms, have privileged access is the international capital market: particularly the Eurodollar and Eurobond markets. The remarkable rise of the Eurodollar market is well known. From a size of $5b. in 1963 it rose to an estimated $35b. by the end of 1969. International firms have played a prominent part in the market on both the demand and the supply side. On the side of demand, international firms have used Eurodollars for both transaction and speculative purposes. In Sweden and Canada we know that corporations hold Eurodollars on current account to meet working capital needs: much intra-firm trade is financed with Eurodollars, as are the issues of long-term securities in Europe, particularly those denominated in dollars.[24] In Britain itself, the Treasury restrictions on financing domestic expenditure from short-term foreign currency borrowing announced in January 1971 brought forth the comment from the National Westminster Bank, 'We shall have to review the credit position of every one of our customers. Many of them have come to consider this money as essential'.[25] It was officially estimated that such foreign currency borrowing in the UK amounted to £200m. in 1970 alone. As far as speculation goes, the evidence is less authoritative: all one can say is that those most closely involved with this market appear to assume that Eurodollars are used to finance speculation, and this assumption became an outcry (in some quarters) during the Deutschmark crisis of May 1969.[26]

On the supply side international firms have used the market for short-term investment of transaction funds and excess cash balances (Squib in Ireland for example), and for short-term investment of money raised on the European security market (capital is raised in advance of need and is invested meanwhile) – thus in the 18 months up to June 1966 US corporations raised $530m. of foreign funds through their affiliates, though they used only $157m. for direct investment outside the US during the same period, and are said to have invested a good deal of the balance on the Eurodollar market.[27]

A similar pattern is observable on the Eurobond market. This market, which has served as a market for long-term debt as against the short – and increasingly medium – term function of the Eurodollar market, has grown from a figure of $164m. in 1963 to $3,517m. in 1968 – altogether a total of $8·6b. worth of bonds having been issued over that period or 75 per cent of all international bond issues (foreign bond issues totalling $2·9b. over the same period). Government and para-government bodies were the predominant issuers in the early years of the market (accounting for 94 per cent of the issues in 1963 and 80 per cent in 1964). They have now been superseded by corporations (accounting for 77·5 per cent of the issues in 1968), who were forced to turn to the market because of the Interest Equalization tax of 1963, and the Johnson measures of 1965 and 1968.

In both the Eurodollar and the Eurobond markets international firms, and particularly American firms, have had a clear advantage over national ones. In the Eurodollar market, it is the large international firms which have the credit names to satisfy the Eurodollar lenders; they commonly have extensive relationships with the US banks whose branches play so important a part in the market; and their size allows them to deal in a market (whose transactions are seldom for less than $1m.) in a way which is not open to most national British firms. Chase Manhattan put it thus: 'only large companies with excellent credit standing are ordinarily eligible for Eurodollar credits . . . even relatively strong overseas subsidiaries of major American companies are frequently required to supply the lending bank with a parent-company guarantee, insuring the lender that an unquestionable source of dollars is in reserve should the subsidiary's own dollar sources fail'.[28]

In the Eurobond market the point is even clearer. The usual range of an issue is $10–25m. It will typically involve three or more managers, a further twenty banks and investment houses in the underwriting group, and up to eighty or so other financial institutions in the selling group; both underwriting and placement houses will be selected by the banks who are managing the issue to ensure a wide geographical spread. Thus the bonds are internationally underwritten and internationally placed. They are sold very much on the name of the issuer and accordingly the large international companies have had a clear advantage. Again in the words of a bank, this time Morgan Guarantee: 'In their investment decisions on Eurobond and the note issues they [the investors] have been inclined to weight heavily the prominence of the company, its sponsorship, and their own familiarity with one or the other. These factors have helped the large, internationally known US corporation to obtain the best terms'.[29] To this we should add that the popularity of convertibles (as a better guard against inflation, and because of the more generous returns offered by convertibles as against the dividend of the underlying stock) has also favoured the large American companies. European firms with the exception of the Dutch have found difficulty in floating convertibles, international investors clearly favouring those bonds convertible into US common stocks.

The point I have wanted to establish is that, in the British economy, international firms, particularly American ones, have a privileged access to the resources of the Eurocurrency markets. As in the case of internal funds, a large part of this privilege comes from size: but there is evidence that in the raising of loans on the Euromarkets the fact that a company has an international spread of operations is a significant advantage.

The access of international firms to substantial internal sources of finance and to the international capital market will clearly have an adverse effect on government policy aimed at restricting domestic investment by the availability or price of credit.[30] But the effect of the international capital market on British monetary policy can be put more generally. For it is now an established theorem in the neo-classical international monetary literature that international capital flows weaken the effects of domestic monetary policy under a system of fixed exchange rates. 'In a world of perfectly mobile international capital, monetary policy will be completely frustrated by monetary flows, at least for any small or medium-sized country, in its efforts to change domestic interest rates relative to the level of rates prevailing internationally'.[31]

In Britain, for example, an increase of the interest rate, through the bank rate or a decrease in the money supply, will cause an inflow of foreign capital into the country (responding to higher interest rates). If the effect of the inflow is not sterilized, reserves will increase as will the money supply, on certain assumptions. The inflow of capital will mean that the Bank is offered dollars which it buys with Treasury Bills. The question then becomes, what will the holders do with the Treasury Bills? If they buy government debt, monetary policy would be safe, for the government would, in effect, be borrowing the amount of the inflow to finance the exchange authorities' purchase of the foreign exchange. If, on the other hand, the demand of the holders of the Treasury Bills is for bank deposits or local authority debt then there would be an effect. In the first case, for example, bank liquidity would increase, as a multiple of the new Treasury Bill holding because of the liquidity ratio. The increase in the money supply would then counteract the putative disinflationary effects of the original rise in the interest rate. The more perfect the international capital market the weaker the effect of monetary policy on domestic income. Given that the development of the Euromarkets has been so closely bound up with the internationalization of corporate capital, and given the impact of these markets on the international mobility of short-term capital, and thus on domestic monetary policies, we can see here a further form in which the growth of international firms may challenge the state's short-term stabilization instruments.

Controls are of course possible and the measures announced in January 1971 are an example of one form of restriction. They removed from the banks the latter's delegated authority to sanction foreign currency loans, and required applications to be made directly to the Bank of England. Permission to borrow was normally only to be given when the loan was for a period of at least five years, since these long-term borrowings could be expected to be used for fixed investment rather than short-term working balances, and they would also be less vulnerable to speculative or precautionary flows back across the exchanges.

Yet these restrictions have been introduced at a somewhat unusual period of post-war British economic history, when the balance of payments is stable and there is pressure on the upper ceiling of the pound. The problem is too much short-term currency from abroad rather than too little. In the more usual periods of balance of payments strain, short-term capital inflows have been encouraged in spite of their acknowledged effects on the domestic 'liquidity effect'.[32] Thus while the British government have shown that it may be possible to insulate a restrictive domestic monetary policy from the effect of international capital inflows during a period of secure visible foreign balances, it would be unlikely that this insulation would continue in a period of payments deficit and sterling weakness.[33]

PART 3

Fiscal Policy

In our discussion of monetary policy we saw that the internationalization of corporate capital had two effects: one was to diminish the overall effect of monetary policy particularly as it applied to international firms; the second was *de facto* to weaken the competitive position of national capital since, following our argument, a rise in the price or availability of credit would hinder accumulation of national relative to international capital. Our principal emphasis was on the first of these points. When we come to fiscal policy again both points hold: but, our emphasis will be on the second, the degree to which fiscal policy has weakened national relative to international capital.

In neo-classical theory, while international capital mobility reduces the effectiveness of monetary policy it increases the effectiveness of fiscal policy. Say there is a tightening of fiscal policy. Taxes will rise or government expenditure will be cut. Either way, government debt falls; this will depress interest rates and ease credit. Further, the fall in GNP will lead to an improvement on current account, an increase in reserves, and an expansion of the money supply. The easing of the monetary situation thus serves to counteract the restrictive fiscal policy. This argument applies to an economy with no international capital mobility. The introduction of such mobility changes the situation, for the fall in interest rates now leads to an outflow of capital through the exchanges, a decrease in reserves, and a tightening of the money supply. The counteracting monetary effect is itself counteracted, and fiscal policy takes full effect.[34] According to the neo-classicals what international capital mobility takes away from monetary policy it gives back via fiscal policy. Stabilization is safe.

It is not at all clear that such symmetry holds for Britain. To begin with, fiscal policy has been far from successful in stabilizing demand. It is as well to recall Dow's well-known conclusion on British macro-management in the 1950s: 'as far as internal conditions are concerned . . . budgetary and monetary policy failed to be stabilizing, and must on the contrary be regarded as having been positively destabilizing. Tax reductions were made in two or three steep steps, and changes in the regulation of credit were extremely severe'.[35] Dow considered that fiscal policy could have a positive effect if tax changes were made more gradually, but he still had to admit that demand would fluctuate because of cycles in the growth of overseas demand, that it would be difficult to eliminate fluctuations in investment in stocks, that controlling investment by financial means takes time to take effect, and that the disproportionate emphasis on consumers' expenditures on durables 'is not a useful way of trying to control the economy'.[36] Thus even in the 50s when the degree of internationalization was lower, fiscal policy was a far from sharp instrument of domestic macro-management.

The increased presence of international firms in the British economy is likely further to limit the scope of fiscal policy. First, US affiliates in particular appear to have a higher export/total output ratio than do corresponding British firms. The share of US firms in British manufacturing exports is 75 per cent larger than their share of UK manufacturing output, and this holds for sectors as well as in the aggregate.[37] It is noteworthy also that the proportion of exports to GDP for the economy as a whole is rising. In 1962 exports of goods and services stood at 22 per cent of GDP and by 1969 this had risen to 25 per cent. Foreign demand for output from UK-located plants – one of Dow's 'basic causes of instability' – has thus been growing relatively over time.

Secondly, the growth of international firms in the British economy is likely to decrease the effectiveness of depreciation allowances as a short-term instrument, because of the privileged access of such firms to alternative sources of funds as discussed in the previous section. Furthermore, as far as incoming foreign investment is concerned, the size of these allowances, plus, on occasion, other financial rates, may actually be fixed over the long-term at the time the original investment is made. This abdication of the flexibility of financial policy instruments has certainly been common abroad (most clearly in underdeveloped countries but also in the Common Market).

Thirdly, where fiscal policy clearly does have an effect on consumer expenditure, and where such effects run counter to the interests of major international firms, there is clear evidence that the political power of these firms is brought to bear on governments to change the measures. The international motor firms in Britain have applied just this kind of pressure against the HP and tax restrictions on the domestic motor market over the past few years, though with only limited success.

Taken together these factors make up a growing limitation to the overall effectiveness of fiscal policy. But they are far from negating the effects of such policy. Fiscal policy can still have a decisive effect on the domestic economy, but – and this is the second major point I want to make in this section – the effect can only be achieved at the cost of national capital and labour. Those measures which do have effect on the level of domestic activity are those aimed at sectors and classes which cannot get round them. Controls on the level of real spending power (direct and indirect taxation), changes in national insurance contributions and health charges, the limitation of government expenditure notably in the field of public and social services, clean air and so on, these are the forms of regulation to which the British state has increasingly resorted. And when it is a question of cutting investment grants, depreciation allowances, initial grants and so on, it is likely to be the smaller national firms which are most seriously affected.

One further discrimination exists in the field of taxation. International firms have the powers to pay a less than proportionate amount of tax. In the first place, foreign investors often obtain substantial tax and depreciation concessions as a condition for their initial entry. Over the last decade these concessions have increased in size and range as countries have effectively bid against each other for the privilege of acting as hosts to foreign investors. In Belgium the fiscal authorities have powers of discretion to waive the '*taxe mobilière*' on the fixed capital on manufacturing enterprise. American enterprises in the Italian South have often succeeded in winning exemption from municipal and provincial taxes (although such exemption is not recognized in the official Italian programme on aids to foreign investment).[38] Certainly the Commission in Brussels is concerned with this competitive bidding-away of tax revenue and has estimated that, taking the EEC as a whole, the existing amount of foreign investment could have been attracted with aids half the size. Keith Joseph reflected a similar concern when he proposed an international agreement between members of GATT on the level of foreign investment aids.

Once established, international firms have further limited their tax payments by means of tax or quasi-tax havens. This is an often quoted phenomenon, though I know of no study which has shown the aggregate effect of such surplus-switching on the British (or indeed any other) economy. Yet it undoubtedly does happen. The oil companies with their high transfer price on crude imports (resulting commonly in losses being shown for UK operations) is an established example. So is the drug industry: we have the evidence of the Sainsbury Commission, and we know too that Squib switched profits to Ireland from her British exports by transfer pricing, and more recently to Panama.[39] Many international consumer durable firms (such as Electrolux) maximize post-tax surplus realization internationally, as do electrical firms. More generally, Piccione has recently given an account of the operation of tax haven companies by US firms, specifically in Switzerland. He cites the following as having 'THCs' in Switzerland: Chrysler, Dow Chemical, General Electric, Du Pont, US Rubber, Controls of America, General Mills, Singer and Sunbeam, though some have recently been modified following changes in US tax laws and Swiss regulations.[40] It is interesting that Switzerland is listed as the third largest foreign investor in the UK in 1968 with total investments of £226m. Nearly three-quarters of this is concentrated in four sectors, food, drink and tobacco, chemicals and allied industries, mechanical engineering, and electrical engineering, and, as the *Board of Trade Journal* commented in its 1968 survey, 'a substantial part of the investment so recorded probably originated in the United States, the investment being made via a Swiss holding company'.[41] There are no figures on how far these tax haven companies affect the profits of their sister-affiliates in the UK; certainly the UK customs as well as the exchange authorities take considerable trouble to prevent the covert transfer of funds through the exchanges. Nevertheless in almost all the methods of covert transfer some success for the firm is possible, even if the limits are often uncomfortably narrow.

What is true of firms is also true of individuals. The internationalization of corporate capital has widened the possibilities for highly paid managers, consultants, and indeed capitalists to realize at least part of their income in low-tax countries. Dunning and Morgan have suggested that the 1953 and 1956 Finance Acts have failed to stop part of the salaries of foreign executives of UK-based foreign-owned subsidiaries being paid abroad.[42] There is also evidence that British executives are having significant parts of their salary paid abroad in low-tax countries (with Bank of England permission) for purposes of overseas consumption (foreign holidays and travel expenditure, the purchase of consumer goods including cars and yachts, the rent or upkeep of a house or villa abroad and so on).[43]

Thus through initial concessionary agreements, profit transfers and overseas salary payments, international firms and their employees are able to lower their tax payments to the British Government. As a result either government revenue is lower or non-international sources are required to pay higher contributions than they otherwise would. Whichever happens, national capital will tend to suffer relatively to international firms.

PART 4

Balance of Payments Policies

The impact of international firms on short-term macro-policy instruments has been most significant in the field of balance of payments policies under fixed exchange rates. We will discuss three aspects of this impact: speculation, exchange controls, and changes in the exchange rate.

By speculation I mean financial transactions which are intended to minimize losses (hedging) or maximize profits (pure speculation) as the result of a change in the exchange rate. If a firm suspects that a particular currency is likely to be devalued, it may follow any or all of the following policies: increase local borrowings; decrease holdings of locally denominated cash or near cash assets; increase the stock of imports; hold up exports; speed up import payments and slow down export receivables; follow a similar policy of leading and lagging on other intra-company international transactions, debt payments, trade credits, dividends remittance or fees and royalty payments. In all these transactions the aim is to decrease assets and increase debts denominated in the currency which is likely to be devalued.[44]

As far as leading and lagging of payments is concerned the evidence is quite clear that this played an important role in the pre-devaluation instability. Renton and Duffy in an econometric analysis of the balancing item in the Balance of Payments accounts have shown that many of the most marked swings in the balancing items have been in periods characterized by uncertainties about exchange rates, 1958(2), 1959(4)–1960(2), 1965(3) and 1967(2)–(3). The particularly violent swings in the balancing item in 1966(4) and 1967(1) – in all there was an adverse balance of £231m. on the balance of monetary movements in those two quarters – they trace to a large underestimation of exports and to an even larger over-estimation of imports. They write, 'these errors were probably due to extensive leading and lagging in the payment for imports and exports as a result of renewed fears of a sterling devaluation engendered by the seamen's strike'.[45]

Fortune (15 September, 1968) claimed that most firms with European subsidiaries asked them to defer payment for goods from the UK for 6–7 months prior to devaluation. International Harvester, Texas Instruments, and IT & T were all protected by hedging, the first two having sold short on sterling. One study showed that 19 out of 22 firms asked had fully hedged their UK investment. Singer announced in their president's annual report for 1967 that their 'assets were fully protected by borrowing and hedging operations'. BP prepared themselves successfully for devaluation for over two years in spite of the fact that their chairman recently announced that his aim was to run BP in support of the British national interest.[46] ICI, Dunlop, and Bowater were all said to have hedged extensively, as were IBM.[47] For many of these firms their financial management may be said to be defensive, a prudent protection of the value of their assets: others (Esso and Mitsui for example, as well as International Harvester) actively speculate, and their departments of international financial management are reputed to be among the highest profit earners in the firm.[48]

It is difficult, other than by analysis of the balancing item, to obtain satisfactory macro-data of hedging by international companies. Month-to-month hedging is often hidden in annual investment figures. Certainly for 1967 gross disinvestment was up and net investment was down on 1966 for foreign investors in the UK; but this is not hard evidence. Perhaps the nearest to macro-figures we can get is Brooke and Remmers' sample of 115 foreign companies in the UK. They show that there was a spectacular increase in the use of local debt – mainly bank overdraft – in 1964 and 1965, the sample firms increasing their bank borrowing during those years at well over twice the rate shown by British quoted companies. The main reason for this they ascribe to fear of devaluation. Almost 60 per cent of the sample subsidiaries substantially reduced their exposure to exchange loss by reducing their liabilities to parent or affiliated companies (or by increasing their intra-company assets). The American-owned subsidiaries repaid £25·5m. in 1964, a figure which accounted for 20 per cent of their total use of funds and over half their aggregate dividend remittances. The same thing happened in 1967. Large dividends, repayment of inter-company loans, cuts in new inflows from parents: these are longer-term hedges which should be added to the effects of the more volatile short-term leads and lags.[49]

One final piece of evidence on the vulnerability of the British economy to the shorter-term movements is presented in Table 5. This shows the volume of intra-firm international transactions over the British exchanges in 1968 (excluding intra-firm trade credit of £271m.). The total of £4,884m. is, if anything, an underestimate because of the low figures for oil and miscellaneous companies, but even with the total as it stands we can see that a one-month lead and lag on these payments would make a difference of £400m. to the British reserves, and a two-month lead and lag a difference of £800m. It is even possible to lag export payments six months without infringing the exchange regulations.

In part international firms play a significant part in hedging, speculation and leading and lagging because of their importance as traders, and their responsibility for large quantities of the finance flowing through the exchanges. But the fact that these flows are intra-firm transactions, and that many of these firms have extensive, centralized, international financial management, does suggest that such forms of balance of payments instability will be more prevalent when international firms dominate international flows, than in an era of predominantly national capitals.

Table 5

Overall estimate of the significance of international firms for the balance of payments in as far as they administer the flows from both ends, 1968

	£m.	£m.
1. Exports and re-exports	1340	
2. Imports	1040	
TOTAL trade movements		2380
3. Foreign investment through unremitted profits and purchases of loan and share capital (into and out of UK)	847	
4. Foreign disinvestment through negative unremitted profits and sales of loan and share capital by UK companies abroad, and foreign companies in UK	203	
5. Other intra-company indebtedness	353	
6. Dividends and branch profits into and out of UK	429	
7. Interest	15	
8. Royalties and services	156	
9. Oil and miscellaneous companies 25% of 3–8	501	
TOTAL non-trade movements		2504
TOTAL ALL MOVEMENTS		4884

Notes:

1. In 1966, intra-firm exports were estimated at 25 per cent of total exports from the UK. (*Board of Trade Journal,* 16.8.1968.) We have assumed that this ratio holds for 1968. We have no comparable estimates for imports. For the UK we have assumed a figure of 15 per cent for imports, rather less than the comparable figure for the USA.
2. The figures for non-trade movements are derived from various issues of the *Board of Trade Journal.* We have throughout taken the gross movements, and not the net movements over the exchanges, since both inward and outward flows can be subjected to leads and lags.
3. In 1967, foreign investment by the oil industry and miscellaneous sectors into and out of the UK amounted to 50 per cent of the figures for other direct investment or to a total of £310m. We know too from Reddaway (p. 80) that the annual average post-tax income of the three major British oil companies was £135m. over the period 1956–64. If we make allowances for other categories of non-trading movement, and for foreign oil companies with subsidiaries in the UK, we may (conservatively) upvalue the total derived for non-trading movements (items 3–9 in the table) by 25 per cent.

Hedging, of course, has a cost, either directly (in the form of higher interest rates on locally raised working capital) or in the form of profit foregone. Similarly, speculation can have a negative as well as a positive outcome; Philips for example suffered substantial losses on their speculation against sterling. The state can in principle negate the effects of speculation by holding larger reserves, but this too has a cost, in both political and economic terms. Britain has incurred this politico-economic cost by her borrowing and stand-by arrangements with central banks and the IMF: speculation by international firms has directly contributed to the weakening of the UK's economic independence in the face of European and American financial capital. Thus while in principle speculative activity can be offset by the state, in historical practice Britain has been unable to do this without further eroding her economic independence.

When we turn to exchange controls we find a similar consideration applying. Formally, Britain has severe exchange controls as far as extra-sterling area transactions are concerned. Dollars required for portfolio investment have to be bought in the premium market; that is to say, they are subject to an independent floating exchange rate which at times (April 1969) has risen up to 60 per cent above the official sterling/dollar exchange rate. In May 1966 new exchange control rules were introduced which forced UK companies to finance direct investment outside the sterling area via the premium market, and at about the same time the Bank activated its powers under the 1947 Act to require British companies to repatriate some two-thirds of their extra-sterling area profits. These profits, like profits from portfolio investment, have to be remitted at the official rate of exchange and not via the premium market.

As far as incoming capital is concerned, exchange controls are directed mainly at ensuring that the foreign company will be largely self-financing; a prospective investor has to show that sufficient assets are being transferred from abroad to enable business to be conducted without forseeable need to borrow money domestically, except for working capital. Foreign investors have to satisfy two other conditions as interpreted by the Treasury Foreign Exchange Committee: the purchase price for new investments must be fair; and the investment should make an appropriate contribution to reserves in terms of foreign capital inflow.[50]

The controls have undoubtedly had some effect. Investment in the non-sterling area from sources other than remitted profits showed a small rise (an average of £61m. p.a. for the period of 1966–8, as against one of £54m. for the period 1963–5) though proportionately its importance declined.[51] Yet overall the controls have been administered in such a way that it is the means of finance rather than the amount invested which has been chiefly affected. John Chown puts it in this way: 'Fortunately since 1966 the Bank of England and the Treasury have used considerable ingenuity to make sure that the need to protect the reserves does not interfere unduly with the overseas expansion of British business. As a practical matter few really viable overseas ventures are hindered by exchange control'.[52] The Bank has allowed exports to foreign subsidiaries not to be paid for but treated as a contribution to capital; it has allowed back-to-back finance (provided the UK company puts up 15 per cent of the capital involved as a deposit with the Bank in premium dollars) and permitted foreign currency borrowing with a parent company guarantee (interest being paid at the official rate of exchange). It has in short interpreted the regulations liberally since the interests of British international firms were at issue.[53]

The controls on inward investment have also been used with effect, but again not so much to limit investment as to improve the terms under which foreign firms entered. British governments have firmly refused to protect their national capital by restricting the inward flow of foreign investment, and they have equally avoided placing any restrictions on the repatriation of profits.

The point being made therefore is that while British governments undoubtedly have the power to affect capital movements through exchange control they have been careful to limit the effects of these controls on the freedom of capital movement by international firms.

Yet we should also note that this power is far from absolute even were it to be used seriously to curb the investments of international firms. We have already mentioned ways in which international firms can circumvent exchange controls: transfer pricing; the payment of fees and royalties at various rates; the scheduling of intra-company debt; the allocation of overheads internationally; the timing of dividend payments, trade payments and so on. These are all bound by limits, but taken together they allow a considerable volume of funds to be transferred through the exchanges without control. Further, there is much back-to-back financing which it is most difficult to detect if it is undeclared, while at crisis periods there is at least some straight smuggling. Where controls are too severe and/or unavoidable, politico-economic pressure may be applied. The CBI campaign against the overseas investment curbs has been one example – an informally successful one as we have seen.[54] At a time of international expansion the difficulty of enforcing exchange controls may not be serious; but it would become critical in the event of an international crisis.

We will now consider the effect of the internationalization of capital on changes in the exchange rate. It has traditionally been assumed that a devaluation will have its most significant effect in the short run. Given that the price elasticity of demand for British exports is greater than unity, and that British export prices fall in dollar terms, then export receipts will rise. In the long run, however, this competitive advantage to the devaluing country will tend to be eroded by domestic inflation following on high import prices and wage demands. The domination of the exchanges by international firms is likely to alter this picture for the following reasons:

(1) International firms mostly operate in oligopolistic markets where prices are sticky; it may not be profitable to the exporting firm to start a price war by lowering final prices by the amount of the devaluation.[55]

(2) International firms tend to allocate national markets to different sources of the firm's supply (this is true of the car industry and electronics); markets which after a devaluation it would have been profitable for a British exporter to enter would accordingly be ruled out if that exporter were a subsidiary of an international firm.

(3) Alternatively, markets may be allocated by an international oligopolistic agreement, with the same consequences as in (2). The metal container market in Western Europe is divided and frozen in exactly this way.

(4) The British plant may be part of an intra-firm international division of labour. The sterling component of the final product may be so small as to make an insignificant difference to the total cost and would certainly be unlikely to justify a price change in the end product. Let us assume that the British export in question is

a part composing one-tenth of the value of the final product. An effective devaluation of 10 per cent (after making allowance for the cost of imports, etc.) would make a difference of 1 per cent in the total cost of the final product.

Such an international division of labour is a growing feature of international corporate production. IBM are the best known example (the exports from the Greenock factory were significantly unaltered as a result of the 1967 devaluation), but other companies have moved and ate moving towards similar national specialization (Ford and Massey Ferguson are two examples).[56]

(5) Exports may be the subject of an agreement between a foreign firm and the British government *ab initio.* Such an agreement was made with Chrysler when they took over Rootes; in this case the requirement was that Rootes should have as high an export percentage as the average for the British car industry, so that in this instance Rootes would probably have increased their exports after devaluation.

I don't wish to over-emphasize these points. A number of them apply in only a rudimentary fashion. Furthermore, most econometric analysis suggests that British exports are sensitive to variations in relative export prices (most guesses on the price elasticity of substitution between British and world exports of manufacturers to the industrial countries centre round −1·5 to −2·0 for the short-term and −2·5 to −3·0 for the long-term).[57] On the other hand, in support of our argument, there does appear to be a tendency towards a division of labour internationally within the firm, and towards more trade becoming intra-firm trade. We know, too, from micro-evidence that international firms exporting from the UK to others of their subsidiaries do not alter their short-term flow of goods in response to exchange-rate changes. This is borne out in the macro-statistics on the monthly volumes of manufactured goods exported from the UK. Volumes were slow to rise after devaluation (if we exclude the effect of leads and lags), and the overall sluggishness of response by exports to devaluation (which seemed to puzzle some commentators) cannot all be ascribed to long lead times on engineering goods.

Devaluation may be expected to have less of a short-term effect on exports than it would have done in a system of purely national capitals. Its limited effect on imports in the short-term is better established as far as Britain is concerned, and this short-term inelasticity has been connected with the existence of administered trade (intra-firm transactions and long-term contracts). Will devaluation have any effect at all? Micro-evidence suggests two possible ones: first a discouragement of capital repatriations, and secondly an encouragement of new acquisitions within the UK. In Britain it is the second which has been particularly striking.

After devaluation earnings on foreign investment in Britain rose from £216m. in 1967 to £312m. in 1968; at least part of the rise being accounted for by windfall profits from exports. Of this total, £112m. was remitted as against £92m. in 1967, but the amount re-invested rose from £97m. in 1967 to £164m. in 1968. Foreign companies, particularly US companies, extended their stake in the British economy by re-investing the profits which they derived from the short-term benefits of devaluation. Devaluation, which the Labour Government was forced into by the competitive decline of national capital and by speculation, and which they hoped would give them a push into some notional 'virtuous circle', in fact served only to extend the degree of Britain's incorporation.

CONCLUSION

On the basis of the above I would suggest the following conclusions. First, the effectiveness of a number of macro-economic policy measures has been curtailed by the internationalization of capital; in monetary policy (even where sterilization is possible), in fiscal policy (particularly in the growth of foreign demand), in the field of exchange controls and in exchange-rate policy.

Secondly, the particular long-term crisis in which Britain finds herself, a crisis which I have referred to as a crisis of incorporation, has constrained governments in such a way that they have not implemented potentially effective instruments of control. This is an important point. Policies do exist for controlling many of the consequences which international firms have had on British macro-policy. These could be elaborated, along the lines of the Andean foreign investment code for example. But the possibilities of a capital diversion by foreign investors and capital flight by domestic capital act as a continuing restraint on the effective implementation of such policies. Further, as British firms increase their international involvement, so does the political pressure increase for the weakening rather than strengthening of limitations on British internationals.[58]

Thirdly, measures which governments have taken to stabilize the economy have borne particularly heavily on national capital and the working class. We saw this to be the case with both fiscal and monetary policy: but it is more generally true. The hardy perennial of deflation policy has hit most those relying on the home market. Unit costs rise, accumulation is limited and competitiveness falls. At times it has been as if government policy was actually charged with weakening national capital prior to its incorporation into larger international capital units, or indeed with weakening the national economy prior to its incorporation into a larger political identity.

To sum up, it appears that for Britain at least the internationalization of capital has weakened the power of the state to perform one function which it has traditionally performed in the domestic economy. There are indications that this is also true of a number of its other traditional functions, and that British internationals, aware of this, see Europe as a suitable framework for re-establishing the effective performance of a number of the state functions so affected.

Chapter Sixteen

REVIEW OF THE EVIDENCE ON GROWTH OF COMPANIES AND ECONOMIES OF SCALE

T. Fikri

Graduate Centre for Management Studies, Universities of Birmingham and Aston in Birmingham

This chapter runs in four parts: part 1 discusses the different growth strategies open to firms, concentrating mainly on various aspects of internal versus external expansion as well as on the underlying reasons for diversification and for the trend towards conglomerates. Part 2 tries to analyse and assess – where possible relying on empirical evidence – the advantages that large firms might have over their

Table 1
Growth vectors in diversification

	Customers \ Products	New products: Related technology	New products: Unrelated technology
New missions	Same type	Horizontal diversification	
	Firm its own customer	Vertical integration	
	Similar type	(1)	(2)
	New type	(3) Concentric diversification	Conglomerate diversification

[1] Market and technology related.
[2] Marketing related.
[3] Technology related.

smaller counterparts. Part 3 looks at the reverse side of the coin, namely, the disadvantages that firms might suffer because of their size. In part 4 an attempt is made at macro level to investigate the effect of mergers and firm-size on market structure and hence on market conduct; their consequent influence on economic performance will be the main theme of this final part.

PART 1

A. Strategies for Growth

The growth of firms can be accomplished in two ways:

1. By internal expansion
2. By mergers or acquisitions

Ansoff lists four different growth strategies open to firms:[1]

1. Market penetration: the growth policy whereby a firm seeks to increase the volume of sales to its present customers or to find new customers for present products.
2. Market development: a firm retains its existing product line while it seeks to create new uses or markets for these products.
3. Product development: here existing markets are retained, but new products are created either to complement or extend the product line or replace current ones.
4. Diversification: this type of growth strategy entails departure from existing products or markets and entry into new markets with new products.

At any one time a firm can pursue one or more of the growth strategies. Expansion along the denoted growth vectors can be achieved internally or by external acquisitions. Most mergers involve expansion into new products and/or new markets, and are described, familiarly, as horizontal, vertical or conglomerate types. A more specific analysis of diversification is necessary however to depict the essential roles played by existing or related technology, and completely new technology. Table 1 summarizes the possible alternatives.[2]

If a distinction is made between the two types of management activities, namely *General* (those functions dealing with planning, organizing, directing and controlling) and *Specific* (those concerned with functions of R & D, engineering manufacturing and other functional areas), it is possible to define common thread or synergy in terms of the amount of carry-over of management activities. Synergy is commonly defined as the 2 + 2 = 5 effect when the combined performance is greater than the sum of its parts.

The degree of synergy achieved from the carryover of specific management functions will depend on the similarity of the activities undertaken. If substantially different skills or technologies (e.g., defence v. light consumer durables) are involved, then carryover will be weak. In broad terms, economies of scale may also be used interchangeably with synergy effects.

A casual glance suggests that it would be preferable, other things being equal, to grow in the way that will achieve maximum synergy; hence the long-standing preference for mergers of the horizontal and vertical type. In the former, the merged companies have related products and operate in the same geographical markets; a vertical merger is one in which the merged companies previously had a buyer-seller relationship.

Synergy is weakest in the conglomerate type of merger. The Federal Trade Commission (FTC) subdivided[3] conglomerates into three main types:

Product extension: where the partners are functionally related in production, engineering, or distribution.

Market extension: involves two companies in the same product line but with different geographical markets.

Pure conglomerates: involves companies in unrelated industries. Here there are practically no synergy advantages except those of general management functions which can be extended to almost any type of activity.

Many factors, including the increased threat of public policy on horizontal and vertical mergers, have resulted in a marked increase in conglomerate type mergers, though the other two expansion methods, especially the horizontal, are still predominant in both Europe and the United States.

B. Analysis of Internal v External Expansion with special emphasis on diversification:–

(1) *Why grow by acquisition?*

The reasons normally given for this type of external expansion can be one or more of the following:

a. Mergers often provide the quickest way of entry into other markets and industries. Entry into areas where the expanding firm lacks the right functional capabilities will be both risky and costly, and the benefits of start-up or operating synergies will be absent.

b. Because this type of growth is so rapid, it may provide almost immediately the necessary critical size for a firm to become an effective or even formidable competitor. Managers and directors often find it the quickest way to create an empire. J. Ling and J. Slater have both exploited this means of growth with remarkable dexterity.

c. Opportunities are created for excess capacity to be utilized.

d. Complementary capabilities may be achieved. This in itself can create products and markets where none had existed before. As will be seen later, small firms have on average distinguished themselves more than the large ones in the field of creativity and innovations because of certain virtues specifically connected with small size. There are mutual advantages in a merger between a large and a small company. The large firm can benefit from the creative enterprise of the small firm, and use its resources to develop any innovation into a sustained commercial success of the kind which the small firm would probably find too risky or costly a venture. From the small firm's viewpoint, the advantages of merging with a large firm lie in having access to the greater range of managerial competence and financial resources needed for development.

e. Small firms may have tax reasons for selling out. The few owners can convert their income stream from one on which a high personal income tax rate is levied to one where the capital gains tax rate applies.

f. Firms may also be taken over if they are unable to utilize their assets profitably or are believed to possess idle sums of money.

g. A common inducement for firms to grow by acquisition is a financial one: purchasing firms enjoy increased earnings per share by taking over companies with a lower PE ratio.

k. Government, on occasions, encourage mergers because the larger structural units they create make it easier both to intervene in the economy and to propagate various national economic policies (e.g., indicative planning). Mergers can also provide a quick way to rationalize industries and combat foreign competition.

(2) *Factors stimulating external acquisitions*

a. The nature of the firm and advances in management technology:
R. H. Coase[4] points out that firm size is determined by the relative efficiency with which the firm versus the market performs the functions of information flow and co-ordination. The conclusion that can be drawn from Coase's theory of firm size is that the stronger the impact of technology and the information revolution, the larger and more diversified firms are likely to become.

b. Technological change:
Because of the diffuse and uneven distribution of managerial skills and technical competence amongst firms and industries, firms in declining industries seek to remedy their weaknesses by acquiring new technologies to improve their growth prospects. The uncertainties of applying advanced technologies successfully are great even for a competent firm; a newcomer will find it even more risky, involving big outlays and negative cash flows for a long period of time. Mergers, in cases like this, offer an increased chance of success to such large, big-risk investments.

c. Increased fixed costs of staff functions:
This can be attributed to the increasing complexity of both the internal and the external environments of business firms; technical dynamism in the economy, the use of more sophisticated production and marketing decision models employed, and the growing intricacy of relationships with government and other 'publics', and so on. Small firms often find it uneconomical to support such high fixed costs; by merging with larger companies they can gain access to general management or specialist services.

(3) *Economic aspects of external growth*

a. It is often suggested that a large number of inefficient firms continue to survive because of the relative inefficiencies that exist among industries. Competition eventually weeds these out of the market, but the process may take a long time; mergers however, can result in a rapid dissemination of technologies and of management science throughout industries, with a boost to efficiency all round. Small and lagging firms are the ones most likely to benefit. In this way mergers can both stimulate competition and create a more favourable aggregate investment function.

b. Mergers can enhance various types of economies or synergies: by avoiding any duplication of effort in staff services or specific management functions, and exploiting other benefits of large scale, the average cost of the whole industry is ultimately shifted downwards. The fuller utilization of resources and the improved chances of success accompanying large high-risk investments will have similar cost effects.

c. The combined firms often constitute a wider technological, marketing or financial base which increases, or even creates the potential for radical innovation in many directions. It makes possible a greater utilization of the partners' respective advantages. The rapid spread of innovations will quicken the pace of technological change, and so contribute to lower costs, greater efficiency, higher levels of economic activity and a faster rate of growth overall.

d. Another efficiency aspect of mergers has been their side-effect of boosting other, non-merging firms. With the upsurge of takeovers in the past two decades a healthy share price became almost a necessity to avert a takeover bid, and this threat induced the vulnerable firms to shake themselves up and improve their earnings performance for the sake of survival. The attacking firm generally promises benefits to shareholders in terms of earnings and efficiency which the defending firm tries to match. This can be a healthy spur to efficiency and competition.

e. Diversification by external acquisition may also stimulate new activity. While in one sense acquisition substitutes one management for another, it nevertheless changes their pattern and behaviour. A new combination of entrepreneurial energies is created in terms of new product sectors, cost functions and patterns of rivalry. Existing firms are stimulated to react to these, with further improvements in market performance as a result. As we shall see towards the end of this chapter, mergers may possess inherent dangers and disadvantages. But the point made here, that they may contribute significantly to economic performance, is a fair one. Later assessments will take into account the trickier trade-off and balancing problems.

(4) *Why grow by internal expansion?*

A starting point for enquiry will be to point again to the two main objectives sought in a merger:

a. Pecuniary gains from financial synergy;

b. Gains attainable in post-merger operations.

The most common gain cited, however, is the increased market power. This will receive a fuller investigation in Part 2.

A firm will prefer internal expansion – other things being equal – if financial synergy is weak or non-existent; and with increasing numbers of prospective buyers in the market it will become harder to find:

a. undervalued assets or companies;
b. scope for an immediate increase in earnings per share;
c. substantial tax loss carry-forwards;
d. opportunity for a higher return on equity.

Therefore an expensive premium paid in a merger will reduce earnings per share unless offset by various financial or functional synergies and other types of long-term gains, including non-pecuniary ones such as staying power, new opportunities flexibilities, etc.

If the scope for financial synergy is limited, attention will mostly be directed at the functional synergies possible. Horizontal and vertical mergers are the two types most likely to yield functional synergy. In industries of high concentration in the UK and US however, this type of merger is hampered by government policy, which discourages such economically related mergers because of their probable anti-competitive effects. Product-extension mergers are perceived as the next best avenue for functional synergy as these are relatively unconstrained.[5]

Generally, however, the scope for economic mergers has somewhat diminished; but even if this constraint were lifted, a large body of evidence casts doubt on the significance of scale economies or functional synergies.

J. S. Bain,[6] after analysing twenty manufacturing industries, concluded that in the majority of industries firms exceeded efficient size in one or more of the three areas of production, sales promotion, and physical distribution. He also found that multi-plant or overhead economies were relatively small. Stern[7] concludes that 'the weight of evidence gathered to date shows rather conclusively, that in most producer and consumer goods industries, large size is not a pre-requisite for operational efficiency . . . Large firms generally have several plants whose economies can be matched by smaller firms each operating only one optimally sized plant'.

Further factors may discourage growth by acquisition: for instance, any uncertainty there might be about the quality of the management to be acquired, or about the compatibility of the partners' management teams and the post-merger[8] administrative problems.

(5) *Aspects of internal expansion*

As government policy on mergers suggests, the main weight of argument against mergers is their effect in reducing competition. C. Kaysen and D. Turner[9] make the point that while mergers can have the effect of increasing competition, this result is problematic rather than automatic as it is with internal growth.

John C. Narver,[10] commenting on internal growth, says: 'If in the face of competition a firm grows internally, the resulting growth is the justly earned reward for successfully meeting the test of the market'.

Narver concludes that the present merger policy in the US, together with growing markets, has helped to enlarge the substantive alternatives open to consumers by supporting, directly or indirectly, low concentration and low entry barriers and thus producing social benefits larger than possible social costs.

If, as we have shown, scope for functional synergies is limited and not significant, and real economies in many industries seem to be exhausted at relatively small to moderate scales, internal growth would seem to contribute more effectively to overall performance; furthermore, avoiding obvious merger failures would constitute a real gain to the economy especially since most of the real dangers arise out of half-successes,[11] and market forces cannot effectively weed out the mergers that sit on inefficiencies.

In arguing in favour of internal growth, however, public policy, and many economists, ignore a fundamental issue. It has been shown, especially in consumer goods, that expenditures for marketing, which includes selling, buying, distribution, market research, etc., can constitute up to about 50 per cent of all costs making up the final price to the consumer. Furthermore, in pointing at marketing economies Bain[12] states: 'It appears possible that there is an important category of concentrated industries – those selling highly differentiated consumer goods in situations where nationwide sales promotion is the superior alternative to firms – in which distribution economies of increased firm scale in a sense justify much larger scales of firm and higher degrees of concentration than production economies alone would'.

A study by Buzzel and Nourse[13] also indicates the very high costs of innovations in food processing industries. 'This coupled with high product failure', says Stern,[14] 'explains why such industries are highly concentrated; the resources required to compete successfully provide an extremely high barrier to entry, assuming that potential entrants wish to market branded merchandise'.

This brings us to Galbraith's thesis[15]: the fact that in many consumer goods markets competition takes the form of product differentiation, efficient distribution and product innovation, where small firms, because of their limited resources, find it very hard to keep up.

Anyone wishing to promote competition in these circumstances must foster mergers amongst smaller firms so that they develop countervailing power. Small firms cannot match the competitive resources and managerial talents of large firms; and their efforts to compete and attract attention in the message-saturated, oversold markets will often constitute loss of resources.

To sum up, if large firms, especially in consumer-goods industries continue to dominate the scene, undermerged, small firms must be encouraged to combine into units big enough to operate as effective competitors and achieve marketing economies that contribute towards such effectiveness.

C. Why Firms Diversify

Since the 1960s, both in western Europe and in the US diversification as a growth strategy has become increasingly common, with evidence from both areas showing a proportionate swing towards conglomerate type mergers. There is no evidence to indicate the degree of internal diversification undertaken by firms, though it appears to be considerable. Government policies on mergers may partly account for this trend, but there are more fundamental reasons; we will analyse them under two headings:

1. Changes in the internal environment of the firm.
2. Changes in the external environment of the firm.

(1) *Internal factors*

a. The profound changes which characterize the last fifty years have been most dramatic in the fields of science and technology, which have been combined, with revolutionary effect, to transform all systems of information supply and communication. Today sophisticated modern aids, developments in management science and computerization enable firms to analyse business problems more thoroughly, and rapidly, than ever before. The diseconomies one would expect from firms engaged in various unrelated activities have yet to be proved. The assumption that diversified firms will be unable to co-ordinate and pull all sub-units or sub-systems towards achieving the central objectives is less valid. Today's 'systems management' can maintain a unified command over the business totality, reconciling the dynamic internal world of business with even the more complex and changing external environment.

b. It is often suggested that the emphasis placed on growth stocks by financial institutions and the financial press has had a big impact on both shareholders and companies. Recognition of the effects of growth on share prices has led to a general drive to induce greater growth in earnings per share. The various measures taken to improve earnings include:

(i) Intensive searching for profitable product or market opportunities often in unrelated areas;
(ii) Stimulating mergers of the conglomerate type, mainly to enhance financial synergy;
(iii) Greater use of cost control.

c. A number of companies diversify to utilize excess productive capacity and managerial talent and, in particular, to ease the fixed costs of staff services. These costs can be startlingly high in modern companies; diversification creates a broader base over which to spread them.

(2) *External factors*

These factors provide a weightier argument for both internal and external diversification.

a. The impact of technology, R & D, and changing patterns of demand, coupled with increased competition, are destroying product lines, product boundaries – even industry boundaries – overnight. New products, services, and techniques, and the great emphasis placed on frequent product differentiation have contributed to a shortening of most product life-cycles, especially those of consumer goods. Ansoff[16] has stressed the need for firms in the future to engage in a continuous process of innovation and exploitation.

b. Mass education and mass communications have increased consumer sophistication, and buyers can now exercise greater discretion between and within brands. If firms have to find progressively more varied ways of satisfying consumer needs, diversification will automatically follow. The increased countervailing power of retailers renders them capable of judging the viability of a brand quickly; this contributes to the uncertainity of the market place, and supports the case for entry into new markets by external diversification.

c. An important development in recent years is the decline in consumer loyalty, a combined result of consumer sophistication and heightened competition between sellers, together with the effects of R & D. Buyer behaviour is becoming harder to predict. Today's markets, geared to the affluent society, are getting more segmented. The age of mass markets and universal brands has given way to consumer desire for more varied and frequently changing brands. Firms find it quicker and less risky to adapt to these changing market patterns via diversification, especially through acquisitions.

PART 2 ADVANTAGES OF SIZE

What accounts for the large companies' leading role in recent industrial development? The answer seems to lie in their formidable staying power. This quality contributes most to the monolithic exterior of the giant firms – with good or bad consequences for the economy as a whole, of which more will be said later. Staying power enables large firms to exert considerable influence in three directions: economically, politically and socially. The tripartite distinction offers a useful basis for analysing the considerable micro-level advantages which these powers make possible for large firms.

A. Economic Power

(1) *Entry barriers*

J. Bain[17] estimates potential competition in an industry according to the advantages of established sellers over potential entrant sellers. These advantages, reflected in the extent to which established sellers can persistently raise prices above the competitive level without attracting new firms, are of two types:

a. Scale economies.

b. Absolute cost advantages.

Large firms are able to exploit more fully the benefits of entry barriers and will naturally play a dominant role in how high the entry barriers will be, bearing in mind, of course, public policy constraint.

a. *Scale economies*

On balance, scale economies, especially technical or production economies, except in certain industries particularly some producer goods industries, do not appear to constitute significant entry barriers. Evidence shows conclusively that in most multi-product or multi-plant firms, and a great majority of firms are just that, production economies are even less significant. It appears that small firms do not suffer a great disadvantage in operating sub-optimal sized plants. Using real productivity as the criterion, the optimal scale is typically smaller, in some industries considerably smaller, than is common in the largest firms.[18] It is important to note, however, that all this evidence applies to US industries where the size of markets and scale of competition have induced greater average plant sizes than in Europe; hence while the potential for plant size economies may be small in the US, in Europe these still can be substantial. The small Table 2 below shows the international comparison of plant size (the UK does not suffer much of a disadvantage).

Table 2

Size of 20 largest plants: US = 100		
US	–	100
UK	–	78
France	–	39
Japan	–	34
Italy	–	29

J. S. Bain, *International Difference of Industrial Structure*, 1966.
Note: The comparisons are for 34 industries and refer to 1954 for the US, UK, and France, 1956 for Japan and 1951 for Italy. *National Institute Economic Review, November 1966.*

A study of four industries in UK by Pratten and Dean shows that production economies, other things being equal,[19] are not significant in footwear and book printing, where firms can obtain full economies at only 1–2 per cent of industry's output capacity. Competition will not be hampered, thus entry barriers will be fairly low. For oil refining an output representing 17 per cent of the national output is required to achieve most of the technical economies of scale for a refinery. For sheet steel this proportion is 50 per cent, whilst in bulk steel production, optimal plant size represents 7 per cent of the industry output capacity.

Bain believes that in some industries marketing economies may justify larger firm scales and higher degrees of concentration than production economies would: his argument[20] mentioned earlier is that 50 per cent of all costs making up the final price to the consumer is in many industries taken up by marketing costs. On the other hand Simon[21] emphasizes the absence of evidence with respect to economies in advertising. W. F. Mueller, in substantial agreement with Bain, remarks[22] that 'the best available evidence suggests . . . that economies of large-scale production, invention and innovation are less important in consumer goods industries than in producer goods industries. The apparent reason for the growing concentration in consumer goods' manufacturing is to be found in the advantages of large scale promotion and distribution'.

Much research has still to be done to assess more fully the importance of other aspects of scale economies particularly those relating to management and staff services: general managerial functions yield economies and synergies which, if significant, could be an important feature in a general theory of mergers. Start-up synergies and the importance of 'learning effects' also require closer analysis. A study by Merrett-Howe-Newbould[23] indicates the scale economies in raising finance.

In the final analysis, on the available evidence (which is hardly abundant), one can make two general points as to the effect of scale economies on entry barriers:

(i) Scale economies, with a few exceptions, do not in themselves appear to present significant obstacles to entry.
(ii) Other factors, particularly product-differentiation, play a far more influential part in determining the level of entry barriers.

b. *Product differentiation – Absolute cost barrier*

While economies of scale show movements on the average cost curve as size or scale is varied, absolute cost effects deal with shifts in the average cost curve itself. Because a size-increase in plant or scale involves both of these – a dimensional increase in utilization, and new expenditure on plant extension (a form of absolute cost) – the two effects can often become blurred or confused.

Product differentiation is a form of absolute cost barrier whose impact is greatest in consumer and packaged goods and grocery products. It renders three distinct advantages:

(i) The removal of pressure on producers to sell at a single price, which enables them to set their own pricing policies.
(ii) The opportunity to compete on various other attributes of marketing mix, e.g., product, quality, design, advertising, distribution, etc.
(iii) Product differentiation helps to reduce the demand elasticities facing individual sellers; thus a highly differentiated product from even a small producer, protected by patents, renders high profits and long survival.

Large firms, with access to resources and equipped with various other advantages that come from stability, can engage in product changes far more frequently than small firms. As Buzzel and Nourse[24] indicate, the innovation costs and commercial risks entailed in launching new products can be great, and small firms suffer a distinct disadvantage.

Competition on the elements of marketing mix, especially product mix, is the commonest form of rivalry. Small firms lack not only the resources to advertise heavily in the message-saturated markets, but also the important visual 'source effect' that results from persistent advertising. They lack the resources to innovate and market new products, and are less equipped to survive setbacks and wait for longer pay-off periods.

Other types of absolute cost barriers that present new entrants with a cost disadvantage at any output level are:

(i) Patent protection – entrants will have to pay royalties to get access to know-how or suffer the consequences. In the US protection can be granted for 17 years.

(ii) The exclusion of entrants from supplies of significant or rare inputs. Potential entrants may have to choose between inferior supplies and/or inflated supply prices.

(iii) Often, large capital requirements or set-up costs automatically exclude small firms from an industry. Capital-intensive heavy industries are an obvious example.

Large firms, which by and large enjoy most of the advantages of high-entry barriers, can either choose to raise prices and earn excess profits, or may opt for competitive prices, thus attracting few rivals, and keeping the whole field to themselves. Evidence[25] suggests that highly concentrated industries, whether simply ticking over or earning excess profits, are primarily concerned with keeping the field to themselves.

(2) *Cross-subsidization*

Some products have typically long life-cycles and pay-off periods. Large multi-product firms subsidize the negative cash flow periods of such products from others with positive returns. This contributes towards the stability of profits. Small firms can neither undertake the range of activities required to produce this sort of leverage, nor can they wait for long pay-off periods.

(3) *Deep pocket theory*

This occurs when large firms engage in heavy, aggressive advertising and promotional activities, and unnecessary model changes, hence out-daring and out-spending small firms in the marketing field. While this practice can amount to abuse, and is usually an extravagance in terms of efficiency, prohibiting it may also impede desirable forms of competition like product performance and improvement. The fact is that consumers do not object to new products or advertisements, and that being the case, consumer sovereignty will ensure that these costly forms of non-price competition continue, especially in the absence of any objective standard to tell firms how much and how often to spend on them.

(4) *Reciprocity*

This refers to the leverage that large purchasers have *vis-à-vis* suppliers: suppliers fear, or might actually be threatened, that if reciprocal transactions are not conducted the large buyer might switch to other suppliers. Reciprocity in the USA is an illegal practice and overt action is necessary to exert reciprocity pressure in order to increase sales.

T. Levitt[26] argues that with the rising sophistication of sales forecasting, production scheduling and other forms of planning and control, large buyers will increasingly favour purchase contracts. He is convinced that the substantial cost-saving potentials of centralized purchasing will change the traditional purchasing practices appropriate to divisional autonomy and decentralized profit centres. He concludes that as buyers have a greater say in defining the product characteristics they want, and the activities of buyers and sellers become more integrated, there will be more synergistic amalgamation of buyers and sellers; these will form the vertically-integrated conglomerates which Levitt defines as the 'Verglomerate'.

B. Political and Social Power

(1) *Political power*

a. Giant concerns can influence certain aspects of foreign policy, e.g., the quasi-sovereign power of oil companies, or the active role in international politics of big companies with large foreign investments.

b. The publicity effects of large firms, independently or with collective support through the CBI or Trade Associations can create effective resistance to particular economic or even political decisions on the part of the government. Government policy-makers may therefore be forced to take into account the bargaining power of big firms.

c. Where local employment depends on a few large giants or where the bulk of economic activity is maintained by a few large firms, they will automatically possess great potential influence *vis-à-vis* the government.

d. The success of government policies in rehabilitating depressed areas will also depend to a great extent on large firms. Their co-operation and initiative in schemes of this kind will often be vital for gaining the support of smaller or medium sized firms.

(2) *Social power*

Linked with political and economic power, but far less quantifiable, is the social power of big business. In the US, particularly, this is considerable. America comes close to being a 'business society', in which the glamourized lives and occupations of executives represent a widespread social ideal. Large firms are also powerful trend-setters in many products or services, and they can influence consumer tastes and irrationalities a great deal.

PART 3 ARGUMENTS AGAINST 'BIGNESS'[27]

A. Effect of Size on Creativity and Innovations

Business prophets have repeatedly stressed the importance of R & D and innovations. T. Levitt[28] comments that: 'Nothing typifies American business so much these days as the continuing rhetoric about the unqualified necessity of constantly creating new products'. P. Drucker[29] stresses the fallacy of the assumption that 'entrepreneurship and innovations lie outside the management scope'; the new management reality is that, in contrast, 'entrepreneurial innovation will become the very heart and core of management'. H. Ansoff,[30] similarly, stressed that tomorrow's firms will need to adopt a 'bi-modal' behaviour, combining innovation and exploitation in a continuous process, i.e., a firm which is inventive and which can market these inventions but at the same time maintain or improve its position with established products in traditional markets.

Levitt[31] maintains that though large corporations produce numerous new products or services, when it comes to creating really dramatic newness they have not visibly distinguished themselves. He gives an endless list of big new industries and radically new methods emanating from the small beginnings of small outsiders. Why, in view of their larger R & D and test market budgets, and their great enthusiasm and effort, are the inventive efforts of large corporations not more productive? Levitt cites not a general lack of flexibility, but two other reasons:

1. 'The larger the company gets', he claims, 'the more effectively it will be organized, operated and motivated to carry out relatively routine rather than relatively new tasks. Hence the larger organization develops a managerial style that is not particularly amicable to activities that conflict with its central continuing purpose'. Operating efficiency and targets are the key motivators of most managers. People and managers tend to reject any infusion of new and uncertain tasks which might hamper the day-to-day performance or even threaten their job security.

2. Another hurdle that large firms face concerns the nature of demand for a new product, as well as the changing patterns of existing demand. At both levels large firms often find that 'thinking big' is a handicap, even though in the past it was just this very psychological approach that helped to create the modern industrial state. There seems to be a built-in conflict between thinking big and creating dramatic newness; with possible exceptions in heavy industries most new things by their very nature tend to possess attributes of smallness at the levels of production, administration and marketing. 'People who successfully fight their way to the top echelons of giant organizations learned many years before that what counts is to think big'.

J. Q. Wilson[32] suggests: 'the very factors that increase the probability that organizational participants will devise and present innovatory proposals are precisely those which decrease the probability that the organization will adopt them'. He believes the reasons for this lie in the structured bureaucratic nature of large firms which the diversity and magnitude of their tasks makes unavoidable. Organizational size and structure tends to smother in operation the very thing that size so uniquely produces in fact: powerful new ideas.

March and Simon suggest with Wilson that diversity in the organization's sub-cultures stimulates proposals, but unlike Wilson they believe that centralized authority will lead to their acceptance.[33] Levitt agrees that centralized authority can act fast, and respond to new ideas quickly – but it is more likely to do neither. He maintains that few large complex organizations, however authoritarian, can effectively give to top officials enough power to get things done as rapidly and as effectively as small firms. The larger the organization the more the leader is forced to compromise.

Another factor giving the competitive edge in creativity to small firms is the way that creativity works at the human and organizational level. The search for really new things requires a departure from routine systems; it requires an adventurous, energetic spirit and the freedom to develop new ideas without too many sobering restrictions. The results of such ventures are not easy to predict, measure or demonstrate beforehand; and corporate planning, involving budgets and calculated risks, does not encourage them.

Large firms often try to counteract their deficiencies regarding innovation by various methods designed to inject the entrepreneurial independence associated with smallness into the larger organizations; for example, R & D departments, decentralized activities, Du Pont's New Venture Management System, and 3M's New Business Development Division project approach are all deliberate attempts to turn managers into entrepreneurs. While these methods can be useful, the special divisions often tend to be regarded as operating departments and to be swallowed into the mechanistic structure of the parent company, whereas they were created specifically to be liberated from stifling scrutiny, conventionality and bureaucracy.

In conclusion, one can say that in creating dramatic new things large firms suffer organizational difficulties, and this coupled with exaggeration of the ease and simplicity with which new things can be accomplished, has led to considerable reliance, despite the anti-trust laws, on growth through acquisitions rather than through internal expansion. This trend has also been encouraged by the complementary effects derived from largeness: the built-in stability that makes large firms better able to support creativity and commercialize new innovations.

B. Size v. Profitability

A recent study by F. Wittnebert[34] shows that since 1960 large US manufacturing companies have suffered declining profit performance, while smaller ones enjoyed improving results. This reversal of trend was on both accounts; rates of return on sales, and rates of return on stockholders' equity.

Possible factors accounting for this new trend include the following:

(1) *Accelerating change*

The fast-changing external environment of firms – due to dynamism in the market place, etc. – imposes on them the need for highly flexible internal environments. The bigger the firm, the keener the impact of change; at the same time, the rigidities of large scale organization make it costly to unravel to cope with changing environments, and these costs rise as the pace of change quickens. Disadvantages of this kind will be less evident in diversified firms and conglomerates where change is expected, than in the tightly organized, routinized, integrated firms, i.e., those in the process and mass production industries.

(2) *Dissatisfied employees*

Large-scale organization depends on a considerable degree of inflexibility and prescriptive power to ensure that pressing jobs are done efficiently and on time. This kind of adherence to rules and procedures, coupled with the pursuit of productivity through automation, specialization, and job simplicity often conflicts with the modern worker's needs of involvement, self-actualization and individual autonomy. Most large organizations are unsuited to creating an environment which the workers find motivating, personal, and conducive to the value system of small organizations. In small companies the pursuit of personal goals, individual accomplishment and official recognition are highly effective incentives.

In automated and mass-production industries, workers often use their more obvious countervailing power, whose root cause is motivational dissatisfaction or possibly plain disruption, in demanding more pay through industrial unrest and strikes. The motor car industry is a vivid example. Loss of production and efficiency is also often due to the low motivational environment of the work place.

Despite the efforts of some big firms to decentralize and 'enrich' or 'enlarge' jobs, the great majority of firms remain impersonal, complex and centralized.

(3) *Post-merger problems*

The large corporations that often owe a proportion of their size to external acquisitions may face various administrative problems. John Kitching,[35] after studying 69 acquisitions, concluded that in the US three out of four mergers fail. The figure D. Hargreaves[36] gives for the UK is eight out of nine, success being measured by long-term increases in earnings per share, the achievement of merger objectives, and enhancement of the acquiring company's reputation. Size is part of the problem. Searby has pointed to one trap, the inadequate appraisal of the complexities before the merger takes place combined with a tendency to relax after it.[37] Levinson has pointed to another problem of large organizations, the rigidity which makes it difficult to organize and plan a successful merger.[38]

(4) *New equalizers*

a. Mass education, mass communication and increased competition are making 'know-how' more readily available to small firms; know-how which acted as a potent source of entry barrier is also becoming obsolete more rapidly.

b. The availability of services and skills on contract and time-sharing facilities on computers also favours the small concerns.

(5) *Public hostility*

Mass education and the mass media have helped to create a climate of general unease concerning inequalities of wealth and opportunity. When this unease mounts to active resentment, it often focuses on the business world, and particularly on the large corporations which symbolize, in a very concrete way, the power of the 'haves' in a society increasingly concerned with the plight of the 'have-nots'. Against this background it is worth noting the growing public conscience and understanding of the business world itself. Large firms, both out of choice and out of constraint, tend to care more for the national interest and human welfare than do smaller ones.

(6) *New demand patterns*

In affluent countries, a considerable proportion of individual spending goes on non-essentials the purchase of which is dictated by personal taste. The non-group quality of this type of spending (on leisure pursuits, for example) makes small firms better suited to catering for the segmented, differentiated tastes of the buyers.

(7) *Government support*

Although large firms can benefit considerably from government support, government subsidies and contracts inevitably expose them to greater official scrutiny. They are expected to act rather like nationalized industries, responding appropriately to public interest and the government's social or economic policies. All such constraints automatically eat into the profit margins.

(8) *Competition*

Large firms, because they bulk so large in the economy, are more likely to be targets of competitive rivalry at home or abroad. Their price and cost advantages are more likely to be eroded than those of small firms.

(9) *Problems of co-ordination*

Other much discussed problems of large firms are the costs of co-ordination, effective communication and flexibility. Modern technological aids have made these problems less burdensome, but they still involve costs which small firms do not need to incur.

F. A. Crusco[39] explains the downward profitability trend of large firms in Wittnebert's charts somewhat differently. He believes that the study covers a period when money was tight. This subsequently encouraged the disappearance of small unprofitable firms, whereas the large unprofitable ones, because of their staying power, survived. This has decreased the overall profitability of large firms.

Crusco also thinks that declining profits are a natural characteristic of entrenched large companies since, as their products age, the subsequent price of a particular product becomes the 'natural' price thus lowering the profit margins. Depending on the usefulness of the product, this aspect has favourable welfare consequences in terms of lower prices and increased consumption.

Thirdly he argues that when a large company brings out a new product it only needs to 'stay in business', hence it accepts higher risks and lower profitability than small firms would.

One can add the point that most large companies are more capital-intensive than small ones and this can also depress profitability figures.

While the explanations offered by Crusco seem plausible they do not necessarily refute the reasons[40] given earlier on, and attempting to quantify such reasons is an ambitious task; moreover certain disadvantages that large firms suffer need not always be reflected in terms of lower profitability.

PART 4 MACRO IMPLICATIONS

A. Assessment from Economic Viewpoint

Some reference has already been made to the macro-economic implications of increasing firm size. In this final section these now receive fuller analysis.

An obvious starting point might be to find out what sort of market structure and consequent market conduct is most likely to lead to optimal market performance. For this, empirical evidence will be used, and where necessary, judgement, inference and qualitative analysis.

R. Caves[41] defines market performance as an industry's contribution, relative to its potential, towards achieving the following economic goals:

1. Maintenance of full employment with acceptable levels of inflation.
2. Equity in the distribution of income.
3. Growth and progressiveness in improving the flow of goods and services.
4. Efficiency in the use of resources.

It is likely that the professed goals of a nation will be social and political as well as economic; and optimizing the vector of these three variables is an incredibly complex task, not only in terms of accommodating a community welfare function, but – most importantly – in terms of reconciling the three objectives themselves, since in the short run they are bound to conflict. These enormous balancing difficulties make it usual to settle for a second- or third-best solution, at least in the short term; and as most countries have a strong preference for enjoying the fruits of economic growth, economic goals will be the terms of our analysis.

It is important to note that the main elements of market structure – concentration, product differentiation, entry barriers, the growth rate of market demand, elasticity of market demand, etc. – will influence the behaviour, or market conduct of firms. As would be expected market conduct, in turn, influences market structure. Through legislation various governments try to shape market structure and market conduct so as to achieve a better market performance. The detailed effects of public policy and legislation will not be discussed here, though the results of past measures will be implicit in any analysis of market structure and behaviour. Discussion of the effects of large firms on market performance will also be confined to the main structural attributes associated with them, namely concentration, product differentiation and entry barriers.

(1) *Full employment and price stability*

One conclusion reached by Caves[42] is that little evidence exists to show that concentration and other dimensions of market structure affect stability of output and employment. Others have felt that concentration leads to more stable investment plans and investment rates. With respect to prices some feel that the rigid pricing policy of certain oligopolists causes more fluctuations in employment over a business cycle than if prices were flexible. Caves agrees with this, but adds that some degree of price rigidity may have its advantages. Another common problem in both the UK and the US is the tendency of oligopolists and concentrated industries vulnerable to trade union pressure to raise prices in proportion to their costs, even if excess capacity exists. This makes full employment without inflation hard to achieve. In competitive industries excess capacity may choke off price increases. The impact of monopolistic groups (e.g., steel firms) on price levels has been significant in hampering the pursuit of full employment, because high prices affect balance of payments adversely.

(2) *Income distribution*

Here there is a relatively weak connection between equity and industrial structure. Equity objectives are better achieved by the use of fiscal and monetary policies.

(3) *Progressiveness*

The degree of progressiveness will influence the rate of wealth accumulation, the quality and variety of goods available, technical competence, etc. As we noted earlier, this aspect of industries will play a dominant role in the overall achievement of market performance and efficiency.

a. *Patents*

Caves maintains that while patents serve to protect both the innovation and the innovator, hence encouraging more innovators, they entail, at the same time, social costs: the holder of a patent might not only try to exploit the protection given as profitably as possible but also pave the way for a permanent monopoly position after the patent has expired. This may also induce firms to enjoy the fruits of protection and innovate less frequently. A US study[43] in 1959 showed that large firms did not distinguish themselves in procuring more patents, in proportion to their size, than smaller firms. In fact they got less, except for a few giant firms.

b. *Innovations and productivity gains*

Levitt, Ansoff and Drucker, on the importance of R & D and innovations, have already been cited. Levitt's point perhaps deserves re-emphasis; when it comes to creating dramatic newness in services, products or methods – in comparison to small firms – large firms have not been outstanding. However, in terms of developing innovations into a commercial success, making product improvements or producing innovative imitations, the advantages of size and staying power give the lead to large firms.

Other writers, failing to make the vital distinction between innovations that bring complete 'newness', and other less radical types of innovation, deal with the subject at a more general level. O. E. Williamson[44] says that 'the present evidence, while hardly abundant, suggests that, as a general rule, the R & D expenditures of the four largest firms in an industry are neither as large proportionately nor as productive as those of their immediately smaller rival'.

With respect to size in the USA, Mansfield[45] found that the ratio of innovations to firm size reached a maximum at about the sixth largest firm for the petroleum and coal industries, and much lower down the scale for steel. Elsewhere Mansfield reports that the largest firms in petroleum, drugs and glass spent rather less on R & D relative to sales than did somewhat smaller ones. In chemicals they spent rather more, in steel they spent less but the difference was not statistically significant. Hamburg[46] and Horowitz[47] found a positive correlation between R & D expenditures and concentration.

Scherer[48] concludes from his study of patent behaviour in a group of 448 firms selected from the *Fortune* list of the 500 largest industrial corporations in 1955 that: 'the evidence does not support the hypothesis that corporate bigness is especially favourable to high inventive output'.

On productivity, Mansfield[49] comments that 'in most industries the productivity of an R & D program of given scale seems to be lower in the largest firms than in somewhat smaller firms'. Stigler[50] also found, in an earlier study, 'hints that industries with lower concentration had higher rates of technological progress'. Williamson,[51] using Mansfield's data, found a negative correlation between the proportions of innovations introduced by the four largest firms and industrial concentration. Kendrick,[52] on the other hand, found no significant correlation between productivity changes and industrial concentration.

Williamson[53] points out that all this fails to answer the question of what market structures most enhance progressiveness, and that evidence concerning this is fairly mixed. From the inconclusive evidence available he infers that mergers between two small firms rarely have negative effects on progressiveness. For lower-middle-sized firms his judgement remains the same. For large firms, however, where market power comes into play, he sees a case for thorough scrutiny.

Research by Merton J. Peck[54] shows that in both the US and the UK 350 or so firms account for 85 per cent of non-governmental R & D. The best UK performance is in 'group C industries' – sectors of relatively simple and static technology like food, textiles, furniture. Performance was average in 'group A industries' (complex and rapidly-advancing technology, e.g., aircraft, machinery, chemicals), and poorest in 'group B industries', which include rubber, metals and paper. 'Group A' and 'Group B' show no significant difference when aircraft is excluded from the former and paper from the latter. The picture is similar for the US. From these findings Caves[55] concludes that since concentration, on average, is lower in 'Group C' industries in both the UK and the US, it offers no support for mergers or monopoly in order to promote R & D expenditure.

It is generally accepted that excessive concentration may slow the pace of technical progress. Caves[56] infers from existing evidence that, 'a large proportion of industrial births are founded on prospects engendered by a new product or a new process. High entry barriers may well shut off this form of progress and we might expect low barriers to hasten the pace of technical change. His overall conclusions are the following:

a. No evidence proves that seller concentration in research-orientated industries has to be as high as it now is to keep up the flow of innovation. This is consistent with several findings already quoted.

b. Large firms in general carry on more research than small ones, but in those industries where most of the research goes on, small firms spend proportionately as much as large ones and perform just as well.

(4) *Efficiency*[57]

Like most economic topics 'efficiency' is not without its share of complexities. Perhaps a first step to a more simplified analysis is to distinguish between three main types of economic efficiency:

a. Technical – firms or industries will be technically efficient if they operate on the lowest possible cost curve. This will depend on the optimality of plant scales and the ability to achieve production or marketing objectives with the least costs possible.

b. Progressiveness – this reflects not only the ability of firms to create or adapt new methods or processes but also their ability to create new products and/or markets and the degree of flexibility and skill they possess in exploiting profitable investment opportunities. The degree of progressiveness will have profound cost and revenue effects.

c. Market efficiency – this indicates whether the industry in general produces the optimal mix of goods and services. This calls for an allocation of factors such that each earns the same marginal rate of return. Market inefficiency will prevail if resources are trapped in declining industries or if monopoly or collusive arrangements distort resource allocation among industries. This aspect of efficiency is also influenced by welfare arguments and value judgements, i.e., resources might earn high returns in producing products perceived by many as socially undesirable, e.g., harmful drugs. Distribution of production factors is therefore an added problem.

It is difficult to analyse overall efficiency in precise terms since progressiveness will influence technical and market efficiency and *vice versa*, hence the identification problem as to sources of inefficiency. Leibenstein[58] distinguishes between allocative and internal or X-efficiency. The former deals with movements along a production surface towards greater allocative efficiency whilst the latter portrays movements from a lower production surface to a higher one. He found that the amount to be gained by increased allocative efficiency is often trivial while the amount to be gained by increasing X-efficiency is frequently significant. If this is true, technical and progressiveness aspects of efficiency which are mainly internal will be of greater importance than market efficiency which is mainly allocative. Efficiency should then be viewed more as a function of management rather than solely of market. It is possible to take this further to advocate a policy aimed at managers rather than at market structure since the most important elements of increased efficiency are to be found in the process and rate of growth rather than with size as such. In fact evidence[59] exists to show that growth and profitability or growth and efficiency are positively correlated; less is known however about their causal relationships. An equally thorny problem is the measurement of efficiency. 'Ideally', Caves[60] says, 'we would possess data on the market value of output and the opportunity cost of all inputs for a set of firms producing identical outputs and using identical intermediate inputs. In reality, the mix of outputs is never the same from firm to firm; utilization rates will differ from firm to firm for irrelevant reasons; the degree of vertical integration will vary, and divergent accounting practices will cloud the statistical record of those already varied situations'.

Despite the difficulties, by using the rate of return on investment to reflect the index of efficiency we might come to some useful conclusions as to relationship between size and profitability, bearing in mind the various qualifications above.

Economists' notion of profits above normal will be the result of uncertainty bearing, risk and innovations. Profits that cannot be attributed to these will be the result of monopoly of market power. In the short-run, however, various supply and demand factors will also bring windfalls in profits.

A number of studies suggest that concentration and high entry barriers tend to produce high profits. J. S. Bain's[61] study of 40 US industries for the period 1936–40 shows high profits to be consistent with high concentration. His results also indicate that at very high levels of concentration there is a break in profitability as oligopolistic interdependence comes into play. The 8 largest firms, controlling more than 70 per cent of sales, seemed to run to higher profits than industries with lower concentration.

The conclusion offered by this and other evidence is not that all concentrated industries earn excessive profits and lead a quiet life. The evidence merely suggests that, on average, high concentrations of sellers tend to earn more profits than low or moderately concentrated sellers, and compared to the latter are less likely to provide substantive alternatives to consumers, though the latter conclusion is often disputed.

The UK Inland Revenue,[62] in compiling data for UK companies' contribution in a trade to total turnover and total profits for 1949–50, found that in most of the 27 individual industry groups, companies responsible for only one-third of total turnover earned about two-thirds of the total profits. The industry figure for wholesale distribution was 71 per cent, for food processing 68 per cent, building and contraction 67 per cent, and for electrical engineering 66 per cent. Data of this sort which uses a common efficiency measure, profits and turnover, runs into comparability problems since this measure would not reflect the efficiency of a vertically integrated firm. Such a measure therefore assesses at best the dispersion of variance of efficiency but not the level of efficiency in all firms.

A more recent study[63] by J. M. Samuels and D. J. Smyth found that firms operating in highly concentrated industries have less variable profit rates than firms operating in less concentrated ones; thu. although firms in highly concentrated industries do not necessarily obtain higher-than-average profits, they are better able to withstand difficult trading periods and other adversities.

P. E. Hart,[64] in a similar study, using US data, found that profit rates were independent of firm size if deficient corporations were excluded from the data. The inclusion of these, however, shows that profitability increases with size, but at a decreasing rate. The former result seems to lend support to views of economists like Marris[65] and Penrose[66] that profitability and size are independent. The latter finding is consistent with Baumol's[67] belief that the conditional distribution of profitability for given company size increased continuously but at a decreasing rate.

Singh and Whittington's[68] findings for UK profit-earning companies also support the independence result. The maxim that 'bigger is not necessarily better' is recurrent.

Considering the recent downward trend in the profitability of large firms, can we conclude that they are getting less efficient? Not necessarily. It could be that for various reasons the efficiency of large companies is not reflected in high profitability; in fact, greater efficiency will almost certainly not be measured by larger profitability if the welfare aspects of efficiency are considered.

Looking at the cost or unit cost aspect of efficiency, the UK Monopolies Commission[69] concludes that investigation into the performance of dominant firms before 1956 shows a 20 per cent range between unit costs of high-cost and low-cost firms or plants. The Monopolies Commission also concludes that dominant firms are the high-cost producers overall. This was due to restrictive practices relieving competitive pressure on inefficient firms. RPM and other types of restrictive practices have also protected a lot of small-scale, inefficient firms, especially in retail distribution. Generally speaking, in most UK industries small scale accounts for only a small percentage of cost disadvantage. In the US more than in the UK small scale is rarely a crippling disadvantage. Ignoring transport costs and other qualifications to economies of scale, 10 to 30 per cent of the capacity of many industries which have been studied seem to lie in plants too small to exploit the potential scale economies. This is partly attributable to the frequent need for product differentiation.

Whilst evidence shows no diseconomies arising with increasing size, it does show that for many multi-product firms, plant economies are often insignificant; in fact it is argued that many US firms do not have large plants, but have, more often, a large number of identical plants. This is consistent with the frequent observation that the long-run average cost curves of most firms is L-shaped or even slightly U-shaped. This has prompted a number of writers to argue in favour of demerging companies with little cognizance, however, of the other types of economies and benefits discussed in parts 1 and 2.

A note on efficiency aspects of advertising and promotion

In view of the large sums devoted to advertising, promotion, and the competitive aspects of product changes, it is unfortunate that there is no objective standard to indicate whether these amounts are excessive or inadequate. Undoubtedly many large firms spend on this scale simply because they can afford it: and at the micro-level, this is not hard to justify. Various studies, especially an extensive one by Neil H. Borden Jr,[70] show that the most effective element in securing trade acceptance for products is consumer advertising; and Philip Wrigley, when asked why he continued to advertise his internationally famous chewing gum so heavily, replied, 'once you get the plane up in the air, you don't shut off the propellors'. Another company chief, in justifying his advertising expenditure, remarked: 'half of my advertising expenditure is wasted but I don't know which half'.

Justification from the economic view point, however, is fairly complex. While advertising and promotion can help to inform consumers, broaden product range, increase competition (except where they act as barriers to entry), contribute to aggregate demand, etc., they can, at the same time be wasteful. There is also a relevant argument in favour of fewer, more durable products instead of more product varieties and model changes. These, though, are matters of value judgement, and difficult to assess.

It is worth noting FTC's recent[71] move to attack heavy advertising as a source of barrier to entry and the spread of market power. Research in the US tends to justify FTC policy Apart from defending the waste it may entail, marketers who want to make a case out of the scale effects of advertising must prove their contribution to operating efficiency and not to absolute cost advantages.

B. Market Conduct and Performance

The behaviour of firms in an industry is defined as market conduct. Public policy in both the UK and the US has been directed mainly to this aspect of industrial organization. Especially in the UK public policy on market structure has taken a pragmatic stand. It is not the purpose in this chapter to analyse the role of government legislation and intervention into industrial organization; we will nevertheless try to assess the effect of market conduct on performance.

Aspects of market conduct which have raised concern from the economic viewpoint include the following:

1 Concentration leads to high prices and lower output. While some evidence exists that concentration raises entry barriers and profit rates, no evidence exists to confirm common high prices and lower output, i.e., sheer monopoly power. In fact, competition amongst giants and oligopolists could be stronger than between smaller firms (e.g., soap powder prices in UK kept unusually low because of such fierce competition). The high profits attributed to concentration might be due not to high prices but to lower unit costs or higher turnover. It is difficult to come to a firm conclusion on this, especially since firms so often prefer to compete not on price but on quality and durability, etc.

2. Some argue that in highly concentrated industries consumer choice might be reduced. There is no evidence that positively supports this view, though it is conceivable that large firms could co-ordinate their product and promotional policies: e.g., the frequency of model changes and life expectance of goods could be agreed upon thus depriving consumers of range and quality. It can also be argued that because this may lead to better investment plans, it is necessary from the efficiency point of view. In the final analysis product collusion does not appear to be a common practice, and clearly, large firms have played a significant role in broadening product range and variety.

3. Another anxiety expressed about large firms, which can be traced to their staying power, is the likelihood that they might invest just sufficiently for cover against falling markets with little or no emphasis on the most profitable investment opportunities. It is possible that a number of large firms will survive in this way, helped by relative inefficiencies amongst firms. There is, however, no evidence suggesting that a significant body of large firms pursue the objective of preventing the average rate of return from falling rather than attempting to maximize it. On the whole, no satisfactory evidence exists as to the effect of concentration on investment.

4. The main types of market conduct that work to reduce competition and distort resource allocation – though they might have benefits as well – are the various ways in which firms co-ordinate prices, agree on market share, cartel and price-leadership arrangements. Public policy requires that such practices conform to the public interest. They are often practices associated with oligopolies; however, it is important to note that price and product collusions can reflect either market power or competitive rivalry and isolating the two is highly difficult.

Caves[72] maintains that the great majority of US industries 'seem to be more independent in their product policies than in their policies towards prices. Price adjustments, far more often than product adjustments seem to aim at protecting maximum joint profits of the industry'. [73] He also concludes that overt collusion will not necessarily increase with heightened concentration. In fact, less concentrated industries resort to restrictive practices more often via Trade Associations or formal agreements. Concentrated industries can gain the same ends less visibly through price leadership or tacit collusion.

Extreme forms of restrictive practices, more often known as coercive conduct, will clearly result in increased concentration, entry barriers and mis-allocation of resources. These often take the form of reciprocity, predatory pricing, cross-subsidization, all of which were discussed earlier and are under constant scrutiny by public policy. While such forms of coercive conduct will undermine market performance (and there is indication that certain industries[74] engage in them more often than others), less coercive forms of conduct like price and product collusion are difficult to evaluate in terms of their effect on performance.

Conclusion

Time and again the important conclusion reached by many economists is that several shortcomings in industrial performance are due not to problems in the organization of industries but to the inadequate quality of management.

In the final analysis a continuous programme of development to produce competent management teams will determine the success of mergers or of giant firms. Moreover, the professed economic goals and values of a nation are variable hence at best we can only rely on the 'rule of reason' when advocating what form of industrial structure is best suited to serve the interest of the community. Distortions, disagreements, mis-allocations are bound to arise.

NOTES

CHAPTER 1

1. 'Report on the proposed merger of Unilever Limited and Allied Breweries Limited', *The Monopolies Commission*, HMSO, June 1969.
2. Amey, L. R., *The Efficiency of Business Enterprises*, Allen & Unwin, 1969.
3. Rowley, C. K., *The British Monopolies Commission*, Allen & Unwin, 1966.
4. Marris, R., *The Economic Theory of Managerial Capitalism*, Macmillan, 1964.
5. Samuels, J. M., and Tzoannos, J., 'Takeovers and Share Price Evaluation', *Business Ratios,* 1969, Issue 2.
6. Gort, M., 'The Economic Disturbance Theory of Mergers', *Quarterly Journal of Economics,* November 1969.
7. Kitching, J., 'Why do Mergers Miscarry', *Harvard Business Review*, November–December 1967. See Chapter 4 of this book.
8. Levinson, H., 'A Psychologist Diagnoses Merger Failures', *Harvard Business Review*, March–April 1970. See Chapter 5 of this book.
9. Weston, J. F., and Mansinghka, S. K., 'Tests of the Efficiency Performance of Conglomerate Firms'. *Journal of Finance*, September 1971. See Chapter 3 of this book.
10. Farrent, P., 'The Truth about Mergers', *Management Today*, May 1970.
11. *Op. cit.*
12. Hogarty, T. F., 'The Profitability of Corporate Mergers', *Journal of Business,* July 1970.
13. *Op. cit.*
14. Searby, F., 'Control of Postmerger Change', *Harvard Business Review*, September–October 1969.
15. Wallace, Forrest D., 'Some Principles of Acquisitions', in *The Corporate Merger* (ed. Alberts, W.), University of Chicago Press, 1966.
16. *Op. cit.*
17. Ansoff, H. I., *Corporate Strategy*, McGraw-Hill, 1965.
18. *Op. cit.*
19. Sutherland, A., *The Monopolies Commission in Action*, Cambridge University Press, 1969.

CHAPTER 2

1. The research was financed by the Houblon-Norman Fund at the Bank of England. The author gratefully acknowledges their assistance.
2. Compare Tables 1 and 8.
3. Again, for brevity, 'four weeks before the first public announcement of the intention to proceed with a takeover' is replaced by 'four weeks before the first bid' even though on occasions the two are not strictly the same.
4. It will be seen in Part IV how absent 'bargains' were.
5. These increases would of course include any benefits accruing to the bidding firm as a whole from the takeover. The interpretation of the following results must therefore take into account the extent to which one believes in the existence of synergy, and the relative sizes of the two firms.

For a larger study by Dr Newbould, from which this paper is taken, see his book, *Management and Merger Activity*, Guthstead, 1970.

CHAPTER 3

1. Research support was provided by the Research Program in Competition and Business Policy, UCLA. Helpful comments were received from A. A. Alchian, M. Goudzwaard, N. H. Jacoby, R. H. Mason and K. Smith. Research assistants participating in data compilation included Kent Alves, Scott Dittrich, Jorge Ramos, Whitt Jones and Nanci Grottke. Ronald Shrieves carried a major responsibility in the computer calculations.
2. See Fama, E. F., 'Risk, Return and Equilibrium: Some Clarifying Comments', *Journal of Finance*, **23**, January, 1968, pp. 29–40; Lintner, John, 'Security Prices, Risk and Maximal Gains from Diversification', *Journal of Finance*, XX, December, 1965, pp. 586–91; Markowitz, Harry, *Portfolio Selection*, Wiley, 1959; Sharpe, William F., *Portfolio Theory and Capital Markets*, McGraw-Hill, 1970; and Tobin, James, 'Liquidity Preference as Behavior Towards Risk', *Review of Economic Studies*, **67**, February, 1958, pp. 65–86.
3. A useful sample would include Gort, Michael, *Diversification and Integration in American Industry*, Princeton, National Bureau of Economic Research, 1962, and 'An Economic Disturbance Theory of Mergers', *Quarterly Journal of Business*, **83**, November, 1969, pp. 624–42; Mueller, Dennis C., 'Theory of Conglomerate Mergers', *Quarterly Journal of Economics*, **83**, November, 1969, pp. 643–59; Narver, John C., *Conglomerate Mergers and Market Competition*, University of California Press, 1967, and 'Some Observations on the Impact of Antitrust Merger Policy on Marketing', *Journal of Marketing*, **33**, January, 1969, pp. 24–31; Reid, Samuel R., *Mergers, Managers and the Economy*, McGraw-Hill, 1968; Stone, James M., *Conglomerate Mergers: Their Implications for the Efficiency of Capital and the Theory of the Firm*, unpublished thesis, Harvard University, March 27, 1969; Udell, Jon G., 'Social and Economic Consequences of the Merger Movement in Wisconsin', *Wisconsin Economy Studies*, Number **3**, May, 1969; Weston, J. Fred, 'Diversification and Merger Trends', *Business Economics*, **5**, January, 1970, pp. 50–7, and 'The Nature and Significance of Conglomerate Firms', *St John's Law Review*, **44**, Spring, 1970, pp. 66–80; Weston, J. Fred, and Peltzman, S., (Eds), *Public Policy Toward Mergers*, Goodyear Publishing Company, 1969, Part V on Conglomerate Mergers; and also 32 other papers in the Spring 1970 edition of the *St John's Law Review, Conglomerate Mergers and Acquisitions*, **44**, Special Issue.
4. Some of the relevant papers are Asch, Peter, 'Conglomerate Mergers and Public Policy', *MSU Business Topics*, **15**, Winter, 1967, pp. 61–7; Bicks, R.A., 'Conglomerates and Diversification Under Section 7 of the Clayton Act', *Antitrust Bulletin*, **2**, November-December, 1956, pp. 175–86; Blair, J. M., 'The Conglomerate Merger in Economics and Law', *Georgetown Law Journal*, **46**, Summer, 1958, p. 672; Bock, Betty, *Antitrust Issues in Conglomerate Acquisitions*, Studies in Business Economics, Number 110, National Industrial Conference Board, 1969, and 'Conglomerate Mergers, Joint Ventures, and Potential Competition', *The Conference Board Record*, **5**, February, 1968, pp. 2–6; Day, Richard E., 'Conglomerate Mergers and the Curse of Bigness', *North Carolina Law Review*, **42**, 1964, p. 539; Patterson, James M., and Patterson, Jeanne, 'Conglomerates: The Legal Issues', *Business Horizons*, **11**, February 1968, pp. 39–48; Turner, D., 'Conglomerate Mergers and Section 7 of the Clayton Act', *Harvard Business Review*, **78**, May, 1965, pp. 1313–95; and 18 papers in the Spring 1970 edition of the *St John's Law Review*, *op. cit.*
5. Various aspects are treated in Ansoff, H. Igor, 'Strategies for Diversification', *Harvard Business Review*, September–October, 1957, pp. 113–24, and 'A Model for Diversification', *Management Science*, **4**, July, 1958, pp. 392–414; Berg, Norman, 'Strategic Planning in Conglomerate Companies, *Harvard Business Review*, **43**, May–June, 1965, pp. 79–92; Weston, J. Fred, 'Mergers and Acquisitions in Business Planning', *Rivista Internazionale di Scienze Economiche e Commerciali*, XVII, April, 1970, pp. 309–20; and in a number of management journal articles.
6. See especially the Discussion in Cabinet Committee on Price Stability, *Studies by the Staff of the Cabinet Committee on Price Stability*, US Government Printing Office, 1969, pp. 69–81; see also Federal Trade Commission Staff, *Economic Report on Corporate Mergers*, US Government Printing Office, 1969, with the introductory statements by Senator Philip A. Hart of Michigan and by members of the Federal Trade Commission.

7. Gort, Michael, and Hogarty, Thomas F., 'New Evidence on Mergers', *Journal of Law and Economics*, XIII, April, 1970, pp. 167–84; Heiden, Edward J, 'Mergers and Profitability', unpublished manuscript, University of Wisconsin; Hogarty, Thomas F., 'The Profitability of Corporate Mergers', *Journal of Business*, **43**, July, 1970, pp. 317–27; Kelly, Eamon M., *The Profitability of Growth Through Mergers*, The Pennsylvania State University, 1967.
8. The 1171-page special edition of the *St John's Law Review*, *op. cit.*, on conglomerate mergers contains no article with empirical data on the comparative performance of conglomerate firms. Two empirical articles in the volume deal with other aspects of performance. The paper by S. E. Boyle analyses the pre-merger growth and profitability characteristics of acquired companies. The paper by T. F. Hogarty reviews earlier historical studies of the success of mergers generally.
9. Reid, Samuel R., *Mergers, Managers and the Economy, op. cit.*
10. Lorie, James H., and Halpern, Paul, 'Conglomerates: The Rhetoric and the Evidence', *Journal of Law and Economics*, XIII, April, 1970, pp. 149–66.
11. Since this kind of 'funny money' (Lorie and Halpern's term) was alleged to be characteristic of conglomerate mergers, their sample of firms is presumed to be of 'conglomerates'. However, no formal criteria for selection were employed.
12. Smith, K. V., and Schreiner, J. C., 'A Portfolio Analysis of Conglomerate Diversification', *Journal of Finance*, **24**, June, 1969, pp. 413–28.
13. Myers, Stewart C., 'Procedures for Capital Budgeting Under Uncertainty', *Industrial Management Review*, **9**, Spring, 1968, pp. 1–19.
14. The Heiden and Reid studies ended in 1961, and the Kelly and Hogarty studies ended in 1963 and 1964, respectively. The conglomerate merger movement did not really get underway until the mid-1960s, and peaked in 1967 and 1968. In fact, a fair test of the conglomerate merger movement is not possible even today since a number of additional years would be required for implementation of the strategies associated with these corporate development programs.
15. For a more complete discussion, see Weston, 'Diversification and Merger Trends' and 'Mergers and Acquisitions in Business Planning', *op. cit.*
16. For further development of these criteria see Weston, 'Diversification and Merger Trends', *op. cit.*, pp. 52–4.
17. Previous studies have not employed analytical criteria for identification of conglomerate firms. Hence this paper sets forth the selection criteria explicitly.
18. We relied on a number of sources to provide candidates for potential inclusion in our study including the Federal Trade Commission reports and a number of lists compiled by financial magazines and brokerage firms.
19. These were computed from the growth in total assets between the year of acquisition and the terminal 1968 date, from the Federal Trade Commission-Securities and Exchange Commission *Quarterly Financial Report on Industrial Corporations*, or national income generated in the industrial category, from the national income statistics of the United States Department of Commerce as reported in various issues of the *Survey of Current Business*. We sought to employ the 3-digit standard industrial classification category where available.
20. The *Fortune* Product Directory was the main source of data. Where information was not otherwise available, we sought on a judgement basis to determine the degree of diversification through review of the product descriptions and descriptions of the nature of subsidiaries provided in the annual investment manual, *Moody's Industrials*. In contrast to the procedure in the FTC's report on mergers, we did not include a company where the firm was involved in only one major merger *and* where at the end of the period the firm did not meet our Screening Rule no. 2 with regard to the degree of diversification.
21. Six firms which passed our two screening rules were not utilized in the final study because of unavailability of required data.
22. The companies that had already been included in the conglomerate group were excluded. We did not, however, in order to avoid bias, exclude the companies that had already been picked in our random sample No. 1. Five companies appeared in both samples.
23. The lists of the two random samples and supplementary data may be obtained from the authors.

24. Since we did not attach great importance to the findings of our growth measures, the selection of the period 1958–68 was determined by the ready availability of data from standard financial information sources. We also used the period 1960–68 since 1960 was the initial year in some studies reported in the Federal Trade Commission staff's *Economic Report on Corporate Mergers*, *op. cit.* Both initial years are years of depressed business activity, while 1968 was a year of inflationary growth. However, data for our control samples covered the same period.
25. The growth figures utilized in the averages were obtained by calculating a compound annual rate of increase between the initial years and the terminal years. Such a measure of growth may give undue weight to either the initial or terminal year, but since all the growth measures are averaged over some sixty companies, such random influences will tend to be averaged out. Also, the same procedures were utilized for the conglomerate firms as for the two random samples of firms.
26. The compound annual growth rates were computed for each company and were used to calculate the unweighted arithmetic means for the number of companies in each sample.
27. The significance was at the 1 per cent level in 35 of 42 observations.
28. For a precise measure, we would deduct non-interest-bearing liabilities from total assets and then calculate the ratio of earnings before interest and taxes or the ratio of earnings before interest alone to total assets minus non-interest-bearing liabilities. However, since the non-interest-bearing liabilities do not ordinarily represent a large percentage of total assets, for comparing groups of companies it is more convenient to use total assets.
29. See, for example, the discussion in Miller, M. H. and Modigliani, F., *American Economic Review*, LVI, June, 1968, pp. 333–91.
30. The sample of industrial companies (RI) exhibited earnings performance in 1958 higher than the conglomerate companies by a difference with significance at the 1 per cent level for all three comparisons.
31. In analyzing the data on preferred stock, we noted a substantial disparity between the stated balance-sheet values of preferred stock for the conglomerate firms and estimates of more realistic values of the preferred stocks based on prevailing dividend yields, call prices or liquidating values. For 1968 we calculated adjusted earnings' rates on total assets, adding to the total assets of each of the three sets of companies, the difference between our estimate of an appropriate balance sheet value of preferred stock and the stated value. As shown in Table 3, the differences in the earning power among the three groups of companies remained non-significant.
32. If the price/earnings ratio was greater than 100 times, or a negative multiple of 50 or more, we excluded it in the second set of calculations.
33. For 1958, the second set of price/earnings ratios, excluding the large negative ratios for some of the conglomerate firms, raised the average for the remaining conglomerates somewhat above the average price/earnings ratios of the other two samples. However, the differences in the means remained non-significant.
34. Random Sample No. 2 included banks and utilities, accounting for leverage ratios higher than those for industrial firms.
35. Other aspects of a theory of the timing of the conglomerate mergers movement are discussed in Weston 'Diversification and Merger Trends', *op. cit.* pp. 50–2.
36. This could also be expressed as changing the product market mix of the firm's portfolio of capital budgets. Again, from the standpoint of the economy as a whole, it would make no difference whether investors provided their own diversification or whether the individual firms achieved diversification, under the assumptions of no bankruptcy costs and no costs of rebuilding an effective organization.
37. An elaboration of how the conglomerate firms achieve these functions is set forth in Weston, 'Diversification and Merger Trends', and 'Mergers and Acquisitions in Business Planning', *op. cit.*
38. It is probable that some individual conglomerate firms will go through reorganization or bankruptcy. This would not be inconsistent with the above proposition. The point is that more of these entities would have been forced into reorganization and bankruptcy if they had not achieved successful defensive diversification.
39. Reid, Samuel R., 'Mergers for Whom: Managers or Stockholders?' *Hearings before the Subcommittee on Antitrust and Monopoly of the Committee on Judiciary,* United

States Senate, 89th Congress, Second Session, pp. 1914–31, and *Mergers, Managers and the Economy, op. cit.* There are a number of justifications for examining the Reid study in somewhat more detail. Most of the other studies dealt with the success of mergers or merging firms generally. These studies are at least indirectly relevant since if merging generally is unsuccessful for firms, by implication the probability is that conglomerate merging would also be unsuccessful. But the possibility exists that diversification and other characteristics of conglomerate mergers could also increase the probability of their success. These possibilities provide a rationale for studies focused on conglomerate merger activity.

40. Reid, *Mergers, Managers and the Economy, op. cit.*, Tables 9. 3–9. 8, pp. 186–8. 'Significant in the wrong direction' indicates that the performance of the conglomerates was superior to the control groups.
41. See Reid, *Mergers, Managers and the Economy, op. cit.*, Table 9.1, p. 185.
42. See any standard textbook on business finance.
43. For details see Gupta, Manak C., 'The effect of Size, Growth, and Industry on the Financial Structure of Manufacturing Companies', *Journal of Finance,* XXIV, June, 1969, pp. 517–29.
44. These sources provide rankings which permit easy determination of median values. Our worksheet analysis of alternative measures of central tendency indicated that the median values are relatively free of the distortions produced by weighted or 'unweighted' averages. Therefore the medians were used for the *Forbes* and *Fortune* data test. Use of the median values precludes utilization of the usual statistical tests of significance. However, the observed differences between the medians were either so large as to be clearly significant or so small as to be clearly non-significant.
45. *Forbes*, vol. **103**, January 1, 1969, vol. **104**, January 1, 1970.
46. *Forbes* defines conglomerate companies as those which have found a central focus for their operations, while the agglomerate companies have diversified without finding a central thread. The two categories are combined for analysis of 'multi-industry' firms.
47. The five-year growth percentages are measured by Forbes by averaging the three initial years and calculating the growth to the values for the terminal years. For example, in the January 1, 1970, issue of *Forbes*, the three initial years averaged were 1963, 1964 and 1965; the terminal year was 1969. The five-year growth rates for sales and earnings per share are medians of the compound annual growth rates calculated for individual companies. For market prices, the total percentage changes for the five-year periods are calculated.
48. *News Front*, June-July, 1969, p. 70.
49. *News Front*, June-July, 1969, p. 56. The averages computed by *News Front* are the weighted arithmetic means.
50. We have also studied a number of aspects of the dispersion of returns, comparing measures of dispersion among the conglomerate firms with the two samples of firms. In addition, we are analyzing the risk/return characteristics in the framework of a capital asset market model. The results will be presented in a separate paper.
51. On the one hand, if the earnings performance of the conglomerate firms had been markedly superior to industry generally, they would be subject to charges that they possessed monopoly power, as have other large firms which have achieved high profitability rates over a period of time. On the other hand, because their earnings as a group have not been significantly higher than industry generally, the conglomerate firms have been charged by their critics with not contributing to improvements in economic efficiency. But to improve earnings up to the average, as to avoid falling below the average, represents a contribution to economic efficiency.
52. Reid, S. R., 'A reply to the Weston/Mansinghka criticisms dealing with Conglomerate mergers', *Journal of Finance*, September, 1971, pp. 937–46.
53. Reid, S. R., *Mergers, Managers and the Economy,* McGraw-Hill, 1968.
54. Hogarty, T. F., 'The Profitability of Corporate Mergers', *Journal of Business*, July 1970, pp. 317–27. The results of this study are referred to in Chapter 1 of these readings.

CHAPTER 4

1. *Mergers and Acquisitions* is published by Mergers and Acquisitions, Inc., 1725 K Street, N.W., Washington, D.C.
2. W. T. Grimm & Co., *1966 Merger Review,* Chicago, Illinois, 1967.
3. Bureau of Economics and Federal Trade Commission.

CHAPTER 5

1. See, for example, Searby, Frederick Wright, 'Control Postmerger Change', *Harvard Business Review,* September–October, 1969, p. 4.
2. See Levinson, H., *The Exceptional Executive,* Harvard University Press, 1968.
3. See Davis, Richard E., 'Compatibility in Corporate Marriages', *Harvard Business Review,* July–August, 1968, p. 86.
4. See Lawrence, Paul R., and Lorsch, Jay W., *Organization and Environment,* Division of Research, Harvard Business School, 1967.
5. Welles, Chris, 'The Battle for United Fruit', *Investment Banking and Corporate Financing,* Spring, 1969, p. 27.

CHAPTER 6

1. The Board of Trade statistics are derived from the following sources:
   (a) 'Acquisitions and amalgamations of quoted companies 1954–61', *Economic Trends,* April, 1963.
   (b) 'Acquisitions and amalgamations of quoted companies 1962–3', *Economic Trends.*
   (c) *General observations on mergers,* published by the Monopolies Commission with the reports on 'Unilever Ltd and Allied Breweries Ltd' and 'The Rank Organization Ltd and the De La Rue Company Ltd', 9 June, 1969.
   (d) 'Acquisitions and mergers of companies in the first three quarters of 1968', *Board of Trade Journal,* 24 January, 1969.
   (e) 'Acquisitions and mergers of companies in 1968', *Board of Trade Journal,* 14 March, 1969.
   (f) 'Acquisition and mergers of companies in 1969', *Board of Trade Journal,* 25 February, 1970.
2. Berle, A. A., and Means, G. C., *The Modern Corporation and Private Property,* New York, 1932.
3. Larner, Robert, J.,'Ownership and Control in the 200 Largest Nonfinancial Corporations, 1929 and 1963', *American Economic Review,* September, 1966, p. 779 for classification of control by minority stock ownership.
4. Sargant Florence, P., *Ownership, Control and Success of Large Companies,* London, 1961.
5. Utton, M. A., *Industrial Concentration,* Harmondsworth, 1970, chapter 3.
6. *Current Trends in Merger Activity, 1968 Statistical Report,* Bureau of Economics, Federal Trade Commission, March, 1969, p. 3.
7. Reid, Samuel R., *Mergers, Managers and the Economy,* McGraw-Hill, 1968, pp.22–3.
8. Ansoff, H. Igor, *Corporate Strategy*, New York, 1965, p. 116.
9. Pratten, C. F., 'A Case Study of a Conglomerate Merger', *Moorgate and Wall Street Review,* Spring, 1970.

CHAPTER 8

1. Davies, J., Secretary of State for Trade and Industry, 17 December, 1970, *Hansard,* vol. 808, no. 58, Col. 1577.
2. Hereafter referred to as the Commission.

3. The Board of Trade (hereafter, the Board) lost merger policy to DEP in October, 1969.
4. The Industrial Reorganization Corporation was formally dissolved by the Industry Act, April 1971.
5. The National Board for Prices and Incomes was dissolved in March, 1971.
6. DTI was created under the *White Paper* on the 'Reorganization of Central Government', October, 1970, Cmnd. 4506.
7. Stevens and Yamey, *The Restrictive Practices Court,* 1965, p. 41.
8. Since Mr Davies' speech (*op. cit.*) the Commission has an enhanced role both in the 'trigger' and learning/monitoring process.
9. Rowley, 'Mergers and Public Policy in Great Britain', *Journal of Law and Economics,* 1968.
10. Sutherland, A., *Monopolies Commission in Action*, Cambridge University Press, 1969.
11. Sutherland, A., *Management of Merger Policy,*
12. *Mergers; a guide to Board of Trade practices,* HMSO, 1969.
13. Speech at Manchester Chamber of Commerce, 28 February, 1969 (quoted in *Mergers, op. cit.*, p. 58).
14. *Op. cit.*, p. 7.
15. *Op. cit.*, p. 108.
16. *Op. cit.*, *Management of Merger Policy,* p. 21.
17. *Ibid.*
18. Monopolies Commission, *GKN/Birfield report,* para. 126.
19. 1965 Monopolies and Mergers Act, Section 6(2): 'The Commission shall also investigate and report whether the enterprises having ceased, in the circumstances of the case, to be distinct enterprises operate, or may be expected to operate against the public interest'.
20. *Op. cit.*, p. 19.
21. The President exemplified his point by reference to the guidelines employed in the USA but implicit in his argument was a general wariness of guidelines in themselves.
22. Van Cise, Jerrold, G., *The Federal anti-Trust Laws,* 1965, p. 5.
23. Department of Justice, *Merger Guidelines,* 1968.
24. Speech in House of Commons, 17 April, 1969; quoted in *Mergers,* p. 62. Examples of 'assurances' are given in the Appendix to the chapter.
25. *Mergers,* p. 28; Chrysler/Rootes; GEC/AEI;* International Computers Ltd.; EMI/ABPC; GEC/EE; General Foods/Rowntree; Ross/AF;* Distillers/United Glass.
26. These cases occurred between summer 1969 and spring 1970.
27. *Op. cit.*, p. 20.
28. Under the 1965 Act a non-newspaper merger can be considered for reference to the Commission either on the grounds of asset size (£5m) or on the technical monopoly rule (over a third of market share). Under the same Act a monopoly can only be referred if it satisfies the market share rule. Hence mergers cannot be referred after a six-months' lapse unless they satisfy the technical monopoly criteria. Of the non-newspaper, non-banking, non-building society mergers considered by the Board up until June, 1969 (318 in all), 61 per cent came under the asset rule alone, 26 per cent under the monopoly rule alone, and 13 per cent under both.
29. This also seems to be reflected in the Conservative Government's intention to make the Commission responsible for continuous review of *ex-ante* and *ex-post* merger situations.
30. BMC/Pressed Steel; GKN/Birfield; BICC/Pyrotenax.
31. Sutherland, A., *Monopolies Commission in Action, op. cit.*, p. 63–4.
32. A list of the assurances is attached as an appendix to provide examples of potential monopoly detriments.
33. It is worth pointing out here that the Commission has no formal power to accept assurances, and this casts some doubt on the standing of the assurances undertaken in the BICC/Pyrotenax case, since the Board was not involved in the negotiations on them at all, and presumably feels no responsibility positively to monitor their implementation.
34. We would note that when the Ross/AF Merger came before the Board for the second time (April 1969), assurances were extracted, the intentions (although not the form) of which

*We would note that in these particular cases where assurances were secured, the IRC was involved in support of the merger.

were very similar to the assurances that were sought and rejected by the Monopolies Commission earlier (May 1966).

35. Monitoring is not a positive act by the responsible department; it depends on complaints by interested parties such as customers and suppliers. The question to be asked consequently is whether such interested parties are aware of all the particular assurances undertaken.
36. Williamson, O. E., *Economies as an Anti-Trust Defence, AER,* March, 1968.
37. The following discussion is based on M. Beesley's 'Economic Effects of National Policies towards Mergers and Acquisitions' in *Long Range Corporate Planning* (Ed. B. Denning), Longman, 1969.
38. An interesting line of thought now is whether the merger control lobby will have more support within DTI, especially with the dissolution of a counter pressure group (i.e., the IRC – whose existence certainly hamstrung the merger control division), and with Mr Davies's apparently greater commitment to the Commission.
39. Monopolies Commission, 'General Observations on Mergers', Annex to *Rank/de La Rue* and *Unilever/Allied Reports,* June, 1969, para. 32.
40. The tentative Conservative proposals give the Commission a chance to study the problem of information and merger effects in more depth, and to become, as Mr Davies put it, an authorative source of information and knowledge on situations of imperfect competition, undertaking a 'general scrutiny of the efficacy of competitive impulses in the economy'. (Mr. Davies, *op. cit.*)
41. *Op. cit.*, chapters III and IV.
42. Ansoff, H. I., *Corporate Strategy,* 1965.
43. Allen, R. M., 'Expansion by Merger' in *The Corporate Merger* (Eds Alberts and Segall), 1969.
44. Rowley, *op. cit.*
45. Sutherland, *Management of Merger Policy, op. cit.*
46. *Ibid.*, p. 25.
47. Monopolies Commission, *op. cit.*, para 32.
48. Edwards, Corwin, 'Public Policy and Business Size' in *Readings in Industrial Organization and Public Policy, AEA,* 1958. Edwards is discussing here the operation of legislation in respect of price discrimination.
49. NBPI, *Second General Report,* 1966–7, para 80.
50. Press notice to *Merger Guidelines,* Department of Justice, May, 1968.
51. Monopolies Commission Report (Session 1966–7, HC 490). The report concerned itself with the production and distribution of mineral insulated cable, rather than other aspects of the case.
52. All quotes are from the Commission report, *op. cit.*

CHAPTER 9

1. Honourable mention should be made of the Acton Society study, *Mergers: the Impact on the Shop Floor* published in 1966, and based on fieldwork investigation of eight case studies.
2. The case for emphasizing these groups will be found in an invaluable article in the May, 1962 issue of the *National Institute Economic Review*; the title is 'Research and Development: a comparison between British and American industry' (author C. Freeman).
3. See Board of Trade, *Mergers,* especially Chapter VI.
4. The phrase 'creative destruction' is, of course, from Schumpeter, J., *Capitalism, Socialism, and Democracy,* and the chapters in which he expounds his view must rank as among the most important in twentieth-century economics. As for the multi-national company, Louis Turner in *Politics and the Multi-national Company* (Fabian Research, 279) quotes figures showing 62 out of the 100 largest American firms, and 49 out of the 100 largest non-American firms, having production facilities in at least six countries.
5. For those who want to pursue the tangled threads of interunion dispute over the unionization of the BSC's white-collar employees there is not only the *Pearson Report* (Cmnd.

3754) but also a considerable amount of detail in the TUC *General Council's Report* for 1968 and for 1969.

6. Commission on Industrial Relations, *Report no. 2* (Cmnd. 4247).
7. The treatment of trade union growth and structure is here set down in highly abbreviated form. It is more fully explored in the Royal Commission on Trade Unions, *Research Paper no. 5,* Part 1, 'Trade Union Structure and Government' by John Hughes.
8. The argument has been most cogently put in the Royal Commission on Trade Unions' *Research Paper no. 3,* 'Industrial Sociology and Industrial Relations' by Alan Fox.
9. See the IRC's *Report* for year ended 31 March, 1969, p. 14.
10. The BOT booklet *Mergers* indicates how limited are the industrial relations questions that the Mergers Panel 'may consider'; see *Mergers*, p. 14.
11. There is an interesting account of the problems experienced in one locality in 'The GEC/AEI Takeover and the Fight Against Redundancy at Harlow' by Stan Newens in the *Trade Union Register* for 1969.
12. There is useful material about GEC/AEI/EE and a number of other combines in an article in *DATA Journal* for May, 1970, 'Organizing the Combines' by W. B. Shields.
13. The information is taken from the Chairman's statement to the 1970 AGM of National Westminster.
14. TUC *Report* for 1969, p. 492.

CHAPTER 10

1. Throughout this paper, reference to the shareholder as a user or needer of information is intended to include the professional analyst and others whose task it is to advise investors.
2. The terms 'bid' and 'merger' are used interchangeably in this paper.
3. A useful summary of the opposing arguments is given in Chapter 3 of *The Stock Market and Economic Efficiency* by W. J. Baumol, Fordham University Press, New York, 1965.
4. Cmnd. 1749, para 333.
5. Hereafter referred to as 'the Institute'.
6. In Statement S.8 issued to its members, the Institute specifically states that 'the purpose for which annual accounts are normally prepared is not to enable individual shareholders to take investment decisions'.
7. See *Accounting for Stewardship in a Period of Inflation* published by The Research Foundation of the Institute of Chartered Accountants in England and Wales, 1968.
8. *Published Accounts-your yardsticks of performance?* published by the Centre for Interfirm Comparison Ltd, 1968, gives some examples of the difficulties encountered in comparing audited accounts. It also mentions that, in one industry, company profits calculated on an agreed uniform basis ranged from 50 per cent to 150 per cent of the audited figures and, in another industry, the range was from 50 per cent to 120 per cent.
9. Reported in the leading daily newspapers on 12 December, 1969, and also in *Accountancy,* January, 1970.
10. See Edey, H. C., 'Accounting Principles and Business Reality', reprinted in Carsberg, B. V., and Edey, H. C. (eds), *Modern Financial Management,* Penguin, 1969.
11. e.g., employees, bankers, debenture holders, creditors, Monopolies Commission and interested government agencies. In fact, nearly all those interested in company performance are more concerned with prospective rather than past performance, an exception, under existing legislation, being HM Inspectors of Taxes in their tax assessment role.
12. *The City Code on Take-overs and Mergers,* April, 1969, obtainable from the Issuing Houses Association, hereafter referred to as 'the code'.
13. Reproduced in *Accountancy,* June, 1969.
14. 'Accountants and the Public Interest' by R. Leach in *The Times,* 22 September, 1969.
15. Hereafter referred to as 'the biddee'.
16. It is hoped that the list is exhaustive but a case would inevitably be overlooked if the *Investors' Chronicle* did not report that forecasts for more than a year ahead had been published.

17. It later transpired that AEI's forecasts had been examined by the same auditing firm. Extracts from their report are included in the Appendix.
18. TR stated that it had changed the basis of calculating depreciation and would continue with the new basis in future. However, it quantified the effect of the change in basis, thereby enabling the reader to make an adjustment if he had wished.
19. Required under Rule 15 of the Code.
20. An uneasiness confirmed by A. C. Rayner and I.M.D. Little in their book *Higgledy Piggledy Growth Again*, Basil Blackwell, 1966.
21. According to the survey reported in *The G.E.C. bid for A.E.I.*, published by J. Walter Thompson Co. Ltd, 1968, the majority of City respondents 'came to the conclusion that the AEI forecasts were realistic, given the 'new' management situation'.
22. EAC's forecast was not included in the present study as it was made early in 1968.
23. During the period examined, the government's dividend freeze policy was in force so companies would not have been allowed to increase their payments without good cause, even if they had wished to.
24. A perusal of *Moodies' Investment Digest 1969* shows that, since 1957, 65 per cent of the 550 companies listed had either maintained or increased their gross equity dividends each year.
25. An examination of sixty bid documents in the six months from 1 September, 1969, indicates that companies are still reluctant to make long-term forecasts as only one company in this sample did so.
26. Rule 15 of the Code requires directors to state the assumptions, including the commercial assumptions, upon which their forecasts are based. An examination of thirty recent cases where forecasts were published shows that the accompanying information is rarely quantitative in nature and sometimes tends to be rather vague.
27. The annual rate of growth in pre-tax profits had been:

	%
1961	3·0
1962	11·5
1963	10·6
1964	15·4
1965	4·9

28. This figure was not even achieved by the following year in which pre-tax profits worked out at £857,000. The unsatisfactory result for 1969/70 was said to be due to a decline in the profits of the EAC side of the business,
29. This would require a profit after tax and preference dividend of £212,000. The actual figure achieved was only £62,000 and the dividend paid was 10 per cent.
30. This was revised downwards on 25 April, 1970 when, according to the *Financial Times*, 'It is confidently expected, however, that a figure of over £500,000 will be shown, which will be a record'.

CHAPTER 12

1. See, for example, Fraser's *Golden Bough* and Bertrand Russell's *Power*.
2. The respects in which it is not similar must also be noted. Whereas military power is destructive, economic power is pursued against a background of the productive process. Economic power is nearly always the result of achieving a balance between gain and conflict.
3. Bertrand Russell, *Power. A New Social Analysis*, Allen & Unwin, 1938, p. 15.
4. See Acton, *Lectures on Modern History*, Macmillan, 1906, p. 204, quoting with approval Vane and Harrington.
5. Return defined as the ratio of net profits to balance sheet net asset values. Samuels, J. M., and Smyth, D. J., 'Profits, Variability of Profits and Firm Size', *Economica*, May, 1968, vol. **35**, no. 138. See also chapter three of this volume.
6. *Financial Analysts Journal*, New York, 1968, quoting a committee advising the US Commerce Department.

7. See Goodman, R., *The Impact of Size,* Acton Society Trust, 1969.
8. Keynes, J. M., *Essays in Persuasion,* Macmillan, 1931, 'The End of Laissez-Faire', 1926. pp. 312–17.

CHAPTER 13

1. See Lundberg, Ferdinand, *The Rich and the Super Rich,* Nelsons, 1969, p. 36.
2. Speech to the 15th CIOS International Management Congress, Tokyo, 1969.
3. See, for example, Watkins, Melville H., and others, *Foreign Ownership and the Structure of Canadian Industry*, Ottawa: Privy Council Office, 1968.
4. Barclay's Unicorn '500' Trust.
5. See Drucker, P. F., *The Practice of Management,* Heinemann, 1955.
6. See Brooke, M. Z., and Remmers, H. L., *The Strategy of Multi-national Enterprise,* Longman, 1970, Chapter 4, note 24. Further references to this book will be abbreviated to *Strategy.*
7. The reference here is to the fact that the succesful engineer is promoted to line management. This point is discussed in Gerstl, J. E., and Hutton, S. P., *The Engineers,* Tavistock, 1966. Other examples of the misuse of skill in the large concern are considered in Pym, Denis, *Industrial Society*, Penguin, 1968.
8. *Strategy,* Chapter 2.
9. See *The Times,* 19 March, 1970.
10. In the text the phrase 'home country' refers to country of origin of the company, 'host country' to the country in which a particular foreign subsidiary is operating.
11. Gray, A. P., and Abrams, Mark, *Construction ESSO Refinery, Fawley.* British Institute of Management, 1954.
12. See Granick, D., *The European Executive,* Doubleday, 1962.
13. See *Strategy,* p. 153.
14. For the detailed evidence for these statements see *Strategy*, pp. 151–208.
15. See *Strategy,* pp. 68–83.
16. For some carefully thought out and detailed proposals for further developments along these lines see Goodman, Edward, *The Impact of Size,* London: The Acton Society Trust 1969, especially pp. 66–75, and Chapter 12 of these readings.

CHAPTER 14

1. There is no reason why the restructuring should be arbitrarily limited to the European continent. Trans-national mergers that included US corporations would make a great deal of economic sense. If half of the European computer industry, for instance, combined with Control Data and the other half joined with Honeywell or Univac, both the Americans and the Europeans would be in a far better position to compete with IBM. But here again there is the problem of balance, of creating a company that the Americans would not dominate, and, of course, of national or European pride.
2. For an account of the changing attitudes towards Monopolies and Mergers in Britain, see Victor Morgan, E., 'Annual Survey of Monopolies, Mergers and Restrictive Practices', *Government and Business,* Journal of the Economists Advisory Group, June, 1971.
3. Statement to House of Commons by the Minister for Trade and Industry, *Hansard,* 17 December, 1970. Statement by Ministry of Trade and Industry, 26 October, 1971, see *The Times*, 27 October, 1971.
4. Toulemon, R., 'The Industrial and Technological Policy of the EEC', *European Intelligence,* 29 July, 1971.
5. 'Market Domination: from Cans to Performing Rights', *European Intelligence,* 15 July, 1971.
6. 'EEC Policy on Competition – A Balance Sheet of Recent Divisions', *European Trends,* May, 1971.

CHAPTER 15

1. Vernon, R., *Manager in the International Economy,* Prentice Hall, 1968, p. 186.
2. Kindelberger, C. P., *American Business Abroad,* Yale, 1969, p. 207.
3. Bukharin, N., *Imperialism and World Economy,* Martin Lawrence, 1927, p. 138.
4. See Hexner, E., *International Cartels,* Pitman, 1946, Chapter VIII.
5. Duncan, Sir Val, 'The Multi-national Corporation as seen through British Eyes', paper presented to the Seminar on the Multi-national Corporation, Council of Foreign Relations, New York, November, 1970.
6. I have discussed these points more fully in a paper 'The Internationalization of Capital and the Nation State',, in (ed.) Dunning, J. H., *Essays on the International Corporation,* Allen and Unwin, 1971.
7. This item in the table is not entirely made up of Euro-currency transactions. It also includes the Bank of England's foreign currency balance held with their correspondents abroad (working balances held for their day-to-day business overseas) as well as balances held on behalf of UK customers who have exchanged control authority to retain foreign currency.
8. Dunning, J. H., *The Role of American Investment in the British Economy,* PEP, February, 1969, p. 120.
9. Department of Trade and Industry, *A Survey of Mergers 1958–68,* HMSO, 1970, Appendices 8 and 9. On the question of growth via acquisition or through internal expansion the survey (p. 14) comments: 'The largest American companies seem to have ignored the prospects of growth by acquisition both in the US and other countries, concentrating instead on self-generated growth; they have become multi-national by setting up plants in countries where they foresaw possibilities of expansion and an increasing flow of profits. On the other hand, most of the largest United Kingdom companies have relied to a considerable extent on acquisitions for growth'.
10. These estimates are based on published figures for the flows and stocks of foreign investment into and out of Britain which have been related to the ratios on the significance of inward investment calculated by Dunning (see note 6 above). We should also note that the direct investment figures we have been using for both inward and outward investment are net of disinvestment. Gross flows are higher. In 1968 while net outward investment from the UK was £410m the gross figure was £607m and for inward investment the figures were £283m (net) and 475m (gross). See *Business Monitor*, Board of Trade, Misc., Series, M4, Overseas Transactions, HMSO, 1970, Tables 7 and 14.
11. Committee on Invisible Exports, *The Role of International Companies,* 1969, p. 7.
12. Rowthorn, R., with Hymer, S., *International Big Business 1957–67,* Cambridge U.P 1971, p. 62. Comparable estimates for other countries are: Canada 46%, Netherlands 43%, Italy 30%, Japan 20%, Germany 16%, US 15%, and France 7%. The method of calculating these figures is given in Appendix 4.
13. Ford for example has 2% of its sales in Britain, 3% of its earnings and 15% of its employment. Shell Transport and Trading has over 75% of its sales, as well as its operations, outside Western Europe.
14. Four of these firms in the distribution sector would not have entered the top 50 companies if ranking were by capital employed rather than sales. The bias towards the distribution sector is a well-known feature of rankings by sales.
15. *Board of Trade Journal,* 21 July, 1967.
16. *The Times 1000 Leading Companies in Britain and Overseas,* 1970–71, p. 7.
17. See Utton, M. A., *Industrial Concentration,* Penguin, 1970, Chapter 4, pp. 60–5.
18. *Survey of Mergers 1958–68, op. cit.*, p. 36.
19. This discussion has, if anything, understated the capital controlled by international firms within the British economy and by British firms overseas, for the following reasons:
(1) Foreign investment figures are given in book values. If we included investment at market value British investment abroad and (probably) foreign investment in Britain would be higher. Thus Reddaway estimated that the market value of the companies he surveyed (excluding oil) exceeded the book value by 36 per cent at the end of 1964. See Reddaway, W. B., *et al, Effects of UK Direct Investment Overseas,* Interim Report, Cambridge, 1967, p. 56. The most recent Board of Trade Enquiry into the value of overseas investments found that for the 75 per cent of companies replying, 'the book value of investment in

associates in their own books was on average some 35 per cent below that shown in the associates' books'. If this under-estimation was general the survey estimates that the value of outward direct investment would be £210m higher in 1968. *Board of Trade Journal*, 23 September, 1970.

(2) Book values only represent a firm's share in net assets according to equity participation; the figures therefore underestimate capital controlled to the extent that the overseas subsidiaries contain minority interests. We have no exact figures for the size of these minorities: foreign investors in Britain at the end of 1965 had three quarters of their investment in wholly-owned subsidiaries and branches: for British firms abroad the figure was only 50 per cent with another 34 per cent in subsidiaries with UK share of 75 per cent or more. The figures are therefore likely to understate capital controlled more for UK investment abroad than for foreign investment in the UK. See *Board of Trade Journal*, 26 January, 1968, pp. iii, v.

In the light of these two points we should allow an upvaluation of at least 50 per cent for British investments overseas. It is interesting to note that Professor Dunning suggests that US firms controlled $9,000m of assets in British industry at the end of 1965 (as against a declared book value of $4,400m at the same date); see Dunning, PEP, *op. cit.*, p. 126.

20. Department of Commerce, *Survey of Current Business*, January, 1967.
21. Brooke, M. Z., and Remmers, H. L., *The Strategy of Multi-national Enterprise*, Longman, 1970, p. 157. They also point out the importance of supplementary finance from abroad for local subsidiaries in a credit squeeze, p. 196.
22. *Business Monitor, op. cit.*, Table 7, 9 and 24.
23. Theoretically neo-classicals might argue that there is no difference between internal and external funds, that a rise in the interest rate on external funds raises the opportunity cost of internal capital. However, internal are quite distinct from external funds in that they are effectively cheaper because of: (1) tax considerations, (2) transactions costs, (3) implicit disclosure costs.
24. Klopstock, R. H., 'The Eurodollar market. Some Unresolved Issues', *Princeton Essays in International Finance*, no. 65, 1968. See also Chalmers, E., (ed.) *Readings in the Eurodollar*, Griffith, 1969, p. 10.
25. *Financial Times*, 13 January, 1971. For evidence of the use of the Eurodollar market by American and British drug companies, see Teeling-Smith, G., (ed.) *Innovation and the Balance of Payments: the experience in the Pharmaceutical Industry*, Office of Health Economics, 1967, pp. 79 and 82.
26. Article by Anthony Thomas in *The Times Business News*, 12 June, 69.
27. Chalmers, E., *op. cit.*, p. 56, and Pizer, S., and Cutler, F., 'Foreign Investments 1965–1966', in *Survey of Current Business*, September, 1966.
28. Chase Manhattan Bank, *Eurodollar Financing*, 2nd ed., September, 1968, p. 16.
29. Morgan Guaranty Trust Company, *op. cit.*, p. 12.
30. Brash, D., *American Investment in Australian Industry*, Australian National University Press, 1966, pp. 91–92. It is interesting, too, that Dow suggests that restrictions on Building Society lending and HP controls were the important instruments of British monetary policy in the 1950s (to both of which we would not expect our argument to apply) whereas the impact of restriction on advances was negligible: Dow, J. C. R., *The Management of the British Economy 1945–60*, Cambridge, 1964, p. 260.
31. Caves, R. E., and Reuber, G. L., *Canadian Economic Policy and the Impact of International Capital Flows*, University of Toronto Press, 1969, p. 48. See also Mundell, R. A., 'Capital Mobility and Stabilization Policy under fixed and flexible exchange rates', *Canadian Journal of Economics and Political Science*, XXIX, November, 1963, pp. 475–85
32. For comments on the effect of the Euromarkets on British domestic monetary policy, see the contributions of R. J. Clark of the National Westminster Bank and P. Davidson of Rutgers University in Croome, D. R., and Johnson, H. G., (ed.) *Money in Britain, 1959–69*, OUP, 1970, pp. 142 and 194.
33. Klopstock makes an interesting comment on the problems of controlling international capital flows when he writes, 'The efficacy of the controls and restrictions should not be over-estimated. The international economy is dominated by multi-national corporations financed by banks whose network of branches or affiliates stretch over several countries. In such an environment controls applicable only to a few countries or to a limited group

of financial institutions do not always work well. And rigidities of interest rates in domestic loan and deposit markets often cause funds to move through the markets perversely contrary to central bank objectives and despite appropriate regulations'. Klopstock, *op. cit.*, p. 22. This lends further support to our general argument.

34. It has been traditionally assumed that the expenditure effects of fiscal policy outweigh the monetary effects by a considerable margin. Rhomberg's study of the Canadian economy (*Journal of Political Economy,* February, 1964) suggests that the converse holds. See Caves and Reuber, *op. cit.*, pp. 51–2.
35. Dow, *op. cit.*, p. 384.
36. *ibid.*, pp. 406–12.
37. Dunning, J. H., *op. cit.*, p. 148.
38. Piccione, U. 'Strategie Operationelle des Investissements Americains a l'étranger'. Annex VII of *Les Investissements Directs des Pays Tiers dans le C.E.E. CCE,* 1969, p. 10.
39. Report of the Committee of Enquiry into the Relationship of the Pharmaceutical Industry with the NHS, 1965–67, Cmnd. 3410.
40. Piccione, *op. cit.*, pp. 11–21, and 39–42.
41. *Board of Trade Journal*, 26 January, 1968, and for figures, *Board of Trade Journal,* 23 September, 1970. It is worth noting that in 1967 Switzerland had the fourth highest stock of US investment of all European countries, and that in the same year the volume of reinvested earnings by US overseas affiliates was higher in Switzerland than in any other country in the world.
42. Committee of Invisible Exports, *The Role of International Companies, op. cit.*, p. 22. This report contains a number of proposals aimed at lowering taxation on international business and their executives based in the UK. For a discussion of these proposals see the *Working Party Report* (chairman Sir Richard Powell), 'The Role of International Companies', published by the Committee on Invisible Exports, March, 1971.
43. Raw, Charles, 'Subtle boost for the directors' salaries', *Guardian,* March, 1971. For a more extensive discussion of tax-haven operations as well as the use of offshore funds by British investors, see: Doggart, T., and Voûte, C., *Tax Havens and Offshore Funds,* ER Special no. 8, Economist Intelligence Unit, 1971.
44. A brief but useful article on hedging is: Lietner, B. A., 'Management risks in foreign exchange', *Harvard Business Review*, March–April, 1970.
45. Renton, G. A., and Duffy, M., 'An Analysis of the UK Balancing Item', London Business School Econometric Forecasting Unit Discussion Paper no. 6, October, 1968.
46. Article on BP by William-Powlett, Barton, *Times Business News,* 5 January, 1970.
47. The reference is from an interview with Charles Levinson, Secretary-General of the International Federation of Chemical and General Workers Unions, Geneva, published in the *Guardian*, n.d. He is quoted as saying, 'Multi-national corporation money management has become a major aspect of their international policy . . . . Because of the vast amount involved this has become virtually another area of banking, and as the multi-national company grows it will increasingly exercise a dominant influence on exchange rates and speculation. Such activities by some of the major British companies like ICI, Dunlop, Bowater, etc., have contributed much more to the recurring weakness of sterling than any number of strikes or consumer buying'.
48. A number of references in this paragraph are taken from Turner, Louis, *The Rise of the Multi-national Company,* Hamish Hamilton, 1970, p. 87.
49. Brooke and Remmers, *op. cit.*, Chapter 7.
50. For the first part of this paragraph see Bank of England, *A Guide to United Kingdom Exchange Control;* and for the second part of the paragraph see Dunning, *op. cit.*, pp. 161–2.
51. Components of UK Overseas Investment 1963–8.

Sterling Area	1963	1964	1965	1966	1967	1968
Total	135	161	186	119	142	177
Unremitted profits	71	98	100	89	94	119
Other sources	64	63	86	29	48	58

Non-sterling Area						
Total	100	102	122	157	139	233
Unremitted profits	47	49	66	94	95	157
Other sources	53	53	56	64	44	76
Total	236	263	308	276	281	410

Source: *Business Monitor,* M4 Overseas Transactions, HMSO, 1970.

52. Chown, John, 'Exchange Control', *Financial Times*, 17 December 1969.
53. It is of some interest that Shell has a special agreement with the British Treasury, dating from the end of the second world war, under which Shell undertakes to keep its cash balances in London on the condition that it has freedom of overseas capital investment. Shell submit a list of their investments to the Treasury, and undertake detailed discussions of major projects, but they are not compelled to justify their investments in the same manner as UK regulations normally require.
54. Ways and means of circumventing the restrictive effects of the dollar premium for portfolio investment are discussed in Whittaker, John, 'Minimizing the Burden of the Dollar Premium', the *Investment Analyst,* October, 1969. The three strategies suggested all take a large part of the return in capital gains which, unlike dividends, the premium does not scale down.
55. In formal terms, devaluation effectively cuts the exporters' marginal cost measured in dollars. However, if the post-devaluation marginal cost schedule still passes through the discontinuity in the marginal revenue schedule of a kinked demand curve, then it will not be worth the exporter cutting his price.
56. Turner, L., *op. cit.*, pp. 16–25.
57. Duffy, M., and Renton, A., 'A Model for Forecasting UK Exports of Manufactures to Industrial Countries'. London Business School Econometric Forecasting Unit Discussion Paper no. 9, August, 1969.
58. See the proposals lowering restrictions on overseas investment put forward in Confederation of British Industries, 'Overseas Investment – Why and How?', October, 1967; Confederation of British Industries, 'Overseas Investment: two CBI Occasional Papers', September, 1969; The Industrial Policy Group (comprising the heads of major British internationals); 'The Case for Overseas Direct Investment', Paper 4 January, 1970; and the Report of the working party of the Committee on Invisible Exports, 'The Role of International Companies', March, 1971 (see note 42 above).

CHAPTER 16

1. and 2. Ansoff, H. I., *Corporate Strategy,* McGraw-Hill, 1965.
3. This definition of conglomerates appears to incorporate the concentric diversification indicated in Table 1.
4. Coase, R. H., 'The Nature of the Firm', *AEA Readings in Price Theory,* R. D. Irwin, 1952.
5. More recently, public policy in US expressed anxiety about some product extension mergers. See Stern, L. W., 'Mergers Under Scrutiny', *Harvard Business Review,* July-August, 1969.
6. Bain, J. S. 'Advantages of the Larger Firm', *Journal of Marketing,* April, 1956, vol. 20.
7. Stern, L. W., 'Perspectives on Public Policy: Comments on The Great Debate', *Journal of Marketing,* January, 1969, pp. 33.
8. For post-merger problems see:
   (a) Searby, F., 'Control of Postmerger Change', *Harvard Business Review,* Sept–Oct, 1969.
   (b) Kitching, J., 'Why do Mergers Miscarry ?', *Harvard Business Review,* November–December, 1967, and Chapter 4 of these readings.
   (c) Levinson, H., 'A Psychologist Diagnoses Merger Failures'. *Harvard Business Review,* March–April, 1970, and Chapter 5 of these readings.
9. Kaysen, C., and Turner, D., *Antitrust Policy,* Harvard University Press, 1959.
10. Narver, John C., 'Some observations on the Impact of Antitrust Merger Policy on Marketing', *Journal of Marketing,* January, 1969.
11. See Searby, *op. cit.*

12. Bain, *op. cit.*
13. Buzzel, R., and Nourse, R., *Product Innovation in Food Processing,* Harvard University, 1967.
14. Stern, *op. cit.*
15. *Ibid.*, p. 36.
16. Ansoff, H. I., 'The Innovation Firm', *Long Range Planning,* vol. 1, no. 2, December, 1968.
17. Bain, J. S., *Barriers to New Competition,* Harvard University Press, 1956.
18. See *Hearings on Economic Concentration,* US Senate, 89th Congress, or Stigler, G. J., '*The Case Against Big Business*', in Mansfield, Edwin, *Monopoly Power and Economic Performance,* Norton, 1964.
19. The more diversified and numerous the product varieties, the less will be the scale economies, also *depending* on the length and number of production runs. See Pratten, C., and Dean, R. M., 'The Economies of Large-Scale Production in British Industry', University of Cambridge Department of Applied Economics, Occasional Papers no. 3, Cambridge University Press, 1970.
20. Bain, *op. cit.*
21. Simon, J. L., 'Are There Economies of Scale in Advertising?', *Journal of Advertising Research,* vol. 5, June, 1968.
22. Mueller, Williard F., 'The Celler-Kefauver Act: 16 Years of Enforcement', Washington, D.C., US Govt. Printing Office, 1967.
23. Merrett, A. J., Howe, M., Newbould, G., *Equity Issue and The London Capital Market,* Longmans, 1967, Chapter 8.
24. Buzzell, Robert D., and Nourse, Robert E. M., *Product Innovation in Food Processing, 1954–1964,* Division of Research, Graduate School of Business Administration, Harvard University, 1967.
25. Caves, R. E., *American Industry: Structure, Conduct and Performance,* Foundation of Modern Economies Series (2nd ed.), Prentice Hall, 1969, p. 50.
    G. Newbould, in a recent study of mergers in UK comes to similar conclusions, *Management & Merger Activity,* Guthstead, 1970.
26. Levitt, T., *The Marketing Mode,* McGraw-Hill, 1969, pp. 295–7.
27. Siekman, Philip, 'Europe's Love Affair with Bigness', *Fortune,* March, 1970 (see Chapter 14 of these readings).
28. Levitt, *op. cit.,* Chapter 5, p. 83.
29. Drucker, Peter F., 'Management's New Role', *Harvard Business Review,* November–December, 1969.
30. Ansoff, *op. cit.*
31. Levitt, *op. cit.*
32. Wilson, J. Q., 'Innovation in Organization: Notes towards a theory', in Thompson, James D., (ed.), *Approaches to Organizational Design,* The University of Pittsburgh Press, 1966, pp. 193–218.
33. March, James G., and Simon, Herbert A., *Organizations,* Wiley, 1958, pp. 172–210.
34. Wittnebert, F. R., 'Bigness versus Profitability', *Harvard Business Review,* January–February, 1970.
35. Kitching, *op. cit.* (see Chapter 4 of these readings).
36. See Tugendhat, L., 'The Complexities of a Merger', *Financial Times,* 5 December, 1969.
37. Searby, *op. cit.*
38. Levinson, *op. cit.* (see Chapter 5 of these readings).
39. Crusco, F. A., *Harvard Business Review,* March–April, 1970 (letters to the Editor).
40. For some of these reasons see Wittnebert, *op. cit.*
41. Caves, *op. cit.*
42. Caves, *ibid.*
43. Scherer, F. M., 'Firm Size, Market Structure, Opportunity and the Output of Patented Inventions', *American Economic Review,* vol. LV, December, 1965.
44. Williamson, O. E., 'Economics as an Antitrust Defense: The Welfare Trade-offs', *American Economic Review,* vol. *LVIII, March, 1968, p. 29.*
45. Mansfield, E., 'Industrial R & D Expenditures: Determinants, Prospect and Relation to Size of Firms and Inventive Output', *Journal of Political Economy,* August 1964, p. 29, footnote 7.

46. Hamburg, D., *R & D: Essays on The Economics of Research & Development,* New York, 1966.
47. Horowitz, I., 'Firm Size and Research Activity', *Southern Economic Journal,* January, 1962.
48. Scherer, *op. cit.,* p. 1114.
49. Mansfield, *op. cit.,* p. 338.
50. Stigler, G. J., 'Industrial Organization and Economic Progress' in White, L. D., (ed.), *The State of Social Sciences,* Chicago, 1956, p. 278.
51. Williamson, O. E., 'Innovation and Market Structure', *Journal of Political Economy,* February, 1965.
52. Kendrick, J. W., *Productivity Trends in The United States,* Princetown, 1961.
53. Williamson, 'Economics as an Antitrust Defence: The Welfare Trade-offs', *op. cit.*
54. Peck, M. J., 'Science & Technology', *Britain's Economic Prospects* by Caves, R. E., and Associates, Allen & Unwin, 1968.
55. Caves, R. E., Associates, *Britain's Economic Prospects,* p.299.
56. Caves, *op. cit.,* p. 103–4.
57. The reader will notice that 'progressiveness' has already been treated as a separate economic goal; this was for reasons of emphasis rather than presentation.
58. Leibenstein, H., 'Allocative Efficiency versus X-efficiency', *American Economic Review,* vol. 56, 1966.
59. Downie, J., *The Competitive Process,* Gerald Duckworth, 1958, p. 181.
60. Caves, R. E., & Associates, *Britain's Economic Prospects,* p. 291.
61. Bain, J. S., 'Relation of Profit Rate to Industry Concentration: American Manufacturing 1936–1940', *Quarterly Journal of Economics,* August, 1951.
62. Caves, R. E., & Associates, *Britain's Economic Prospects,* p. 292.
63. Samuels, J. M., and Smyth, D. J., 'Profits, Variability of Profits and Firm Size', *Economica,* May, 1968.
64. Hart, P. E., and Mellors, J., 'Profitability and Size of Firms', University of Reading, Discussion Papers in Economics no. 15.
65. Marris, R. L., *Economic Theory of Managerial Capitalism,* MacMillan, 1964.
66. Penrose, E. T., *Theory of the Growth of the Firm,* Blackwell, 1959.
67. Baumol, W. J., *Business Behavior Value and Growth,* Harcourt Brace, 1959.
68. Singh, A., and Whittington, G., *Growth, Profitability and Valuation,* University of Cambridge, Department of Applied Economics, *Occasional Paper* no. 7.
69. See Rowley, Charles K., *The British Monopolies Commission,* Allen and Unwin, 1966, Chapter 16.
70. Borden, Neil H. Jr., *Acceptance of New Food Products by Supermarkets,* Harvard Graduate School of Business Administration, Division of Research, Boston, 1968.
71. See Stern, L., 'Mergers Under Scrutiny', *Harvard Business Review,* July–August, 1969.
72. Caves, *op. cit.* p. 49.
73. The more independent the firms are, ignoring the possibility of their moves being offset by counter strategies of their rivals, the higher will be the total costs of the industry.
74. Some monopolies which existed in industries like aluminium, nickel and shoe machinery showed that they were more interested in keeping the field to themselves than in earning high profits – see Caves, *op. cit.,* p. 50.

NOTES ON AUTHORS

M. E. Beesley	Professor of Economics and Faculty Dean, London Graduate School of Business Studies. The author of many articles on monopolies, restrictive practices and the government.
K. Bhaskar	When the cases were prepared the author was a research student at the London School of Economics and Political Science. He is now a Lecturer at the University of Bristol.
M. Blanden	Journalist with the Financial Times.
R. J. Briston	Senior Lecturer in Finance, University of Bradford. Author of *The Stock Exchange and Investment Analysis.*
M. Z. Brooke	Lecturer in Management Sciences, The University of Manchester Institute of Science and Technology. Author of a book and many articles on multi-national business.
Susan Dev	When this paper was presented she was a P. D. Leake Teaching Fellow at the London School of Economics and Political Science. She is now a Lecturer in Accounting there.
T. Fikri	At the time of writing the paper he held the position of Research Associate at the Graduate Centre for Management Studies, Birmingham. He is now working with the Cyprus Productivity Council.
R. Goodman	Director of the Joseph Rowntree Social Service Trust and Vice-Chairman of the Acton Society Trust.
J. Hughes	Vice-Principal, Ruskin College, Oxford.
J. Kitching	Wrote this article whilst studying at the Harvard Business School during the year 1966–7. He brought to the study considerable experience both as an operating executive and as a consultant in the United Kingdom. He is now an independent consultant, active in the field of mergers and acquisitions in Britain and on the Continent.
H. Levinson	Visiting Professor of Business Administration, Harvard Business School. Author of numerous articles on management problems.
S. K. Mansinghka	Assistant Professor of Finance at the University of California, Riverside, USA.

R. Murray	Was a Research Associate at the London Business School when he presented the paper at the Conference in 1970, but has since moved to the Institute of Development Studies at the University of Sussex.
G. Newbould	Reader at the Manchester Business School and has written a number of articles and books on Finance. He is the author of *Business Finance, Management and Merger Activity* and co-author of *Equity Issues and the London Capital Market*.
D. G. Rhys	When he wrote the paper he was at Hull University. He is now Lecturer in Economics at the University College, Cardiff.
J. M. Samuels	Professor of Business Policy, Graduate Centre for Management Studies, Universities of Birmingham and Aston in Birmingham.
P. Siekman	Journalist with the *Fortune* magazine.
J. F. Weston	Professor of Business Economics and Finance at the University of California at Los Angeles. One of the most respected figures in Finance in the United States. He has written numerous books including one of the best selling text books on Managerial Finance.
G. M. White	Research Officer, London Graduate School of Business Studies.

SUBJECT INDEX